The New York Times
ESSENTIAL LIBRARY

Classical Music

The New York Times
ESSENTIAL LIBRARY

Classical Music

A Critic's Guide to the 100
Most Important Recordings

ALLAN KOZINN

TIMES BOOKS

Henry Holt and Company   New York

Times Books
Henry Holt and Company, LLC
Publishers since 1866
115 West 18th Street
New York, New York 10011

Library of Congress Cataloging-in-Publication Data

Kozinn, Allan.
    The New York Times essential library : classical music: a critic's guide
to the 100 most important recordings / Allan Kozinn.—1st ed.
      p. cm.
    Includes index.
    ISBN 0-8050-7070-2
    1. Sound recordings—Reviews. 2. Music—Discography.
I. New York times. II. Title.

ML156.9.K7 2004
780.26'6—dc22   2003057047

First Edition 2004

Frontispiece: Conductor Bernard Herrmann

Printed in the United States of America
1 3 5 7 9 10 8 6 4 2

Contents

Preface   **xxiii**

1. HILDEGARD OF BINGEN, *O Jerusalem*
   (Sequentia)   1

2. GUILLAUME DE MACHAUT, *Messe de Notre Dame*
   (Ensemble Organum, Marcel Pérès, conducting)   4

3. JOSQUIN DESPREZ, *Missa Fortuna Desperata,* "La
   Plus des Plus," "Bergerette Savoysienne," "Adieu
   Mes Amours," "Consideres Mes Incessantes/
   Fortuna" (The Clerks' Group, Edward Wickham,
   conducting)   7

4. CARLO GESUALDO, Madrigals, from Books III,
   IV, V, VI (Les Arts Florissants, William Christie,
   conducting)   9

5. JOHN DOWLAND, *First Booke of Songes* (The Consort of Musicke, Anthony Rooley, lutenist and director)   12

6. *SHAKESPEARE SONGS AND CONSORT MUSIC* (Alfred Deller, countertenor; Desmond Dupré, lutenist; the Deller Consort)   15

7. CLAUDIO MONTEVERDI, *Vespro della Beata Virgine* (1610) (The Monteverdi Choir; the London Oratory Junior Choir; His Majesties Sagbutts & Cornetts; the English Baroque Soloists, Sir John Eliot Gardiner, conducting)   19

8. CLAUDIO MONTEVERDI, *Madrigali Guerrieri ed Amorosi* (Madrigals, Book VIII) (Concerto Vocale, René Jacobs, conducting)   23

9. HENRY PURCELL, Odes for St. Cecilia's Day and Music for Queen Mary (Taverner Consort, Choir and Players, Andrew Parrott, conducting)   26

10. JOHANN SEBASTIAN BACH, *Brandenburg* Concertos (Il Giardino Armonico)   29

11. JOHANN SEBASTIAN BACH, Sonatas and Partitas for Unaccompanied Violin (BWV 1001–1006) (Christian Tetzlaff, violinist)   32

12. JOHANN SEBASTIAN BACH, Mass in B minor (BWV 232) (The Bach Ensemble, Joshua Rifkin, conducting)   35

13. JOHANN SEBASTIAN BACH, *Glenn Gould—
A State of Wonder: Goldberg* Variations (Glenn
Gould, pianist)   38

14. GEORGE FRIDERIC HANDEL, *Water Music*
(English Baroque Soloists, Sir John Eliot Gardiner,
conducting)   43

15. GEORGE FRIDERIC HANDEL, *Israel in Egypt*
(The Choir of King's College, Cambridge; The
Brandenburg Consort, Stephen Cleobury,
conducting)   45

16. GEORGE FRIDERIC HANDEL, *Messiah* (Choir of
Christ Church Cathedral, Oxford, Simon Preston,
director; Academy of Ancient Music, Christopher
Hogwood, conducting)   48

17. DOMENICO SCARLATTI, Sonatas (Wanda
Landowska, harpsichordist)   53

18. ANTONIO VIVALDI, *Il Cimento dell'Armonia e
dell'Inventione* (Europa Galante, Fabio Biondi,
solo violinist and conductor)   58

19. WOLFGANG AMADEUS MOZART, Piano Concertos,
no. 20 in D minor (K. 466); no. 27 in B-flat (K. 595);
no. 26 in D major (K. 537); no. 23 in A major (K. 488);
no. 24 in C minor (K. 491); (Sir Clifford Curzon,
pianist; English Chamber Orchestra, Benjamin Britten,
conducting; London Symphony Orchestra, István
Kertész, conducting)   61

20. WOLFGANG AMADEUS MOZART, Symphony no. 41
    in C, *Jupiter* (K. 551), Concerto for Clarinet and
    Orchestra in A (K. 622), and Concerto for Bassoon
    and Orchestra in B-flat (K. 191) (Jack Brymer,
    clarinetist; Gwydion Brooke, bassoonist; Royal
    Philharmonic Orchestra, Sir Thomas Beecham,
    conducting)   64

21. WOLFGANG AMADEUS MOZART, Divertimento
    in E-flat (K. 563) (Gidon Kremer, violinist; Kim
    Kashkashian, violist; Yo-Yo Ma, cellist)   67

22. WOLFGANG AMADEUS MOZART, Requiem (K. 626,
    completion by Franz Xaver Süssmayr) (John Alldis
    Choir, BBC Symphony Orchestra, Sir Colin Davis,
    conducting)   70

23. FRANZ JOSEPH HAYDN, String Quartets (The
    Emerson String Quartet)   74

24. FRANZ JOSEPH HAYDN, The *London* Symphonies,
    Vol. I (Royal Concertgebouw Orchestra of
    Amsterdam, Sir Colin Davis, conducting)   77

25. FRANZ JOSEPH HAYDN, *Die Schöpfung* (The
    Creation) (Stockholm Radio Chorus, Stockholm
    Chamber Choir, and Berlin Philharmonic, James
    Levine, conducting)   81

26. JUAN CRISÓSTOMO ARRIAGA, Symphonie à Grande
    Orchestre, *Los Esclavos Felices* Overture, and Overture
    for Nonet (Le Concert des Nations, La Capella Reial
    de Catalunya, Jordi Savall, conducting)   84

27. LUDWIG VAN BEETHOVEN, The Nine Symphonies, Overtures (Cleveland Orchestra, Cleveland Orchestra Choir, George Szell, conducting)   86

28. LUDWIG VAN BEETHOVEN, Concerto for Violin and Orchestra in D major (Jascha Heifetz, violinist; Boston Symphony Orchestra, Charles Munch, conducting); JOHANNES BRAHMS, Concerto for Violin and Orchestra in D major (Jascha Heifetz, violinist; Chicago Symphony Orchestra, Fritz Reiner, conducting)   93

29. LUDWIG VAN BEETHOVEN, *The Late Piano Sonatas* (Richard Goode, pianist)   96

30. FRANZ SCHUBERT, *Lieder* (Ian Bostridge, tenor; Julius Drake, pianist)   99

31. FRANZ SCHUBERT, *Winterreise* (D. 911) (Dietrich Fischer-Dieskau, baritone; Alfred Brendel, pianist)   103

32. FRANZ SCHUBERT, Quintet in C for Two Violins, Viola, and Two Cellos (D. 956) (The Alban Berg Quartet, with Heinrich Schiff, cellist)   105

33. FRANZ SCHUBERT, Sonata for Piano no. 21 in B-flat (D. 960), and Three Klavierstücke (D. 946) (Mitsuko Uchida, pianist)   108

34. HECTOR BERLIOZ, *Symphonie Fantastique* (Royal Concertgebouw Orchestra of Amsterdam, Sir Colin Davis, conducting)   111

35. FELIX MENDELSSOHN, Symphony no. 4 in A major, *Italian* (op. 90); and overture and excerpts from the Incidental Music for *Midsummer Night's Dream* (Orchestra of the Age of Enlightenment, Sir Charles Mackerras, conducting)   115

36. FRÉDÉRIC CHOPIN, Twenty-four Preludes (op. 28), Berceuse (op. 57), Barcarolle (op. 60), Piano Sonata no. 2, "Funeral March" (op. 35), and the Impromptu in G-flat (op. 51) (Arthur Rubinstein, pianist)   117

37. ROBERT SCHUMANN, *Carnaval* (op. 9), *Novellette* (op. 21, no. 1), *Nachtstück* (op. 23, no. 4), *Romance* (op. 28, no. 2), and *Fantasiestücke* (op. 12) (Arthur Rubinstein, pianist)   120

38. FRANZ LISZT, Sonata in B minor, *Bénédiction de Dieu dans la solitude, Waldesrauschen, Gnomenreigen,* and *Vallée d'Obermann* (Claudio Arrau, pianist)   124

39. JOHANNES BRAHMS, *Ein Deutsches Requiem* (A German Requiem) (op. 45) (Arleen Augér, soprano; Richard Stillwell, baritone; Atlanta Symphony Orchestra and Chorus, Robert Shaw, conducting)   127

40. JOHANNES BRAHMS, Symphony no. 1 in C minor (op. 68), Symphony no. 2 in D (op. 73), Symphony no. 3 in F (op. 90), Symphony no. 4 in E minor (op. 98), *Tragic* Overture, and *Academic Festival* Overture (Chicago Symphony Orchestra, Sir Georg Solti, conducting)   130

41. JOHANNES BRAHMS, String Sextet in B-flat (op. 18), String Sextet in G (op. 36), Quintet for Piano and

Strings in F minor (op. 34), Quintet for Strings in F (op. 88), Quintet for Strings in G (op. 111), and Quintet for Clarinet and Strings (op. 115) (Cecil Aronowitz, violist; William Pleeth, cellist; Christoph Eschenbach, pianist; Karl Leister, clarinetist; The Amadeus Quartet)   134

42. BEDŘICH SMETANA, *Má Vlast* (My Country) (Czech Philharmonic Orchestra, Rafael Kubelik, conducting)   138

43. MODEST MUSSORGSKY, *Songs* (Sergei Leiferkus, baritone; Semion Skigin, pianist)   143

44. MODEST MUSSORGSKY, *Pictures at an Exhibition* (Ravel orchestration), *Khovanshchina* Prelude (Shostakovich orchestration), *Night on the Bare Mountain* (Rimsky-Korsakov orchestration), and *Sorochintsky Fair* Gopak (Liadov orchestration) (Vienna Philharmonic, Valery Gergiev, conducting) 145

45. PETER ILYICH TCHAIKOVSKY, Symphony no. 4 in F minor (op. 36), Symphony no. 5 in E minor (op. 64), and Symphony no. 6 in B minor, *Pathétique* (op. 74) (Leningrad Philharmonic Orchestra, Evgeny Mravinsky, conducting)   147

46. NIKOLAI RIMSKY-KORSAKOV, *Scheherazade;* ALEXANDER BORODIN, Symphony no. 2 in B minor (Royal Concertgebouw Orchestra of Amsterdam, Kiril Kondrashin, conducting)   150

47. EDVARD GRIEG, *Holberg* Suite (op. 40), *Two Elegiac Melodies* (op. 34), *Peer Gynt* Suite no. 1 (op. 46) and Suite no. 2 (op. 55), and "Evening in the Mountains" and "At the Cradle" from *Lyric Pieces* (op. 68, nos. 4 and 5) (Academy of St. Martin-in-the-Fields, Sir Neville Marriner, conducting)   153

48. *Music from Saratoga:* LUDWIG VAN BEETHOVEN, *Kreutzer* Sonata for Piano and Violin no. 9 in A (op. 47); CÉSAR FRANCK, Violin Sonata in A (Itzhak Perlman, violinist; Martha Argerich, pianist)   156

49. ANTONÍN DVOŘÁK, Symphony no. 9 in E minor (op. 95), *Carnival* Overture (op. 92), and Slavonic Dances, nos. 1 and 3 (op. 46) (New York Philharmonic, Leonard Bernstein, conducting)   158

50. CAMILLE SAINT-SAËNS, Symphony no. 3 (op. 78); PAUL DUKAS, *The Sorcerer's Apprentice* (Simon Preston, organist; Berlin Philharmonic, James Levine, conducting)   162

51. GIUSEPPE VERDI, Requiem and *Four Sacred Pieces* (Elisabeth Schwarzkopf, soprano; Christa Ludwig, mezzo-soprano; Nicolai Gedda, tenor; Nicolai Ghiaurov, bass; Janet Baker, mezzo-soprano [in the *Four Sacred Pieces*]; Philharmonia Orchestra and Chorus, Carlo Maria Giulini, conducting)   165

52. GABRIEL FAURÉ, Requiem (1893 version, op. 48); *Cantique de Jean Racine* (op. 11); Messe Basse; *Tantum Ergo* (op. 65, no. 2); and *Ave Verum Corpus* (op. 65, no. 1) (Mary Seers and Isabelle Poulenard, sopranos; Michael George, baritone; Corydon Singers; John Scott,

organist; English Chamber Orchestra, Matthew
Best, conducting)   168

53. GUSTAV MAHLER, Symphony no. 4 in G (Judith
    Raskin, soprano); *Lieder eines fahrenden Gesellen
    (Songs of a Wayfarer)* (Cleveland Orchestra, George
    Szell, conducting; Frederica von Stade, mezzo-soprano;
    London Philharmonic Orchestra, Andrew Davis,
    conducting)   170

54. GUSTAV MAHLER, Symphony no. 9 (Berlin
    Philharmonic, Leonard Bernstein, conducting)   175

55. JEAN SIBELIUS, Symphony no. 2 (op. 43) (Royal
    Philharmonic, Sir John Barbirolli, conducting)   178

56. LEOŠ JANÁČEK, String Quartet no. 1, *The Kreutzer
    Sonata;* and String Quartet no. 2, *Intimate Letters;*
    ALBAN BERG, *Lyric Suite* (Juilliard String
    Quartet)   181

57. CLAUDE DEBUSSY, *La Mer, Jeux, Le Martyre de Saint
    Sébastien* (orchestral fragments), *Prélude à l'après-midi
    d'un faune, Images, Nocturnes,* and *Printemps*
    (Montreal Symphony Orchestra,
    Charles Dutoit, conducting)   185

58. CLAUDE DEBUSSY, Preludes, Books I and II (Paul
    Jacobs, pianist)   188

59. MAURICE RAVEL, *The Orchestral Works* (Philippe
    Entremont, pianist; Camerata Singers; New York
    Philharmonic and Cleveland Orchestra, Pierre Boulez,
    conducting)   190

---

60. ERIK SATIE, *L'Oeuvre pour Piano (The Piano Works)*
    (Aldo Ciccolini, pianist)   193

61. MANUEL DE FALLA, *El Sombrero de Tres Picos,*
    Interludio y Danza from *La Vida Breve,* and *El Amor
    Brujo* (L'Orchestre de la Suisse Romande, Ernest
    Ansermet, conducting)   196

62. RICHARD STRAUSS, *Tone Poems* (Staatskapelle
    Dresden, Berlin Philharmonic, Karl Böhm,
    conducting)   200

63. ARNOLD SCHOENBERG, Suite (op. 29), *Verklärte
    Nacht* (op. 4), and Three Pieces for Chamber Orchestra
    (Members of the Ensemble InterContemporain,
    Pierre Boulez, conducting)   203

64. IGOR STRAVINSKY, *Petrushka* and *Le Sacre du
    Printemps* (Columbia Symphony Orchestra, Igor
    Stravinsky, conducting); or *Le Sacre du Printemps*
    and *L'Oiseau de Feu* Suite (Columbia Symphony
    Orchestra, Igor Stravinsky, conducting)   207

65. IGOR STRAVINSKY, *The Mono Years* (The Cleveland
    Orchestra and a chamber ensemble, Igor Stravinsky,
    conducting)   212

66. REYNALDO HAHN, *La Belle Époque: The Songs of
    Reynaldo Hahn* (Susan Graham, mezzo-soprano;
    Roger Vignoles, pianist)   215

67. AGUSTÍN BARRIOS, *From the Jungles of Paraguay:
    John Williams Plays Barrios* (John Williams,
    guitarist)   217

68. SIR EDWARD ELGAR, *English String Music;*
Introduction and Allegro (op. 47), Serenade in E minor
(op. 20), *Elegy* (op. 58), and *Sospiri* (op. 70); RALPH
VAUGHAN WILLIAMS, *Fantasia on a Theme by
Thomas Tallis* and *Fantasia on Greensleeves* (Sinfonia
of London; Allegri String Quartet; New Philharmonia
Orchestra, Sir John Barbirolli, conducting)   222

69. SERGEI RACHMANINOFF, Concerto no. 3 in D minor
for Piano and Orchestra (op. 30); SERGEI PROKOFIEV,
Concerto no. 3 in C major for Piano and Orchestra
(op. 26) (Van Cliburn, pianist; Symphony of the Air,
Kiril Kondrashin, conducting; Chicago Symphony
Orchestra, Walter Hendl, conducting)   224

70. EDGARD VARÈSE, *Ionisation, Amériques,* and *Arcana*
(New York Philharmonic, Pierre Boulez, conducting);
Offrandes, Octandre, Intégrales, and *Density 21.5*
(Ensemble InterContemporain, Pierre Boulez,
conducting)   228

71. CHARLES IVES, *Three Places in New England*
(Orchestral Set no. 1) and Orchestral Set no. 2; CARL
RUGGLES, *Sun-Treader* and *Men and Mountains;*
RUTH CRAWFORD SEEGER, Andante for Strings
(Cleveland Orchestra and Chorus, Christoph von
Dohnányi, conducting)   231

72. GEORGE GERSHWIN, *Rhapsody in Blue* and *An
American in Paris;* FERDE GROFÉ, *Grand Canyon
Suite* (Columbia Symphony Orchestra and New York
Philharmonic, Leonard Bernstein, conducting, and
pianist in the *Rhapsody*)   235

73. AARON COPLAND, *The Copland Collection—Orchestral and Ballet Works, 1936–1948* (Henry Fonda, narrator; Benny Goodman, clarinetist; New Philharmonia Orchestra, London Symphony Orchestra, New England Conservatory Chorus, Columbia Symphony Strings, Aaron Copland, conducting)   238

74. SAMUEL BARBER, Adagio for Strings (op. 11), Overture to *The School for Scandal* (op. 5), Second Essay for Orchestra (op. 17), *Medea's Dance of Vengeance* (op. 23a), *Andromache's Farewell* (op. 39), and Intermezzo from *Vanessa* (op. 32) (Martina Arroyo, soprano; New York Philharmonic and Columbia Symphony Orchestra, Thomas Schippers, conducting)   241

75. KURT WEILL, *Kleine Dreigroschenmusik, Mahagonny Songspiel, Happy End, Berliner Requiem*, Pantomime I (from *Der Protagonist*), *Vom Tod im Wald*, and Violin Concerto (Mary Thomas and Meriel Dickinson, mezzo-sopranos; Philip Langridge and Ian Partridge, tenors; Benjamin Luxon, baritone; Michael Rippon, bass; Nona Liddell, violinist; London Sinfonietta, David Atherton, conducting)   244

76. ALBAN BERG, Violin Concerto; WOLFGANG RIHM, *Time Chant* (Anne-Sophie Mutter, violinist; Chicago Symphony Orchestra, James Levine, conducting)   247

77. DMITRI SHOSTAKOVICH, Symphony no. 5 in D minor (op. 47) and Symphony no. 9 in E-flat major (op. 70) (New York Philharmonic, Leonard Bernstein, conducting)   250

78. DMITRI SHOSTAKOVICH, Concerto for Violin and Orchestra no. 1 in A minor (op. 77), Concerto for Cello and Orchestra no. 1 in E-flat (op. 107) (David Oistrakh, violinist, New York Philharmonic, Dimitri Mitropoulos, conducting; Mstislav Rostropovich, cellist, Philadelphia Orchestra, Eugene Ormandy, conducting)   253

79. BÉLA BARTÓK, The Six String Quartets (Emerson String Quartet)   256

80. BÉLA BARTÓK, Concerto for Orchestra; *Music for Strings, Percussion, and Celesta;* and *Hungarian Sketches* (Chicago Symphony Orchestra, Fritz Reiner, conducting)   259

81. KARL AMADEUS HARTMANN, *Concerto Funèbre;* Symphony no. 4; and Chamber Concerto (Isabelle Faust, violinist; Paul Meyer, clarinetist; Petersen Quartet; Munich Chamber Orchestra, Christoph Poppen, conducting)   262

82. OLIVIER MESSIAEN, *Quatuor pour le Fin du Temps (Quartet for the End of Time)* (Tashi)   264

83. HEITOR VILLA-LOBOS, *Bachianas Brasileiras,* nos. 1, 2, 5, and 9 (Victoria de los Angeles, soprano [in no. 5]; Orchestre National de la Radiodiffusion Française, Heitor Villa-Lobos, conducting)   267

84. BENJAMIN BRITTEN, *War Requiem* (op. 66) (Galina Vishnevskaya, soprano; Peter Pears, tenor; Dietrich Fischer-Dieskau, baritone; Simon Preston, organist; Melos Ensemble; Highgate School Choir; Bach Choir; London Symphony Orchestra and Chorus, Benjamin Britten, conducting)   271

85. BENJAMIN BRITTEN, *The Young Person's Guide to the Orchestra* (op. 34), *Simple Symphony* (op. 4), and *Variations on a Theme of Frank Bridge* (op. 10) (London Symphony Orchestra, English Chamber Orchestra, Benjamin Britten, conducting)   274

86. WITOLD LUTOSŁAWSKI, *Symphonic Variations,* Symphony no. 1, *Musique Funèbre,* Symphony no. 2, Concerto for Orchestra, *Jeux Vénitiens, Livre pour Orchestre,* and *Mi-Parti* (Polish Radio Symphony Orchestra, Witold Lutosławski, conducting)   276

87. LEONARD BERNSTEIN, *Candide* Overture, Symphonic Dances from *West Side Story,* Symphonic Suite from *On the Waterfront,* and *Fancy Free* (New York Philharmonic, Leonard Bernstein, conducting)   279

88. BERNARD HERRMANN, *The Film Scores* (Los Angeles Philharmonic, Esa-Pekka Salonen, conducting)   282

89. MILTON BABBITT, *Three Compositions, Duet, Semi-Simple Variations, Partitions, Post-Partitions, Tableaux, Reflections* for Piano and Synthesized Tape, *Canonical Form,* and *Lagniappe* (Robert Taub, pianist)   286

90. JOHN CORIGLIANO, Concerto for Clarinet and Orchestra; AARON COPLAND, Concerto for Clarinet, Strings, Harp, and Piano; IGOR STRAVINSKY, *Ebony* Concerto; LEONARD BERNSTEIN, *Prelude, Fugue, and Riffs,* on *Richard Stoltzman: The Essential Clarinet* (Richard Stoltzman, clarinetist; London Symphony Orchestra, Lawrence Leighton-Smith and Richard Stoltzman, conducting)   289

91. STEVE REICH, *Early Works* (Steve Reich and Russell Hartenberger, clapping; Nurit Tilles and Edmund Niemann, pianists)   292

92. STEVE REICH, *Tehillim* and *Three Movements* (Schönberg Ensemble with Percussion Group The Hague, Reinbert de Leeuw, conducting; London Symphony Orchestra, Michael Tilson Thomas, conducting)   294

93. PHILIP GLASS, *Music in Twelve Parts* (Philip Glass Ensemble, Michael Riesman, conducting)   296

94. PHILIP GLASS, *Koyaanisqatsi* (Albert de Ruiter, bass; Philip Glass Ensemble, Western Wind Vocal Ensemble)   299

95. JOHN ADAMS, *Shaker Loops* (1978, revised 1983) and Violin Concerto (1993) (Orchestra of St. Luke's, John Adams, conducting; Gidon Kremer, violinist, London Symphony Orchestra, Kent Nagano, conducting)   302

96. GREGORIO PANIAGUA, *La Folia* (Atrium Musicae de Madrid)   305

97. ARVO PÄRT, *Tabula Rasa, Fratres* (Violin and Piano version), *Cantus in Memory of Benjamin Britten, Fratres* (Cello Ensemble version) (Gidon Kremer and Tatiana Grindenko, violinists; Keith Jarrett and Alfred Schnittke, pianists; the Twelve Cellists of the Berlin Philharmonic; Stuttgart State Orchestra, Dennis Russell Davies, conducting; Lithuanian Chamber Orchestra, Saulus Sondeckis, conducting)   307

98. HENRYK GÓRECKI, Symphony no. 3 (op. 36) (Dawn Upshaw, soprano; London Sinfonietta, David Zinman, conducting)   310

99. EINOJUHANI RAUTAVAARA, Symphony no. 7, *Angel of Light;* and *Annunciations* (Concerto for Organ Brass Group and Symphonic Wind Orchestra) (Kari Jussila, organist; Helsinki Philharmonic Orchestra, Leif Segerstam, conducting)   312

100. BRIGHT SHENG, *H'un: In Memoriam 1966–1976, The Stream Flows, Three Chinese Love Songs,* and *My Song* (New York Chamber Symphony, Gerard Schwarz, conducting; Lucia Lin, violinist; Lisa Saffer, soprano; Paul Neubauer, violist; Bright Sheng, pianist; Peter Serkin, pianist)   316

Another 100: More Albums You Should Own, or at Least Know About   321

Illustration Credits   337

Index   339

Preface

There was once a late-night TV ad that touted a couple of eight-track tapes, with the promise that they included "All the Classical Music You Will Ever Need!"

Please don't think of this book as the print version of that collection.

The selection here—annotated entries about one hundred recordings, as well as a supplementary list of another one hundred—covers considerable ground, touching on many of the major composers and works of the classical repertory, and exploring a few obscure but extremely worthy byways. Yet if anything seems truer to me now than before I started writing, it's that there is no such thing as *all you will ever need.*

This book covers, after all, about nine hundred years of music history, and from a musical perspective, none of those years was uneventful. Some decades—say, 1818 to 1828, 1910 to 1920, or even 1974 to 1984—could easily have yielded one hundred entries or more. For that matter, so could several of the composers represented on either list. For an open-minded listener, there are always new composers to discover, or works by favorite composers that have somehow escaped attention.

And then there is the matter of performance. A great work can be interpreted innumerable ways, and while some of them add nothing to the unfolding dialogue among a composer, a work, and an audience, it is surprising how many readings yield fresh insights about works that have been kicking around for a couple of hundred years. There is no single, absolute, correct way to play a piece, and although it can be argued that there are plenty of wrong ways, the fact is that an approach that one listener will consider insupportably eccentric may illuminate a work completely for someone else.

I've heard both those things said about performances by Glenn Gould and Leonard Bernstein, among many others; and in some cases I've fully understood both reactions to a performance and either loved it, hated it, or been entirely indifferent to it regardless of the forcefully stated opinions swirling around it. Once you come to love a particular piece of music, you are likely to be interested in hearing just about any point of view a musician might offer on it. That doesn't mean you'll be pleased by all those points of view: you are likely, in fact, to develop strong ideas (ideally, informed ones) about what works or doesn't, and why. But those preferences may have wide parameters.

So, what, you may be asking by now, makes the list of recordings discussed between these covers an *essential library*? What makes a recording or a work *essential* when the repertory is so vast, interpretations of work within that repertory are so plentiful, and there are no absolutes? The goal, clearly, was to assemble a collection of a hundred recordings that should be in any collection, whether that of someone new to classical music, or of a longtime collector who may have overlooked them.

Obviously, a personal calculus is involved, and ground rules about the nature of the collection had to be established before specific choices could be made. The first concerned how the list would be organized. If this were a jazz or rock list, that would have been comparatively easy. A critic compiling a jazz list that includes Miles Davis's *Kind of Blue* or John Coltrane's *A Love Supreme,* or a rock list that includes the Beatles' *Sgt. Pepper's Lonely Hearts Club Band* or Bob Dylan's *Blonde on Blonde,* doesn't have to worry about choosing among sixty or seventy competing performances, as is the case with, say, a Beethoven symphony or Bach's *Goldberg* Variations.

And in choosing those albums, not only are great specific works covered, but their creators and performers are covered at the same time, since in most cases, a jazz or rock recording is both the performance and the composition. On the classical music side, a critic choosing George Szell's Beethoven symphonies, or Richard Goode's Beethoven piano sonatas, will hear a nagging voice fretting about whether other favorite conductors or pianists will be represented.

To begin with, I had to banish that nagging because it would have limited my choices in an unacceptable way. It would have meant, for instance, that if Szell were the choice for Beethoven (as he is), I would have to choose another conductor's Mahler's Fourth, for the sake of broader representation, when in fact my honest choice for that work is also Szell's recording.

Still, the issue itself is important. There are two plausible ways to organize a book about classical recordings. One is by performer, and would involve making a list of up to one hundred great performers, and selecting for each a recording or two that best represents their artistry. If one were to go back early enough in the history of recording, one could use such a list to trace the history of how performance style has changed (and it has, considerably) through the 125 years that recordings have been made. That can be fascinating: I once taught a course at the Juilliard School based on that approach, and it was great fun.

But it can also be a bit specialized for readers who aren't that interested in how the use of vibrato changed, or how trills were played between 1920 and 1970, or who might be curious to hear Brahms play the piano—but not so curious as to consider listening several dozen times to the single extant cylinder he recorded in 1889, in the hope that a vaguely piano-like sound might arise from the layers of crunching noise.

That's an extreme case, of course, and although in the end I decided that contemplating classical music through the prism of performance was too limiting, I did keep in mind the desirability of presenting different historical performing styles among the selections. So while my general preference, in the performance of music from the baroque and classical eras, is for performances on period instruments, driven by late-breaking discoveries (or, at least, theories) about how the music was performed in its time, I also have a fondness for supposedly archaic approaches to this music—thus, the inclusion of Wanda Landowska's Scarlatti, Sir Thomas Beecham's Mozart, or Glenn Gould playing the *Goldberg* Variations on the piano rather than the more musicologically proper harpsichord.

The obvious alternative to organizing the collection by performers, of course, is to organize it by composers and works. There is a good, practical reason to do this in a book recommending recordings: record stores, after all, are organized that way. Unlike most record stores, though, I am presenting composers and their works chronologically, so that readers can take in the grand sweep of musical history as they page through the book. There are some chronological quirks, of course, because composers' lives and works overlap. Haydn, for example, was twenty-four years older than Mozart and was hard at work by the time Mozart was born. But most of the Haydn covered herein is late music, composed near the end of Mozart's life, or after his death. I didn't want the Haydn and Mozart entries to be interspersed, so on the basis of the music, rather than the dates of birth and death, I placed Haydn after Mozart rather than before him. Things get even thornier in the mid-twentieth century, but I think the rationale for placing the entries where they are will be apparent.

With a few exceptions that had more to do with disc couplings than anything else, the second list presenting another hundred recordings does not overlap the main one: it is an expanded list of works, not a list of alternative performances. (Alternative performances are, in many cases, noted within the essays about the hundred recordings on the main list.) Moreover, the recordings included on it should not be considered also-rans: just about anything on that list could easily have had a place in the main part of the book, and quite a few of them almost did. At that, there are quite a few composers and performers whose work I greatly admire, but who are not represented on either list. A third list of one hundred more recordings that deserve a place in your collection could have been easily assembled as well.

As it turned out, even arranging the selections by composer had its pitfalls. Certain composers (Bach, Mozart, Haydn, Beethoven, Schubert, and Brahms, for example) were so prolific in their creation of essential works, and are such central figures in the historical parade, that they demand multiple entries. They have them, though not as many as they would if the list were not limited to one hundred. I decided that it was more important to represent a greater number and variety of composers and styles—and to include composers and works that are too often overlooked—than to try to be comprehensive about the works of composers who are universally acknowledged as great. I believe I have done those composers justice, in a rough sort of way; but I decided that for the sake of variety and breadth, no composer should have more than four or five entries in the main list.

Among the dividends of this decision was an ability to look in on the formation of various national styles in the nineteenth and twentieth centuries, and to look at contemporary composers whose work is central to the way classical music is being made now—an important issue for those of us who believe that this is a living art, not just a fossil collection.

That said, limiting the number of entries available to any single composer also allowed for the display of a few fossils that deserve greater exposure than they've traditionally had. The early-nineteenth-century Spanish composer Juan Crisóstomo Arriaga, or the early-twentieth-century Paraguayan guitarist-composer Agustín Barrios, for example, may seem decidedly inessential or downright eccentric to some readers. But Arriaga and Barrios, working outside the mainstream, produced some fantastic, distinctive work. It's music I love, and you should hear it. That, in fact, is the guiding principle for all the recordings I have included here.

There are some oddities at the more contemporary end of the spectrum, too. Gregorio Paniagua's *La Folia* is one. This is a disc that has probably eluded most collectors, but which has a lot to say about the history of composition and—apart from all that—is a great deal of fun. Fun should not be an alien concept here. I considered it an essential quality of several of the discs I included, and until the very end of the project, I had been intent on including one of Peter Schickele's P.D.Q. Bach albums, with their brilliant parodies of classical style and pretention. In the end, an unbidden fit of responsibility led me to include one more Brahms or Haydn entry instead, but P.D.Q. is on the supplementary list. Schickele's analysis of the opening movement of

Beethoven's Fifth Symphony, presented as a sportscast, should be in every collection.

Choosing performances required a set of ground rules as well. As a purely practical matter, I felt it was important to choose performances that are currently available on CD. That rule proved a nightmare, given the unsettled state of the record industry. Recordings, even venerable and revered ones, go in and out of print regularly. Record labels are gobbled up by other record labels, their recordings either warehoused or reissued. Other labels go out of business, leaving their recordings in various states of limbo—some gone for good, others (where, for example, the masters are owned by a producer or the performers) to have a new life on another label.

This is another difference between a book of this kind about jazz or rock and one about classical music. My colleague Ben Ratliff, in the Jazz volume in this series, recommended several recordings that never made the transition from LP to CD. Because the recording is both the work and the performance in jazz, once Ben decided that such a recording was essential, there was no way around that. In the case of classical music, though, even if a favorite performance was never issued on CD, the work itself most likely has been, in performances that can be wholeheartedly recommended.

As with virtually all the rules I set out, I made a couple of exceptions to the "in print" rule—although even in these cases, the recordings were, at some point recently, available on CD. The fact is, the Internet has made it possible to define "available" loosely. Searching the Net, I have found used copies of discs that were long out of print, and I have found discs long unavailable in the United States on the websites of Japanese, British, Canadian, and Australian record shops. Mostly, though, the CDs listed here are available domestically.

I also tried to avoid catch-all boxed sets. A collection of a composer's complete works is fine if you know the composer well enough to know that you want it all. But for the purpose of this book, I felt that sets of that sort were cheating: it was my job to explain why specific works and performances were essential, and simply glomming all of a composer's music at once seemed an abdication of that responsibility. I also felt it was important that my recommendations be affordable, particularly for readers who were experimenting, and ten-CD boxes generally are not.

Here, too, there are exceptions. It seemed justifiable, even necessary, to recommend a complete set of the Beethoven symphonies. I felt less strongly about recommending a complete Mahler cycle, but you'll find one on the second list of one hundred. In fact, the rule about boxed sets is considerably relaxed in that list.

Both lists also include a few compilations that I might normally have considered thrown-together assemblies of unrelated performances, but which offered within them recordings that I felt were essential, and that were no longer available in any other form. A case in point (which ended up on the supplementary list) is a Leoš Janáček compilation on the Decca label. I had wanted to recommend a 1982 recording by Sir Charles Mackerras that included the composer's Sinfonietta and *Taras Bulba,* and it turned out that although the original disc was long out of print, it was incorporated whole into a two-CD compilation that also included orchestral and chamber works performed by other ensembles—all at a price less than that of the original CD. I might have misgivings about Decca's approach, but disqualifying the current set on those grounds didn't seem sensible.

Another rule, to which I adhered fairly loosely, was that except where there were extenuating circumstances, the recordings recommended in the main list should be sonically up-to-date. This may be overcompensation for a sin of my youth—some distant episodes of indefensible snobbism during my college years, when I had a part-time job at a record store. When customers would innocently ask for, say, a Beethoven Fifth, I would ask whether they wanted a great performance or great sound. "But," they would invariably ask, "can't I get both?" "Oh no," I would tell them, peering over the top of my glasses, offering the choice of an ancient mono radio recording that bristles with energy but sounds distorted and constricted, or a brand-new splashy recording that will show off a fancy sound system, but has no interpretive depth whatever.

This was outrageous, of course: there is so much ground, interpretively and sonically, between the Arturo Toscanini and Zubin Mehta recordings I had in mind. In these pages, I have discounted some fantastic but terrible-sounding recordings when equally fantastic great-sounding discs were available as well. And great-sounding, in this context, does not mean recorded last year, or even digitally. Many of the recordings here were recorded in the 1950s and 1960s and sound absolutely spectacular. Some go back farther than that; the Landowska recordings already mentioned are from the 1920s.

Some of the performances I've included may seem surprising. Some even surprised me. Like anyone who has spent a lifetime listening to classical music recordings, I came to this project with long-standing favorites for virtually every one of the hundred selections. But as I listened to those recordings, along with competing performances (including very recent ones), I found that in many cases, my preferences had changed, and, in some cases, brand-new recordings struck me as more vital—or, at least, better representative of the way I feel about the music now—than recordings I loved since childhood.

This is as it should be: I have real problems with the Golden-Age-ism that is an article of faith for so many classical music listeners—the belief that the performers of decades past were giants in whose footprints today's players vanish. There were great players, singers, and conductors back then; there are great players, singers, and conductors now. One can prefer the style of one era to another's, in performance just as in composition; but the whole point of an interpreted art is that interpretive ideas change with time. And I felt that it was important, where possible, to include both recordings that are classics of long-standing and those by the best young musicians performing today, whose work deserves to vie with that of their predecessors for the attention of the classical music audience.

The Bach Sonatas and Partitas for Unaccompanied Violin, for example, are works that have long been close to my heart, and in the 1970s I was partial to Nathan Milstein's then-new Deutsche Grammophon set. In the 1980s, that was displaced by Gidon Kremer's traversal. Now I prefer the Christian Tetzlaff recording recommended here, and in ten years my favorite may be a recording by a player who cracked open the score for the first time last Tuesday.

Classical music listeners are an opinionated bunch, and no doubt these lists will elicit complaints about the selections I've made or not made. While assembling them, though, I found an interview with the conductor Nikolaus Harnoncourt (published in the liner notes for his 1997 Brahms symphony recordings) that puts interpretation in perspective nicely.

"The relationship between one generation of interpreters and the next is like that between two intelligent friends whose discussions inevitably spark off an argument simply because they feel the need to adopt differing views, even though they do not really occupy differing standpoints. If a conductor and orchestra perform a piece in a particular and highly convincing way for one generation, then this interpretation at the same time encourages dissent and begs the question why it has to be played in one way and not another. . . .

"While I was teaching at the Salzburg Mozarteum, I would sometimes play the students old gramophone recordings. What interested me most—and sometimes also drove me to despair—was the way in which the taste and aims of one generation (in other words, what one might describe as yesterday's fashion) were always treated with contempt by the next. And yet anyone who listens seriously will recognize approaches which, important and interesting though they undoubtedly are, nowadays tend to be overlooked since today's performers are following another trend. We need to be clear in our own minds that the same will happen to our own readings in twenty or thirty years' time. Indeed, it is bound to happen, since a work does not have a single fixed form that is valid for all time."

The New York Times
ESSENTIAL LIBRARY

Classical Music

1. HILDEGARD OF BINGEN

O Jerusalem

SEQUENTIA

(Deutsche Harmonia Mundi 05472-77353-2)

Includes the title work as well as Quia felix puerita—Magnificat, O felix apparitio, O beatissime Ruperte, O tu illustrata, Cum erubuerint, O frondens virga—Gloria patri—Ave generosa, O quam preciosa, O ignee spiritus, O quam magnum miraculum est, *and instrumental works.*

Recorded 1995

It took until the second half of the twentieth century for women to come into their own as composers, that is, for more than one or two to be recognized as important voices in the global musical dialogue. But women have always composed, and the earliest known female composer, Hildegard of Bingen (1098–1179), was also one of the great intellects of her era. Having experienced religious visions from the age of five, Hildegard took up studies at the monastery at Disibodenberg when she was fourteen. Eventually a convent was established there, and Hildegard succeeded her teacher, Jutta von Spanheim, as its prioress, in 1136. In around 1150, Hildegard established her own convent at Rupertsberg, near Bingen; and when that house became too crowded, in 1165, she established another at Eibingen.

Hildegard's writings include *Scivias,* a collection of fourteen extended poems in which she describes twenty-six revelations that came to her in her visions, as well as works on science and medicine, a trilogy of allegorical religious works, and the lives of Saint Disibod and Saint Rupert. Having achieved a reputation for prophecy and working miracles, Hildegard maintained correspondence with popes, emperors, and other leaders, and when challenged on matters of religious doctrine or practice, she held her ground.

As a Benedictine abbess, Hildegard naturally devoted her musical energics entirely to sacred works, most of which are settings of ecstatic texts drawn from her own poetry. There are a few basic hallmarks in her musical language. She wrote long before the invention of the modern scale and the system of keys that we now take for granted. For Hildegard, music was rooted in the church modes, which you can think of as (roughly speaking) a series of scales based on the white keys of the piano keyboard, with no sharps or flats. Each of these modes had a distinct character, and was used to stir a particular kind of feeling: works in the mode beginning on G, for example, were joyous; those on D evoked purity.

Also, Hildegard's music is monophonic: her compositions are single melodies, with no harmony or counterpoint (polyphony), whether performed by one singer or many. Yet a single line is hardly a limitation: sometimes Hildegard sets her texts simply and syllabically, but often a word is painted with expansive, soaring melismas that, in extreme cases, reached more than seventy notes.

Among Hildegard's musical works is a morality play, *Ordo Virtutum,* in which the soul is tempted by the Devil, but is persuaded back to the right path by the Virtues. Sequentia recorded this extraordinary work twice (in 1982 and 1997, both for Deutsche Harmonia Mundi). But the group's vividly sung *O Jerusalem* collection seems a better and more varied introduction to her music. It proposes an imaginative (if also imaginary, or at least fanciful) reconstruction of the dedicatory ceremony at Rupertsberg. Several of the pieces, including the title work, include paeans to Saint Rupert; indeed, considered in the context of a dedication ceremony, there is a suggestion that the convent represents an earthly analog to the vision of a spiritual Jerusalem that Hildegard's text describes.

Several early-music ensembles have recorded these works, and typically they have given the pieces straightforward, devotional performances that bring out their beauty but, compared with Sequentia's reading, sound a bit staid. Sequentia gives its performance of the title work a context: the first sounds one hears are the bells and ambience of the Bamberg Cathedral. Like other ensembles, Sequentia gives most of the work to its female singers, although one—"O ignee spiritus"—is performed by men. (Men's and women's voices would, of course, not have been heard together in the church music of Hildegard's time.)

But here, too, Sequentia takes a different path than most groups. Although in works performed by compact vocal forces (two or three voices) they sing with polish and precision, those qualities are not presented as an ideal. Rather, in works for the massed ensemble, Sequentia's singers give the pieces the slightly rough-hewn, earthy, real-life sound that one might actually have heard in a convent or monastery. The vibrant acoustical ambience of St. Pantaleon, Cologne, abets this feeling.

I question the group's inclusion of three brief instrumental works based on themes from Hildegard's vocal pieces, but if they seem out of place in the context of this reconstruction, they offer an opportunity to hear Sequentia's players, and to hear Hildegard's music from a different perspective. Certainly less harm is done here than in, say, *Illumination* (Sony Classical, 1997), a poorly conceived melding of Hildegard's music and new age electronic instrumentation.

The notes booklet for *O Jerusalem* includes superb annotations by Barbara Thornton, who founded Sequentia with Benjamin Bagby in 1977. Included are quotations from Hildegard's mystical writings and correspondence, all of which bring her to life nearly as vividly as the music. Thornton, who died of a brain tumor in 1998 at age forty-eight, was the driving force behind Sequentia's Hildegard project, which yielded several other highly recommendable recordings, including *Ordo Virtutum* (I prefer the 1997 version), *Canticles of Ecstasy* (1994), *Voice of the Blood* (1995), and *Saints* (1998), all on the Deutsche Harmonia Mundi label.

There are two non-Sequentia Hildegard recordings worth special mention as well: *A Feather on the Breath of God* (Hyperion, 1984), a varied overview, beautifully rendered by Gothic Voices; and *11,000 Virgins* (Harmonia Mundi USA, 1997), Anonymous 4's exquisite collection of chants for the feast of Saint Ursula, mostly by Hildegard but also including works from as late as the fifteenth century.

2. GUILLAUME DE MACHAUT

Messe de Notre Dame (Notre Dame Mass)

ENSEMBLE ORGANUM, MARCEL PÉRÈS, CONDUCTING
(Harmonia Mundi 901590)

Recorded 1995

For most record collectors with a special fondness for early music, the works of Guillaume de Machaut (c. 1300–1377) represent the pinnacle of the fourteenth-century French style, and, indeed, Machaut was esteemed in his day, both as a composer and as a poet. Little is known of his early life, but in around 1323 he became a clerk in the household of Jan de Luxembourg, king of Bohemia, a position that involved considerable travel in Europe, and in 1340 he became a canon at the Cathedral of Rheims, for which he wrote this justly celebrated Mass in the early 1360s.

To modern ears—especially ones that haven't taken in a lot of medieval music—the Notre Dame Mass will probably have a decidedly alien quality. And well it should. The ideas about harmony that drive the classical and romantic styles didn't begin to evolve until more than a century after Machaut, and they didn't coalesce into the musical language that we now consider standard until the seventeenth century. By then, the compositional notions of Machaut's day (how rhythm worked, how voices related to one another, and what constituted acceptable harmonies) were supplanted and forgotten.

Still, the Notre Dame Mass is a seminal work in the history of Western music: in some ways it represents the dawn of the age of the modern composer, and of new ways to think about music. It is the earliest known four-part polyphonic setting (that is, a work in which four distinct vocal lines move independently) of the complete Mass by a single known composer.

That's a mouthful, and it requires some parsing.

First, one has to define what is meant by a Mass, from a musical perspective. There are two components: the five sections of the Ordinary—Kyrie, Gloria, Credo, Sanctus, and Agnus Dei—are texts that remain constant, and have therefore been prime candidates for musical setting through the ages (since, from a completely utilitarian view, they could be used at any time in the liturgical year). The other sections, which make up the Proper, are tied to specific feasts or seasons. Typically a church in Machaut's time, and for centuries after, would use polyphonic settings of the Ordinary, with the Proper drawn from the plainchant (traditional church chant melodies) related to the occasion. So the designation of Machaut's work as the first complete setting of the Mass refers to its status as a composition of all five sections of the Ordinary plus, in Machaut's case, the concluding Ite Missa est section.

Before Machaut, the standard practice appears to have been for cathedral musicians to assemble Masses from settings of the individual movements, written by different composers at different times. It may be that the six sections of the Machaut Mass were composed at different times as well, but the scholarly consensus is that the Notre Dame Mass is a coherent setting, composed and meant to be performed together. In the Kyrie, Sanctus, Agnus Dei, and Ite Missa est, the cantus firmus—actually a plainchant melody—is sung in long notes in one of the lower voices, while the higher voices move more quickly above and around it. The Gloria and the Credo use a different form: all four voices move together, chordally, in the same rhythm.

Equally important is the fact that Machaut signed the work. His predecessors generally worked anonymously; in fact, the only reason we can affix the names of certain earlier church composers to specific works is that traveling musicians took the trouble to discover the music's authorship, and included transcriptions, with attribution, in their own manuscripts. (Oddly, the compilers of many of these manuscripts are themselves anonymous.) Indeed, Machaut devoted much effort during the final decade of his life to the task of collecting and editing his works, musical and poetic, for preservation.

There have been several notable recordings of the Mass over the years, and they show the degree to which scholarly thinking about the performance of this music has changed. Two classic versions—those by the Deller Consort (Vanguard, 1961) and the Munich Capella Antiqua (Teldec, 1970) were based on the belief that although the work would have been sung by an all-male chorus, the top voices would have been countertenors, or male altos. Those recordings also present the work with instrumental accompaniment (using early instruments, of course); and they offer only the polyphonic Mass movements.

Those remain important recordings, but by the mid-1980s ideas had changed. When Andrew Parrott and his Taverner Choir recorded the Mass (Angel, 1984), they used only bass and tenor voices, and dispensed with the instrumental accompaniment on the grounds that one would not have been used in church music of that time. (Unlike the scores of later eras, the performing forces were not indicated in medieval manuscripts.) Moreover, since research by then had established that the Mass was written for one of the four annual Feasts of the Blessed Virgin, Parrott chose one (the Feast of the Nativity) and included the relevant plainchant.

But Marcel Pérès ups the ante further. Like Parrott, he presents the Mass in an unaccompanied vocal performance, and has interpolated the plainchant for a Marian feast (this time the Feast of the Purification). Pérès's innovation, though—and what makes this such a fascinating disc—is to try to revive the ornamentation and even the timbre and sense of ensemble that Machaut's choir would have had.

This effort is almost entirely conjectural, and we will never know how close or far Pérès is to the sound Machaut heard. The hallmarks of his approach are, first of all, a very plain style of singing: instead of the smooth, highly polished timbres and tight ensemble one would expect of a modern group, the Ensemble Organum gives a reading that is earthy and slightly rough at the edges (though by no means slovenly). And the upper vocal lines are adorned with an unusual form of improvisatory ornamentation—everything from wiggled notes and sliding attacks to more ambitious expansions.

As Pérès writes in his liner notes, "Ornamentation is essential, for it creates the active force of the work, renders its rhythmic substance tangible, ensures the transition from one harmony to another and sometimes unbalances a chord to strengthen the sound of the next one. By means of ornamentation, the singer betrays the extent of his involvement with the work."

Recordings of antique church music don't get more involved than this.

3. JOSQUIN DESPREZ

Missa Fortuna Desperata

THE CLERKS' GROUP, EDWARD WICKHAM, CONDUCTING

(ASV Gaudeamus GAU 220)

Includes Josquin Desprez's Missa Fortuna Desperata, *"La Plus des Plus," "Bergerette Savoysienne," "Adieu Mes Amours," "Consideres Mes Incessantes/Fortuna"; "Fortuna Desperata" attributed to Antoine Busnois; Heinrich Isaac's "Bruder Contrat/Fortuna"; Ludwig Senfl's "Herr Durch Dein Bluet/Pange Lingua/Fortuna"; Matthaeus Greiter's "Passibus Ambiguis/Fortuna"; and an anonymous composition entitled "Fortuna Zibaldone."*

Recorded 2000

Around the time this recording was released, Edward Wickham and his Clerks' Group—a superb English ensemble that specializes in early choral music—were touring the United States with *The Original Josquin,* a concert of works by Josquin Desprez (c. 1450–1521), the French composer widely regarded as the towering figure of Renaissance polyphony. It is not only in hindsight that Josquin enjoys such high regard: he held positions at various courts and chapels in France and Italy—including the papal chapel, in Rome, from 1489 to 1495—and with the invention of the printing press and moveable music type, his works became extremely well traveled. The early publisher Petrucci opened his four collections of motets with works by Josquin, and his publication, *Misse Josquin* (1502), was the first printed book of music devoted fully to the work of a single composer. By 1514, Petrucci had published two more volumes of Josquin masses.

While it could undoubtedly be argued that Josquin's fame at the turn of the sixteenth century made him attractive to a publisher like Petrucci, it is also true that publication expanded his fame considerably, a point that Wickham openly explored during their concert tour. Had music publishing been invented a couple of decades later, at the time of Josquin's death, it is possible that we might regard him merely as one of many great composers of the age, rather than as the greatest. Josquin was, in this view, an early media star who benefited from the printing press in much the same way Madonna benefited from music videos nearly five centuries later.

Still, Josquin's music magnificently represents the prevailing styles and practices of its age. This recording includes works by both Josquin and his contemporaries, but the centerpiece is Josquin's Missa Fortuna Desperata, a Mass based on (and named for) a popular chanson that is generally attributed to Antoine Busnois (1430–1492). In Josquin's time, "Fortuna Desperata" was well known throughout Europe, and today early music collectors run into it periodically in versions by several composers. The Clerks' Group, though, proceeds from the logical assumption that "Fortuna" is no longer hummed in every household, so they open the disc with the presumed Antoine Busnois setting (Wickham, in his notes, expresses doubts about the attribution), followed immediately by the Mass.

In some ways, this is an expansion of a practice we encountered in Machaut's Notre Dame Mass: an existing melody—plainchant in Machaut's case, a popular tune in Josquin's—becomes the theme (or cantus firmus) around which the work is built. Still, there are touches that make this more than a straightforward cantus firmus Mass. The melody makes its principal appearances not only in the tenor, but in each of the voices, and there are times when the Mass text is fit to all three vocal lines of the Busnois version—a technique known as parody.

Josquin, of course, does a great deal more than bend "Fortuna" to the contours of the Mass; rather, he uses the melody as the starting point for a brilliant, wide-ranging contrapuntal structure (counterpoint, like polyphony, is the interplay of independent musical lines), and within that structure, the "Fortuna" theme is treated—rhythmically, harmonically, and melodically—to elaborate processes of variations and expansion. Listen, for example, to the quotation of the theme at the start of the Agnus Dei, where it is stretched and embellished almost beyond recognition—and, in fact, turned upside down, a move that one twentieth-century analyst suggested may have been meant to symbolize Fortune's wheel turning.

Wickham and company fill out the recording with other works

that quote from "Fortuna Desperata," sometimes mixed with other popular melodies. A few are by Josquin, most notably "Adieu Mes Amours," in which the complaints are financial rather than amorous, and the gently suggestive "Bergerette Savoysienne," in which the singer propositions a young shepherdess from Savoy. Included, too, are "Fortuna"-based songs by Heinrich Isaac (c. 1450–1517), Ludwig Senfl (c. 1486–c. 1542), and Matthaeus Greiter (who flourished between 1535 and 1550), and an anonymous Florentine skit, "Fortuna Zibaldone."

The Clerks' Group has adopted the practice of singing from a single, large choirbook, as singers in Josquin's day would have done, rather than using individual parts, as modern singers do. One could object, perhaps, that the use of a female soprano is contrary to the practice in Josquin's day, but there is no arguing with the result. This ensemble sings with a purity of tone and an exquisite blend. More to the point, it approaches Josquin's music as part of an evolving continuum, not as an object of reverence.

4. CARLO GESUALDO

Madrigals, from Books III, IV, V, VI

LES ARTS FLORISSANTS, WILLIAM CHRISTIE, CONDUCTING
(Harmonia Mundi HMC 901268)

Recorded 1987

The place of a musician in the social hierarchy, from medieval times through the early nineteenth century, was typically that of an employee, sometimes fairly exalted and sometimes not, depending on the musician's fame or the degree to which an aristocratic patron valued music. Rulers who actually composed were not unheard of: after all, musical training was regarded as part of a well-born person's education, and one can find, in odd corners of the record catalog, a few extant songs by Henry VIII of England, as well as modest works by

Archduke Rudolph of Austria (a student of Beethoven) and King Frederick II of Prussia. But whatever their legacies as rulers may have been, they were musical dilettantes.

That cannot be said of Carlo Gesualdo, prince of Venosa and Count of Conza (c. 1561–1613). Gesualdo was thoroughly devoted to music, and spent much of his life holed away on his estate composing madrigals and sacred works, many of which were published and highly regarded by other composers during his lifetime. Partly because of his melancholy temperament, and also, no doubt, because his position allowed him to follow his muse with no concern about pleasing a patron, Gesualdo was innovative in the extent to which he used chromaticism (a technique in which the music moves beyond the natural notes of the home key) and dissonance to suggest the pain and tensions in the texts he set.

Many of those texts—and certainly those of most of the madrigals in this compellingly sung collection by the French ensemble Les Arts Florissants—are about unrequited love, uncontrollable passion, the metaphorical association of love and death, or just plain death. And as much as one may want to resist pop psychology associations between the music and Gesualdo's life, the links seem pretty clear.

Although Gesualdo was born only a year after his father was given the principality of Venosa, he came from a well-established family: his mother was the niece of Pope Pius IV, and two of his uncles were cardinals. When he succeeded his father as prince, in 1586, he married Maria d'Avalos, who was also from an aristocratic family (and Gesualdo's cousin).

By 1588, however, Maria began conducting an affair with Fabrizio Carafa, the Duke of Andria, and when Gesualdo discovered them in flagrante delicto, on October 16, 1590, he did as any right-thinking prince with a grievously wounded pride and a reputation to protect would do: he murdered them both. The incident became the stuff of legend, immortalized in the poetry of Tasso and several contemporary Neapolitan poets, expanded upon in novels, and commemorated in twentieth-century studies of the composer like *Carlo Gesualdo, Prince of Venosa: Musician and Murderer,* published in 1926 by Cecil Gray and Philip Heseltine (the latter a composer best known by his pen name, Peter Warlock).

Three years after the double murder, Gesualdo married Leonore d'Este, the niece of the Duke of Ferrara. The renowned musical resources at the ducal court in Ferrara inspired Gesualdo to build a resident ensemble of his own. And as his second marriage also proved miserable, though not lethal, Gesualdo increasingly withdrew into composing and music-making. He published his first two books of madrigals under a pseudonym (Gioseppe Pilonij) in 1594, but distanced himself from the style of those works by the time he published Book III, under his own name, in Ferrara in 1595. Book IV followed in 1596; Books V and VI were published in 1611.

What is immediately striking about Gesualdo's music is his responsiveness to the vivid imagery of the texts he drew upon. This takes the form of oddly shaped melodies using intervals that were unusual at the time; phrasing that is dictated by both the rhythms and emotional force of the poetry, even when those rhythms are jagged; and assertively dissonant harmonies.

A particularly striking example, on this disc, is *Sparge la morte al mio Signor,* from Book IV, a piece with twisted religious imagery. The opening lines ("Death spreads over my Lord's face / Over its bleak pallor") are harmonized conventionally and sung with a velvety serenity. But as the narrative continues—particularly the repetitions of the final lines ("But he who sees him shrinking back / Bows his head, hides his face, and dies")—the music moves increasingly through unexpected keys before returning, on the last repetition of the last line, to the serenity of the opening.

In "Mercè grido piangendo," from Book V, Gesualdo doesn't wait so long to reach a state of emotional extremis. "Mercy, mercy, I cry," the vocal quintet begins, each word more tightly ratcheted with emotion. The third word, "grido" (I cry), is virtually a scream of pain. And if the continuation ("But who hears? Ah, alas, I am failing; So I shall die in silence") is couched more gently, the harmonic modulations and sudden dissonant turns are even more extreme than those in "Sparge la morte."

It should come as no surprise that several of the great composers of the twentieth century—most notably Igor Stravinsky, who regarded himself as an iconoclast in the Gesualdo mold—took this music to heart. But Gesualdo's work has not been well served on disc. As of this writing, there are fine recordings available of Gesualdo's sacred music, by the Tallis Scholars (Gimell) and the Hilliard Ensemble (ECM), yet there are no complete collections of his astounding madrigals currently in print.

Of the available compilations, the most satisfying by far is this CD by William Christie, an American conductor and harpsichordist who has built his career in Paris and is best known for his productions and recordings of French baroque opera. The selection of madrigals is superb, and Christie's fine singers are equal to the challenges of Gesualdo's harmonic, rhythmic, and coloristic peculiarities.

Another appealing touch here is the inclusion of instrumental works—mostly renderings of madrigals—as palate-cleansers to separate the selections from each of Gesualdo's madrigal books. They are performed as harp works, either unaccompanied or as duets with lirone (a precursor of the cello) or theorbo (a large lute), by Andrew Lawrence-King, a harpist who, in the decade following this recording, went on to become an early-music world star in his own right.

5. JOHN DOWLAND

First Booke of Songes

THE CONSORT OF MUSICKE, ANTHONY ROOLEY,
LUTENIST AND DIRECTOR
(L'Oiseau-Lyre 421 653-2)

Recorded 1976

English music came into its own, at least temporarily, during the reign of Elizabeth I, when composers in and around her court produced a vast body of songs and madrigals—many of them driven by the same bawdy double-entendres one finds in Shakespeare and other playwrights of the time—as well as sacred works. John Dowland (1563–1626) was certainly the greatest of the many composers who flourished in and around the Elizabethan and Jacobean court, at least in the realm of secular music: although he composed some exquisite psalm settings and other sacred works, both early and late in life, William Byrd surpassed him as a composer of sacred works. Dowland lived an intriguing, if frustrating, life. At seventeen, he traveled to France in the employ of Sir Henry Cobham, the English ambassador to the French court, and during his stay he apparently perfected his technique as a lutenist, and made the decision—politically unwise for a subject of Protestant England—to convert to Catholicism. Back in England in 1588, he earned a degree in music from Oxford University, but by then he was already famous enough to be included in Dr. John Case's *Apologia Musices* as one of the best-known musicians of the day.

His name crops up regularly in records of royal festivities. But the one thing he wanted most, an official position at the English court, eluded him until he was fifty, a slight he attributed to official prejudice against Catholics. In the mid-1590s, he traveled in Europe, performing at various German courts and assimilating the compositional styles prevalent there and in Italy.

By his own account, Dowland turned down several court positions in Germany, but in 1598, still lacking an offer of an equivalent English post, he accepted a position in the service of King Christian IV of Denmark, where he remained (apart from several extended visits to England) until 1606. Back in England, he continued to win the support of individual patrons, to whom he dedicated his popular books of songs, and in 1612 he finally won an appointment as a lutenist (one of five) in the court of King James I, a position he apparently held until his death in 1626.

Music publishing was a fairly new business in Dowland's time, and after discovering that some of his lute pieces had been published without his consent, and in versions he regarded as inaccurate, he undertook the publication of his own works. All told, he produced four books of songs (the first three were simply numbered; the fourth was published as *A Pilgrimes Solace*) between 1597 and 1612, as well as a collection of consort works that included seven differently characterized versions of one of his most famous songs, "Lachrimae," also known as "Flow My Tears." In addition, a group of sacred pieces not included among these publications has survived, as have more than ninety lute works, some demanding a level of virtuosity that has kept them at the heart of the modern guitar and lute repertory.

The First Booke of Songes or Ayres of Fowre Partes with Tablature for the Lute, to use the full title and spelling that appears on the title page of the first printing, from 1597, is the cream of Dowland's vocal music. Among its twenty-one songs are many that had proven popular in the early years of his career, and were included largely in the hope that "authorized" versions would circumvent the market for pirated editions. They display all the hallmarks of Dowland and his age, from affectations of dolefulness, often associated with unrequited love, to a lively eroticism, and quite a few of them—"Can She Excuse," "If My Complaints," "Come Again," and "Come, Heavy Sleep," for example—remain among the most frequently performed of the era's rich lute song repertory.

The Consort of Musicke's recording of this collection—the first installment of a complete traversal of Dowland's music, finished in 1982—established this group of young singers and players as the best of what was then the new generation of British early-music groups. The singers—Emma Kirkby, soprano; John York Skinner, countertenor; Martyn Hill, tenor; and David Thomas, bass—each brought a fresh, distinctive vocal timbre and judicious use of vibrato to the project. Kirkby, in particular, sings here with a purity of tone that gives this recording much of its character, but it is often the blend of the four voices that makes the performance so magical.

The ensemble's choices in what today would be called the "arrangement" of the music shape the sound delightfully. Unlike a modern score, which specifies such details as the kinds of voices and instruments to be used, and exactly what the instrumental accompanists are to play, Dowland's books leave these issues to the performers. This music was, after all, meant for performances of all kinds—at court or in private homes, by professionals or amateurs, soloists or ensembles. For each song, he provided four lines of vocal counterpoint, as well as tablature for an accompanying lute part. They could be performed by a single voice with lute (or lute and bass viol) accompaniment, or with the accompaniment of a full consort of viols; or, perhaps, by two voices with lute, or even as four-part madrigals, with or without accompaniment. They could even be performed instrumentally, by groups of viols, or recorders, or both.

The Consort of Musicke comprises voices, lute, and viols, and Anthony Rooley deploys them in just about every possible way, and sometimes in several different ways as a song unfolds. In "Go, Crystal Tears," for example, the first verse is performed by tenor and lute, the second by four voices. On the 1976 LP release, the variety was even greater: the two verses were separated by a version for four viols. That instrumental rendering, and similar ones in "Would My Conceit" and "Come, Heavy Sleep," were removed when the recording was transferred to CD, in order to fit the set (originally on two LPs) onto a single CD. It's a pity, and I would advocate searching for the original LP.

Still, regrettable as these trims are, none of the music or text of the *First Booke* has been sacrificed, and even in its truncated form, this is a disc I would take to the proverbial desert island. Listen to the opening song, the sweetly melancholy "Unquiet Thoughts," often performed as a work for solo voice and lute. The Consort of Musicke instead uses its full vocal complement, yielding an arrangement in which each verse begins with an arresting sequence of four solid chords, followed by imitative contrapuntal interplay as the verse unfolds. I can't imagine a listener not being seduced, immediately and completely, both by the music and by this ensemble's sound.

6. SHAKESPEARE SONGS AND CONSORT MUSIC

ALFRED DELLER, COUNTERTENOR; DESMOND DUPRÉ, LUTENIST; THE DELLER CONSORT
(Harmonia Mundi HMA 195202)

Includes William Byrd's Non Nobis Domine; Francis Cutting's Walsingham Variations; Robert Johnson's "Where the Bee Sucks" and "Full Fathom Five"; Thomas Morley's "It Was a Lover and His Lass" and "O Mistress Mine"; Thomas Weelkes's "Strike It Up, Tabor"; John Wilson's

"Take O Take Those Lips Away"; and the unattributed songs "Willow Song," "How Should I Your True Love Know," "We Be Soldiers Three," "When Griping Griefs," "Calleno Custure Me," "Then They for Sudden Joy Did Weep," "Bonny Sweet Robin," "When That I Was," "Kemp's Jig," "Greensleeves," and "He That Will an Alehouse Keep."

Recorded 1969

The gulf between popular and high culture that exists today was not so pronounced a few centuries ago. That isn't to say that a gulf of sorts didn't exist, but its parameters were entirely different. The infatuation with a settled canon of works created in the past, which is at the center of today's definition of high and low art, did not arise until the nineteenth century. In earlier times, the categories were more functional: sacred works, composed for the chapels of kings and princes, or for church use generally, were the equivalent of high art, and everything else might be considered popular. Within that world of secular music, there were distinctions, of course, but an anonymous folk melody could be as beloved as a song by a favored composer.

This was certainly the case in Elizabethan England, and this classic collection of songs—popular songs in their day, art songs by today's reckoning—fully conveys the flavor of the age. With the obvious exception of John Dowland, many of the greatest composers of the time are included, among them Thomas Morley (c. 1557–1602), Thomas Weelkes (c. 1576–1623), John Wilson (1595–1674), and Robert Johnson (c. 1583–1633). What most (but not all) of these songs share is an association with the plays of William Shakespeare. Some are merely mentioned in passing, but quite a few are actually performed. Morley's "It Was a Lover and His Lass," for example, is sung by the Second Page in act 5 of *As You Like It,* and the clown, Feste, sings a verse of the same composer's "O Mistress Mine" in act 2 of *Twelfth Night.*

Shakespeare did not commission composers to write these songs; on the contrary, he preferred to use songs so popular that anyone hearing the play could be expected to know the song and its lyric—and, therefore, what it said about the character or situation in which it appears. What could be more suitable for Ariel to sing to the survivors of the shipwreck in *The Tempest* than Robert Johnson's "Full Fathom Five"—or, when he is promised his freedom, Johnson's ebullient "Where the Bee Sucks."

Probably the most famous of these, however, is the "Willow Song," which Desdemona sings in act 4 of *Othello,* just before her jealous husband murders her. An anonymous lament that touches on faithlessness and lost love, it concludes with a verse that Shakespeare did not incorporate in his text, but which his audience would have known: "Take this for my farewell and latest adieu / Write this on my tomb, that in love I was true." Even without its foreshadowing, this intensely melancholy song is perfect for the moment, and this Elizabethan original is, in my view, immensely more moving than the version Verdi composed for *Otello.*

The performances here are by the great English countertenor Alfred Deller, a true early-music pioneer. The countertenor voice, essentially a male alto, is meant to convey something of the sound produced in centuries past by castratos—talented singers who were castrated before their voices changed, so that they could retain their high vocal range. The practice hardly bears contemplation now, but there were ample compensations, at least for those castratos who became famous opera stars, some of whom (the eighteenth-century soprano Farinelli, for example) remain famous to this day. The last-known castrato, Alessandro Moreschi, was born in 1858 and lived long enough to make a handful of recordings around 1902.

Deller began his career in the 1940s, and was particularly evocative in the works of Purcell and the Elizabethan composers, but he had a broad repertory, and created the role of Oberon in Britten's *Midsummer Night's Dream.* Today's countertenors have built on the foundation that he provided, and the best of them—singers like David Daniels and Brian Asawa—sing with a roundness and power of projection far beyond what Deller was able to achieve. But Deller's voice had a quality that any great singer works hard to cultivate: a distinctive personality that is immediately recognizable. His recordings capture that beautifully, and they remain treasures of their era.

On this one, Deller is in most cases accompanied by the lutenist Desmond Dupré, who also has the spotlight to himself for a few lute solos, including the lovely *Walsingham* Variations by Francis Cutting

Countertenor Alfred Deller

(1583–c. 1603) and two anonymous works that have long been staples of Elizabethan lute recitals, *Kemp's Jig* and *Bonny Sweet Robin* (also sometimes called *Robin Is to the Greenwood Gone*). Deller is also heard in a few selections with members of the Deller Consort, the vocal ensemble he founded in 1950.

Among these is an interesting oddity: Non Nobis Domine, a beautiful liturgical setting by one of the era's greatest composers of sacred music, William Byrd (1543–1623). It is a short piece, and it closes the program on a note of serenity. But it also touches on the continuity of the musical tradition, since it is based on a rising musical figure that many later composers have used—most notably Johann Sebastian Bach, in the Dona Nobis Pacem that closes his Mass in B minor.

7. CLAUDIO MONTEVERDI

Vespro della Beata Virgine (1610)

THE MONTEVERDI CHOIR; THE LONDON ORATORY
JUNIOR CHOIR; HIS MAJESTIES SAGBUTTS & CORNETTS;
THE ENGLISH BAROQUE SOLOISTS,
SIR JOHN ELIOT GARDINER, CONDUCTING
(Archiv 429 565-2, two CDs; also available on DVD)

Ann Monoyios, Marinella Pennicchi, sopranos; Michael Chance, countertenor; Mark Tucker, Nigel Robson, Sandro Naglia, tenors; Bryn Terfel, Alastair Miles, basses.

Recorded 1989

Because musical eras don't click into place with the clockwork precision suggested in music appreciation classes, the generally agreed—and certainly deserved—stature of Claudio Monteverdi (1567–1643) as the first great baroque composer requires at least a small asterisk. To the extent that he participated mightily in the development of one of the great new forms that helped define the early baroque—that is, opera—and in the sense that he was an ardent exponent of a new, vividly expressive style of madrigal composition that was also a significant leap into the new era, he was clearly a baroque composer. It should be borne in mind, however, that the sounds that Monteverdi knew—the instruments he wrote for—were those of the Renaissance, and quite different from the comparatively modern models available to later baroque composers.

That said, this brilliant set of Vespers tells us a lot about the roots of the ornate baroque style, and also about Monteverdi's considerable contributions to its foundation. Monteverdi composed it sometime after 1607, when he had been a musician at the Gonzaga court in Mantua for more than fifteen years and was seeking new employment. He was, by then, recognized as an important composer, whose works were known well beyond Italy. He was also a devoted modernist, which is to say that he adhered to the new notion that held that music must be responsive to the meaning of the text, and he had engaged in a war of published treatises with the conservative theorist Giovanni Maria Artusi, who argued for the primacy of music over words.

He had already written the first of his celebrated operas, *L'Orfeo*, in 1607, as well as the lost opera *Arianna* (1608). But the intrigues and demands of the Gonzagas, as well as what he regarded as poor compensation, had led him to look elsewhere. When the Vespers were published, in 1610, they carried a dedication to Pope Paul V, possibly in the hope of a musical post in Rome. Nothing came of that, but upon the death in 1613 of the maestro di cappella at the Basilica of St. Mark's, in Venice, Monteverdi sent the Vespers as part of his application for the post. For his audition that August, he was required to provide the complete music for the Feast of the Assumption, one of several feasts in honor of the Virgin Mary in the course of the liturgical year, and an occasion for which these Vespers are ideally suited. Four days after the audition, Monteverdi was confirmed in the post.

It's hard to imagine a more smashing audition piece than these Vespers. The evening service begins, amazingly, with the same brass Toccata that opens *L'Orfeo*, fitted out here with the chorus intoning— amid the swirl of celebratory noise—a plainchant reading of the line that opens Psalm 70, "Oh God, turn to me in my adversity." What follows is a series of psalm settings, a hymn, and a closing Magnificat—movements that all the Marian feasts have in common—scored for five- and even ten-part choirs, sometimes placed antiphonally around the basilica, with the support of the range of winds, brass, strings, and continuo instruments (organ, lutes, and sometimes a harpsichord) that Monteverdi had at his disposal.

Between each of the psalms, Monteverdi supplies vocal movements he called Concerto and Sonata (terms that did not yet specifically connote instrumental works), which use texts from the Song of Songs, Isaiah, and other sources, and are often overtly theatrical. "Pulchra es" and "Duo Seraphim," for example, are dialogues that would not have been out of place in one of Monteverdi's operas; and "Audi coelum" uses a distantly placed singer to create an echo effect, something Monteverdi also uses in the Magnificat.

There was another element as well: space. The acoustics of the Basilica of St. Mark's are extremely resonant, and although we don't know exactly where Monteverdi's various forces were placed, we do know what a performance of the Vespers sounds like at the basilica, since that is where Sir John Eliot Gardiner and company made this recording. Notable, as well, is the fact that the recording is drawn from concert performances. First, an audience diminishes the reverberance of a hall somewhat, and since a congregation would have been on hand in 1613, it made sense to have one available for the recording. And from a performance perspective, there is much to be said for the sweep of a live recording, rather than the start-and-stop methods typical of studio recordings today.

One of the pleasures of following the early-music world is watching conductors, musicologists, and conductor-musicologists adopt theories about how the music was meant to be performed, and then square off against one another in polemical battles, fought not only in the pages of scholarly journals, but also in the liner notes for recordings and in the performances themselves. Monteverdi and Artusi would be smiling. In the case of the Monteverdi Vespers, most performers took the 1610 published version at face value until the 1980s, when younger musicologists began wondering whether the published version reflected (or was even meant to reflect) the order and contents of a Vespers service in Monteverdi's day. Interpreting the evidence differently from their predecessors, they proposed new ways of ordering the psalms and concertos, and duly recorded them.

This, Gardiner argues in a detailed liner essay, is nonsense. He cites various documents showing that the inclusion of the concertos and sonatas was typical in Venice around that time, and finds the evidence of the published order more compelling than speculative reconstructions.

Still, he adds an innovation of his own. Most conductors, before and since the release of this recording, have added plainchant appropriate for one of the Marian feasts as a preface to each of the psalms, on the theory that this would have been done as a matter of course, with the plainchant offering the congregation a moment for reflection before the grandeur of the choral psalm setting. Not so, according to Gardiner. For one thing, Monteverdi included the plainchant within his ornate settings—indeed, one of the great innovations of this work is the simultaneous use of the old (plainchant) and new styles— so singing it on its own would be redundant. Moreover, he argues, the between-psalms concertos were meant to take the place of the plainchant.

In the end, though, it isn't the musicology that carries the day for this recording, it's the sheer exuberance of the performance. Tempos are brisk, the instrumental playing is remarkably polished, and both the choral and solo singing are full of character and spirit. The setting of Psalm 127, Nisi Dominus, is the most viscerally exciting account I've heard on disc, and the boys' choir performance of the Sonata Sopra Sancta Maria has an uncommon sweetness and transparency, even in the echoic St. Mark's. Mainly, what makes this recording come alive is that the performers sound as if they are passionately convinced of everything they are singing and playing.

8. CLAUDIO MONTEVERDI

Madrigali Guerrieri ed Amorosi
(Madrigals, Book VIII)

CONCERTO VOCALE, RENÉ JACOBS, CONDUCTING
(Harmonia Mundi HMC 901736.37; two CDs)

Recorded 2000

Composers who are primarily revered for works built on a grand scale quite frequently devoted themselves with equal vigor and imagination to pieces that, on the surface, seem more modest. In Monteverdi's case, a handful of surviving operas and the Vespers are the monuments that have won him a place in musical history, yet he was equally devoted to the more intimate art of the madrigal, a song form that flourished in the sixteenth century (we have already savored some by John Dowland and Carlo Gesualdo), but had essentially died out as a popular form by the seventeenth.

Monteverdi published this amazingly varied collection of madrigals in 1638, when he was seventy-one, and he seems to have intended it as a grand manifesto, intended to show what he regarded as the expansive capabilities of the madrigal. More specifically, he meant the book to illustrate an approach to expressive text setting that he had been perfecting for several decades. Drawing on madrigals going back as far as the 1620s, Monteverdi compiled a work that stood as a showcase for what he called the *concitato,* or "agitated" style. He described his aims and methods in a preface, which he began by asserting the novelty of his approach:

"Having considered that our mind has three principal passions, or affections—anger, temperance and humility or supplication—as the best philosophers affirm and, indeed, considering that the very nature of our voice falls into a high, low and medium range. Music theory describes this clearly with the three terms: 'agitated,' 'languid' and 'temperate.' In all the works of past composers, I have indeed found examples of the 'languid' and the 'temperate,' but never of the 'agitated,' a style described by Plato in his third book, 'On Rhetoric.' . . . I therefore, with no little research and effort, set myself the task of discovering it."

As its title suggests, the work is divided into two sections, the first devoted to songs of war (*Canti Guerrieri*), the second to songs of love (*Canti Amorosi*). Both subjects, of course, lend themselves to the "agitated" style that Monteverdi was intent on exploring, and indeed, the two are by no means mutually exclusive here. In the *Canti Guerrieri*, the skills of the good warrior are sometimes likened to those of a persistent lover, and although some of the songs are literally about battle, others are love plaints steeped in the imagery of war. The crossover in the *Canti Amorosi* is less overt, but there is a suggested association between the pain of unrequited love and that of wounds suffered in battle.

Monteverdi's *concitato* style is, above all, pictorial: in both mood and physical gesture, the music directly and immediately reflects the emotions and action of the poetry, whether implicit or explicit. The opening verse of "Hor che' le ciel e la terra," for example, describes a placid scene: heaven, earth, and wind are still, beasts and birds are asleep, and the sky is starry and calm. Writing for vocal sextet (other works here are for as few as one or as many as eight voices), Monteverdi sets this text to a slow-moving, velvety chord progression, as sublimely peaceful as the scene the text describes. But at the line "Veglio, penso, ardo, paingo" (I wake, I ponder, I burn, I weep), the transformation is sudden: the words are sharply enunciated and the volume builds with each declaration.

Another picturesque example, "Vago augelletto" (Pretty Little Bird), is a setting of a Petrarch sonnet, for seven voices, which begins with a flighty vocal figure that evokes the bird song mentioned at the start of the poem. But that lasts for only one line of text: when Petrarch continues the thought—"or weeping your bygone days"—Monteverdi abruptly switches to dark, slow-moving, mournful music. In a verbal description, it sounds disjointed, but of course, this music is meant to be heard, not described—and hearing it, with the text at hand, a listener is drawn fully into Monteverdi's world.

The most striking example of the *concitato* style—and for me, one of the most exquisite of Monteverdi's works—is "Il Combattimento de Tancredi e Clorinda." This intensely dramatic scene for bass (the narrator), tenor (Tancredi), and soprano (Clorinda) lasts nearly twenty minutes, and is meant to be played with costumes and staging, as it was at its first performance in 1624 or 1625. It is closer in spirit to opera than to madrigal, but its tone painting is so visceral that one scarcely needs to understand Italian to see the action unfold. The galloping of Tancredi's horse as he apprehends Clorinda, who is disguised as a knight, is captured in the rhythm of the string writing, and as the singers enact the battle described in the Tasso text (and sung by the narrator), the instrumental ensemble mimics the thrusting of swords and the shield and helmet butting of armored combat.

The work really soars, though, after Clorinda's defeat. Its final moments are transfixing: Clorinda requests water to wash away her sins before she dies, and Tancredi, complying, discovers her identity and administers the last rites. Monteverdi makes Tancredi's anguish palpable, but even that pales beside the last notes heard in the piece—the ascending chromatic figure, followed by a graceful turn, to which he sets Clorinda's dying words, "S'apre il ciel: io vado in pace"—"Heaven opens, I go in peace."

René Jacobs and Concerto Vocale have made several first-rate Monteverdi recordings over the years, and this complete *Madrigali Guerrieri ed Amorosi* is a stunning addition to its discography. The performances are vital and fresh, and they are executed with Monteverdi's expressive notions fully in mind.

All told, Jacobs uses a dozen singers, deployed in well-balanced combinations and supported by a finely polished instrumental ensemble. There are some unusual touches here. Ensembles approaching these madrigals have generally kept to the prescribed instrumentation, strings and continuo. Jacobs adds brass and percussion instruments, in ways that are sometimes subtle and sometimes not, but which are always justified by the texts, and which enliven the performances.

The continuo group is equally expansive. Time was when a continuo consisted of a harpsichord and a cello; Jacobs has the full range of potential continuo instruments on hand—among them, organ, harpsichord, lute, theorbo, guitar, harp, and bowed bass instruments—and has selected combinations that suit the texts.

Economy is an attraction here as well: Jacobs and company get the full collection onto two discs. The Consort of Musicke, in its own superb traversal (Virgin Classics, 1989–1990), required three, principally because the works are presented at generally slower tempos. That set was recently reissued on two discs, but at a cost: the twenty-minute "Ballo della Ingrate," an important component of the book, was deleted.

9. HENRY PURCELL

Odes for St. Cecilia's Day and Music for Queen Mary

TAVERNER CONSORT, CHOIR AND PLAYERS,
ANDREW PARROTT, CONDUCTING
(Virgin Veritas 5 61582 2, two CDs)

Emma Kirkby, soprano; Michael Chance and Kevin Smith, countertenors; Rogers Covey-Crump, Charles Daniels, Paul Elliott, Neil Jenkins, and Andrew King, tenors; Michael George, Simon Grant, David Thomas, and Richard Wistreich, basses; Robert Woolley, organ. Includes Welcome to All the Pleasures *(Ode for St. Cecilia's Day, 1683),* Funeral Sentences, Come Ye Sons of Art *(Birthday Song for Queen Mary, 1694),* "Funeral Music for Queen Mary," Hail! Bright Cecilia *(Ode for St. Cecilia's Day, 1692).*

Recorded 1985, 1988

There is something appealingly quaint about the tradition, current in late-seventeenth- and early-eighteenth-century England, of musicians and music lovers assembling every November 22 to celebrate Saint Cecilia's Day—Saint Cecilia being the patron saint of musicians—with an evening's entertainment that included a feast and the performance of a specially composed ode. For some thirty years, starting in 1683, the London focus of these feasts was Stationer's Hall. Henry Purcell (c. 1659–1695), the most celebrated English composer of the age, contributed odes to the very first of these feasts, in 1683, and to others in 1685 and 1692.

The first of those odes, *Welcome to All the Pleasures,* as well as Purcell's expansive 1692 contribution, *Hail! Bright Cecilia,* are the centerpieces of this beautifully played collection led by the early-music specialist Andrew Parrott. Gathered with them, though, are some equally characteristic Purcell works—the early *Funeral Sentences,* composed in 1680, *Come Ye Sons of Art,* the last and most famous of the six birthday odes he wrote for Queen Mary, in 1694, as well as the sublime music he provided for her funeral in March 1695—music that was used again for Purcell's own funeral at Westminster Abbey only nine months later, when he died at the age of thirty-six.

Purcell's career was extraordinary. The son of a court musician, he was immersed in music from childhood. As a boy, he was a chorister in the Chapel Royal of King Charles II, and at eighteen he was appointed composer for the king's violins, and soon became an organist in the Chapel Royal as well. By 1680, he was composing not only for the royal court and chapel, but was writing theater works. Purcell maintained his status as a court composer during the reign of James II and after the accession of William III and Mary, in 1689, although by then his composition for the court was eclipsed by his work for the theater.

Many influences impacted Purcell's style: his overtures, with their elegant dotted rhythms, mirror the style of French opera composers like Jean-Baptiste Lully, and his florid text settings show traces of both French and Italian models. Yet Purcell's own uniquely English musical accent comes through distinctly, and influenced composers of the next generation: Handel's English works, for example, sometimes have a hint of Purcell's ghost lingering over them.

Of the works included here, the most expansive is the 1692 ode, a setting of a poem by Nicholas Brady, the royal chaplain, that glorifies the art of music—both in the abstract (as a "Celestial Art" and "Universal Tongue") and with reference to specific instruments (among them, organ, flute, fife, trumpet, and drum) and the spirit they evoke—and venerates "Bright Cecilia" as the "Great Patroness of Us and Harmony." The purely Purcellian charms in this thirteen-movement work include an opening symphony that begins with an antiphonal dialogue for trumpets and strings, magnificently florid arias for the vocal soloists, and robust, spacious choral writing.

Parrott's performance adheres to the scholarly style that, in the 1980s, also proved to be the most exciting way to bring this music to life. The vocal soloists use vibrato sparingly and expressively, rather than lathered over the line as a matter of course, and the singers—Emma Kirkby and other stars of the English early-music world—are expert at that approach. The accompanying ensemble performs on period instruments, also using comparatively little vibrato, and producing a sound that varies from bracingly astringent to sublimely polished, as the music dictates. And instead of tuning to today's standard concert pitch of A=440 (that is, the A above middle C on the keyboard vibrates at 440 cycles per second), Parrott and company acknowledge the fact that pitch has crept upward since Purcell's time by using a tuning of A=392. Going by modern pitch standards, 392 cycles per second is actually the note we know as G, meaning that the performance is pitched a full step lower than it appears on the page. In practical terms, this proves good news for tenors and sopranos, for whom the vocal writing becomes somewhat more comfortable.

Parrott offers a fairly audacious innovation as well. Since two of the movements—"With That Sublime Celestial Lay" and "Wond'rous Machine"—are paeans to the organ, he interpolates an organ work, Purcell's Voluntary in D minor, between them. There are arguments to be made for and against—it is certainly in the spirit of the piece, but it is unlikely that the work was actually presented in this manner. But it's a fine performance and the risk pays off.

The two CDs in this midprice reissue were originally issued separately at full price. As is so often the case in the record industry, bargains are not without cost. The original issues, released by EMI/Angel in the late 1980s, had booklets that included extensive notes as well as texts for the vocal works. The concisely packaged Virgin Veritas reissue offers a condensed three-paragraph gloss on Purcell and these pieces.

Opera, of course, is beyond the purview of this book, but my favorite Purcell recording—and one of my favorite recordings in any genre—is Parrott's 1981 account of *Dido and Aeneas*, with Emma Kirkby and David Thomas in the title roles (Chandos). The ensemble textures, the purity of the soloists' vocal sound, the care given to interpolating dance pieces where the score indicated that short dances were intended, and the sheer energy of the performance all make it a must for anyone interested in this composer's finest work.

10. JOHANN SEBASTIAN BACH

Brandenburg Concertos

IL GIARDINO ARMONICO
(Teldec 4509-98442, two CDs)

Recorded 1997

How does one begin to choose among the recordings of J. S. Bach's music—or even the best recordings of his greatest music? Both prolific and prodigiously inventive, Bach composed well over a thousand works and addressed virtually every genre (opera being a notable exception) common in the first half of the eighteenth century. Along with comparatively few others—Mozart and Beethoven come to mind—Bach could easily account for all one hundred selections in this volume.

The Bach performance tradition, captured on more than a century's worth of recordings, reflects innumerable shifts in taste and changes in performance practice. Not least among these is a healthy (and sometimes bellicose) give-and-take between advocates of period instruments who insist that Bach's music should be performed using the sounds that were in Bach's ear, and champions of modern instruments who insist—*pace* Marshall McLuhan—that the medium is not the message. Beyond that, the decades have seen changing theories on everything from the basics (what tempos are appropriate, how large ensembles should be) to the finer points (whether performers should add ornamentation to Bach's already florid lines, and if so, how much improvisatory leeway they should have).

The popular thumbnail view of Bach is that he was the central figure of the baroque era, which ran roughly from 1600 to 1750. Yet Bach's renown is largely posthumous. During his lifetime (1685–1750) his music was often at odds with the prevailing tastes. An early position as a church organist in Mulhausen ended abruptly when congregants complained that his harmonization of their favorite chorales was too modern. Late in Bach's life, when the contrapuntal complexities that were his musical lifeblood gave way to rococo simplicity, Bach's works were considered fussy and old-fashioned.

Still, as music history has shown time and again, things have a way of shaking out, and now Bach has it all: musicians and scholars revere him for his supreme mastery of counterpoint, and laymen who don't necessarily care about the details find both exquisite beauty and visceral excitement in many of Bach's works. One set of pieces that embodies both qualities—the visceral side may have the slight edge— is the suite of concertos that Bach compiled for Christian Ludwig, the Margrave of Brandenburg, in 1721.

I used the word *compiled* rather than *composed* because despite their association with the margrave, the *Brandenburg* Concertos were not actually written for him, and it is likely that Christian Ludwig never heard them performed. His own Berlin orchestra was of only modest accomplishment, and was most likely not up to the task. These are works for virtuoso instrumentalists—players who are first-rate both as soloists and as ensemble players. One need only listen to Il Giardino Armonico's brisk period instrument performances—with special attention to the solo trumpet part in the Second Concerto, the expansive harpsichord part in the Fifth Concerto, and the tandem horn writing in the First Concerto—to appreciate the technical challenges.

The idea that these six works are a unified collection is a modern notion. True, the beautifully written manuscript that Bach sent to the margrave—probably as a subtle job application—gives that impression. But Bach certainly didn't compose them as a cycle. Some movements date back as far as 1713, and Bach would reconfigure them for use in other contexts (as cantata movements, for example) as late as 1729. To Bach, these were simply part of a vast inventory of useful pieces.

Yet Bach brought these particular works together for a reason, and they continue to work incredibly well as a set. Each concerto is scored for a different ensemble makeup. Horns, oboes, a bassoon, and a violin (actually a violino piccolo, a small violin tuned to higher pitch than the standard instrument) give the First Concerto its particular coloration. In the Second, trumpet, flute, violin, and oboe hold the spotlight. The Third and Sixth are scored for string ensembles—but where the Third is conventionally balanced (violins, violas, and cellos), the Sixth is for darker, low-lying instruments (violas, gambas, and cellos). A pair of recorders and a solo violin give the Fourth its bright, woody character. And although the Fifth has ear-catching solo parts for violin and flute, it is the enormous harpsichord cadenza in the first movement that is the work's calling card.

Virtually every period-instrument band on the planet has tried its hand at the *Brandenburgs,* and among Il Giardino Armonico's most estimable competitors are sets by the English Concert (Archiv, 1982), the Academy of Ancient Music (L'Oiseau-Lyre, 1984), and the New London Consort (also on L'Oiseau-Lyre, 1993). Modern-instrument groups occasionally try their hand at the works as well, and now that so many younger musicians play on both old and new instruments, the modern performances no longer have the ponderousness that used to weigh them down. There is even a quirkily interesting traversal on the synthesizer, by Wendy Carlos, who included the Third on her classic *Switched-On Bach* album for CBS in 1968 (reissued by East Side Digital).

Il Giardino Armonico's sheer sparkle gives it the edge. This Italian group was founded in 1985, and is directed by Giovanni Antonini, one of its flutists. It plays with an uncommon zestiness and precision, but probably the most immediately thrilling aspect of the performance is its bright and sometimes unusual timbres. The horns in the First Concerto, for example, are brash and gamey, but they are also thoroughly in tune, and they sit perfectly in this robust reading.

Notable, too, is the speedy string playing in the Allegro and Presto movements, the consistently brilliant solo playing, and an approach to dynamics that is so beautifully nuanced that the music always sounds fresh and surprising. And when Bach offers a bit of improvisatory space, the Giardino players take it: where some groups simply (and disappointingly) play the two-noted chords that appear between the two movements of the Third Concerto, Giardino sees those chords as an invitation to play a brief cadenza, which one of its violinists does with consummate taste.

11. JOHANN SEBASTIAN BACH

Sonatas and Partitas for Unaccompanied Violin
(BWV 1001–1006)

CHRISTIAN TETZLAFF, VIOLINIST

(Virgin Classics 45089 2; two CDs)

Recorded 1993

When we think of Bach as a practical, performing musician, the image that comes immediately to mind for most of us is that of a keyboard player. It's only natural: his duties as a church organist yielded a copious amount of music for that instrument, ranging from pious chorale preludes to more free-spirited toccatas, fantasias, and passacaglias. And, of course, the harpsichord literature is blessed with countless Bach works, from the *Goldberg* Variations, the Chromatic Fantasy and Fugue, and the *Inventions* to the *English* and *French* Suites, the keyboard concertos, and the two astonishing books of preludes and fugues called *The Well-Tempered Clavier*—to say nothing of the concertos.

Bach's son Carl Philipp Emanuel Bach remembered him differently, though. In a letter to Johann Nicholas Forkel, Bach's first biographer, in 1774, the younger Bach wrote that his father "liked best to play the viola, with appropriate loudness and softness. In his youth, and until the approach of old age, he played the violin cleanly and penetratingly, and thus kept the orchestra in better order than he could have done with the harpsichord. He understood to perfection the possibilities of all stringed instruments."

That explains something about his ability to write such virtuosic yet fully idiomatic music for the violin and cello, for which he produced both accompanied sonatas and unaccompanied works.

At a glance, it might seem odd for Bach to have expended such effort writing contrapuntal works for instruments that are optimally configured to play single musical lines. When playing within an ensemble or with other instruments providing harmonic support, the violin or cello might evoke anything from quiet, lilting introspection to soaring, daredevil virtuosity. But the instruments are not made for counterpoint or chordal writing, or for supporting their own melodies with built-in accompaniments. In asking musicians to do all these things in his unaccompanied works, Bach demands that they bend the instrument to their will, and his.

In the case of the violin works, there was a vogue for unaccompanied virtuoso pieces among German violinists in the first decades of the eighteenth century, many of whom composed or improvised their own works. Bach might have written these works to play himself, or he might have written them for a friend with the considerable technique they demand. Or he may have written them as a theoretical exercise—one of several important works (including the *Brandenburgs,* the Mass in B minor, and the *Art of Fugue*) compiled mainly to show what could be done within the confines of the format. All we know for certain is that they have survived in a beautifully written manuscript dated 1720.

With Bach, of course, the phrase "what could be done within the confines" is hardly as limiting as it sounds. Consider the layout of the six works. Three are sonatas, a distinction that indicates a formality that Bach observed in his slow-fast-slow-fast design, with expansive fugues—glorious contrapuntal structures in which a theme is first stated in a single musical line and then repeated at the start of each new line as it is added to the increasingly complex and interlocking texture—as their second movements. The other three are partitas, or suites of dance movements somewhat freer and more varied in their structure. One might expect the center of gravity to be in the sonatas, yet it is at the end of the Partita no. 2 that Bach provides an extraordinary Chaconne—a grandly exploratory set of variations that is one of the highlights of Western classical music.

Just about every great violinist who has made recordings has turned his or her attention to these works at least once, and indeed there are great recordings from the full parade of legendary violinists, starting with Yehudi Menuhin (EMI, 1934–1936), and including Jascha Heifetz (RCA, 1952), Arthur Grumiaux (Philips, 1960), Nathan Milstein (Deutsche Grammophon, 1973), Gidon Kremer (Philips, 1980), and Itzhak Perlman (1986–1987).

The recording I have chosen, though, is a recent traversal by Christian Tetzlaff, a young German violinist at the start of what promises to be a captivating career. Tetzlaff was just twenty-seven when he recorded this set, yet technically and interpretively the performance is breathtaking. He displays an exquisitely focused sound, seemingly limitless agility that puts his preference for brisk tempos well within his grasp, and a truly surprising ability to avoid many of the compromises that violinists naturally make in these contrapuntal works.

Bach's chordal writing, for example, is rendered with remarkable solidity rather than in the more conventional arpeggiated style (that is, with the notes of a chord played one at a time) that the curve of the violin's bridge would seem to impose. He uses slurs reluctantly, preferring to articulate every note, even in the swiftest passages. One might expect such fastidiousness to sound mannered, but that is not at all the case. Instead, it contributes to a performance of unusual clarity. In fast movements—the Prelude to the Partita no. 3, for example—the melodic line stands in relief against the arpeggios and running figuration within which Bach has placed them; and in the fugues, Tetzlaff manages to give each strand of counterpoint complete independence.

Often, he creates the illusion that these works are duets, not solo pieces. And he matches these technical accomplishments with a more conceptual one: he distinguishes between the sonatas and the partitas by giving the sonatas a comparatively dark, regal sound, and allowing greater nimbleness in his coloration of the partitas.

12. JOHANN SEBASTIAN BACH

Mass in B minor (BWV 232)

THE BACH ENSEMBLE, JOSHUA RIFKIN, CONDUCTING
(Nonesuch 79036-2, two CDs)

Judith Nelson, Julianne Baird, sopranos; Jeffrey Dooley, countertenor; Frank Hoffmeister, tenor; Jan Opalach, bass.

Recorded 1981–1982

There is nothing like settling in to hear a performance of Bach's Mass in B minor, and letting the huge choral texture of the opening Kyrie eleison—"Lord, have mercy on us"—wash over you like a vast, cleansing wave.

Or so many of us thought until 1981, when the musicologist Joshua Rifkin published a paper that questioned how big a chorus Bach had in mind when he composed the Mass. And his answer, demonstrated in this groundbreaking recording, was that if Bach were thinking in purely practical terms—that is, in terms of the forces he had available to him in Leipzig—the chorus would have been a mere five singers, or one voice to a part, with a similarly tiny instrumental ensemble supporting them. Moreover, the work's soloists would have to do double duty: when they weren't singing their solos and duets, they were the choir.

That huge wave of sound, Rifkin argued—and indeed, the entire concept of a separate chorus to sing ensemble material—was a nineteenth-century innovation, alien to Bach and his time.

It was a view that caused some consternation at the time, even among fans of early music on period instruments, who already knew that baroque performing forces were smaller than those of later eras and felt that a chorus of twenty or so was historically suitable. Objections were raised on a variety of grounds, including the fact that there is no evidence that Bach composed the B minor Mass for an actual performance.

There are, for example, no surviving performance parts, as there are for many of his other works, only a full score. And the layout of the movements suggests that the Mass would not have been appropriate for either the Catholic or the Lutheran rite. Moreover, virtually everything in it was originally composed for another purpose, and adapted to use in the Mass. Although these components hold together brilliantly, they actually represent an array of compositional styles—traditional and modern—available to a composer in Bach's time. All this suggests that Bach may have intended the Mass as an exemplary compilation, like the *Art of Fugue* and the *Brandenburg* Concertos—in which case the practicalities of how many singers Bach had in his choir is beside the point.

A look at the work's history clarifies Rifkin's conclusions, though. First, within the Mass is a kind of proto-Mass, a Missa (that is, the Kyrie and Gloria sections only), composed in 1733. Bach compiled the Missa as an offering to the Elector Friedrich II, in Dresden, and he delivered it, along with a dedicatory letter in which he complained of having endured various slights in his church positions in Leipzig—a situation that could be relieved were the elector to give him at least a titular office. It took three years (and a reminder from Bach), but in 1736 the elector named him a composer in his chapel.

Whether the elector actually heard the Missa is uncertain, but when Bach delivered the score, he included individual parts for the singers and instrumentalists. They included two soprano parts, and one part each for an alto, tenor, and bass; two first violin parts and single parts for second violin, viola, and cello; as well as a continuo part probably intended for an organ. Rifkin has established that there would have been no practical way for more than one singer or instrumentalist to read from a single part. Therefore, the number of parts represents the number of players.

The full Mass is another matter. The newly added material—the second half of the score, which includes the Symbolum Nicenum (or Credo), the Sanctus, and a final section that includes the Osanna, Benedictus, Agnus Dei, and Dona Nobis Pacem—has sections that involve instruments not required for the Missa, and there were some scoring touch-ups in the Gloria as well. But the vocal ensemble is basically the same. In Bach's time, the convention was for the singers, called *concertists,* to sing both solo and choral lines. If a musical establishment was particularly well appointed, extra singers, or *ripienists,* could be added for extra heft in the choruses. This, however, was not a luxury Bach knew: there were eight singers on the chapel roster, but he complained in his letters that any given week, some singers would be out because of illness; plus, when instrumentalists were ill, the singers had to take their places, diminishing the choir further.

Might Bach have envisioned a larger choir? Perhaps—but since a larger choir was contrary to both his experience and the conventions in which he worked, there is no reason to assume he did.

In the years since Rifkin published his findings, some conductors continued working as they always had; some reduced their choirs, but not as drastically as Rifkin; and some took the next logical step, performing huge works like the *St. Matthew Passion* using one voice to a part. If you can set aside the expectation of a grand choral sound, there are many immediate rewards in Rifkin's chamber version. Complete textural transparency is the most obvious: in the choral movements, the voices have the same clarity they have in the smaller ensembles, and with only one on a part, there is a personal, human quality—a definite sense of each singer—that cannot be approached in a massed choral performance. The textural lightness benefits the instrumental work as well; yet the emotion in sections like the Qui tollis is as powerful as in larger performances.

One thing that makes Rifkin's single-voice-to-a-part version work as well as it does is the fact that he has a superb cast. The sopranos, Judith Nelson and Julianne Baird, sound fresh and lithe. Jeffrey Dooley's countertenor is accurate and centered in ensemble sections, and lovely when heard on its own, as in the Agnus Dei. Frank Hoffmeister, the tenor, and Jan Opalach, the bass, give firm, shapely readings. There is a modest quality in the instrumental playing—not a lack of polish, exactly, but also not the superbuffed sound that period-instrument ensembles have developed since 1982—that makes this performance seem realistic. That said, there is a measure of artifice here as well: a concert in New York performed soon after this recording was released did not hold the same cohesiveness.

There are, of course, ample alternatives. The 1960 recording by Robert Shaw with his Robert Shaw Chorale and Orchestra (RCA), with its tremendous sound, modern-instrument textures, and leisurely tempos, is the polar opposite of the Rifkin. Shaw, actually, said that he found Rifkin's ideas interesting and instructive, and that they led him to rethink his approach to the work, at least a bit. When he recorded the work again with the Atlanta Symphony Orchestra and Chorus in 1990, he used what sounds like a slightly smaller choir. But there remains a seductive lushness in this somewhat brisker reading, which boasts a fine slate of soloists, including Sylvia McNair, Delores Ziegler, Marietta Simpson, John Aler, William Stone, and Thomas Paul (Telarc).

Sir John Eliot Gardiner offers a reasonable compromise in his 1985 recording with the English Baroque Soloists and Monteverdi Choir. The choir ranges from twenty-four to thirty voices, depending on the chorus, and the solo lines are divided among fifteen soloists, most from the choir. The orchestra, too, is several times larger than Rifkin's, and its continuo group uses both organ and harpsichord, where Rifkin's uses only organ. Still, the period-instrument ensemble and the vocalists trained in baroque style produce a somewhat trimmer sound than you'll hear in either of the Shaw performances.

13. JOHANN SEBASTIAN BACH

Glenn Gould—A State of Wonder

GLENN GOULD, PIANIST
(Sony Classical S3K 87703, three CDs)

Includes two performances of the Goldberg Variations, *plus outtakes, and a discussion between Glenn Gould and Tim Page about his performances of the* Goldberg Variations *recorded on August 22, 1982.*
Recorded 1955, 1981, 1982

I have friends who are so enamored of Glenn Gould's recordings of the *Goldberg* Variations that they believe that anyone else who takes up the work—particularly anyone playing it, like Gould, on the piano rather than the harpsichord—must inevitably live in Gould's shadow. I won't go that far: something about these thirty magnificently diverse variations on a graceful aria draws out the inventiveness in many musicians. Long before Gould, and since his death at age fifty in 1982, pianists have approached the *Goldbergs* as a canvas on which to paint rich-hued self-portraits, more or less in Bachian garb. Nor have keyboardists maintained an exclusive grip on the work: citing Bach's penchant for rescoring his own works, organists, guitarists, brass ensembles, string trios, and chamber orchestras have performed and recorded it, in some cases with surprisingly good results.

Still, it is undeniable that Gould made his mark on the performance history of this great work—and the work made its mark on Gould. His two studio recordings bracket his career: he recorded the *Goldbergs* as his debut for CBS Masterworks in 1955, when he was twenty-two, and he revisited it twenty-seven years later, in 1981, offering a radically different view that was released less than a week before his death. Both recordings are included here, along with a disc of bonus material, all for about the price of a single top-line CD. Heard side by side, these performances offer an extraordinary picture of the degree to which music is, or can be, as much an interpreter's art as a composer's.

As interpreters go, Gould was particularly strong-willed, and he could be both persuasive and maddening. His repertory was quite large; he recorded nearly ninety discs for CBS, and although much of that discography was devoted to the major works of Bach, Gould also explored music by Byrd, Haydn, Strauss, Hindemith, Schoenberg, Shostakovich, Poulenc, and others. His musical perversities were many. He considered Mozart and Beethoven overrated, for example, and his recordings of their sonatas might be described either as idiosyncratic or irredeemable, depending on your tolerance for eccentric tempos, balances, and sonorities. Leonard Bernstein, who was also known for strong interpretive viewpoints, once prefaced a New York Philharmonic performance of the Brahms First Piano Concerto with a brief speech in which he distanced himself from the interpretation that Gould was about to offer.

Eventually, Gould abandoned the concert hall altogether, arguing that concerts were unmusical spectacles ("a spectator sport," was how he put it), rendered superfluous by radio, television, and recordings. His glib characterization of concerts aside, he came to feel that only the recording studio offered him the atmosphere and level of control he needed to create his art. But his departure from the stage was by no means an abandonment of his audience. Gould was clearly a musician who needed to communicate, and in addition to making piano recordings, he composed (sometimes whimsically), conducted, wrote essays and reviews, and produced radio documentaries.

The degree to which that communication had to take place on Gould's terms can be heard on the bonus disc included in this set, the centerpiece of which is an interview that was meant to promote Gould's 1981 remake of the *Goldbergs*. Conducted by Tim Page, then a New York freelance critic, now the chief critic for the *Washington Post*, it is a detailed, informative look at how Gould's view of the work had changed since he first recorded it in 1955. Yet, as Page points out in an accompanying essay, it was actually less an interview than an acting job. Every aspect of the conversation, from the questions and answers to the pauses, jokey asides, and chuckles, was scripted by Gould.

The main business of *A State of Wonder* is, of course, the *Goldbergs,* in Gould's two readings. The work itself is surrounded by ample lore. Published in 1741 as the fourth and final section of the *Clavierübung*—a collection of works that surveyed the art of keyboard composition as it stood in Bach's time—its official title is *Keyboard Exercise, consisting of an Aria with Diverse Variations, for a Harpsichord with Two Manuals.*

It acquired the *Goldberg* nickname because of a story in an early biography of Bach by Johann Nicholas Forkel. Forkel asserted that the work was commissioned by Count Hermann Carl von Keyserlingk, the Russian ambassador in Dresden, who was an insomniac and wanted an involved work for his harpsichordist, Johann Gottlieb Goldberg, to play for him in the wee hours. Goldberg was a renowned keyboard virtuoso, and may have been a student of Bach's, but there are reasons to doubt this legend. One is that Bach tended to include lavish dedications with works commissioned from him, and there is none in the published version of the *Goldbergs*. Another is that in 1741 Goldberg was barely fourteen years old.

At any rate, it's difficult to imagine either of Gould's recordings soothing an insomniac's restless nights. In the 1955 recording, he takes generally brisk tempos, and the overall impression is of an eruption of energy. Listened to closely, though, the subtleties shine. The Aria, while played more quickly than many readings, nevertheless has room to breathe comfortably, and by the fourth or fifth variation, speed and transparency begin to emerge as hallmarks. Still, as driven as Gould's readings are, they never feel rushed, and even the most fire-breathing of them—nos. 5, 12, and 20, for example—sacrifice nothing in clarity. Every note is there, crisply articulated and distinct, and every strand of counterpoint stands out against the others.

There is also ample flexibility and surprise. The dotted rhythms of the seventh variation and the graceful turns that propel no. 13 emerge with uncommon elegance. Gould gives no. 16—which Bach called an Overture, and which is the clear dividing line between the first and second halves of the work—the Gallic accent and the architectural grandeur that its title suggests. And then there is no. 25: just as he takes many of the variations at an unusually bristling clip, Gould lingers over every note of this one, making it an almost Mahlerian meditation. It is a reading so enveloping that the explosive account of no. 26 that follows it sounds all the more bracing.

Of Gould's two versions, I greatly prefer the earlier one, but the differences are enlightening. In the score, Bach characteristically calls for each half of each variation to be repeated, but not all performers regard the repeats as obligatory. In 1955, Gould did not take any of them. In 1981, he took several of the repeats, but not all of them. He had also come to regard his 1955 tempos as youthfully impetuous. Now the Aria is a good deal slower, and so are some of the variations. But the changes in speed are only part of the picture. In its best moments, his later reading is more nuanced than its predecessor, but it also tends toward a weightier, more intense approach that can be a bit odd. What remains a preoccupation, though, is clarity of texture, and differences in detail between the interpretations are pointed up by that clarity.

Other highly recommendable accounts of the *Goldbergs* are plentiful, and especially given Gould's quirkiness, a few should be mentioned. On the harpsichord, Kenneth Gilbert offers a carefully sculpted account, with modest coloration and selective repeats (Harmonia Mundi).

Trevor Pinnock offers a thoughtful traversal (Archiv), and there is an appealing energy in the various accounts by Gustav Leonhardt (Vanguard, Teldec). These recordings were all made between the 1960s and the 1980s, but to see how thoughts about the work have changed—even in the historically minded world of the harpsichord—listen to the rich-hued versions recorded by Wanda Landowska in 1933 (EMI Classics) and Karl Richter in 1958 (Teldec).

There are also fine piano performances by Andras Schiff (Decca), Andrew Rangell (Dorian), Vladimir Feltsman (Musicmasters), and the jazz pianist Keith Jarrett (ECM). Add to that several recordings by Rosalyn Tureck, who specialized in Bach through virtually all of the twentieth century's revolutions in performance practice. Her last version of the *Goldbergs,* released in 1999, includes all the repeats, taken at stately tempos, as well as CD-ROM material that allows computer users to follow the score—either unadorned or with the individual voices color-coded—and read both a variation-by-variation analysis and an illustrated biography of Bach.

Pianist Glenn Gould in the recording studio, humming along to his performance

Johann Sebastian Bach

14. GEORGE FRIDERIC HANDEL

Water Music

ENGLISH BAROQUE SOLOISTS,
JOHN ELIOT GARDINER, CONDUCTING

(Philips 289 464 706-2)

Includes Water Music *Suite no. 1 in F (HWV 348), Suite no. 2 in D (HWV 349), Suite no. 3 in G (HWV 350);* Music for the Royal Fireworks *(HWV 351); and variant movements from* Water Music *(HWV 331, nos. 1 and 2).*

Recorded 1983, 1991

Compared with Bach, who labored in a handful of relatively small German towns, George Frideric Handel (1685–1759)—his exact contemporary—enjoyed a notably more cosmopolitan life, and considerably greater fame in his time. Born in Halle, the son of a surgeon at the court of the Duke of Saxe-Weissenfels, he seemed destined, by parental fiat, for a career in law. As a child, he studied the keyboard secretly, playing the sotto-voce clavichord in the family's attic, until the duke heard him play the organ at age nine and persuaded the elder Handel to give his son music lessons. He took his first church post in Halle in 1702, but a year later he went to Hamburg to pursue opportunities as an opera composer.

In 1706, he journeyed to Italy, where—in Florence, Rome, Naples, and possibly Venice—he composed sacred choral works and had some success as an opera composer before returning to Germany in 1710. That year, he was engaged as Kappelmeister at the electoral court in Hanover, a position that allowed him considerable freedom to travel. Handel used that freedom principally for working visits to London, and when he was dismissed from his Hanover post, in 1713, it was in London that he remained. As it turned out, he was reunited with the Elector of Hanover in 1714, when his former employer became King George II of England.

It was for a musical boating party on the Thames, thrown by King

---

George in July 1717, that Handel composed his popular *Water Music* suites. The *Daily Courant,* a London newspaper, reported that in addition to the king and his guests, "many other Barges with Persons of Quality attended, and so great a Number of Boats, that the whole River in a manner was cover'd; a City Company's Barge was employ'd for the Musick, wherein were 50 Instruments of all sorts, who play'd all the way from Lambeth (While the Barges drove with the Tide without Rowing, as far as Chelsea), the finest Symphonies, compos'd express for this Occasion, by Mr. Hendel, which His Majesty liked so well, that he cas'd it to be plaid over three times in going and returning."

The dance pieces that make up these suites show the degree to which Handel had absorbed the prevailing accents of English musical life, and allowed them to gain dominance over both his native German and acquired Italian influences. This music is much closer in spirit to Henry Purcell than to J. S. Bach or Dietrich Buxtehude. It adopts Purcell's partiality to the French rhythmic style, as well as certain French dances, like the Bourrée and Rigaudon; yet there are distinctively English hornpipes here, too, and echoes of English country dances.

On this zesty recording, Sir John Eliot Gardiner brings out this music's essential combination of earthiness and courtly charm. His ensemble, the English Baroque Soloists, is a period-instrument group, so its brass parts, played on the perilous valveless horns of Handel's time, have a textured and slightly tart sound that brings this celebratory music to life. The gentler Suite in G—placed between the two more ebullient F major and D major suites on this disc—has other attractions, most notably a nimbleness in the string and recorder playing, and a silky quality that seems to support the contention by some musicologists that this suite was actually meant not for the boat trip but for a royal supper later in the evening.

Joining this reissue of Gardiner's 1983 *Water Music* is the conductor's 1991 account of the *Music for the Royal Fireworks,* the majestic suite composed to celebrate the peace of Aix-la-Chapelle in 1749. Gardiner sensibly forgoes what is believed to have been the "outdoor" scoring of just winds, brass, and percussion, in favor of the more varied concert version with strings. The Bourrée and La Paix, therefore, offer a courtly contrast to the grandiose brass-and-percussion-driven

Ouverture and Réjouissance, and the Minuets have it both ways—strings at first, then winds, brass, and percussion on the work-closing repeat.

The *Fireworks* music shares and magnifies many of the qualities heard in the *Water Music,* and here, too, Gardiner and his players—especially the brass—keep the energy levels high while conveying a sense of the music's inherent stateliness.

15. GEORGE FRIDERIC HANDEL

Israel in Egypt

THE CHOIR OF KING'S COLLEGE, CAMBRIDGE;
THE BRANDENBURG CONSORT,
STEPHEN CLEOBURY, CONDUCTING
(Decca 452 295-2, two CDs)

Susan Gritton, Libby Crabtree, sopranos; Michael Chance, Robert Ogden, altos; Ian Bostridge, tenor; Stephen Varcoe, Henry Herford, basses.

Recorded 1995

Handel wrote his first English oratorio, *Esther,* in 1718. It remained an isolated effort until 1732, when a London revival of *Esther* led to the composition of two more biblically based dramatic settings, *Deborah* and *Athalia,* followed, over the next quarter century, by a rich variety of subjects—*Saul, Solomon, Joseph and His Brethren, Jephtha, Joshua, Judas Maccabeus, Messiah,* and *Israel in Egypt* among them.

Still, at the time he began expanding his oratorio inventory, Handel's principal interest was Italian opera, a form that offered greater possibilities than oratorio, both in terms of subject matter (opera could draw freely on history and mythology; oratorio dealt only with the sacred) and as sheer spectacle (opera was staged; oratorio was not). But a variety of circumstances pushed Handel to consider oratorio more seriously. One was the establishment, in 1733, of the Opera of the Nobility, a new company formed to compete with Handel's productions at the King's Theater.

Because London's audience for Italian opera was too small to be split between rival companies, the new effort eventually failed. But before Handel could win his audience back, the opera season was interrupted by the death of Queen Caroline. And when it resumed, there were too few subscribers to support Handel's plans.

There was, however, an audience for his oratorios, which, after all, were in English and about subjects and people the audience knew well. For the 1739 season, he composed two: *Saul* and *Israel in Egypt*. He had also composed an extensive funeral anthem for Queen Caroline, *The Ways of Zion Do Mourn,* based on a wide-ranging selection of biblical verses, and he seemed intent on reusing it. His first plan was to include it in *Saul* as an elegy to both Saul and Jonathan, but in the end he reworked that section to include other music.

The funeral anthem found life elsewhere. By changing the opening line from "The ways of Zion do mourn" to "The sons of Israel do mourn," and by making a few other judicious alterations, Handel and his librettist, Charles Jennens, were able to transform the anthem, whole, into "The Lamentations of the Israelites for the Death of Joseph"—or, Part I of *Israel in Egypt.*

Actually, the text—much of which comes from the Books of Job, Lamentations, Ecclesiastes, and Psalms—makes no explicit reference either to Joseph or to the plight of the Israelites in Egypt, but it provides an emotional backdrop against which the work's larger drama unfolds. And having based the work on biblical texts, Handel decided to try something new. Instead of having a newly composed libretto fashioned from a biblical story, he would draw the entire text from the Bible. It was an approach Handel only adopted one other time—in *Messiah.*

With the reworked funeral anthem as a prologue, Handel began Part II, "Exodus," with a tenor recitative announcing the ascension of a new king, and a chorus that describes the oppression of the Israelite slaves with music that is alternately hard-driven and built around a gentle sighing figure. The text is drawn partly from Exodus and partly from the retelling of the liberation from Egypt in Psalm 105. Along the way, Handel appears to have lost count of the plagues: his work describes only nine of the ten ("wild beasts" is passed over), but they are conveyed through exquisitely picturesque music.

When Egypt's waters turn to blood, Handel gives the chorus a melody so full of unexpected leaps as to sound like the work of a much later composer. The plague of the frogs, an alto aria, is accompanied by a "hopping" violin figure, and the violins are similarly evocative in the next chorus, "He spake the word," where their quick, buzzing figures dart around the chorus's mention of "all manner of flies and lice." In "He gave them hailstones for rain," the declamation is threateningly hard-edged, and supported with punchy brass chords that suggest the impact of those hailstones. The plague of darkness is drawn with a terrifying faux-serenity—a slow, smooth style that is brimming with tension. And the final plague, the death of the Egyptian firstborn, has an almost military stridency: the accompanying string chords come down like whips punctuating the choir's lines.

The plagues dispatched, Part II continues with the exodus itself, conveyed in "But as for his people," a movement that begins jauntily but pauses for a lovely pastoral moment, complete with oboes (usually used to represent shepherds' pipes in baroque music), on the second line, "He led them forth like sheep." The parting of the Red Sea, if less dramatic than one might expect, has a painterly grandeur, and Handel depicts the Egyptians' pursuit of the Israelites, and the Red Sea closing on them, with suitably vibrant battle music, followed by a magnificently contrapuntal expression of faith.

For Part III, "Moses's Song," Handel drew his text entirely from the first twenty-one verses of Exodus 15—the song sung by Moses and the Israelites after seeing the Egyptian army annihilated.

Structurally, the work ranges in unexpected and sometimes strange directions, compared with the quasi-operatic style that Handel generally pursued in his oratorios. Part I is composed entirely for chorus. In Part II, there are two tenor recitatives and a single alto aria, but the rest—thirteen of the sixteen numbers—are, again, for chorus. And in Part III, which might logically be presented as fully choral, the twenty-three numbers include a soprano duet; a bass duet; an alto and tenor duet; solo arias for tenor, soprano, and alto; two tenor recitatives; and fifteen choruses.

This was too much for the sizeable part of Handel's audience that was already feeling aggrieved about the loss of the opera productions, with their florid arias, and which had hoped to hear the same in the oratorios. Handel responded to their complaints in subsequent performances and revivals by removing Part I entirely and grafting in arias from other works. But most conductors today, Stephen Cleobury among them, embrace *Israel in Egypt* as Handel intended it.

Some have gone to unusual lengths in pursuit of authenticity. A lovely 1993 recording by Harry Christophers and the Sixteen, on the defunct Collins Classics label, included an organ concerto between Parts I and II, on the grounds that the original advertisements promised one. That seemed a bit much, and Cleobury, thankfully, does not go that far. But his version has all the virtues of a modern period-instruments performance, including tight ensemble playing and singing (a must in the plague choruses), and tempos closely geared to the spirit of the text, but generally on the brisk side. On hand as well is a solid, attractive slate of vocal soloists, who sing the music stylishly and with just enough vibrato to keep the line expressive.

16. GEORGE FRIDERIC HANDEL

Messiah

CHOIR OF CHRIST CHURCH CATHEDRAL, OXFORD, SIMON PRESTON, DIRECTOR; ACADEMY OF ANCIENT MUSIC, CHRISTOPHER HOGWOOD, CONDUCTING
(L'Oiseau-Lyre 289 430 488-2, two CDs)

Judith Nelson, Emma Kirkby, sopranos; Carolyn Watkinson, contralto; Paul Elliott, tenor; David Thomas, bass.

Recorded 1980

This most famous of Handel's English oratorios has become a staple of Christmas concerts, but there is no reason, historically or otherwise, to think of it only in that context. Handel composed it in twenty-four days during the summer of 1741, and although Charles Jennens, the work's librettist, hoped that the work would be performed that Christmas, its first performance wasn't until April 1742. Its various revivals during Handel's lifetime cast it as an Easter work as well, and it wasn't performed regularly as a Christmas piece until well into the nineteenth century.

That shouldn't be surprising: only the first third of the work is devoted to the Christmas story, and its text is drawn mostly from Isaiah and other prophetic books of the Bible (plus a few psalms), with only a few excerpts from the New Testament, and none of the traditional imagery of mangers or gift-bearing kings. The larger part of the work deals with the Crucifixion and the promise of redemption, topics more germane to Easter. Of course, to those who believe in these texts, the work is germane all year. And part of the magic of *Messiah*—more than, say, the Bach Passion settings—is that one needn't subscribe to the work's theological underpinnings to admire or even truly love this miraculous marriage of music and text.

Much of the work's power and charm lies in its simple, direct pictorialism. From the gentle falling melody to which Handel sets the opening words ("Comfort ye") to the ebullience of the "Hallelujah" chorus and the ornate, celebratory counterpoint of the final "Amen," there is scarcely a line of text that Handel does not illustrate. When the libretto tells of rough places being made plain, Handel's melody moves from a jagged, wiggling line to a single, steady note. A sweetly turned pastoral melody buoys "He shall feed his flock," but when the text speaks of the people as sheep who have gone astray, the winding chorus lines evoke that chaos, as well as a hint of bleating. To describe "the people that walked in darkness," Handel gives the solo bass an eerily vacillating chromatic melody to convey the sense of being lost; but as the sentence continues—"have seen a great light"—the darkness is lifted with a bright, upward leap.

Often the action is as much in the accompaniment as in the vocal music. In the central section of "But who may abide," the quick bowing of the strings suggests the blast of the refiner's fire that the text mentions. Later in the work, a similar effect accompanies the question, "Why do the nations rage?" The orchestration, too, yields sublime moments. Handel used the trumpet sparingly in *Messiah,* but when it suddenly appears in the accompaniment to "Glory to God" and again in "Hallelujah," the effect is electrifying—as it is, in a more theatrical way, in the bass showpiece, "The trumpet shall sound."

The tangled history and rich performance tradition of *Messiah* complicate the business of choosing a single version on disc. From the earliest commercial recording of a *Messiah* aria—W. D. McFarland's truncated, piano-accompanied account of "Every valley shall be exalted," recorded for Berliner Gramophone in 1899—to this year's models, conductors and soloists have consistently found fresh ways to perform the score. One could trace this interpretive freehandedness back to Mozart, who in 1789 (thirty years after Handel's death) prepared a version of *Messiah* with added winds, rescored aria accompaniments, and other dramatic touches. But even that wouldn't be going back far enough: Handel himself reworked *Messiah* for each of its revivals between 1742 and 1759, leaving a stack of variant versions of several numbers in his wake.

One can chart the passing styles of baroque performance from *Messiah* recordings. Until the 1960s, the dominant approach favored large orchestras and choruses and even a bit of reorchestration, all in the service of grandly sweeping musical gestures. With the distortion of hindsight, we now think of this as a "Victorian" approach, but reports of mammoth, roof-raising *Messiah* performances can be traced back to 1784. Still, beginning in the 1960s, a leaner, more texturally transparent "historical" approach prevailed. Reduced orchestras playing on period instruments or, at least, applying period techniques to modern ones, and singers rendering the arias with free (but usually not excessive) ornamentation, but very little vibrato, all sought to reproduce the *Messiah* sound that Handel would have heard. Recently, an ecumenical approach to stylistic issues has yielded various hybrids.

Over the years, most conductors have assembled their ideal *Messiah* scores by picking and choosing from among Handel's variants—certainly a legitimate approach, and one Handel used himself. But the *Messiah* I've been fondest of since its release on LP in 1980 is this lithe account by Christopher Hogwood and his Academy of Ancient Music. Hogwood's goal was to re-create a specific version—the one performed, under Handel's direction, at the Covent Garden Theater and the Foundling Hospital, in London, between April 5 and May 15, 1754. Why this version? For one thing, it was well documented: the original score has been preserved, as have financial records that tell us exactly how many performers were used (or, at least, paid) for the performances.

There is some give-and-take here: on the deficit side, it's a pity that Handel opted to use the short version of the *Pifa* (the beautifully ruminative *Pastoral* Symphony that serves as an interlude within the first part of the oratorio) in this edition. "Why do the nations?" is heard in a short version as well. On the other hand, "But who may abide," usually heard in its bass or alto versions, is presented here in a reworked edition for soprano, and it is sung gloriously by Emma Kirkby, the soprano whose pure tone and graceful phrasing defined early-music singing in the 1970s and 1980s.

The other vocal soloists make fine contributions as well, and the transparent sound of both the Academy orchestra and the all-male chorus are also among the joys of this robustly played, bright-hued performance.

A period-instrument fancier who doesn't want to be limited to Hogwood's choice of the 1754 score—or, for that matter, anyone fascinated with Handel's variants—should seek Nicholas McGegan's recording of the work with the San Francisco–based Philharmonia Baroque, the U.C. Berkeley Chamber Chorus, and a superb cast of soloists that includes Lorraine Hunt, Janet Williams, Patricia Spence, Drew Minter, Jeffrey Thomas, and William Parker (Harmonia Mundi, 1991). The performance is vibrant, with some wonderful ornamentation from the singers and brilliant orchestral playing, but, best of all, McGegan included every one of Handel's variants in appendix sections at the end of each disc, as well as a handy guide showing which selections Handel used at different times, all of which allows listeners to reprogram the work to create any edition they prefer.

Among modern-instrument *Messiah* recordings, Sir Thomas Beecham's performance with the Royal Philharmonic Orchestra, using a spectacularly expansive rescoring (there are cymbal crashes!) by Eugene Goosens, is an exhilarating representative of the grand tradition (RCA, 1959). And Sir Colin Davis's London Symphony recording stands as a fine example of a texturally trim, spiritually opulent reading that honors the score without hitting the extremes of either the Beecham school or the early-music orthodoxy.

A page from the score of Handel's *Messiah*

17. DOMENICO SCARLATTI

Sonatas in C (K. 159, K. 423, K. 515), C-sharp minor
(K. 24), D (K. 397, K. 430, K. 490, K. 492), D minor
(K. 32, K. 141), E (K. 20, K. 380), F (K. 107, K. 256),
F minor (K. 481, K. 519), F-sharp minor (K. 447),
G (K. 124, K. 259, K. 328), G minor (K. 8, K. 234),
A minor (K. 109), and B-flat (K. 440)

WANDA LANDOWSKA, HARPSICHORDIST

(EMI Classics 64934 2)

Recorded 1934, 1939, 1940

or

All the sonatas on the previous disc, plus the Sonatas
in C-sharp minor (K. 247), D (K. 29, K. 96, K. 281,
K. 400, K. 443), D minor (K. 9, K. 32—two versions),
E (K. 206), E-flat major (K. 193), F (K. 6, K. 17,
K. 276), F minor (K. 69, K. 462, K. 519), G minor
(K. 450), A (K. 429), B-flat (K. 544), and B minor
(K. 27, K. 377)

WANDA LANDOWSKA, HARPSICHORDIST

(Pearl GEMS 0106)

*Also includes Johann Sebastian Bach's Fantasia in C minor (BWV 906),
George Frideric Handel's Air and Variations in B-flat, Carl Philipp
Emanuel Bach's Concerto in D for Harpsichord and Strings. Orchestra
conducted by Adolf Kodolfsky on C. P. E. Bach.*

Recorded 1923–1943

Technologically, stylistically, and purely in terms of vintage, Wanda
Landowska's recordings of these two dozen sonatas by Domenico
Scarlatti (1685–1757) are treasurable antiques. As the earliest recordings of Scarlatti on the harpsichord, they have a place in the history of
modern performance. They are historical in a broader way as well:
the latest recordings here are from sessions in Paris in March 1940

---

during the months between France's declaration of war on Germany and Germany's invasion. One of the recordings—the Sonata in D (K. 490)—captures not only the sound of Landowska's harpsichord, but also the blasts of antiaircraft fire near the studio.

There was a time, during the height of modern early-music purism, in the late 1970s and early 1980s, when Wanda Landowska's recordings were regarded as hopelessly anachronistic representations of the harpsichord and its music. That view is not entirely without merit—indeed, Landowska's approach irritated musicologists even in her own day—but it misses the point. In the essays that she published prolifically, Landowska acknowledged forthrightly that her big, brawny Pleyel harpsichord had resources considerably beyond those of the harpsichords that J. S. Bach, François Couperin, and Scarlatti knew, and that her interpretations were not historical re-creations.

"At no time in the course of my work have I told myself, 'this is the way it must have sounded at the time,'" she wrote. "Why? Because I am sure that what I am doing in regard to sonority, registration, etc., is very far from the historical truth. To the purists who say to me, 'This was done in such a manner; you should conform, etc.,' I answer, 'Leave me alone!' . . . At no time in the course of my work have I ever tried to reproduce exactly what the old masters did. Instead, I study, I scrutinize, I love, and I recreate."

And yet, for all that, there was a great degree to which Landowska really was a crusader for authenticity. Born in Warsaw in 1879, she was trained as a pianist and a composer, but she became increasingly drawn to the music of the seventeenth and eighteenth centuries, particularly after she moved to Paris in 1900. Landowska performed this music on the piano until about 1910, but she also began investigating the harpsichord, which she first played publicly in 1903. She quickly came to believe that the harpsichord was the proper instrument for baroque music—a commonplace idea today, but one that met considerable resistance from listeners who believed that the harpsichord had been rightly supplanted by the piano, with its stronger sound and its greater coloristic and dynamic resources.

Landowska responded on two fronts. She frequently published articles on the superiority of the harpsichord for baroque music, and she designed her own two-manual (or dual keyboard) harpsichord, complete with a pedal mechanism that made quick changes in registration (the color, quality, and weight of the sound) possible. The Pleyel was a double-edged sword. It allowed her to produce performances that had the timbre of a harpsichord but the nuance and variety of the piano—performances that listeners who preferred the piano might find persuasive. Yet to the part of the music world intent on rediscovering the sounds of the baroque era, the instrument was heretical.

A listener today has the luxury of standing apart from that battle. Recordings of the Scarlatti sonatas on proper reproductions of baroque harpsichords are plentiful and they range from straightforward readings that balance energy and elegance, by players like Gustav Leonhardt (Sony Classical/Seon), Trevor Pinnock (Archiv), Colin Tilney (Dorian), Scott Ross (who recorded the entire set for Erato), and Luc Beauséjour (Analekta), to idiosyncratically ornamented interpretations, like those of the Dutch harpsichordist Ton Koopman (Capriccio). On the piano, Vladimir Horowitz made a specialty of Scarlatti, and several discs of his exquisitely chiseled readings are available on CD (Sony Classical); John Browning also recorded a collection of refined piano performances (Musicmasters).

Landowska's reputation has rested largely on her Bach recordings, quite a few of which are available on RCA reissues. But these Scarlatti recordings are in a class by themselves. Scarlatti, of course, was an exact contemporary of Bach's, but stylistically they might as well have been born a generation apart. To put it simply, where Bach reveled in polyphonic complexity and extended form, Scarlatti wrote works in which a few ideas—often colorful, descriptive ones—were explored economically within tight, compact structures. Scarlatti was born in Naples and was the son of the opera and oratorio composer Alessandro Scarlatti. His first professional jobs were in Venice and Rome, where he followed in his father's footsteps, writing vocal works for both the church and the stage.

In Rome, the Portuguese ambassador, the Marquis de Fontes, commissioned Scarlatti to compose "Applauso genetlíaco," a serenade, to commemorate a birth in the Portuguese royal family in 1714. Thus began an association that led to the creation of these sonatas. In 1719, Scarlatti visited Lisbon, where he was received at court with great acclaim, and reportedly sang a concert to an accompaniment played by the queen. He was given a post as music master at the royal chapel, as well as teaching responsibilities. One of his more talented charges was the Princess Maria Barbara, who eventually became Scarlatti's patron as the queen of Spain, and for whom he composed his more than 550 sonatas. It is not known how long Scarlatti remained in Portugal; he was apparently back in Italy at various times between 1724 and 1727. But in 1729, after Maria Barbara married Ferdinand, the heir to the Spanish throne, Scarlatti moved to Spain to serve in their household.

It should be understood that these are sonatas in the baroque sense: the word comes from the Italian *sonare* (to sound), and is applied to an instrumental or ensemble work, generally in a binary form—a first section, with a repeat, then a second, also with a repeat. The more elaborate classical form that Mozart and Beethoven knew, in which the themes were put forth in an exposition, then explored in a development section, and recapitulated at the end, had not yet evolved. The designation was used so loosely in Scarlatti's time that when the first collection of his sonatas was published in 1728, the works were called "Essercizi." That title conveys their origins, as learning pieces for Maria Barbara; but the set as a whole includes some sophisticated and entertaining music, well beyond what the "Essercizi" label and the sonatas' brevity may suggest.

One of Scarlatti's achievements in these pieces is grafting a measure of local color—musical gestures picked up as he traveled through Spain with Maria Barbara and Ferdinand—onto the niceties of the Italian keyboard style. Among the works included here, for example, one hears Andalusian arabesques in the Sonatas in C-sharp minor (K. 247) and F minor (K. 519); celebratory fanfares, tinged with the accents of Spanish dance music, in the Sonatas in C (K. 159) and E (K. 380); and the gracefully dotted rhythms of the sarabande in the Sonata in G minor (K. 8). Throughout his sonatas, Scarlatti also leaned toward harmonies full of open fourths, arpeggiated accompaniments, and rolled chords, all meant to emulate the sound of the Spanish guitar.

Implicit in this music is an invitation to the interpreter to bring out the music's picturesque qualities, and that Landowska did, unabashedly using her harpsichord's extended registration possibilities to go beyond what even a pianist could do. Quite often—in most of these pieces, in fact—she uses her array of sounds in an orchestral way, changing the timbre to offset phrases or parts of a phrase, or to differentiate between the melody and accompaniment figures. A few particularly compelling examples of her approach include her use of a muted (lute-stop) sound in some of the repeated passages in the Sonata in D (K. 430), or the juxtaposition of a clear, ringing sound played on one manual with a muted sound on the other in the Sonata in B-flat (K. 440)—a work to which she also adds harmonies to fill out Scarlatti's spare textures.

Generations of musicologists have raised eyebrows at these liberties. But I suspect that many also secretly admire the verve, inventiveness, and sheer force of personality that these performances project.

As with many recordings that have gone out of copyright, compilations of these recordings are available on several labels. The EMI set offers a fine overview of the sonatas included in the two Scarlatti albums (which in those days were booklike sets of 78 rpm discs, hence the name "album") she recorded in Paris in 1934 and 1939–1940. Pearl, a label for historical recording fanciers, offers a more complete view, at about three times the price. This comprehensive edition begins with a pair of Scarlatti sides Landowska recorded in 1923 (in New York) and 1930 (in London), followed by all forty of the sonatas included in the two Paris albums, as well as remakes of K. 443 and K. 32, recorded in New York in 1946. For good measure Pearl includes a vigorous 1930 recording of J. S. Bach's C minor Fantasia, a 1937 account of Handel's B-flat major Air and Variations, and a performance of a concerto by Bach's son, Carl Philipp Emanuel, recorded by the Canadian Broadcasting Corporation in Toronto in 1943.

18. ANTONIO VIVALDI

Il Cimento dell'Armonia e dell'Inventione (op. 8):
Twelve Concertos, including *The Four Seasons*
(Concertos nos. 1 through 4); *La Tempesta di Mare*
(Concerto no. 5); *La Piacere* (Concerto no. 6);
and *La Caccia* (Concerto no. 10)

EUROPA GALANTE, FABIO BIONDI,
SOLO VIOLINIST AND CONDUCTOR
(EMI/Virgin Veritas 5 45465 2, two CDs)

Recorded 2000

First I must dispatch that old joke about Vivaldi (1678–1741)—the one about how he wrote one concerto and photocopied it five hundred times. Only someone who has used Vivaldi's concertos as background music, without according them the attention they deserve, could make such an assertion, even in jest.

Vivaldi's concertos are nearly as varied as they are numerous. Many are in the concerto grosso form, in which the orchestra is divided into two groups—a smaller concertino group, and the full ensemble, which engage in dialogues or battles, as the case may be. Vivaldi was also drawn to the solo concerto, a newer approach in which a solo instrument stood against the full ensemble. That is the model he adopted in *Il Cimento dell'Armonia e dell'Inventione* (The Contest of Harmony and Invention) and, of course, it remains the dominant concerto format to this day.

Many of Vivaldi's concertos date from the years he was employed to teach the violin to the young ladies at the Ospedale della Pietà, in Venice. But if the practical intent of his efforts was didactic, Vivaldi nevertheless lavished considerable inspiration on them. Often, the concerto became a canvas for bold experiments in expressive tone painting, and there are no finer examples of that than the first four concertos of *Il Cimento,* known independently of the rest of the collection as *The Four Seasons.*

These four concertos are so familiar and so frequently recorded that one would think an ensemble tackling them anew would search hard to find a novel approach. Sadly, of the dozens of *Four Seasons* recordings on the market, a great many simply rip through the concertos as if they were little more than dazzling showpieces. They embody that character, but Vivaldi was aiming higher. The works were published, after all, with a set of explanatory sonnets that describe the pictures, sounds, feelings, and experiences that Vivaldi meant to evoke in every bar of these works. All a performer need do is take these poems to heart.

Fabio Biondi and Europa Galante do exactly that, but they also take a great many interpretive liberties. Tempos and dynamics are manipulated for dramatic effect; the strings and harpsichord are sometimes wildly percussive, and Biondi regularly adds tiny cadential flourishes and ornamentation to the solo line. He also uses variant scores. Instead of relying on the score that was published in Amsterdam in 1725, Biondi assembled his edition from manuscripts held in libraries in Manchester, Dresden, and Turin—versions that differ in many details from the standard reading. All this makes for performances that may seem idiosyncratic at times, but are undeniably fresh and electrifying.

By way of a quick overview, "Spring" is announced with a bright, brisk ensemble figure, as well as the solo violin's evocation of birdsong and of gently rippling streams. But it is the imminent thunderstorm that catches Biondi's interest, and in the Manchester score, its gusts and lightning bolts are especially violent. In the slow movement, the sweetly etched violin line represents the dreams of a napping goatherd, and the two-note viola figure that accompanies it is his dog's barking. It is astonishing how many violists simply play those notes straight and clean, as if suggesting a barking dog were difficult or embarrassing. This ensemble's violist doesn't flinch: a sharp, percussive bow attack creates the effect, and the line is played loudly enough to rival the violin line as the central event of the movement.

The slow introduction to "Summer" captures the languor of a day under the blazing sun, and here again Vivaldi offers birdcalls as well as zephyrs that become fierce winds. Another thunderstorm—this time of the torrential midsummer variety—is painted in the speedy violin writing of the finale. Biondi and company sharpen the accents and manipulate the dynamics and tempos, making this storm unusually insistent.

"Autumn" begins with a dance to celebrate the harvest, complete with drunken revelers. The season's balmy evenings are evoked in the middle movement, and in the finale, we are taken on a hunt, full of horn calls and the noise of galloping horses chasing a wounded fox.

And just as the opening of summer suggests the blistering heat, the quick string figures that begin "Winter" create a frosty atmosphere. Biondi's reading is at its most iconoclastic: a harpsichord emerges from among the string chords, and the dynamics grow from a whisper to a shout. Still, the imagery—shivering in the first movement, and later the comfort of the fireplace, the unsteady crunch of boots on ice, and the howling of the winter wind—is conveyed in every tactile detail.

Biondi's aggressively individualistic readings reflect the latest trend in *Four Seasons* performances. A close rival among recent recordings is the version by Il Giardino Armonico, with Enrico Onofri playing the solo violin lines (Teldec, 1993). Like Biondi's reading, this version combines period-instrument timbres and stylish ornamentation with a modern sense of dynamic fluidity and a continuous reconsideration of balances to create an obsessively nuanced reading.

One reason I chose Biondi's set, though, was that it includes equally robust accounts of the other eight concertos in *Il Cimento*. Some are overtly pictorial, others are more abstract explorations of form and tonality, but each offers a listener insight into the musical concerns of a baroque master.

Recognizing that the Europa Galante and Il Giardino accounts may be too on-the-edge for some tastes, let me recommend a few more conventional recordings in which the performers are mindful of Vivaldi's poetic imagery. The violinist Giuliano Carmignola has recorded a fine, energetic performance with Andrea Marcon and the Venice Baroque Orchestra (Sony Classical, 1999). Carmignola appears to use the Manchester manuscript as well—as do the violinist Simon Standage, with Trevor Pinnock conducting the English Concert, in their classic reading (Archiv, 1982).

There are also very good modern-instrument recordings by Vladimir

Spivakov, with the Moscow Virtuosi (BMG/RCA Red Seal, 1988), and Anne-Sophie Mutter, with the Trondheim Soloists (Deutsche Grammophon, 1999). No barking dogs on either, but some fine, beautifully focused playing.

19. WOLFGANG AMADEUS MOZART

Piano Concertos: no. 20 in D minor (K. 466), no. 27 in B-flat major (K. 595), no. 26 in D major (K. 537), no. 23 in A major (K. 488), and no. 24 in C minor (K. 491)

SIR CLIFFORD CURZON, PIANIST; ENGLISH CHAMBER ORCHESTRA, BENJAMIN BRITTEN, CONDUCTING NOS. 20 AND 27; LONDON SYMPHONY ORCHESTRA, ISTVÁN KERTÉSZ, CONDUCTING NOS. 23, 24, AND 26

(Decca 468 491-2, two CDs)

Recorded 1967–1970

For the vast majority of musicians and listeners who spend any time with classical music, Wolfgang Amadeus Mozart (1756–1791) is an iconic figure who represents both the zenith of the Viennese classical tradition, and creative genius as an independent ideal. That said, one might take note of his detractors, if only for the sake of perspective. The iconoclastic pianist Glenn Gould famously disliked Mozart's piano sonatas and recorded them in eccentrically speedy performances. Influential listeners in Mozart's own time had reservations as well: although he dazzled Europe when he toured as a child performer and composer, it was matter of continual frustration, in his last years, that he was unable to obtain a court position, and that works as brilliant as *Le Nozze di Figaro* and *Don Giovanni* were not immediately embraced by the Viennese public.

Mozart's position in the musical cosmos became clearer after his death, and while on the one hand it didn't take long, there is a degree to which our view of this composer remains in flux. New research into his life and works, and occasional discoveries of manuscripts or copies of unknown scores (usually not of seismic importance, but interesting nevertheless) continue to sharpen our image of Mozart.

There have been correctives for the extravagances of Mozart worship. Some are inadvertent: when Lincoln Center decided to commemorate the bicentennial of his death by having every last scrap of his music performed, it became clear that much of what he wrote as a teenager, while certainly admirable, is actually not that interesting. The same Lincoln Center overview included scholarly lectures, one of which was given by a prominent musicologist who, apparently feeling overwhelmed by the mythologizing in popular Mozart biographies from the 1950s through Peter Shaffer's *Amadeus,* thought it necessary to advise listeners that Mozart's music was not actually dictated by God.

Mozart's piano concertos hold a special place among his works, not only because they were composed as vehicles through which Mozart could display his own prodigious powers at the keyboard, but also because they embrace the best qualities of both his symphonic and his keyboard writing, and hint at his operatic sensibilities as well. Many an annotator has noted the operatic spirit of Mozart's slow movements, which push the pianist to make the instrument sing, as well as the dramatic qualities of the movements that begin and end each work, particularly in the late concertos. Even so, there can be no generalizing about the mature concertos, five of which are included in this superb compilation featuring Sir Clifford Curzon, a pianist revered for the patrician quality of his playing. Each creates a distinct world.

The earliest of Curzon's five, the Piano Concerto no. 20 in D minor (K. 466), was Mozart's first concerto in a minor key—he only wrote one other, no. 24 in C minor (K. 491), also included here. The key signature is not merely a minor point: in Mozart's time, keys had distinct attributes (a notion that goes back to the Platonic characterization of the different modes), and D minor's connotations include tempestuousness and foreboding, qualities one senses immediately in the menacing triplet figure in the bass during the work's very first bars.

Completed on February 10, 1785, and given its premiere the following day (without the benefit of a full rehearsal), the work must have struck its first listeners as revolutionary. Its storminess is more akin to the Sturm und Drang spirit of Beethoven's time than the classicism still prevalent in Mozart's. Characteristic of Mozart's time as well, however, was the expectation of a happy ending, and after three movements of battle and dialogue between the solo line and the orchestra, the piece ends in the surprisingly bright—yet entirely natural sounding—key of D major.

The Concertos nos. 23 in A (K. 488) and 24 in C minor (K. 491) were composed three weeks apart, in March 1786, at a time when Mozart was also putting the finishing touches on the opera *Le Nozze di Figaro*. They are in many ways mirror images of one another, although their keys suggest their differences: the A major Concerto is a cheerful work, at least in its outer movements, with a bittersweet, lilting Adagio sandwiched between them to give the concerto a more sober hue, and the outer movements of the C minor Concerto have an abidingly dark, tragic quality, with a comparatively innocent, tranquil Larghetto separating them.

By 1788, Mozart's popularity in Vienna had started to wane, and the bright-spirited Concerto no. 26 in D (K. 537) was part of an attempted comeback. But Mozart's greatest successes with this work were out of town, so to speak: in 1789 he performed it in Berlin, where it was well-received, and in 1790 he performed it in Frankfurt at Leopold II's coronation as Holy Roman Emperor. It was that appearance that gave the work its nickname, the *Coronation* Concerto.

The Concerto no. 27 in B-flat (K. 595) was completed on January 5, 1791, after six relatively fallow months during which Mozart, worried about his health and facing discouraging financial prospects, composed very little. Yet his travails are not apparent here: this last concerto is a supremely graceful work, and a hint of the elevated spirituality that marks several other works of Mozart's final year can be heard here as well, most notably in the serene central Larghetto.

Touching the spiritual core of Mozart's music was Curzon's particular specialty, and in that regard, these performances are unequaled among Mozart concerto recordings. Listen to any of the slow movements here: the singing melodies have a dynamic arch that evokes not only the suppleness of the voice but, more important, the ebb and flow of passions that can be conveyed in an aria's text but are necessarily sub-rosa in an instrumental work. In the fast movements, too, Curzon had a way of evoking a great range of colors and moods, a palette necessary in this collection of works.

He was also famously demanding. During the 1967 sessions with István Kertész (a gifted conductor who died in a drowning accident in 1973) that produced these recordings of Concertos nos. 23, 24, and 26, he also recorded no. 27, but refused to approve either no. 26 or no. 27 for release. Three years later, when he recorded no. 20 with the composer Benjamin Britten on the podium, he tried no. 27 again, and again refused to approve it, reportedly having reconsidered certain interpretive details not long after the sessions. He finally agreed to release the Britten collaboration in 1978, but only after securing a promise that Decca would allow him to record it again. Sadly, he died in 1982, before having another go at the work. The collaboration with Kertész on no. 26 was released posthumously. In each case, it's impossible to imagine what Curzon's objections were, or how he could have produced more profound or more thoroughly considered readings.

20. WOLFGANG AMADEUS MOZART

Symphony no. 41 in C, *Jupiter* (K. 551), Concerto for Clarinet and Orchestra in A (K. 622), and Concerto for Bassoon and Orchestra in B-flat (K. 191)

JACK BRYMER, CLARINETIST; GWYDION BROOKE,
BASSOONIST; ROYAL PHILHARMONIC ORCHESTRA, SIR
THOMAS BEECHAM, CONDUCTING
(EMI Classics 67601 2)

Recorded 1957–1959

It may seem odd to suggest a Mozart recording by Sir Thomas Beecham at a time when period-instrument performances—or modern-instrument readings that take period style into account—are the fashionable norm for preromantic music. Transparent textures, nimble tempos, and, at times, astringent timbres are the hallmarks of up-to-date Mozart performances, and Beecham's performances are the willful antithesis of all that. They are from an age earlier than this disc's recording dates suggest, a time when different ideas about Mozart performance prevailed. And listeners willing to accept them on their own terms will find them remarkably persuasive. If the excitement of a sleek new period-instrument performance is visceral to a significant degree, the thrill of a Beecham recording has more to do with musical lines that are carefully and lovingly shaped to bring out their beauty and suppleness.

There is no reason both approaches cannot coexist. After all, the whole point of an interpretive art is that vastly different views of a work can be equally compelling or moving to a listener—particularly one who isn't unalterably invested in the quest to re-create the sounds a composer and his original audience heard. To Beecham, that quest was beside the point. He was fairly contemptuous of the nascent period-instrument world of his time, and was less interested in how a Mozart symphony sounded to Mozart than in the implications of what Mozart put on paper.

That's why, when you listen to this 1957 performance of the *Jupiter* Symphony—Beecham's third recording of the work (the earlier ones date from 1934 and 1950)—you will hear a broad orchestral texture, heavy on the bass and with principal melodies cast as sharply articulated, shapely lines. Details of the score's inner workings—the violins bowing away at a sixteenth-note figure when the theme is in the winds, for example, or a gentle wind counterpoint to a prominent string line—are spotlighted without being given an unnatural weight. And punctuating figures that support phrase endings are played with the same attentiveness as lines that lead up to them.

Beecham's tempos are leisurely by today's standards, and when Mozart indicates a dynamic change, Beecham magnifies it, making the quiet passages more graceful and the loud ones grander. In the Minuet, his dynamics are subtler still: within both the piano and forte passages in this stately account, virtually every note is shaded differently. There are changes to the score, as well, including having the horns play their part an octave higher than written in the Andante cantabile, and adding a completely Beechamesque timpani roll to the work's closing chord.

All this makes for a far more manipulated reading than is typical today, but there is something enduringly vital about Beecham's interpretation—a sense that the musical line must breathe naturally and develop as an organic whole.

The companion pieces—two of Mozart's wind concertos, with principals from the Royal Philharmonic as the soloists—have similar attractions. In the outer movements of the Clarinet Concerto, Beecham makes the orchestral music dance, and Jack Brymer follows suit in the clarinet solos, which are phrased with the same pointedness as Beecham imposes on the orchestral tuttis. Between those movements is a sublime Adagio, one of the most soulful of Mozart's instrumental movements, and played here entirely in that spirit.

Conductor Sir Thomas Beecham

Wolfgang Amadeus Mozart

The performance of the Bassoon Concerto is a bit more unusual. As in the other two works, Beecham's terraced dynamics and detailed phrasing give the reading a consistent freshness, but here they also endow it with an operatic character, at least in the first two movements. This theatrical quality—the sense that individual movements are transcribed arias—is something many of Mozart's concertos share. It is abetted here by Gwydion Brooke's mellow bassoon tone, which evokes the dusky sound of a mezzo-soprano, particularly in the central Andante ma adagio. But the real surprises are in Brooke's own cadenzas. The one in the second movement is simple and to the point, but the vocabulary of the first one is so freewheelingly modern as to sound wildly un-Mozartean, as is the short cadenza added to the finale. Yet these brief solo turns do what a traditional cadenza was meant to do: they entertain and dazzle.

Brooke's playing here, no less than Beecham's conducting, is part of a historical dialogue between composer, performer, and listener. One can admire or disagree with aspects of it, but it is the possibility of that dialogue that makes these works worth maintaining in the repertory for century after century.

21. WOLFGANG AMADEUS MOZART

Divertimento in E-flat (K. 563)

GIDON KREMER, VIOLINIST; KIM KASHKASHIAN, VIOLIST;
YO-YO MA, CELLIST
(Sony Classical MK 39561)

Recorded 1984

A divertimento is, as its title implies, a light entertainment, and indeed, for the opening five minutes or so of this one, scored for string trio, a listener might get the impression that Mozart was merely following the dictates of the form. By the time he composed this one, in

1788, he had written quite a few, most of them fairly light in both spirit and substance.

But keep listening: this is the first work Mozart had called a divertimento since 1780, and it is on an entirely different level from its predecessors. It is a stealth symphony, disguised as a string trio; one could even say that beneath a thick layer of courtliness—a layer that is shed quickly—it offers a foretaste of the passions that would begin to glow a quarter century later, in the middle works of Beethoven. I would argue that the Divertimento in E-flat is one of Mozart's true masterpieces. That it is so often overlooked when lists of Mozart's greatest works are drawn up is astonishing: I have introduced quite a few friends to it over the years, and they have invariably come to the same conclusion well before the end of the performance.

The circumstances of the work's composition suggest reasons for its depth. During the summer of 1788, Mozart was chronically in debt, with no prospect of a high-paying post to alleviate the financial pressures. He was physically worn down as well, and ill. He completed the *Jupiter* Symphony—his last work in that form—in early August, and then wrote very little for six weeks.

But at the end of September, he entered this divertimento into his catalog, and noted in one of his letters that he composed it for Michael Puchberg, a wealthy merchant who, like Mozart, was a Freemason. Puchberg had responded generously to the first of Mozart's pleas for financial help the previous June and he would continue to lend Mozart money, no doubt aware that there was little prospect of repayment, until shortly before the composer's death in 1791. This six-movement, fifty-minute divertimento, Mozart's longest chamber work, was apparently a gesture of thanks.

One of the most immediately distinctive qualities of the work is the equality of the three string lines: each may take the spotlight momentarily, but the other lines are rarely just accompaniment. Even in the Adagio second movement, in which Mozart followed his habit of giving his slow movements an operatic character, there are passages that sound more like duos or trios than like arias. The third-movement Minuet offers all the qualities of a lively conversation. The fifth-movement Minuet, by contrast, is a chordal setting, built around a motif that suggests a horn call, and it might have been at home in an earlier Mozart divertimento except that the modulations in the first of the two Trio sections are among the moments when the work reaches toward the Beethovenian future.

Between the Minuet movements is an Andante that, like many of the work's movements, begins in a way that hardly hints at its denouement. The theme here is simple and courtly, an elegant dance. But an extraordinary set of variations follows, packed with invention, internal dialogues, both lively and intensely meditative, and stretches of triple counterpoint.

So why is this work such a connoisseurs-only affair? One reason may be that its thoroughly democratic balance, though one of its greatest strengths, from a listener's point of view, poses significant hurdles in purely practical terms. It demands three first-rate players, musicians who are equals in tone and technique, and who have ample time to rehearse it. If this were a quartet, that would be no problem: full-time quartets are plentiful, and they get under a work's skin not only through intensive rehearsal, but by playing it on tour over many months and years. Dedicated string trios, by contrast, are comparatively few, which means that when the work is performed, it is likely to be either by members of a quartet who have decided to adopt the piece (and let one of the violinists sit out half a concert) or by the kind of ad hoc ensemble that is likely to get through the piece respectably but without finding all that it has to offer.

The trio on this recording is unusual as ad hoc ensembles go: Gidon Kremer is an exceptionally probing violinist who demands much of the musicians he works with. Kim Kashkashian is a technically brilliant violist and an eloquent interpreter. And Yo-Yo Ma, apart from being one of the greatest cellists of his time, is a musician whose particular energy and devotion to chamber music has a way of inspiring the musicians with whom he plays. At the time the recording was made, this trio was touring together, as it continued to do intermittently over a few seasons, sometimes filling out as a quartet with the violinist Daniel Phillips. They made several recordings, of which this is the most sublime.

22. WOLFGANG AMADEUS MOZART

Requiem (K. 626, completion by Franz Xaver Süssmayr)

JOHN ALLDIS CHOIR, BBC SYMPHONY ORCHESTRA,
SIR COLIN DAVIS, CONDUCTING

(Philips Silver Line Classics 420 353-2)

*Helen Donath, soprano; Yvonne Minton, contralto; Ryland Davies,
tenor; Gerd Nienstedt, bass. Also available as a Decca Penguin Classics
460 670, with an essay by Stephen Jay Gould.*

Recorded 1967

One of the pivotal dramatic conceits in Peter Shaffer's *Amadeus* is the
plot by the composer Antonio Salieri to poison Mozart and appropriate his Requiem, which Salieri had anonymously commissioned. In
Shaffer's tale, Salieri meant to keep Mozart alive until the work was
finished, and then to pass it off as his own tribute to his colleague as
soon as Mozart died, thereby guaranteeing that posterity would
remember him as the composer of at least one masterwork. This is
fantasy, of course, and Shaffer labeled it as such: although it has
become a popular bloodsport among critics and musicologists to vil-
ify Shaffer for his portrayal of Mozart and for the historical liberties
both in his play and in the Milos Forman film version (for which Shaffer reworked and expanded the play considerably), Shaffer has always
made the point that his work is not intended as a biography of
Mozart. Rather, it uses Mozart and the glories of his music as the
starting point for a meditation on the nature of genius and mediocrity.

On its own terms, it has a lot to offer, and the film version, thanks
to the flexibility of the medium, includes a handful of scenes that
show exactly how Mozart's music works. One of these finds Mozart,
on his deathbed, dictating sections of his Requiem to Salieri. The
scene is fiction, although a handful of Mozart's friends visited him on
December 4, 1791—the day before his death—and sang through the
completed sections of the Requiem, and *The New Grove Dictionary*

of Music and Musicians suggests that Salieri may have visited as well. But if the scene that Shaffer wrote almost certainly never took place, the dramatization of Mozart dictating the piece—singing individual lines, assigning them to specific voices or instruments, and then doing the same with the harmonies and orchestral support—illuminates some of the music's structural niceties from the inside. For viewers who don't read orchestral scores, this was surely an ear-opening way to hear the piece.

Shaffer, of course, was by no means the first to endow the history of the Requiem with a dramatic fictional overlay; the difference is that his effort was properly labeled, not passed off as fact. Mozart's early biographers were not so careful, and stripping away the mythology they created—stories of a death-obsessed Mozart persuaded that he was writing his own Requiem and chafing under the burden, for example—has kept generations of musicologists busy.

Mozart was commissioned to write the Requiem in July 1791 by a benefactor who wished to remain anonymous—not Salieri, but Count Franz von Walsegg-Stuppach, who may have intended to pass off the work as his own at a memorial service for his wife, who had died earlier in the year. The composition, rehearsals, and first performances of *Die Zauberflöte* and *La Clemenza di Tito* kept Mozart from devoting himself fully to the work until the fall, at which time his final illness (the consensus is that he died of rheumatic fever) slowed him down.

He completed and orchestrated the Introitus (the Requiem Aeternam), establishing the work's unusual, dark-hued sound world. He also wrote out the vocal lines, with accompanimental indications, for the Kyrie, Dies Irae, Tuba Mirum, Rex Tremendae, Recordare, and Confutatis, as well as eight bars of the Lacrimosa and parts of the Offertorium. The rest of the work was left incomplete: parts of it were undoubtedly sketched out, but because the sketches no longer exist, it is impossible to know with certainty how detailed Mozart's notes were. This was by design: Mozart's wife, Constanze, was intent on having the work completed, and on pulling a veil of secrecy over how much of the Sanctus, Benedictus, and Agnus Dei were composed by her husband.

Constanze first asked the composer Joseph Eybler to finish the work, and when he declined she turned to Franz Xaver Süssmayr,

Mozart's student. Constanze later asserted that Süssmayr was given instructions on how the work was to be completed by Mozart himself, the day before he died. Süssmayr completed his version within two months of Mozart's death, and although musicians and critics have been second-guessing him ever since, his version has remained the standard edition of the score. Not that it is the only choice. An edition by Franz Beyer corrects what Beyer considered Süssmayr's orchestrational missteps. Richard Maunder's compositional surgery involved dropping the Sanctus, Benedictus, and Agnus Dei, in the belief that they were entirely Süssmayr's, and reorchestrating the rest using late Mozart scores as models. And Robert Levin, convinced that Mozart had at least sketched out the final three sections, retained them but made numerous innovative changes in the orchestration and arrangement of the materials throughout the work.

My own preference is for Levin's completion, which has already had respectable recordings by Martin Pearlman with Boston Baroque, on period instruments (Telarc), and Bernard Labadie with Les Violons du Roy and La Chapelle de Québec, on modern instruments (Dorian). But it hasn't yet had the knockout recording it deserves, or that can match the sheer emotional power and wrenching beauty of Sir Colin Davis's 1967 BBC Symphony account, using the Süssmayr edition.

The recording captures Davis fairly early in his career, four years before the start of his fifteen-year tenure as music director of the Royal Opera at Covent Garden. Still a young firebrand, he had captured the attention of the London musical world with lively, insightful performances of the Mozart operas with the Chelsea Opera Group, as well as with the works of Berlioz. Both composers, along with Sibelius, remained Davis's lifelong specialties, and this Requiem goes a long way toward explaining why his Mozart readings have been so highly regarded.

The soul of this performance is in the degree to which Davis uses contrast—in dynamics, textures, and tempos—to project the work's grandeur. One could argue, in fact, that some of these contrasts make for a decidedly romantic conception, but to me they describe the contours of a deeply felt expression of faith. Most of all, there is an urgency in the performance, a quality already palpable in the Introit and the magnificent fugal Kyrie, but magnified greatly in the Dies

Irae, where Davis's brisk tempos and full-throttle dynamics fully suggest the terrors of the "Day of Wrath." He creates a similar effect later in the Rex Tremendae, but at a more expansive tempo, and in the Confutatis, where he makes the most of the contrast between the fiery writing for basses and tenors and the alternating passages for angelic sopranos and altos.

The Tuba Mirum showcases not only the fine vocal quartet that performs here—most notably Helen Donath, who sings the soprano line with the kind of clarity and lightness one hears in Emma Kirkby's recording of the truncated Maunder edition, with Christopher Hogwood (L'Oiseau-Lyre)—but also some very solid solo trombone playing by Jack Pinches. There is a wonderful bloom in the vocal phrasing, both among the soloists and in the choral sections, and where fluidity and expansive tempos suit the needs of the text—in the Recordare, the Benedictus, and, especially, in the grand proclamations of the Sanctus—Davis gives the music all the room it needs.

There are dozens of fine recordings of the Mozart Requiem, a few of which have already been mentioned in passing. As an alternative, Sir John Eliot Gardiner's 1986 recording with the English Baroque Soloists, the Monteverdi Choir, and an excellent slate of soloists that includes Barbara Bonney, Anne Sofie von Otter, Hans Peter Blochwitz, and Willard White (Philips) is performed with virtuosic clarity on period instruments. Gardiner takes a more straightforward approach, but if he manipulates his tempos and textures less overtly, his reading by no means lacks the personal touch that will bring a listener back to the recording again and again.

23. FRANZ JOSEPH HAYDN

String Quartets: op. 20, no. 5; op. 33, no. 2 (*The Joke*); op. 54, no. 12; op. 64, no. 5 (*The Lark*); op. 74, no. 3 (*The Rider*); op. 76, no. 2 (*Fifths*); and op. 77, no. 1

THE EMERSON STRING QUARTET

(Deutsche Grammophon 289 471 327-2, two CDs)

Recorded 2000–2001

Music history, or at least music history as conveyed in the survey courses that used to be called "music appreciation," has played a mean trick on Franz Joseph Haydn (1732–1809). It has made him into "Papa" Haydn, a revered figure of the old school—not an under-appreciated genius like Mozart or a revolutionary iconoclast like Beethoven, but a happily bewigged musical servant, eager to please the Esterházy princes for whom he wrote hundreds of solid, lovely pieces, many of which still sound great to modern ears.

Such a reductive account completely distorts both his career and his life's work. It overlooks the ample friction of his early court career, as well as the fact that for the last few decades of his life he was an independent, entrepreneurial composer with an enormous following all over Europe. And by casting Haydn as the blandest of the three Viennese greats (Mozart and Beethoven being the others), it gives short shrift to music that can be charming and courtly, but also play-ful, earthy, and dramatic.

There is also the question of Haydn's seminal place in the history of two of classical music's central genres, the symphony and the string quartet. Although it is not true to say (as music appreciation texts once did) that he invented both compositional forms, certainly his early experiments helped shape and establish the symphony and quar-tet as we know them today, and he stands unquestionably as the first important contributor to the symphony and quartet canon. In quan-tity as well as quality, that contribution was huge: going by the latest musicological reckoning, he wrote 106 works that can properly be called symphonies, and sixty-eight string quartets.

In truth, both forms evolved along with Haydn's career. The symphony found its roots in the baroque Sinfonia—the instrumental movement played to arrest an audience's attention at the start of a cantata, an oratorio, or an opera. The most adventurous of these were multipart forms—say, a fast-slow-fast structure—and, ultimately, the sections at different tempos, and with their own themes, drifted off to become the separate movements of the classical symphony. The quartet's evolution was equally direct: the difference between a quartet as Haydn conceived it and one written by a composer during his childhood (Georg Philipp Telemann, say) is that in the baroque version, the cello line would have been supplemented by a harpsichord, and one of the top lines might have been scored for flute instead of violin.

Haydn's earliest quartets (like his earliest symphonies) date from the 1750s: the official but possibly apocryphal story is that the composer was engaged as a violinist by Count Karl von Fürnberg, and asked to write for an ensemble that included another violinist, a violist, and a cellist. When his first works for the group proved pleasing, so the story goes, the count commissioned more, and a form was born.

Did it actually happen this way? It's unlikely that question will be settled to unanimous satisfaction, and it doesn't matter. More to the point is that a few years later, when Haydn was working at Esterháza, in Hungary—fifty miles from Vienna and comparatively isolated—he was free to pursue and refine his experiments. If the early quartets had been light entertainments, those of the 1760s and beyond show Haydn treating the quartet, both corporately and individually, as a virtuoso ensemble. He was clearly inspired by the textural and coloristic variety he could wring from four similar voices, and as one proceeds through his quartets, the writing becomes increasingly inventive, three-dimensional, even picturesque. By the time he reached his final essays in the form, in 1799, his style had moved light-years from where he started, and it would cost Beethoven some effort to catch up with him.

By the time the Emerson String Quartet recorded this superb two-disc survey, it had distinguished itself with recordings covering vast tracts of the repertory, including all the Beethoven, Bartók, and Shostakovich quartets, and a good sampling of other works from the nineteenth and twentieth centuries. Going back to the source seemed only natural, and they play these works with a vision of where Haydn's works would eventually lead, but also with sufficient freshness to allow the music to speak on its own terms.

They capture, for example, a lovely innocence in the opening movements of the F minor Quartet (op. 20, no. 5), the earliest of the works included here, but also a sense that Haydn by this point was no neophyte: the Emersons play the work's closing fugue with the intellectual weight its Bachian contours demand. By contrast, when Haydn lightens up, these players jump into the spirit. There is, for example, the finale of the *Lark* Quartet, which has the energy of dances such as a hornpipe or a gigue, and which the Emersons play with speedy precision; and in the finale of the *Joke* Quartet, where Haydn toys with listeners' harmonic expectations, the ensemble doesn't exaggerate Haydn's comic touches, but lets the composer's moves speak for themselves.

The Emerson String Quartet also gets points for the breadth of its overview—seven quartets on two discs, moving chronologically from op. 20 to op. 77. There are, of course, many fine single discs to choose from as well. The Lindsay String Quartet recorded a magnificent, warm-toned Haydn series (ASV), just about any volume of which will prove enlightening. And of the period-instrument versions, I'm particularly fond of L'Archibudelli's *The Three Last String Quartets* (Sony Classical), which includes op. 77, nos. 1 and 2, the unfinished op. 103, and, in a nice touch, a quartet version of "Der Geis"—the part-song that Haydn wanted published with op. 103 to explain why he stopped composing. "All my strength is at an end," the text reads, "I am old and weak; there's little that brings me cheer but wit and the juice of the vine."

24. FRANZ JOSEPH HAYDN

The *London* Symphonies, Vol. I

ROYAL CONCERTGEBOUW ORCHESTRA OF AMSTERDAM,
SIR COLIN DAVIS, CONDUCTING
(Philips 442 611-2, two CDs)

Includes Symphony no. 95 in C minor, Symphony no. 96 in D (Miracle),
*Symphony no. 98 in B-flat, Symphony no. 102 in B-flat, Symphony
no. 103 in E-flat* (Drum Roll), *Symphony no. 104 in D* (London).

Recorded 1976–1981

It is impossible to contemplate the sheer number of symphonies that Haydn composed without the subsequent history of the form intruding to make his output seem even more vast. Traditionally numbered at 104, but with a couple more recently added by musicologists and catalogers, his symphonic output is more than twice that of Mozart, who produced 41 by the standard canonical numbering, or as many as 56 if you include various works that have been reclassified recently. Beethoven finished only nine, and although some later composers have surpassed that number, the great ones who did are comparatively few.

Mendelssohn and Schubert, both of whom died young, made it to five and nine, respectively (although in Schubert's case, the number of incomplete works, movements, and sketches that he left make it difficult to number his symphonies accurately). Dvořák wrote nine, and Bruckner's numbered symphonies end with the Ninth (although there are two others, called no. 0 and no. 00). And although Mahler sketched a Tenth, he was spooked by the idea of moving past Beethoven's marker, and he died before finishing the Tenth's orchestration.

Of course, the scale of the symphony changed considerably on its way from Haydn's first to Beethoven's last, and so did both composers' and listeners' expectations of the form. For Haydn, a symphony was a fifteen- to twenty-minute work, cast in three or four movements, and intended entirely to entertain. Mozart, Haydn's younger contemporary, was largely content with that role, although from the Twenty-fifth Symphony on, he tended to ratchet up the weight and drama, taking Haydn's evocative Sturm und Drang symphonies of the 1770s as a launching point. Beethoven started out with the Haydn and Mozart symphonies as models, but he quickly expanded the symphony in scope and size, and began using these newly expanded canvases for grandly scaled tone paintings (like the *Pastorale* Symphony) and even political manifestoes (like the *Eroica* and Ninth Symphonies).

To say that Haydn's symphonies were meant to entertain is not to write them off as lightweight. Entertainment, for Haydn, meant a range of things, from the serious to the frivolous. And indeed, among his symphonies one finds imaginatively descriptive music, as in the sunrise evoked in the *Morning* Symphony (no. 6), as well as unbuttoned humor, as in the *Surprise* Symphony (no. 94), with its sudden chordal thwacks, or the *Farewell* (no. 45), in which virtually the entire orchestra walks off the stage in the finale, leaving only two violinists still playing.

I chose this two-CD selection from the *London* Symphonies because these works capture Haydn's symphonic style in full flower and are superbly represented in these trim, zesty readings by Sir Colin Davis and the Royal Concertgebouw Orchestra. Recorded at a time when the period-instrument world was making its way from its former Renaissance and baroque specialization into the larger realm of the standard symphonic canon by way of Mozart, Davis's readings showed that a modern orchestra and a conductor able to bring out the wit and vitality in this music could still offer an enlivening look at Haydn. The finales, in particular—some of Haydn's most vigorous—combine litheness with power in a way that set a high standard for modern Haydn playing.

The commissions for these works came along at precisely the right time. Haydn's longtime employer, Prince Nikolaus I Esterházy, died at the end of September 1790, and although he continued to receive his salary, as well as an annual payment from the prince's estate, there was no reason for him to remain at Esterháza, since the prince's son immediately dissolved its musical establishment. Haydn moved to

Vienna, and turned down at least one position at another court, intent on pursuing the fully independent career for which his considerable fame provided an ample foundation.

It was only two months after Nikolaus's death that Johann Peter Salomon, a German impresario based in London, turned up in Vienna to tempt the newly independent Haydn to visit England—something Salomon had attempted to do, without success, several times in the past. This time, Haydn was amenable. In January 1791, he and Salomon traveled to London, where they presented a series of orchestral concerts led by Salomon, who was a violinist, with Haydn playing the keyboard. For those performances, between March 1791 and May 1792, Haydn composed the first six of the *London* Symphonies, nos. 93 to 98. They were a tremendous success, and Salomon invited Haydn back for a second series—for which he composed nos. 99 through 104—between February 1794 and August 1795.

There are some brilliant touches in these works. The finale of no. 95, for example, begins as a courtly dance, but launches quickly into a fugal section that bears a resemblance to the finale of Mozart's *Jupiter* Symphony (composed in 1788), and may be a tip of the hat to the younger composer, who Haydn had befriended in Vienna. Mozart's shadow may have fallen on no. 98 as well: the sweetly melancholy Adagio is said to have been written just after Haydn learned of Mozart's death, in December 1791, and its opening theme bears a trace of "Dove sono," one of the more moving arias in *Le Nozze di Figaro*. Also, in no. 98, there are some surprises in the finale, in the form of solo passages for the violin and the keyboard (played here on a harpsichord), originally meant to be played by Salomon and Haydn himself.

Symphony no. 102 is notable for its strangely forward-looking qualities. It opens with the kind of foreboding chord, played with a swelling crescendo, that Beethoven would use to great effect about a decade later in his First Symphony and in the *Egmont* Overture; and the development of the opening movement seems also to have an almost Beethovenian heft. Parts of the Adagio look even farther into the future: in terms of harmony and texture, they could almost be mistaken for Dvořák. The opening drum roll that gives no. 103 its nickname provides a novel touch, but equally novel is the length and sobriety of the Adagio introduction. But here—as in no. 104 and several of the others that begin with a slow introduction—the transition to the Allegro con spirito that makes up the movement proper bursts like the sun through a cloud.

This first volume of Sir Colin Davis's *London* Symphonies seemed the marginally more attractive of the two sets into which Philips has divided the twelve works, but the companion collection (Philips 442 614-2, with Symphonies nos. 93, 94, 97, 99, 100, and 101, also on two CDs) is certainly worth having as well. There are, in fact, no weak stretches in Haydn's symphonic output, and if money is no object, I recommend Antal Dorati's extraordinary traversal with the Philharmonica Hungarica, complete with alternate versions of several works

Composer Franz Joseph Haydn

and movements in a boxed set of thirty-three CDs (Decca 448 531). Actually, at a list price of $264—or $8 a disc—these dynamic performances are a bargain.

25. FRANZ JOSEPH HAYDN

Die Schöpfung (The Creation)

STOCKHOLM RADIO CHORUS, STOCKHOLM CHAMBER CHOIR, AND BERLIN PHILHARMONIC, JAMES LEVINE, CONDUCTING

(Deutsche Grammophon 427 629-2, two CDs)

Kathleen Battle, soprano; Gösta Winbergh, tenor; Kurt Moll, bass.

Recorded 1987

Although oratorios rank below symphonies, piano trios, string quartets, and Masses in the hierarchy of works for which Haydn is most celebrated, the handful he wrote are quite striking, and none more so than his exquisite setting of *The Creation*, which turns the opening pages of Genesis, by way of a German libretto by Baron Gottfried von Swieten and a section of John Milton's *Paradise Lost*, into a powerful, three-dimensional drama.

The work was inspired, at least partly, by the great master of the oratorio, Handel. During a visit to London in January 1791—some thirty-two years after Handel's death—Haydn attended a Handel festival at Westminster Abbey that was truly awesome in scope, with one thousand singers and musicians offering *Messiah*, *Israel in Egypt*, and several other works, and with King George III in attendance.

Haydn's impresario in London, Johann Peter Salomon, had been encouraging him to write oratorios, which were extremely popular in England. On Haydn's next visit to England, in 1794, he began work on one, but left it unfinished. When he returned to Vienna in 1795, however, he brought with him a libretto for *The Creation* that had been written for Handel, but which Handel never got around to setting. During his journey, he stopped in Passau, where he heard a version of his own "Seven Last Words," composed in 1787 as an instrumental meditation. In Passau, however, a local composer added choral parts and recitatives, an expansion that intrigued Haydn. Back in Vienna, Baron von Swieten revised the Passau libretto, and Haydn provided his own music for a reworked oratorio version.

He also handed the *Creation* libretto to the baron, who translated it into German and undertook various revisions—cutting some sections, adding to others—and made numerous musical and dramatic suggestions to Haydn in his marginal notes, some of which (for example, having the chorus sing "Let there be light" only once, without the repetition that was typical in such works) the composer adopted. And mindful of Salomon's request, Haydn and von Swieten took care to fashion an English libretto that not only reflected von Swieten's changes, but also fit Haydn's music.

The work plays out in three parts: Part I covers the first four days, from the creation of light (physical as well as spiritual) through the separation of land and sea, the sprouting of trees and fruit, and the appearance of the heavenly bodies. Part II is devoted to the creation of animate life, from animals, birds, and fish to humankind. And Part III focuses on Adam and Eve, stopping short just before their fall. In Parts I and II, the solo roles depict angels—Gabriel (soprano), Uriel (tenor), and Raphael (bass); in Part III, the bass and soprano usually take up the roles of Adam and Eve, as they do in Levine's recording (in some performances, new singers are introduced, although there is no more music for Gabriel and Raphael), with the tenor, still Uriel, opening the section with a description of the happy pair, and stopping in at the end to warn Adam and Eve that they will be "happy for evermore if vain delusion lead you not astray to want more than you have and know more than you should." Robust choruses praising God's power and glory run throughout the score.

The work's first performance was a private one, at the palace of Karl Philip, Prince of Schwarzenberg, on April 29, 1798, and it was an immediate hit with its aristocratic audience. Its public premiere in Vienna occurred nearly a year later, at the Imperial Burgtheater, with an orchestra and chorus of around four hundred, and contemporary reports describe the response as, again, rapturous.

The work's attractions are immediately apparent. As Handel no doubt would have done, Haydn mined the opportunities for pictorialism in the Creation story, beginning with the opening Largo, the orchestral "Representation of Chaos" that draws the listener in before the bass, singing as the angel Raphael, offers the opening line of Genesis as a recitative. The chorus takes up the narrative with a serene, sweetly harmonized vision of the spirit of God moving "upon the face of the waters," and an equally soft-hued rendering of the command, "Let there be light." The first words of the next clause ("and there was . . .") continue in the same manner—slow, calm, pianissimo—only to explode into a sustained fortissimo, for full orchestra and chorus, on the word "light."

Similarly vivid effects illuminate the whole work, and the choruses remain deeply felt, with a blend of the devotional and the celebratory as each of God's acts of creation is described and marvelled at by the angels and the chorus. Yet as vivid as *The Creation* is, to modern ears it also carries a sense of classical orderliness that makes it rather quaint, as if God and his angels presided over the Creation wearing powdered wigs, stockings, and brocade coats.

Levine's robust performance, using a large modern-instruments orchestra and choir, takes account of the classical style in matters of phrasing and balance without bowing to musicological notions about timbre and weight. That's fine: a good, dramatic period-instruments version, by Sir John Eliot Gardiner with the English Baroque Soloists and Monteverdi Choir, is available on the same label (Deutsche Grammophon). But much of the appeal of Levine's reading is in its heft and color—qualities that give this performance a real impact and make its tone painting as vivid and powerful as the subject matter demands. The cast of soloists is also well-balanced and suitably expressive, and Levine draws a beautifully blended, exuberant sound from the combined Swedish choruses.

26. JUAN CRISÓSTOMO ARRIAGA

Symphonie à Grande Orchestre, *Los Esclavos Felices* Overture, and Overture for Nonet (op. 1)

LE CONCERT DES NATIONS, LA CAPELLA REIAL
DE CATALUNYA, JORDI SAVALL, CONDUCTING
(Astrée E 8532)

Recorded 1994

Overshadowed by Mendelssohn and Mozart in the annals of composer prodigies who died young, Juan Crisóstomo Arriaga was an accomplished if little-known composer whose works amply repay investigation. Called "the Spanish Mozart"—or, in more politically charged times, "the Basque Mozart"—Arriaga was born in Bilbao in 1806. He began composing by the time he was eleven, and in quick order he produced remarkably mature works for choir, orchestra, and chamber ensembles, as well as an opera, *Los Esclavos Felices*. When he was fifteen, in 1821, the industrious young composer went to Paris to continue his studies at the Conservatoire. He died in Paris of a pulmonary infection in January 1826, a few days short of his twentieth birthday.

The three works included here constitute virtually all that has survived of Arriaga's orchestral music. Arriaga composed the Overture for Nonet—two violins, viola, double bass, flute, two clarinets, and two horns—in 1818, when he was twelve. The opera, *Los Esclavos Felices,* dates from 1820, and won the young composer considerable fame when news of its first performance in Bilbao spread through Spain and made its way to Paris. Much of the score is lost, but the surviving Overture—a cheerfully Italianate piece—gives the impression that it was a characterful, virtuosic work. And although no date of composition has been firmly established for the symphony, its expansiveness and assurance suggest that it was one of his last compositions.

There is an appealing omnivorousness in Arriaga's music, which is caught in the transition from classicism to romanticism that was taking place as Arriaga learned his art. Consider, for example, that when Arriaga was born, Mozart had been dead for fourteen years; Haydn was alive but had essentially retired; and Beethoven was between his Fourth and Fifth Symphonies.

All three influenced Arriaga profoundly, but although the spirit of classicism is fully alive in his music, you can hear a strong kinship with Beethoven in his works. The early Overture, for example, begins with a slow section that has the dark coloration of late Mozart, but bursts into the light with a bright string figure that would be fully at home in a Haydn finale. Yet, near the end of the piece, one encounters a halting, ascending scale—almost exactly the same figure Beethoven used to begin the final movement of his Symphony no. 1. Arriaga's own symphony, with its Sturm und Drang chordal blasts and winding melodic lines rich in pathos and drama, displays Beethovenian moves as well.

One hears other influences, too—Rossini in the *Esclavos* Overture, Schubert in the symphony—but it wouldn't be entirely accurate to call Arriaga's music derivative. Its real attraction (and the reason for its inclusion here) is its current of originality. However drawn Arriaga may have been to the Viennese and Italian styles, the idiosyncratic perspective of an outsider helped him sidestep some of the more predictable melodic and harmonic conventions—the stock moves, so to speak—of those styles.

These performances are conducted by Jordi Savall, an enterprising Spanish conductor and viola da gamba player who became internationally famous when his gamba performances were included in the film *Tous les matins du monde*. Finding unusual repertory and treating it with care, much as a museum curator might handle a priceless painting, is Savall's specialty, and the playing he draws from Le Concert des Nations, a period-instrument group, is bright, energetic, and alert to Arriaga's penchant for sudden shifts in direction and texture.

Recordings of Arriaga's music are shockingly few, but if you find these pieces intriguing, I would recommend looking into his three string quartets, composed in Paris in 1824. These are beautiful, warm-blooded works, both lively and richly melodic, and they can be heard in finely polished performances on a 1985 recording by the Voces String Quartet (MDG 603 0236-2).

---

27. LUDWIG VAN BEETHOVEN

The Nine Symphonies, Overtures

CLEVELAND ORCHESTRA, CLEVELAND ORCHESTRA CHOIR,
GEORGE SZELL, CONDUCTING

(Sony Classical Essential Classics SB5K 48396, five CDs)

Adele Addison, soprano; Jane Hobbson, mezzo-soprano, Richard Lewis, tenor; Donald Bell, baritone. Includes Symphony no. 1 in C major (op. 21); Symphony no. 2 in D major (op. 36); Symphony no. 3 in E-flat major, Eroica *(op. 55); Symphony no. 4 in B-flat major (op. 60); Symphony no. 5 in C minor (op. 67); Symphony no. 6 in F major,* Pastoral *(op. 68); Symphony no. 7 in A major (op. 92); Symphony no. 8 in F major (op. 93); Symphony no. 9 in D minor,* Choral *(op. 125); with the* Egmont *Overture (op. 84),* King Stephen *Overture (op. 117), and* Fidelio *Overture (op. 72b).*

Also available on five individually packaged CDs: Symphony no. 1 (op. 21); Symphony no. 6, Pastoral *(op. 68), and* Egmont *Overture (op. 84) (Sony Classical SBK 46532); Symphony no. 2 (op. 36), Symphony no. 5 (op. 67) (Sony Classical SBK 47651); Symphony no. 3,* Eroica *(op. 55), Symphony no. 8 (op. 93) (Sony Classical SBK 46328); Symphony no. 4 (op. 60), Symphony no. 7 (op. 92) (Sony Classical SBK 48158); Symphony no. 9,* Choral *(op. 125),* Fidelio *Overture (op. 72b) (Sony Classical SBK 46533).*

Recorded 1958–1968

Let's face it: any classical music collection must include all of the Beethoven symphonies. Individually, these are vibrant, energizing pieces; together they represent a body of work that is so central to our understanding of symphonic music as a genre, that even the less important of them—the First and Second, although some might add the Fourth and Eighth—contribute something to the broader picture, if only the necessary shorter steps between great innovations.

Ludwig van Beethoven (1770–1827) did not, obviously, conceive of the symphonies as a unified cycle: they were simply steps in his creative evolution and parallel the development one sees in his string quartets and piano sonatas, collections that in many ways are equally crucial to an understanding of what he accomplished.

But Beethoven's own musical growth is a microcosm: taken as a group, the symphonies offer a panoramic look at the transformation in the early nineteenth century of the symphonic form as well as the way orchestral instruments were used in the discourse of the concert hall. They trace the path of the Haydnesque conventions of classical style to the storminess, overt emotionalism, and philosophical idealism that would characterize romanticism. Whether Beethoven was the first romantic or a transitional figure can be debated persuasively either way, but he unquestionably laid the foundations of the new movement. The romantics who came after him, from Schubert, Schumann, and Berlioz to Brahms, Liszt, Wagner, and Mahler, revered Beethoven as the fountainhead of an emerging musical language.

Whether it is preferable to have all nine symphonies performed by a single conductor and orchestra, or nine performances cherry-picked from the catalog, is a significant question, and a tough one. There is something to be said for seeking favorite interpretations of each work. But it is also particularly satisfying to listen to a unified overview, offered by a master conductor and a top-flight orchestra.

These performances by George Szell and the Cleveland Orchestra have proven extraordinarily durable, both interpretively and in terms of their recorded sound. In fact, the recordings, made over a decade starting in 1958, barely show their age: they capture the timbres, textures, and incandescent power of the orchestra with remarkable clarity.

Entirely apart from what they tell us about Beethoven and his works, these discs are reminders of how Szell, with his vigorous, demanding, and insightful approach to music-making, transformed the Cleveland Orchestra into one of the world's great ensembles during a tenure that lasted from 1946 until his death in 1970, only two years after the last recording in this cycle. The Austro-German classical and romantic canon was where Szell was most at home, and in some ways these performances—along with a magnificent collaboration with the pianist Leon Fleischer on Beethoven's Five Piano Concertos (also part of Sony's midprice Essential Classics series)—are his crowning achievements.

Beethoven was not yet thirty when he completed his Symphony no. 1, in 1800, and the shadows of Mozart and Haydn still lingered over his music, something particularly evident in the thoroughly courtly contours of this work's Andante cantabile con moto second movement. But before reaching this conservative, songlike movement, a listener will have encountered some of the temperament that, when magnified over the next few years, would drive much of Beethoven's greater work. The symphony begins, for example, not with a straightforward C major chord, to establish its key, but with a peculiar little Adagio chord progression in which seventh chords set up a chain of tensions and resolutions that lead into the brisk Allegro.

Szell lets Beethoven have it both ways: the movements that bow in the direction of Haydn are played with a light, supple touch; the ones that hint at Beethoven's future are played with great vigor and divorced from the past. The broader contours aside, listen for moments when Beethoven puts the spotlight on the brass (the Trio section of the Menuetto, for example) or solo winds for some superb playing.

Symphony no. 2, completed in 1802, moves ahead, ratcheting up the tensions in the opening movement, but also offsetting them with an innocently folksy figure, first played by a wind band (later by the strings). Beethoven also abandoned the Menuetto third movement, which was virtually standard in the classical symphony, in favor of the structurally similar but more light-spirited Scherzo. Actually, the Menuetto in the First Symphony is a Scherzo for all practical purposes, but Beethoven maintained the old nomenclature. Still, while Beethoven can be heard pushing against their limits, the impulses of classicism prevail. Szell's solution to the problem of acknowledging both those elements is heard to best effect in the finale: the start has a positively Mozartean lightness of texture, but the almost chaotic fury of the playing, starting around five minutes into the movement, highlights the degree to which Beethoven's personal style was shedding classical constraints.

It was with Symphony no. 3, the *Eroica,* in 1803, that Beethoven came fully into his own—and very deliberately so, having declared to a friend, soon after finishing the Second Symphony, that he was dissatisfied with his music and wanted to take "a new path." To a degree, the tumultuous times helped him fix his course. Acting on an idea that was first suggested to him in 1798, Beethoven set about writing a symphonic portrait of Napoleon, who had become his political hero by embracing the egalitarian and antimonarchical ideals of the French Revolution and spreading them (militarily) through Europe. In the end, Napoleon crowned himself emperor, and Beethoven destroyed the dedication, but that scarcely changed his ideas about the work itself. The only difference was that now the work described a heroic ideal, rather than an actual hero. Some analysts have suggested that Beethoven may have seen an idealized version of himself in the starring role.

The extramusical issues aside, the symphony broke considerable ground. It is, for starters, roughly twice as long as a conventional symphony of its time—something that many of its first listeners found shocking in itself. The opening movement is a battle piece: it begins with two cannonlike blasts, and, at its climax, there is a long and unprecedented barrage of tension-creating dissonant chords. The opening blasts are followed by a triadic theme that Leonard Bernstein once described as "simplicity made manifest," and from which an extraordinary edifice is built. The second movement tolls a stately funeral march, and after the brief Scherzo, Beethoven offers an unusual finale—a large set of variations based on a theme from his ballet *The Creatures of Prometheus,* and built of recast versions of themes from the first three movements.

Symphony no. 4, first heard in 1807, was something of a retrenchment after the grandeur of the *Eroica.* Looking back nearly four decades later, Robert Schumann described the work as "a slender Greek maiden between two Norse giants." Yet, if it is less explosive than the *Eroica,* it is by no means a retreat to the world of Haydn. The work's slow introduction unfolds dreamily; in Szell's hands, it seems almost like a suspension of time that gradually opens up into a lively Allegro vivace. A slow movement that Szell endows with the drama and pacing of an opera scene follows, as does a Menuetto that, as in the First, should really be considered a walloping Scherzo, and the closing Allegro ma non troppo begins in a Mozartean accent, but quickly takes on the broad-boned style, full of dynamic contrasts and harmonic tension, that Beethoven had been steadily developing.

Those qualities would reappear explosively in the opening movement of Symphony no. 5, completed in 1808 and certainly one of the most familiar works in the symphonic repertory, not least because its four-note opening motif has accrued numerous political and literary associations. For example, because its rhythmic shape—three short and one long note—is that of the Morse code letter V, it came to be associated with Victory during World War II. There is also the notion, put into circulation in 1840 by Beethoven's secretary and biographer, Anton Schindler, that the motif represents fate knocking at the door, an interpretation attributed by Schindler to Beethoven himself. Its meaning notwithstanding, it is worth trying to cut through the work's familiarity to see the innovations in the opening movement, not the least of which is the way Beethoven absolutely pummels this four-note theme to create a grand dramatic structure.

Beethoven composed the Fifth concurrently with Symphony no. 6, the *Pastoral,* yet another departure for him. Cast in five movements, the work is an expansive tone painting, describing an eventful day in the countryside. The movements are marked with indications of Beethoven's vision: the beautifully fluid opening movement is labeled "Awakening of Cheerful Feelings upon Arrival in the Country." A "Scene by the Brook" follows, complete with nightingale, cuckoo, and quail calls in the solo winds. The three final movements, played without pause, evoke a "Merry Gathering of Country Folk" interrupted by a spectacular symphonic "Thunderstorm," which gathers slowly before it explodes, and finally a "Shepherd's Song" of thanksgiving after the storm moves away.

Like the Fifth and Sixth Symphonies, the Seventh and Eighth were composed together, in 1811 and 1812. There are some slight signs of kinship between the Seventh and the *Eroica:* the Seventh also begins with grand chordal blasts, although instead of standing naked, as the chords that begin the *Eroica* do, those of the Seventh are connected by slow, melancholy wind lines. And in the Seventh, too, the second movement is a funeral march. On the other hand, Wagner's characterization of the Seventh as "the apotheosis of the dance" cannot be dismissed. Each movement—including the funeral march—has the character of a dance: the first two are elegantly proportioned, even stately at times; the Presto and the closing Allegro con brio are wilder, with sharp rhythmic accents and a sense of unstoppable propulsion.

The relationship between the Seventh and the Eighth resembles the one between the *Eroica* and the Fourth: both even-numbered symphonies are notably shorter than their immediate predecessors. The Eighth is also free of nonmusical associations, and even attempts to tie it to events in Beethoven's life—his deafness, which was total by then, or his visit to Linz, where he began meddling in his brother Johann's life—are fruitless, since the work's ebullience offers no hint of these problems. Again, Szell's performance is so beautifully etched as to elevate the work's stature within the set. Its attractions include pinpoint wind playing and trim string punctuation in the Allegretto scherzando second movement, brass tracery in the Menuetto (a real one this time), and nimble shifts between delicacy and emphaticness in the finale.

And then, of course, there's the Ninth, started in 1822—a decade after the Eighth—and completed in 1825. It is the longest and most ambitious of the symphonies, an idealistic paean to the concept of universal brotherhood captured in Schiller's "Ode to Joy," the poem that Beethoven set for chorus and soloists as the work's finale. But a description of the Ninth cannot do justice to either the work or Szell's electrifying and remarkably brisk 1961 performance.

It is a measure of how beloved the Ninth remains, and how emblematic it is, that it is frequently called upon to mark momentous occasions—the tearing down of the wall separating East and West Berlin, for example. It also helped determine the capacity of the compact disc: when Sony and Philips were proposing standards for the format in the late 1970s, the president of Sony insisted that a one-hour playing time, though longer than an LP, would not be sufficient: the disc had to play for at least seventy-five minutes so that a performance of Beethoven's Ninth could fit on a single disc. Some performances last almost that long: a 1951 performance by Wilhelm Furtwängler at Bayreuth (EMI) runs 74:55. Szell, by contrast, takes about 67 minutes. Timings aren't everything, of course, but for a sense of the difference in their approach to the work, Furtwängler takes 25:11 for the final movement; Szell takes 17:56.

There are, of course, numerous worthy alternatives to the Szell set. I have always been fond of Leonard Bernstein's first traversal, with the New York Philharmonic (Sony Classical)—recordings that also include Bernstein's illuminating lectures on the *Eroica* and the Fifth. Claudio Abbado's 2001 cycle with the Berlin Philharmonic (Deutsche Grammophon), which includes a Ninth even faster than Szell's, also has many revelatory moments. Toscanini's NBC Symphony performances, recorded between 1949 and 1953 (RCA Red Seal), display classic vigorousness and precision, and in their most recent CD incarnation (1998) these mono recordings sound quite good. Probably the finest of the growing collection of period-instrument traversals is Frans Brüggen's set with the Orchestra of the 18th Century (Philips, 1984–1992).

George Szell conducting the Cleveland Orchestra

Ludwig van Beethoven

Among individual recordings, you cannot go wrong with Carlos Kleiber's muscular yet intellectually rigorous accounts of the Fifth and Seventh with the Vienna Philharmonic (Deutsche Grammophon, 1975–1976), or Fritz Reiner's wonderfully picturesque recording of the *Pastoral* with the Chicago Symphony (RCA Red Seal, 1961).

28. LUDWIG VAN BEETHOVEN

Concerto for Violin and Orchestra in D major (op. 61)

JOHANNES BRAHMS

Concerto for Violin and Orchestra in D major (op. 77)

JASCHA HEIFETZ, VIOLINIST

(RCA 61742-2)

Boston Symphony Orchestra, Charles Munch, conducting (Beethoven); Chicago Symphony Orchestra, Fritz Reiner, conducting (Brahms).

Recorded 1955

Perhaps a listener needs to have grown up in the LP era to fully appreciate what an embarrassment of riches this CD represents, for better and worse. Here are the two greatest violin concertos in the nineteenth-century repertory—some would say in all of music—played by one of history's most brilliant violinists, captured at the height of his powers and accompanied by two of the greatest conductors and orchestras of his time. Each work is big enough, in terms of both duration and musical and emotional breadth, to fill an LP on its own, and that was how these recordings were originally released.

One could argue that in an entirely esthetic sense, that's how it ought to be: as pleased as I am for the bargain this CD represents (not to mention that it allows both works to be handily included as a single selection in a list of one hundred essential recordings), I rarely listen to both the Beethoven and the Brahms in a single sitting. They offer a lot to assimilate if you're listening intently, and taking them in together can rob each of the space and the respect it deserves. As much as I hate to romanticize the LP—it was, after all, a mass-market commodity—in the case of the recordings at hand it strikes me that the LP issues were artistic artifacts, installments in an expanding catalog that documented both the peaks of the repertory and Heifetz's artistry, while the CD, by contrast, is simply a storage medium in which a couple of those installments are handily mothballed. You can unpack them however you like, of course.

The Beethoven was composed in 1806, a productive year in which he also worked on the Fourth and Fifth Symphonies, the *Rasumovsky* String Quartets, the Fourth Piano Concerto, and the *Appassionata* Piano Sonata. As he had done with the symphony, and for that matter, with most of the forms he inherited from the generation of Mozart and Haydn, Beethoven expanded the scale and scope of the concerto: in the Violin Concerto, the first movement alone is longer than most of the violin concertos written by Bach, Vivaldi, or Mozart, although the second and third movements are comparatively short (a structural model followed by Brahms as well).

Beethoven composed the work for Franz Clement, a violinist and conductor who, at twenty-six, was renowned as a virtuoso. Beethoven gave him plenty to work with, including the sweet, beautifully contoured principal theme of the first movement and all the virtuosic drama that flows from it, as well as the graceful, achingly beautiful solo line in the Larghetto and the cheerful theme of the finale.

Now that the work is widely agreed to be one of the pinnacles of the repertory, it is instructive to consider that its premiere was something of a circus by today's comparatively sedate performing standards. Beethoven carried on the baroque and classical tradition of including in his concertos at least one cadenza—an opportunity for the soloist to shine in an unaccompanied solo, often improvised. Clement, who must have been a nineteenth-century precursor of Jimi Hendrix, used the spot to offer one of his own sonatas, performed on a single string, with the violin held upside down.

Later eras were more straitlaced about cadenzas, but because

Beethoven did not supply formal ones, violinists supplied their own well into the twentieth century, and in some cases soloists have commissioned contemporary composers to supply their own perspective. That said, the vast majority of violinists today play the cadenzas written by Fritz Kreisler. Heifetz does not. In the first movement, he uses his own recasting of a cadenza by Leopold Auer, his teacher (and the teacher of several other great violinists of the early twentieth century, including Mischa Elman and Efram Zimbalist); and in the last, he uses his own modification of a cadenza by Joseph Joachim. Like Kreisler's, these use Beethoven's material as a starting point, but they explore different aspects of the music, filtered through the prism of violin technique.

Joachim, in a way, is the link between the Beethoven and Brahms concertos. A prodigy born in 1831, Joachim studied with Mendelssohn when he was twelve, and in 1844, a month before his thirteenth birthday, he made his debut in London with the Beethoven concerto, which became his signature piece for several decades thereafter. In the early 1850s, he became the principal violinist at the Hanover Court Orchestra, and around then he became friendly with Robert and Clara Schumann and Johannes Brahms, who was two years his junior. Joachim quickly became a champion of Brahms's work, but they had been friends for a quarter century before Brahms wrote his violin concerto for the violinist, who provided advice on the shape of the solo line and played the work's premiere in 1879.

Where the Beethoven begins with unabashed lyricism, the Brahms begins with brawny, chordal assertiveness. But Brahms's lyrical side catches up with the work as well: the Adagio is as soulfully melodic a movement as you'll find in the violin literature, and even in the comparatively brisk tempos that Heifetz and Fritz Reiner take here, its nobility and passion come through affectingly, with the lively Hungarian-accented finale as a perfect foil.

Joachim wrote his own first movement cadenza, but violinists have not universally felt compelled to adopt it. The violinist Ruggiero Ricci, on an instructive 1991 recording of the Brahms (Biddulph), offered his own cadenza along with those of fifteen other violinists and composers, among them Ferruccio Busoni, Eugène Ysaÿe, Kreisler, Joachim, Auer, Heifetz, and Nathan Milstein; the listener can use the interactive programming capability of the CD system to select the desired cadenza upon each listening.

Heifetz, naturally, plays his own, a thematically apt, technically challenging showpiece. He recorded both these works within nine months of each other in 1955, and, as is the case with many of RCA's stereo recordings of this era, the sound of both the soloist and the orchestra is captured with a realism that is impressive to this day. What stands out most, of course, are both the shimmering, silvery precision of Heifetz's sound and the patrician bearing that he brings to the music. These qualities have struck some listeners as icy, and there are moments in other Heifetz recordings where they have a point. But these performances cast an appealing light not only on Heifetz's sheer violinistic wizardry, but on his ability to produce a heart-melting sound as well.

29. LUDWIG VAN BEETHOVEN

The Late Piano Sonatas

RICHARD GOODE, PIANIST

(Nonesuch 79211, two CDs)

Includes Sonatas no. 28 in A (op. 101), no. 29 in B-flat (op. 106), no. 30 in E (op. 109), no. 31 in A-flat (op. 110), and no. 32 in C minor (op. 111).
Recorded 1986, 1988

The shape of Beethoven's life and career was such that the most significant bodies of work in his catalog—the symphonies, string quartets, piano sonatas, and concertos—each stand as emblematic (albeit each from a different perspective) of his extraordinary development. The symphonies and concertos were, from first to last, manifestations of the public Beethoven. Like all his works, they evolved from comparatively decorous—or at least, form-adherent—works that were a stone's throw from Haydn into huge canvases that shed preconceptions about form and scope. But they were fundamentally meant for public consumption and embodied ideas that Beethoven wanted to project—ideas that ranged from his new notions of formal grandeur (in, for example, the *Emperor* Concerto) to a utopian vision of universal brotherhood (as in Symphony no. 9).

The quartets and the piano sonatas, by contrast, began as fully private works. Beethoven wrote the sonatas to perform himself, or to publish for sale, and the quartets (and, for that matter, piano trios and other chamber works) to be performed with his patrons and colleagues, and also for publication. But although he continued to make these works available to the public, they became increasingly radical in form and substance, and increasingly personal as expressions of the deaf composer's turbulent inner world. In the works of his final decade or so, Beethoven had moved from stretching the rules and boundaries of classicism to creating a musical syntax far removed from the language he had learned as a student in Bonn and in his early years in Vienna.

The piano sonatas have an especially personal quality: the piano was, after all, Beethoven's instrument, so it should not be surprising that he poured his soul into his piano music more directly than any other medium. Richard Goode, an eloquent interpreter of Beethoven, Schubert, Bach, and several contemporary composers (most notably George Perle), has recorded masterly, insightful readings of all thirty-two sonatas, available either in a complete set, released in 1993 (Nonesuch 79328, ten CDs) or in separate installments, of which the set at hand is one—and the one to have if you want only to sample them.

What makes Goode's readings so exquisite is the degree to which he has tapped into an ideal but elusive combination of the opposing qualities that great Beethoven playing demands—a careful balance of technical rigor and unbridled emotion, spiritual flight and earthy muscularity, improvisatory freedom and thorough control.

The five final sonatas, composed between 1816 and 1822, make startling listening even if you've heard them dozens of times. The opening of the op. 101 Sonata is so easygoing that you can be lulled into expecting an uneventful voyage. And indeed, storms threaten but never quite materialize. Still, near the end of the first movement, Beethoven begins to toy with the ear's expectations, offering a series of syncopated chords that handily sidestep the main beats. The central movement leaves the ruminative quality of the opening one behind and adopts a galloping rhythm that Goode's deft touch keeps from becoming too prosaic. His hallmark is to play pianissimo passages with a lightness that makes them seem almost to float on the air, and to play more robust passages with a flexible weight that keeps the movement in control without making it appear artificially restrained. The finale begins deceptively: a slow, dark chordal introduction (which Goode makes wrenching through careful dynamic gradation) finds its way back to the work's graceful opening theme, by way of a single, winding line, and from there to a brisk episodic finale.

The op. 106 Sonata, nicknamed the *Hammerklavier,* comes roaring in with a brief, insistent chordal figure and then goes, basically, all over the place—from full-power brawniness to the sweetest lyricism. A sprightly, wild-eyed Scherzo that lasts a mere two and a half minutes is interposed between the opening Allegro and the Adagio sostenuto, and, despite its brevity, the movement is packed with head-turning modulations and peculiar moves. After the adventures of the first two movements, the Adagio sostenuto seems to come from another world—or two worlds, actually: parts of it are sublime and prayerful, but there is an undercurrent of theatricality as well in some of the aria-like melodic turns. Ultimately, the sublime triumphs; but from it emerges a vigorous finale, the centerpiece of which is a fugue—a vision of Bachian formality imported into the nineteenth century.

The final trilogy—ops. 109, 110, and 111—expands upon the developments in op. 106, but in a way that is more searching and more exploratory—and also more technically perilous. All three scores have elements that a listener today, with the wisdom of hindsight, might regard as visionary glimpses of things to come, with precursors of Chopin and Liszt and harmonic flights that suggest the free chromaticism of the late nineteenth century. Yet there are backward glances as well: Bach's influence is felt distinctly in the variations in the Andante of op. 109 and the fugue of op. 110.

It is op. 111, though, with its abundant twists and contradictions, that makes the greatest demands on a pianist's technique and imagination, and here Goode is at his finest. Grand extroverted gestures give way to intense rumination; free-flying fantasy becomes a nightmarish struggle and passages of crude ferocity are transformed into stately chord progressions that seem not to be bound by time. Goode's achievement here is making this strange realm of Beethoven's seem plausible and coherent, while maintaining all of the energy and flightiness that make the work the marvel it is.

Goode's cycle inhabits a crowded field, and there are many worthy contenders. Rudolf Serkin's studio recordings of ops. 109, 110, and 111, and quite a few others (Sony Classical) have an appealing patrician quality, but a live recording made in Vienna in 1987 (Deutsche Grammophon) reaches even greater depths in the final three. Maurizio Pollini's recordings of these same five sonatas, from 1975 and 1976, benefit from the technical brilliance and power, supported by intellectual rigor, that are Pollini's defining characteristics. The Irish pianist John O'Conor's recording of the final three (Telarc, available both separately and as part of a fine complete traversal) takes an entirely different view: that of Beethoven as a classicist whose vision took him beyond the bounds of classical style, but who was intent on retaining that style's refinement as he charted new realms.

30. FRANZ SCHUBERT

Lieder

IAN BOSTRIDGE, TENOR; JULIUS DRAKE, PIANIST
(EMI Classics 56347)

Includes "Die Forelle" (D. 550), "Ganymed" (D. 544), "Im Frühling" (D. 882), "An den Mond" (D. 196), "Heidenröslein" (D. 257), "Wandrers Nachtlied II" (D. 768), "Erster Verlust" (D. 226), "Der Fischer" (D. 225), "Fischerweise" (D. 881), "Nacht und Träume" (D. 827), "Der Zwerg" (D. 771), "An die Musik" (D. 547), "Du bist die Ruh" (D. 776), "Auf dem Wasser zu singen" (D. 774), "An Silvia" (D. 891), "Litanei auf das Fest Allerseelen" (D. 343), "Frühlingsglaube" (D. 686), "Im Haine" (D. 738), "Der Musensohn" (D. 764), "Wandrers Nachtlied I" (D. 224), "Seligkeit" (D. 443), and "Erlkönig" (D. 328).

Recorded 1996

Like Mozart, Franz Schubert (1797–1828) produced a copious amount of truly magnificent music in a tragically short life. Unlike Mozart, he lived a life that was both curiously uneventful, for a composer of such breadth and talent, and sadly impoverished. Although it is not known when he began composing, his earliest surviving works were written when he was thirteen. He had assembled a sizeable catalog by the time he was eighteen, and at his death at thirty-one, apparently from syphilis, he left more than a thousand works.

Schubert's output is broader than is widely known. His symphonies (seven complete, three close enough to completion to allow for scholarly reconstruction), works for the piano (sonatas, impromptus, fantasies, and myriad shorter forms), songs and song cycles, and a number of grandly expansive chamber works for varied combinations of instruments are justly famous, having fully retained their power to seduce more than 150 years after his death. But there are also operas and incidental music, dance movements for orchestra, keyboard and chamber combinations, and dozens of choral works, both sacred and secular, including six Masses.

Within this vast body of work, and against such ambitious musical edifices as symphonies and piano sonatas, songs may seem modest creations. Schubert turned out hundreds of them, many lasting only four or five minutes, some a good deal shorter. Their textures are simple and direct: a vocal line sufficiently uncomplicated that the text is clearly understandable, supported by a piano accompaniment straightforward enough not to compete with the singer.

Yet Schubert's songs are among his finest creations, miracles of concision and focus, and although the foregoing description is essentially accurate, it is also deceptive. The melodies may seem simple on the surface, and Schubert's most famous attribute is his gift for a long, lyrical melody. But more crucial is his sensitivity to the word. He read copious amounts of poetry, and the best of it elicited a deeply musical response in him. And if you listen to the songs in this collection with the texts in hand, you will—I guarantee it—be amazed and moved by the degree to which the emotional core of the poetry is given concrete and often remarkably subtle form in Schubert's melodies and phrasing. You will find, as well, that while the keyboard parts do indeed keep out of the way of the vocal lines, they are by no means simple: listen, for example, to the machine-gun chordal figures and sinister chromatic bassline in "Erlkönig."

Interesting, too, is the breadth of subjects to which Schubert was drawn. Among the twenty-two offerings on this disc are three songs about fishing. One—"Die Forelle," the song that also provides the melodic basis Schubert expanded upon in his popular *Trout* Piano Quintet—offers a quick briefing on the best way to hook a brook trout. In another, "Fischerweise," a fisherman extols the joys of fishing, but notes that he isn't about to be hooked by the shepherdess he sees fishing on a nearby bridge. And in the third, "Der Fischer," a fisherman is lured to his death by a water nymph.

Also among these songs are glimpses of love in many of its manifestations, from first flush, in "Ganymed," to first loss, in *Erster Verlust,* with several stages in between touched on in "Im Frühling" and the bright-hued Shakespearean "An Silvia." There is a magnificent paean to music itself—"An die Musik"—as well as meditations on mortality in "Wandrers Nachtlied II," and songs in which the natural and mystical intertwine, among them "Nacht und Träume," "Wandrers Nachtlied I," and "Du bist die Ruh." And there is a pair of almost cinematically macabre fantasies—"Der Zwerg," in which a queen is murdered by a dwarf who was in love with her, and the final song in this collection, Schubert's intensely dramatic setting of Goethe's *Erlkönig,* in which a father races vainly to bring his son to safety as the supernatural Erlking tempts the child's spirit toward death.

The Schubert discography is packed with eloquent readings of these songs, including classic recordings by such incomparable singers as Dietrich Fischer-Dieskau, Hermann Prey, Dame Janet Baker, Peter Schreier, Hans Hotter, Fritz Wunderlich, Elly Ameling, and Elisabeth Schwarzkopf—and that accounts only for singers of the past few generations. Tempting as it was to choose one of their recordings, the generation of singers now before the public is holding up the tradition honorably as well, and given the tendency among classical music listeners always to regard the past as a golden age and the present as a time of decline, I wanted to point up one of the better Schubert recital discs from the more recent crop. Even with that as a criterion, the selection was tough: Matthias Goerne, Thomas Quasthoff, Anne Sofie von Otter, Håkan Hagegård, Christoph Prégardien, Renée Fleming, Bryn Terfel, and Barbara Bonney have recorded Schubert recitals that each makes a strong claim.

Ian Bostridge, in the first of several recordings he has devoted to Schubert, offers a finely balanced collection of songs in performances that are both interpretively astute and beautifully executed. Bostridge, an English tenor who was in his twenties when he made this disc, has a delicately calibrated voice that is ideal for this repertory. But although his tone is beautiful and pure, he seems uninterested in producing a pretty sound for its own sake; rather, he puts that sound to use drawing listeners into the moment as Schubert shapes and defines it.

One of his accomplishments is his ability to establish the persona behind each of the songs. When the mood of the text changes suddenly, or if the narrative breaks to allow a character to speak (both things happen in "Der Zwerg"), Bostridge makes the distinction clear by changing his timbre or altering the amount of power behind it. Probably the clearest illustration is his account of "Erlkönig." There are four distinct voices in the text: the father, the child, the Erlking, and the narrator. Through changes of tone and articulation, Bostridge conveys the child's reaction to seeing the mythical Erlking—a reaction that changes from surprise to distress to sheer terror—as well as the evolution of the Erlking's entreaties, which grow increasingly seductive before suddenly turning menacing. Between these characterizations, Bostridge conveys the father's consoling bravery, as well as the narrator's dramatic detachment.

31. FRANZ SCHUBERT

Winterreise (D. 911)

DIETRICH FISCHER-DIESKAU, BARITONE;
ALFRED BRENDEL, PIANIST

(Philips 289 464 739-2)

Recorded 1985

It may seem frivolous, in a selection limited to one hundred recordings, to include not only a collection of Schubert's songs, but also one of his song cycles, particularly since it means sacrificing one of the other forms in which Schubert excelled. But choosing one or the other was impossible: only a selection of songs drawn from all over Schubert's catalog could give an impression of the variety he brought to the form (and get certain favorites into the discussion), yet the song cycles, in which Schubert set collections of poems that create unified narratives, raise this side of his art to a new level. On the one hand, a cycle's songs have all the hallmarks of the independent ones—concision and an uncanny emotional directness, for example—and each can stand alone if it must. But together, these songs create an arching dramatic whole that goes well beyond what even Schubert was able to achieve in a single four-minute song.

Actually, Schubert may have worked up to the idea of the cycle in some of his earlier songs: it is not unusual for a small group of songs Schubert published in a single opus to have a thematic link of some kind. But the publication of Wilhelm Müller's *Poems from the Posthumous Papers of a Traveling Horn Player* must have suggested even grander possibilities to Schubert, who set the first part of the collection as *Die Schöne Mullerin* in 1823, and took up its final part, *Winterreise,* in 1827.

Winterreise is a bleak collection—the musings of a lovelorn young man who, at the start of the cycle, leaves his town on a dark winter night and thinks back to May, when he was happily in love. Why the relationship fell apart is not explained; we only need to know that it has, and that he is still in love with the lady in question. But if disappointment in love has driven him away, the journey itself seems not to have a healing effect; just the opposite, in fact.

While still close to home, he feels his tears freezing and recalls the warmth of a happier spring. He crunches through the snow, wishing to burrow down to the grass below, where his lost love once stepped. And even though it is dark, he closes his eyes as he walks past a linden tree in which he had carved amorous messages, only to imagine the tree beckoning ominously. As his journey takes him farther, the singer's loneliness and despondency deepen, until in the final song, "Der Leiermann," he sees a kindred spirit in an old, broken-down organ-grinder he observes busking on the outskirts of the village, ignored by the villagers, snarled at by dogs, and standing barefoot on the ice.

Schubert matches Müller's poems with music that reflects their imagery. In "Die Post," the piano mimics the sound of a post horn announcing the arrival of mail from the traveler's town, and the vocal lines catch the traveler's mixed feelings—excitement at the sound of the horn, as well as the forlorn knowledge that he has no reason to expect any mail. In "Im Dorfe," an assertive piano figure suggests the dogs barking at the traveler as he makes his way through the village. And "Der Leiermann" juxtaposes a drone and the repeating melody of the organ-grinder.

Schubert was fully aware of this cycle's power. His oldest friend, Josef von Spaun, wrote that in the fall of 1827, Schubert sang the cycle, to his own piano accompaniment, for a group of friends, telling them first that he had found the composition of the songs particularly upsetting: "He sang the entire *Winterreise* to us in an agitated tone of voice. We were quite dumbfounded by the gloomy mood of these songs, and finally Schober [in whose home the performance took place] said that he liked only one of them, namely 'Der Lindenbaum.' To which Schubert simply replied, 'I like these songs more than all the others, and you will get to like them too.'"

Among contemporary interpreters, the baritone Dietrich Fischer-Dieskau virtually owns this music. A splendid Schubert singer, he can be heard in at least eight recorded versions of the cycle, with nearly as many pianists. His collaboration with Alfred Brendel—who is also an exceptionally eloquent Schubert performer—is one of his more recent accounts, though not his last: he made another with the pianist Murray Perahia in 1990, originally for a television production, but later released by Sony Classical. What makes this version so illuminating is the degree to which Brendel and Fischer-Dieskau are of a single mind toward the music. Both have a thorough understanding of this work, and through phrasing and coloration in which they mirror each other perfectly, they create a reading that explores the wanderer's despair, but not without offering flecks of lightness that give him a human dimension—something that makes his plight all the more pitiable.

32. FRANZ SCHUBERT

Quintet in C for Two Violins, Viola, and Two Cellos (D. 956)

THE ALBAN BERG QUARTET,
WITH HEINRICH SCHIFF, CELLIST
(EMI Classics 7243 566942)

Recorded 1983

In popularity surveys that performing organizations often take, Schubert's *Trout* Quintet, for piano and strings, seems to invariably swim off with the top vote in the chamber music category. The *Trout* is without doubt a great work, but this Quintet in C—nicknamed *Two Cellos* for obvious reasons—has always struck me as the richer, more irresistibly beautiful composition, a kindred spirit to Mozart's Divertimento in E-flat (K. 563).

One of Schubert's last works, it was probably completed in September 1828 and captures several of the virtues of his style in full bloom. Most immediately striking, of course, is his seemingly boundless melodic invention, the faculty that gave his six hundred songs their power and immediacy, and which Schubert was able to expand upon in his instrumental works.

As in the songs, Schubert's instrumental melodies carry a distinct emotional weight. In this work, the emotional tenor is bittersweet, with episodes that range from the ebullient to the tragic. Its ambiguities haunt the first two movements, which move continually between major and minor, as well as in the contrast between the ecstatic Scherzo and its more funereal Trio section. Even in the finale, which begins as a robust Viennese ballroom dance, Schubert derails expectations (if a listener still harbored any) by weaving in gracefully turned episodes more akin to the flowing melodies of the opening movement. And in its final bars, he embellishes the closing cadence, in C, with an abrupt little twist—a move up half a step to D-flat, then back to the main key.

Interesting as well is the textural scope of the piece. Works for string quartet with an extra cello are not plentiful: among Schubert's predecessors and contemporaries, Luigi Boccherini and Georges Onslow come to mind, but quintets with pairs of violins and violas, and a single cello, were far more typical. Both models make sense on their own terms. The viola quintet works on the assumption that the cello sound is sufficiently weighty for one cello to hold the bottom range on its own, while two treble (violin) and tenor (viola) voices counterbalance each other. But as the Schubert Quintet demonstrates, balancing the violins with a pair of cellos allows for an unusual sumptuousness—something Schubert elicited in passages where the two cellos play long melodic lines in tandem, often harmonized in intervals of a third or a sixth.

In this performance by the Alban Berg Quartet, with the superb cellist Heinrich Schiff, the blend and unity the ensemble achieves serves the music in every way, technically as well as emotionally. There is a spaciousness here that is perfectly suited to the work's glowing lyricism, and is especially affecting in the Adagio. And given the importance of contrast and ambiguity throughout the piece, these musicians manage to magnify pivot points without overstating them.

Still, the competition is considerable, and worthy. For listeners willing to make a slight concession in sonic lushness, there is a magnificent all-star performance, recorded in 1952 at the Prades Festival, which was run by the great cellist Pablo Casals (Sony Classical). The players are Isaac Stern and Alexander Schneider, violinists; Milton

Katims, violist; and Casals and Paul Tortelier, cellists—the best interpreters of a couple of generations, from a 1952 perspective. And indeed, there are numerous nuances, turns of phrase, and edgy balances that make this an especially compelling performance. Where the Berg players try to envelop you in a kind of sonic sensuality, these musicians emphasize the music's vigor and drive.

The recording by Casals and company has something else going for it: a 1953 performance of Schubert's Symphony no. 5 in B-flat (D. 485), with Casals conducting the Prades Festival Orchestra. Composed in 1816, it is notably lighter in spirit than the Quintet: the opening Allegro is certainly one of the most cheerful moments in the Schubert canon. As was his wont, Casals leads a regal reading, leisurely in tempo and broad in texture, but remarkable for its attention to detail.

There is one point on which some Schubertians will fault both the Berg and Casals recordings, however: they both omit the exposition repeat in the first movement. Repeats are an issue of some dispute in Schubert. Some argue that the exposition repeat was, by Schubert's time—and in the context of Schubert's music—merely a convention left over from the classical age, when movements were shorter and less involved, and when it made sense to hear the principal themes again before heading into a movement's development section, where those themes would be taken on a transforming journey. Others insist that Schubert's scores include repeats because Schubert wanted the music repeated, and that the architecture even of Schubert's biggest movements requires the repeat for a sense of structural balance.

I am agnostic on this point (and I'm in good company), but if the second argument makes greatest sense to you, or if you just wish the opening movement lasted about five minutes longer (nearly twenty instead of just over fourteen), let me recommend a beautifully played, interpretively flexible account by the Emerson String Quartet, with Mstislav Rostropovich playing the second cello, recorded in 1990 (Deutsche Grammophon). The sound is not quite as burnished as that on the Berg recording, but there is much to recommend this CD beyond the first-movement repeat. The music's lyricism has been given primacy, but the Emersons and Rostropovich tap into its essential energy as well, often by using dynamics and coloration (particularly in contrasting modes of attack) to set those qualities in high relief.

33. FRANZ SCHUBERT

Sonata for Piano no. 21 in B-flat (D. 960) and Three Klavierstücke (D. 946)

MITSUKO UCHIDA, PIANIST
(Philips 456 572-2)

Recorded 1997

The Japanese pianist Mitsuko Uchida first caught the music world's attention as a Mozart player, with a series of elegantly turned recordings of all the sonatas and piano concertos, and recitals that were often even more captivating than the recordings. She branched out in several directions, seemingly intent on not becoming typecast as a specialist in any particular repertory, and offering accounts of music by Chopin, Debussy, Schoenberg, Berg, and Webern that were as perceptive and as persuasive as her Mozart. Then in the 1990s, she found another stopping point: the sonatas of Schubert, with which she has continued to surprise and delight.

The centerpiece of this early installment in Uchida's Schubert series is the Sonata in B-flat, a huge work that Schubert completed on September 26, 1828, less than two months before his death. The sonata was part of a trilogy—the others were the Sonatas in C minor (D. 958) and A major (D. 959)—and beyond that, part of a burst of brilliant composition that marked his final months. The C minor and A major Sonatas are great works as well, but the B-flat major Sonata towers above them. Its attractions are similar to those of the *Two Cellos* Quintet, with melodic ingenuity chief among them, a harmonic facility that yields wrenching results, and an essentially bittersweet cast.

Yet its spirit is different from that of the Quintet—more private and inward-looking, at least in the first two movements, which together account for about three-quarters of the work's length. The first movement unfolds as a slow plaint that grows gradually in intensity, and then pulls back by way of a series of weighty pauses and brusque questioning motifs before moving into the development section. It is almost as if, pursuing an increasingly heated internal dialogue, Schubert is brought up short by a fresh question, or the reminder of a point he had missed. The movement's quiet storminess is abetted by some distinctive landmarks: a rumbling trill in the bass that recurs at crucial structural points, for example, and the insistently repeated, raindroplike accompanying figure.

Second movements typically offer sharp contrasts with those that came before them, but here Schubert moves from one slow tempo (Molto moderato) to another (Andante sostenuto), and ratchets down the mood from ruminative to brooding during the opening and closing sections. At the center of the movement, he shakes off the gloom and takes up a brighter, more assertive theme, only to descend into the darkness of the opening section again at the end. The Scherzo is a complete shift in character: fast, trim, and steeped in a thoroughly innocent beauty, it dances off the keys. Even here, there are clouds in the form of an ominous central Trio section, but they are swept away quickly. The finale, a Rondo marked Allegro ma non troppo, has its emotional ups and downs and its weight shifts as well, but an exuberant coda sweeps in to give the work an upbeat ending.

Making all those mood shifts, sudden and otherwise, hang together is a crucial interpretive concern, and Uchida's persuasiveness is remarkable. Her account of the Molto moderato is the picture of calm expansiveness, and it unfolds with a veiled, velvety sound that is unusual for Schubert and, for that matter, for Uchida. Admirable, too, is her approach to tempo and pacing: she applies a flexible rubato that lets the musical line breathe, and when Schubert pauses and shifts focus (just before the development, for example), Uchida's rhythmic freedom creates the illusion that the compositional choices are being made on the spot. And there are some breathtaking dynamic moves: often, just as Schubert undertakes a daring harmonic change, Uchida pulls back to a triple pianissimo, drawing the listener intimately into the moment.

She brings a similar smoothness of tone, as well as an organic sense of development, to the Andante sostenuto and to a beautifully accented reading of the finale. And between them, her Scherzo is a perfect combination of briskness and delicacy. Uchida seems not to buy the shift toward darkness in the Trio: she applies a sharp-edged rhythmic approach—thoroughly at odds with her flexibility in the first movement—that suggests that this dark turn represents only a superficial threat, and indeed, the quick return of the main Scherzo theme dispatches it.

Uchida fills out the disc with the Klavierstücke (D. 946), a set of three works composed in May 1828. Exactly what Schubert intended for them—whether they were to be parts of other works, or grouped together as they are now—is not known. The set's title was affixed by Johannes Brahms, who edited the pieces for publication in 1868, some forty years after Schubert's death. That generic title ("Piano Pieces") may give the impression that these are trifles, but they are actually substantial explorations.

Pianist Mitsuko Uchida

Franz Schubert

The first, a work in E-flat minor, begins with a tempestuous flurry, a section that recurs, almost as if the movement were a Rondo; but between those recurrences, Schubert moves far afield, toward gentler material. The second and third juggle contrasting passages in different ways, and although the third is the shortest of the set, it includes music that is as enveloping and as heartrending as the outer sections of the sonata's second movement. By their nature, these free, almost rhapsodic pieces demand interpretive elasticity. Uchida gives them that, along with a weight and forcefulness that argue for the importance of these overlooked pieces.

34. HECTOR BERLIOZ

Symphonie Fantastique

ROYAL CONCERTGEBOUW ORCHESTRA OF AMSTERDAM,
SIR COLIN DAVIS, CONDUCTING
(Philips 464 692-2)

Also available as a Decca Penguin Classics 289 635-2, with an essay by Terrence McNally.

Recorded 1974

Long before "Sex, Drugs, and Rock 'n' Roll" became a pop culture catchphrase—something like a century and a half before, in fact—the French composer Hector Berlioz wrote this symphonic vision of a sensitive young artist who, driven by an obsessive passion for a woman, eats opium and has visions of being guillotined and participating in a Witches' Sabbath. It was a blast of fresh air in its day, and can still sound both surprising and viscerally thrilling in the hands of an imaginative conductor. Conductors who can compel this visionary piece into life have been plentiful over the decades, and there are dozens of persuasive accounts in the catalog. But among the conductors of the mid- to late-twentieth century, Sir Colin Davis has proven an incomparably eloquent Berlioz interpreter, and this 1974 recording—the second of his three accounts, all of which are in print—has long been the performance against which all others are measured.

Berlioz (1803–1869) came of age just as the classical style was giving way to romanticism, and although analysts have pointed out his classical roots, the essence of his music is in every way—style, texture, sound, and subject matter—fully romantic. Although he struggled for recognition against harsh criticism, particularly in France, he had his champions elsewhere, most notably in the circles in which Wagner and Liszt wielded influence. It took until well into the twentieth century for the full range of his music, including his gargantuan operas, to be widely appreciated. But the *Symphonie Fantastique* exercised a strong appeal from the start.

Berlioz came to music by way of medicine, although his medical studies were undertaken under some duress, at the insistence of his father, a doctor in La Côte-Saint-André, near Grenoble, where Berlioz was born. At seventeen, Berlioz left for Paris to attend medical school, but he was more interested in music from the start, and the musical life of Paris proved a distraction that his medical studies could not withstand. By his early twenties, he was working on operas (fragments of which are extant) as well as cantatas and other works that have, in recent years, found their way onto recordings, and which show the seeds of an original style. In 1826 he entered the Conservatoire, where his individuality and ambition were regarded with some suspicion.

The seminal event that led to the *Symphonie Fantastique,* though, was not a musical experience: it was seeing a performance of Shakespeare's *Hamlet* by a visiting English company in 1827. The performance was in English, which Berlioz did not speak; but he left the theater an avid fan, as were many others in the French literary avant-garde, who regarded Shakespeare as refreshingly antithetical to French classical theater. Another artistic thunderbolt that paved the way for the *Symphonie Fantastique* was Berlioz's first encounter with Beethoven's Third and Fifth Symphonies, in 1828.

Besides introducing Berlioz to Shakespeare, that 1827 *Hamlet* left him smitten with the company's Ophelia, the Irish actress Harriet

Smithson. His passion for Smithson was apparently all-consuming: in the two years that followed, Berlioz went to see her perform whenever her troupe was in Paris, and went to considerable pains to meet her. Once he accomplished that, he actually persuaded her to marry him. But the marriage was a disaster, since, in Berlioz's mind, Smithson was Ophelia, Juliet, and Desdemona; the real-life Smithson simply didn't measure up.

But pain sometimes yields great art, and the *Symphonie Fantastique,* which Berlioz set to work on at the start of 1830, is bound up in the pain of the composer's relationship with Harriet Smithson. That said, it is not a literal portrait of that failed romance, but rather the equivalent of a semiautobiographical novel.

To be sure that its vividly drawn drama was not lost, Berlioz provided a specific program for the work, which we are to experience through the eyes of the protagonist, an artist who imagines happiness with an idealized vision of love. That vision is embodied in the idée fixe—a gracefully rising and falling theme that makes up the substance of the first movement, "Reveries—Passions," and appears in various guises in each of the others. Berlioz (or his protagonist) then takes us to a nineteenth-century ballroom, bright and colorful, where a swirling waltz is under way, but there's no avoiding the idée fixe there: a version of the theme is heard within the waltz figure, as if in half-heard conversation. The next stop is the countryside, in the hope of a serene, pastoral escape. Naturally, in this "Scène aux champs," as Berlioz called it, with its dialogue of shepherd's pipes, the idée fixe wafts in on the breeze.

Unable to flee his obsession, Berlioz's protagonist turns to opium, but, of course, his hallucinations involve his beloved as well: he dreams that he has murdered her, and is now in the crowd at the guillotine, watching his own execution. In a wonderful moment of tone painting, Berlioz provides the military drumroll that is the signal for the blade to descend. But in the seconds before that happens, the idée fixe appears as a solo clarinet, her theme cut short by the thwack of the guillotine blade, and the movement's closing brass chords. We return to the opium dream, and Berlioz's evocation of a Witches' Sabbath. The orchestration evokes darkness and terror; the idée fixe is transformed into a rhythmic taunt, and the Dies Irae—the traditional

Gregorian chant from the Mass for the Dead—makes its appearance at the bottom of the orchestration, introducing a Witches' Round Dance, which it then becomes part of. There is no redemption here: this is where Berlioz leaves his poor protagonist.

Sir Colin Davis's involvement with this score was long and deep by the time he made this recording, and while there are some specific textual highlights one can point to—this is one of the few recordings to use the cornet part that Berlioz added to the second movement—the real joys are in the way Davis brings Berlioz's scenes to life. Both the opening movement and the pastoral "Scène aux champs," for example, balance the reflectiveness and agitation that Berlioz's lovelorn young artist experiences as his romantic obsession intrudes on his every thought. Tension erupts within the glitter of the ballroom as well. And the two hallucinatory movements are inescapably nightmarish.

As an alternative, Leonard Bernstein's 1963 account with the New York Philharmonic (Sony Classical) provides a vision of the work that may be more over-the-top than Davis's, and some listeners may find that it takes Berlioz's fantasy too far. Still, Bernstein makes the finale howl and thrash and brings a rich-textured dreaminess to the "Scène aux champs." The CD version also has an inviting bonus: one of Bernstein's engaging lectures, a trendy but durable analysis from 1968, which proceeds from an image of Berlioz as a pioneer of psychedelia.

35. FELIX MENDELSSOHN

Symphony no. 4 in A major, *Italian* (op. 90); and overture and excerpts from the Incidental Music for *Midsummer Night's Dream*

ORCHESTRA OF THE AGE OF ENLIGHTENMENT,
SIR CHARLES MACKERRAS, CONDUCTING
(EMI/Virgin Classics 61975)

Recorded 1988

Felix Mendelssohn (1809–1847) belonged to a lost generation of symphonists—composers who maintained an allegiance to the clean contours of the classical style, even though they came of age during Beethoven's last years, when the stormy grandeur of romanticism had already become established as the movement that would propel the nineteenth century. Beethoven, certainly, was among his models—but so were Bach and Handel, odd choices at a time when baroque music was generally considered an antiquarian concern.

No doubt as a consequence, Mendelssohn isn't always given his due. In his own time, opinion was split: Hector Berlioz regarded him as too drawn to composers of the past, but Robert Schumann compared his ingenuity to Mozart's. Listeners today tend to recognize him as a prodigiously talented composer who wrote mature works while still in his teens (the *Midsummer Night's Dream* Overture is a case in point), though not quite on the same plane as Mozart, Beethoven, or Bach.

If there is one Mendelssohn symphonic recording that makes the case for a more favorable reassessment, it's this pairing of the *Italian* Symphony and some of the *Midsummer Night's Dream* music by Sir Charles Mackerras and the Orchestra of the Age of Enlightenment, a London-based period-instrument band. You get a sense of the disc's agenda within the first ten seconds, as the gentle chordal burst and tremolando wind figures that open the *Italian* Symphony give way to the jaunty theme in the violins. The clarity of texture here is extraordinary, even when the brass and winds add their clout. As a result, every line of Mendelssohn's orchestration comes through clearly, leaving a listener with a renewed respect for this composer's inventiveness.

Mendelssohn was twenty-three when he completed the *Italian* Symphony, in 1833, although he began to collect the raw materials during a visit to Italy that took him through Venice, Rome, Florence, and Naples in 1830 and 1831. Curiously, his letters home suggest that he was unimpressed with Italy's musical culture at the time: his descriptions of the native music ranged from "indifferent" to "inferior," and he described the orchestras of Rome as "unbelievably bad."

Perhaps he intended his symphony as an essay in what Italian music could be—in much the same way that Dvořák, nearly seven decades later, offered his *New World* Symphony as a template for American symphonists. But whatever his intention, Mendelssohn produced a piece that, while by no means a travelogue, ingeniously evokes the sights and sounds of the country. You hear the joys of the Italian countryside in the vigorous string and wind writing that drives the opening movement, and the Andante con moto has traditionally been taken as a portrait of pilgrims visiting Rome. And whatever his feelings about Italian music, Mendelssohn used some quite effectively in the finale, which is based on an Italian folk dance, the Saltarello. Few recordings of the work present that finale with the breeziness one hears in the Mackerras version.

The *Midsummer Night's Dream* music is even more miraculous, particularly the Overture, which Mendelssohn composed in 1826, when he was seventeen. This piece has everything—the elegance of the Athenian court, the tenderness of the lovers, the shimmering, mercurial quality of the elves, and the brusqueness of the tradesmen, including a braying sound meant to portray Bottom. George Bernard Shaw, whose music criticism was often as astute as his plays, described the Overture as "the most striking example of a young composer astonishing the world by a musical style at once fascinating, original and perfectly new."

Another seventeen years elapsed before Mendelssohn wrote the rest of the incidental music, on a commission from King Friedrich Wilhelm IV of Prussia. By using some of the themes from the Overture and creating many more afresh, Mendelssohn managed to match the youthful charm of the original piece. The Orchestra of the Age of

Enlightenment offers the best movements of the incidental score, and it plays them with the same combination of transparency and ebullience that it brings to the symphony.

In the more delicate passages, the orchestra's gently racing strings conjure images of the woodland fairies who inhabit Shakespeare's fantasy. Particularly effective are the Scherzo, in which the string and wind textures have a perfect, crystalline quality, and the "Clown's Dance," which is a picture of rustic vividness (but played with sufficient clarity to let a listener admire the brass counterpoint near the end). The real highlight, though, is the "Wedding March." Here is a place where using original instruments makes a tremendous difference. Among the brass, for example, is an ophicleide, a precursor of the tuba. Along with the biting timbres of early trumpets and trombones, as well as a solid percussion underpinning, this obsolete instrument contributes to a sound that is regal and jubilant—everything this too-often-sentimentalized movement is meant to be.

36. FRÉDÉRIC CHOPIN

Twenty-four Preludes (op. 28), Berceuse (op. 57), Barcarolle (op. 60), Piano Sonata no. 2, "Funeral March" (op. 35), and the Impromptu in G-flat (op. 51)

ARTHUR RUBINSTEIN, PIANIST
(The Rubinstein Collection, Vol. 51, RCA 63051-2)
Recorded 1946

Of all the composers who wrote for the piano, few were as firmly and exclusively tied to the instrument's sound and textures as Frédéric Chopin (1810–1849). The vast majority of his works are either for solo piano or piano with orchestra, and the rest—songs, a trio, and a handful of cello works—include the piano as well. It was clearly sufficient for his expressive needs: there are no Chopin symphonies, operas, or string quartets. Yet, as focused as he was on this one instrument, his works range quite expansively, from electrifying technical display to singing lyricism and deeply felt drama.

It is also abidingly personal writing: Chopin's works are an extension of his technique, and although he made them available to other pianists by publishing them—publication was an important source of his income—there is also a real sense that they were conceived principally for his own use. In Poland, where he spent his first nineteen years, he had developed a reputation both as a virtuoso pianist and as a promising composer whose youthful polonaises captured something of the national spirit within the textures and contours of a formal concert work.

Chopin, though, was increasingly uncomfortable with the life of a virtuoso, which did not suit either his sensitive disposition or his preference for the refined and intimate. When he arrived in Paris in 1831, he did his best to avoid the large concert halls, preferring the more upscale atmosphere of salons and soirées. It was at one such occasion, in April 1838, that he met the Baroness Aurore Dudevant, the novelist popularly known as George Sand, with whom he conducted a long and stormy love affair. Actually, he had met Sand at a salon concert a few years earlier, but his heart lay elsewhere and he paid her little regard. In 1838, though, they fell immediately in love, and the works on this recording mark the beginning and end of their romance.

The Twenty-four Preludes—one in every major and minor key—may have been started as early as 1831, but were completed during Chopin's sojourn, with Sand and her two young children, on the Spanish island of Mallorca in 1838. These are aphoristic works—the shortest lasts thirty seconds, the longest just over three and a half minutes—meant to capture fleeting moods or, in a few cases, to follow those moods through a variety of emotional twists. The "Funeral March" Sonata, named for the dark-hued march in its third movement, was started in 1835, but completed mostly at Sand's estate in 1838 and 1839.

The Impromptu, from 1842, dances with an improvisatory spirit, much like the preludes. Included here, as well, are the graceful Berceuse, a cradle song, completed in 1844, and the more emotionally expansive Barcarolle, by definition an instrumental boat-song but clearly a weightier essay, in this case, completed in 1846, when Chopin's relationship with Sand was on its downward slope—as, in fact, was his own health. As is often the case, Chopin's titles are more impressionistic than literal, and they scarcely hint at the riches in the music. The Berceuse is built on a gentle rocking figure in the left hand that justifies its title; but the right-hand line is a great flight of pianistic fantasy. And the Barcarolle, one of Chopin's most commanding works, is full of passion, some of it dark, focused, and meditative, some steamy and nearly out of control. Impressive, too, is Chopin's forward-looking use of chromaticism in the work's final pages.

Great Chopin interpreters are plentiful, and there is no lack of superb recordings to choose from: you can't go wrong with the Chopin performances by Garrick Ohlsson (EMI and Arabesque), Vladimir Horowitz (RCA and Sony Classical), Mitsuko Uchida (Philips), Emanuel Ax (Sony Classical), Vladimir Ashkenazy (Decca), or Murray Perahia (Sony Classical), to cite a few favorites among many.

Yet Arthur Rubinstein's recordings hold a special place in the Chopin discography. That said, this disc might seem a peculiar choice. Recorded at sessions in New York and Hollywood between March and August 1946, they lack the sonic richness of the recordings he made when the technology was more fully developed, and when his own interpretive style was more settled. Rubinstein himself was said not to have been fond of these. But this set includes his only traversal of the Preludes, and the performances have an incisiveness and an edge that makes much of today's Chopin playing sound safe and homogenous.

Because Rubinstein recorded into the 1970s (he died in 1982), it is tempting to think of these as "youthful" recordings—and indeed, their energy and impetuousness, compared with his later playing, give that impression. But Rubinstein was fifty-nine when he recorded these performances, and he had been playing most of these pieces for at least four decades by then. Whatever qualities these performances have, callowness is not one of them.

Perhaps the most immediately striking quality of these recordings is the piano sound, which is somewhat drier than one hears on recordings today. Forget about room ambience and acoustical warmth, or bloom—the microphone focuses on the nuances of Rubinstein's sound, and the results are revelatory. Even in the most unassuming of the Preludes, every strand of Chopin's harmony is perfectly defined, and at times—in Prelude no. 2, for example—the sound of the accompanying figuration is slightly gritty, while the melody rings out clearly. In the "Raindrop" Prelude (no. 15), the repeating note that gives the piece its nickname is played with real dynamic and rhythmic suppleness, but so is the melodic material around it, and the chordal section emerges with an ominous power and solidity before melting into the hymnlike follow-through.

One after another, these performances offer something unusual and provocative. Even the gentle E minor Prelude (no. 4), usually the picture of introspective melancholy, slowly builds to a raw climax, and as Rubinstein makes his way through the twenty-four, it becomes clearer than usual how completely Chopin captured the breadth of emotion, from amusement to rage, despair to joy, in these short pieces. The sonata performance touches on extremes as well: it has its irresistibly lyrical moments, but explosive drama is its real motivating force.

37. ROBERT SCHUMANN

Carnaval (op. 9), *Novellette* (op. 21, no. 1),
Nachtstück (op. 23, no. 4), *Romance* (op. 28, no. 2),
and *Fantasiestücke* (op. 12)

ARTHUR RUBINSTEIN, PIANIST
(The Rubinstein Collection, Vol. 20, RCA 63020-2)
Recorded 1949, 1953

Of all the great nineteenth-century composers, Robert Schumann (1810–1856) probably has the spottiest track record. I'm convinced that his four symphonies, for example, have found a place in the repertory not because they are on the level of the Beethoven, Brahms, Schubert, Mendelssohn, or Mahler symphonies, but for a raft of other reasons: we have become used to them with repeated hearings, and have found bits that we particularly like amid longer stretches that don't work quite as well; our admiration for so many of his other works extends a measure of toleration to these, too; we are generally sympathetic to the Schumann we know from reading biographies (that is, the guy who pursued and married his teacher's daughter against her father's wishes, and who was so intent on improving his keyboard facility that he affixed weights to his fingers, to their general ruin); or we have run into that rare performance by a conductor whose understanding of them yields performances in which they are actually quite moving (Klaus Tennstedt or Wolfgang Sawallisch, for example).

Most of Schumann's piano music does not require rationalization of this sort, and this volume of RCA's *Rubinstein Collection* brings together the best of it in performances that match Schumann's poetic and excitable best. Looking through the Schumann (or Rubinstein) bins, you are likely to encounter another, almost exactly identical compilation—Vol. 51, which includes *Carnaval, Fantasiestücke,* the *Romance,* and the first *Novellette,* but with another *Novellette* (op. 21, no. 2) and *The Prophet Bird* (op. 28, no. 2) in place of *Nachtstück* (op. 23, no. 4). The real difference is that Vol. 20 was recorded in 1949 (only the *Fantasiestücke*) and 1953, in mono; Vol. 51 was recorded in the 1960s, in stereo.

It would be going too far to say to beware of the later version. The performances there are full of the color and temperament that make Schumann's piano music so arresting. Moreover, the fantastically quirky *Prophet Bird* was nearly enough to tilt my choice toward that disc. But of the two sets of performances, the later ones are more relaxed and ruminative, while the earlier ones are more focused and energized, and afford a fuller, more direct sense of the extremes that drive these works. And although the piano sound on the more recent recording is a bit rounder and fuller, as one might expect, the sound of the 1949 and 1953 recordings is quite beautiful and texturally clear.

Composers of the romantic era were motivated by a range of concerns that included everything from an interest in creating distinctly national musical accents to simply expanding the descriptive power of musical language itself. But one quality that most of the romantics shared, and which Schumann had in abundance, was an active sense of fantasy. To a great extent, this had mainly to do with couching their own anxieties, passions, and dreams in imagery that could be presented publicly without fully exposing their psyches. But even when the fantasy was impersonal—as it was, for example, in the splendidly imagined musical landscape that Mendelssohn created in *Midsummer Night's Dream*—there was a clear sense that its expression was the reason composers were expanding their musical language and resources in the first place.

Schumann's vivid imagination is captured in these pieces like an ancient insect in amber. *Carnaval* has an interesting biographical backdrop. Schumann, twenty-four years old when he started the work, was madly in love with two young women during its composition, both associated with his teacher, Friedrich Wieck. One was Wieck's daughter, Clara, a formidable pianist herself, and eventually Schumann's wife. Wieck was not enthusiastic about Schumann's infatuation with Clara, who was only thirteen at the time. Schumann was, it turned out, easily distracted: he also fell in love with Ernestine von Fricken, a seventeen-year-old student of Wieck's.

Ernestine was from the Bohemian town of Asch, and using the German names for the notes of the scale—in which E-flat is called S and B is called H—Schumann was able to fashion a musical theme from the name of her hometown, a name that also includes all of the musically translatable letters of Schumann's own name. This motto, in various permutations, became the theme on which *Carnaval* is based, and Ernestine herself is portrayed in the "Estrella" movement. In the end, Ernestine was removed from Schumann's circle by her foster father, and Schumann's attentions wandered back to Clara, who also makes an appearance in *Carnaval:* the "Chiarina" movement plays on an Italian version of her name.

The work itself is a collection of twenty-one vignettes, set entirely in a fantasy world that is introduced by the zesty "Préamuble," which is part fanfare and part description of a tumultuous crowd milling around during the carnival season (for which the work was named). After this introduction, the characters file in, among them several complementary pairs—the downcast "Pierrot" and the more foppish, lighthearted "Arlequin," for example, are standard commedia dell'arte characters, as are "Pantalon et Colombine"; but the poetic "Eusebius" and the fiery "Florestan" are Schumann's own alter egos. Two composers are in the crowd too: the "Chopin" movement is a delightful gloss on Chopin's style, and "Paganini" captures a sense of that violinist-composer's virtuosic leaps around the fingerboard.

Each of the characters and scenes in the work is sketched with remarkable force, but also great concision: of the twenty-one movements, only the "Préamuble," the "Promenade," and the closing "March des Davidsbündler contre les Philistins"—a little manifesto in which Schumann argued in favor of the free-spirited originality of new music, and against the Philistines who didn't see the point of it—

Pianist Arthur Rubinstein

last longer than two minutes. Amid all this, Schumann included a section called "Sphinxes," the performance of which—that is, whether to perform them and how (since the notes are written as thick black bars, without time values)—is left to the player. Rubinstein, like many pianists going back to Clara Schumann, omitted it.

The movements of the *Fantasiestücke,* composed in 1837, show a greater sense of emotional upheaval. At the time, Wieck was so adamantly opposed to the notion of Schumann marrying Clara that he obtained a court injunction to prevent it. Schumann and Clara were able to marry three years later, but at the time Schumann considered the situation hopeless. Some of this must have spilled into the *Fantasiestücke,* or at least, into the first four movements, which are essentially a dialogue between Eusebius and Florestan, each expanding upon the qualities Schumann gave them in *Carnaval.* The last four in the set are more varied, with humorous touches woven through depictions of tragedy and a parodistic evocation of heroic grandeur.

38. FRANZ LISZT

Sonata in B minor, *Bénédiction de Dieu dans la solitude, Waldesrauschen, Gnomenreigen,* and *Vallée d'Obermann*

CLAUDIO ARRAU, PIANIST

(Philips 289 464 713-2)

Recorded 1969–1970

Among the nineteenth-century composers whose works make up the core of the classical music canon, there are comparatively few whose music still stirs up as much debate as Franz Liszt (1811–1886). In his time, there were many who considered his music unadulterated junk—loud, fast, flashy, and empty. I have friends and colleagues who still believe that, and Liszt had only himself to blame for such harsh judgments. His vast canon, which is dominated by piano works but also includes symphonic essays, choral pieces, songs, and dramatic settings, includes many splashy dazzlers, designed to appeal to both players and listeners for whom pyrotechnic display is an end in itself.

But there is a great deal more to Liszt than that. His most important and enduring works erupt from his spectacular imagination, complete technical command, and prescient sense of the directions in which musical language might evolve. At its best, his music joins the passions of high romanticism with the experiments in chromaticism that became the driving force of twentieth-century music; indeed, quite a few of his piano works prefigure the musical language that Debussy and others among the French impressionists would explore in the decades following Liszt's death.

The Sonata in B minor is in many ways the summit of Liszt's mountain of piano works, although other scores and sets of works— the *Transcendental* Etudes, the *Harmonies poétiques et religieuses*, and the various books of the *Années de pèlerinage*, for example— rival it for inventiveness and surpass it in scope.

One could argue that the sonata is not a sonata at all, but a fantasy held together by some of the formal strictures of sonata development. It's an almost useless distinction: by the time Liszt completed the work, in 1853, the rules of sonata form, rooted in the classical era, had been widely circumvented and all but retired.

Some regard Liszt's sonata as a musical evocation of scenes from Goethe's *Faust*—a work that clearly interested Liszt, who addressed it in symphonic terms—with the opening Allegro energico theme representing the title character, the more sardonic, forceful marcata theme representing Mephistopheles, and the gentler music that recurs periodically representing Gretchen. An alternate, autobiographical reading ascribes the work's varied themes to different aspects of Liszt's own personality. Either or neither may be valid: Liszt never endorsed an interpretation. More to the point, the piece takes listeners on an extraordinary journey, and it requires an interpreter who has the technique to negotiate its considerable difficulties as well as its emotional extremes, a crucial part of which is making the quiet, rising chord progression in the work's final bars seem like a true transfiguration.

The Chilean pianist Claudio Arrau was a splendid Lisztian who kept up an interpretive tradition he inherited from his teacher, Martin Krause, who knew Liszt and devoted much of his life to studying Liszt's music and style. In his 1970 recording, Arrau addresses the sonata's more forceful sections with an almost demonic agitation. But he also maintains a remarkable clarity of texture, so while there is ample thunder, and even an almost reckless drive, the performance is never merely a barrage of sound. In soft-edged passages, Arrau summons the same lyricism that animates his great Chopin recordings.

The companion pieces here fill out the Lisztian portrait somewhat. The *Bénédiction de Dieu dans la solitude,* one of the ten *Harmonies poétiques et religieuses* (composed between 1847 and 1852), is a sublime, meditative work, full of delicate filigree woven around an almost hymnlike melody. *Waldesrauschen* and *Gnomenreigen* are concert studies, essentially descriptive works completed in 1880. The first is a lovely forest ode, the second a more sprightly and pianistically outgoing fantasy that Arrau plays with great crispness of texture. Included here as well is *Vallée d'Obermann* (1837–1838), an often dramatic tone poem inspired by a novel that fascinated Liszt at the time, Etienne Pivert de Senancour's *Obermann.*

By its nature, Liszt's piano music invites and encourages interpretive variety, and if you sit down with a stack of recordings, you begin to appreciate the extent to which markedly different approaches to sound color, texture, dynamics, and tempos—to say nothing of the many possible relationships among those parameters—can yield equally exciting and eloquent results. So having recommended Arrau's account of the sonata, let me point out that other pianists have recorded very different yet equally persuasive interpretations.

I am partial to Alfred Brendel's 1991 recording (Philips), a thoroughly individual account that may strike some listeners as mannered, but which is rich in surprising, provocative phrasing ideas that I find difficult to resist. Much the same can be said—and in bigger, bolder letters—for the barnstorming, supervirtuoso recording that Vladimir Horowitz made in 1932 (EMI, part of a three-CD collection of his early recordings). Other close contenders currently available on CD include fiery performances by Arthur Rubinstein (RCA, 1965) and Jorge Bolet (Everest, 1961).

39. JOHANNES BRAHMS

Ein Deutsches Requiem (A German Requiem) (op. 45)

ARLEEN AUGÉR, SOPRANO; RICHARD STILLWELL,
BARITONE; ATLANTA SYMPHONY ORCHESTRA AND CHORUS,
ROBERT SHAW, CONDUCTING

(Telarc CD-80092)

Recorded 1983

There is a moment in this exquisite *German Requiem* by Johannes Brahms (1833–1897) when it becomes clear whether the performers have fully grasped the composer's intentions. Nearly three minutes into the second movement, the chorus and orchestra repeat the verse that opens the movement, "Denn alles Fleisch is wie Gras" (For all flesh is as grass). In its earlier appearance, the verse is couched in a tender setting, as a truism offered and accepted with ease. But in this repetition, with the choir supported by the full orchestra and a pounding timpani, Brahms is more emphatic. The verse's full emotional weight bears down on the listener as a concrete and personal recognition of mortality.

Yet, as vehemently as Brahms presses this point, the *German Requiem* as a whole delivers a gentler message. Instead of setting the Latin text of the Roman Catholic Requiem Mass, Brahms assembled a text of his own, drawing on verses from the Old and New Testaments, as well as a single verse from the Apocrypha, in German translation. Certain mainstays of the traditional Requiem text—the terror of Divine wrath on the Day of Judgment, for example—are jettisoned entirely, in favor of notes of consolation. In the text Brahms assembled, the mourner is comforted with reminders that the soul thrives in the world to come.

Equally striking is the universalist tone that Brahms adopted. Apart from an assumed belief in God and the afterlife, he deliberately avoids doctrinal and denominational issues; indeed, the work is not even specifically Christian, in the sense that Jesus' name is never invoked. This is a Requiem that can be embraced by anyone. As Brahms himself put it, "I could easily dispense with the word 'German' and replace it with the word 'Human.'"

Brahms labored over the *German Requiem* for a dozen years, and there can be no doubt that its power derives from the very personal nature of its inspiration. He began work on the score in 1856, partly as a response to the death of Robert Schumann, his mentor and early champion, but he completed only two movements before laying the work aside. After his mother's death in 1865, Brahms took up the Requiem again, and completed a six-movement version by the end of 1866. The premiere of that version, at the Bremen Cathedral with Brahms conducting, was the composer's first major success.

Still, he was not fully satisfied that the work said all he wanted it to say. In May 1868, he added the finishing touch: a movement for soprano solo and chorus in which consoling verses from the Books of John and Ecclesiastes surround this verse from Isaiah: "I will comfort you as one whom his mother comforts." Brahms dedicated the movement to the memory of his mother.

The musical influences on the *German Requiem* are in some ways as interesting as the emotional ones. Schumann had listed an idea for a German Requiem in his own book of planned projects, but never began the work. But there was a predecessor that Brahms would have known: the *Musikalische Exequien* (1636) by Heinrich Schütz, a composer whose music (along with Bach's and Handel's) Brahms was studying during the years he worked on the *German Requiem*. Schütz also compiled his own German text from scriptural excerpts, and the close association in his work between brass instruments and men's voices is mirrored in Brahms's score. Although nothing in the Brahms sounds particularly baroque, there are fugal sections in the third and sixth movements.

Robert Shaw's legendary mastery of choral timbres and textures is put to magnificent use in his 1983 recording of the *German Requiem*. In the opening pages—and regularly throughout the work—the choral sopranos sing with a seamless, velvety tone that makes the sound truly angelic. The more robust sections are equally vivid, and consistently gripping, and Shaw's grandly expansive tempos give the work a rich, enveloping quality. Richard Stillwell and Arleen Augér also endow the movements in which they are the soloists with an appealing warmth, and the Atlanta Symphony, which came of age during Shaw's tenure as its director, matches its choir in lushness.

The quality of the sound is notable as well. Although early digital recordings have been criticized for faults ranging from shrillness to sterility, Telarc—which began as an audiophile label—has always taken great care with its productions. Among the charms of this one is a rich bass sound that gives the music the firmness and foundation it needs, but also allows the more ethereal passages to soar freely.

Other recordings present conceptions very different from Shaw's, and for anyone who loves this work, two are particularly worth noting. One is a period-instrument performance by Philippe Herreweghe (Harmonia Mundi, 1996). Where smoothness is an absolute value for Shaw, Herreweghe takes the view that sharply defined instrumental and vocal profiles give the work a measure of flesh-and-blood realism. There is something to that: this recording with La Chapelle Royale, Collegium Vocale, and the Orchestre des Champs Elysées, and the soloists Christiane Oelze, soprano, and Gerald Finley, baritone, offers moments of both heavenly beauty and visceral power.

At the other end of the spectrum is a classic account that Bruno Walter recorded with the New York Philharmonic, the Westminster Choir, the soprano Irmgard Seefried, and the bass George London in 1954 (Sony Classical). Walter uses a hefty ensemble and a choir that is not as finely polished as Shaw's, but his brisk, fluid tempos and his careful use of dynamics and accenting to shape phrases make this a magical reading, particularly in the final two movements.

40. JOHANNES BRAHMS

Symphony no. 1 in C minor (op. 68), Symphony no. 2 in D (op. 73), Symphony no. 3 in F (op. 90), Symphony no. 4 in E minor (op. 98), *Tragic* Overture, and *Academic Festival* Overture

CHICAGO SYMPHONY ORCHESTRA,
SIR GEORG SOLTI, CONDUCTING

(Decca 430 799, four CDs)

Recorded 1978–1979

The tardiness with which Brahms approached the symphony is generally ascribed to the awe in which he held Beethoven's works, and not without reason. Brahms himself was quoted as saying: "I shall never finish a symphony. You have no idea how it feels to hear behind you the tramp of a giant like Beethoven." But Brahms probably knew that he would eventually change his mind. His career path demanded that he turn his attention to either symphony or opera, and opera did not interest him. He was, however, a supremely methodical composer, who would not commit a work to paper until it was ready—and, even then, fretted about his choices until the score was published.

Actually, Brahms began collecting ideas for a symphony when he was in his late twenties. He quietly sketched them out over the course of fifteen years, and wrote several other orchestral works, including the *Haydn* Variations in 1873, before deciding that the time was right. He made that decision in 1876, when he was forty-three. The four-movement work he produced boasts one of the most surprising introductions in the symphonic canon: a slow, dark-hued, harmonically shifting section underpinned by a steady timpani beat. The work itself is rich in distinctively Brahmsian themes, as well as reminiscences of several Beethoven works, most notably the Fifth and Ninth Symphonies. The theme of the finale, in fact, bears a resemblance to the Beethoven Ninth's "Ode to Joy." And although the work was received respectfully when it was given its premiere, in Karlsruhe, there were also those who took to calling it Beethoven's Tenth.

Brahms is said to have found such comments objectionable; but then, the incorporation of Beethovenian themes cannot have been unconscious, and Brahms must have known that they would be heard. From a certain point of view, in fact, this homage may have seemed necessary to him. He was, after all, a conservative composer intent on holding up what he regarded as the traditions of late classicism and early romanticism that Beethoven represented.

There was an opposing view—that of the New German School, of which Liszt and Wagner were the most notable advocates and practitioners. They, too, revered Beethoven, but their view was that the logical extension of his symphonic spirit dictated that even purely symphonic music should have extramusical associations—as, for example, Beethoven's *Eroica* and *Pastoral* Symphonies did. In their estimation, and in that of their very vocal and demonstrative followers, Berlioz and other French composers had the right idea; Brahms represented the old guard. Ultimately, of course, both schools came to be seen as valid expressions of their age but, at the time, the partisan battles were waged with uncompromising vehemence.

Brahms kept to his path, and in 1877, just as the score for the First Symphony was on its way to his publisher, he started the Second, completing it in only a few months. His estimation of this work, conveyed in a letter to his publisher, was that "the new symphony is so melancholy that you won't be able to bear it." He suggested that the pages be printed with black borders. Yet except for the introspective slow movement, the work hardly fits Brahms's own description. Most listeners hear pastoral leanings in the work, and its blazingly bright closing pages seem triumphant rather than melancholy—as is the work's key, D major. When it had its premiere, in Vienna, just over a year after the premiere of the First Symphony, it was an immediate success.

Brahms waited until 1883, when he was fifty, to write his Third Symphony, the most compact of the four, and in some ways the most dramatic, with currents that have led fanciful annotators to describe it as an internal debate about life, with memories of youthful impulses countered by a sense of loss. By quoting the theme of the first movement in the last, Brahms gave the work a cyclical feeling that struck Clara Schumann, at least, as the embodiment of her husband's ideas about compositional unity in extended works. Thus her effusive assessment: "What a work, what poetry, the most harmonious mood runs through it all, all the movements are part of a unified whole, pulsating with life, every movement a jewel."

Brahms undertook the Fourth Symphony in the summer of 1884, in a chilly alpine town called Murzzuschlag, and he finished it in the summer of 1885. A dark, reserved piece, it is often considered as a conscious leave-taking of the symphonic form, but it can also be heard as an assertion of mastery. It begins with a sense of deep melancholy, and the first movement grows stormier as it unfolds. The second is a touching, deeply felt elegy, after which the lively, even humorous third movement comes as a surprise.

The bright mood it creates, however, shatters quickly with the solemn ascent of the threateningly dense brass chords at the start of the final movement. Brahms's finales are all colossal, but that of the Fourth embodies a peculiarly Brahmsian obeisance to the past. It is a Passacaglia, a baroque form in which a theme runs continuously through the bass. Moreover, Brahms based the theme on a chorus from Bach's Cantata no. 150—a work that had not been published at the time, but which Brahms knew from a manuscript given to him by Philip Spitta, the editor of the Bach-Gesellschaft Edition, a pioneering musicological project then in progress. In terms of harmony and gesture, the movement is pure Brahms. But hidden within it was a tribute to a past master.

The four Brahms symphonies can be shoehorned onto two CDs these days, and many labels have taken that approach, particularly with reissues. This set by Sir Georg Solti and the Chicago Symphony is on four CDs, but is still a bargain, selling for less than the price of two top-line CDs.

The principal appeal of Solti's Brahms is the clarity with which he explores both the intellectual and emotional substance of the four symphonies. His judgment on tempos and texture is unimpeachable, and his thoughtful approach to balancing thematic material against inner-voice detailing is consistently enlightening. Possibly because Solti's catalog of recordings is so huge, and also, perhaps, because he made the Chicago Symphony into a gleaming, streamlined music-making machine, his recordings seem to be taken for granted these days, and some of them have been criticized as examples of soulless perfection. But these performances have a directness that is both

Composer
Johannes Brahms

thrilling and moving, and the brilliant brass sound that was a Solti-Chicago trademark serves Brahms well.

Solti approaches Brahms in a large-scale, modern fashion, but not every conductor has made the same choice. Sir Charles Mackerras, leading the Scottish Chamber Orchestra (Telarc, three CDs), set out to reproduce the orchestral weight of the ensembles in Karlsruhe and Meiningen, where Brahms conducted the First and Fourth Symphonies, respectively. The orchestra stands at about half the size of Solti's, but the recording process is a great equalizer: the sound is by no means "small," but there is a greater transparency and clarity of articulation than big-orchestra recordings typically yield. The set also includes an interesting reconstruction of the First Symphony's original

Andante sostenuto, which Brahms retouched between the first performances and the work's publication, as well as the *Haydn* Variations and the *Academic Festival* Overture.

The Brahms recordings that Eugen Jochum made with the Berlin Philharmonic between 1951 and 1956 (Deutsche Grammmophon) represent a wholly different approach. These performances were criticized as needlessly willful when they were new, but they reflect a tradition of extreme tempo manipulation that goes back to Brahms himself, or so one is led to believe by the composer's complaint, in a letter to the violinist Joseph Joachim after leading the Meiningen Court Orchestra in performances of the Fourth, that "in these concerts I couldn't make enough accelerations and slowings." There are, indeed, moments that may seem eccentric, but Jochum's performance is an uncommonly soulful view of these works.

One further recommendation: István Kertész's recordings with the London Symphony Orchestra and the Vienna Philharmonic are both elegant and eloquent, and in their last CD incarnation—as two double-CD sets (Decca)—they were packaged with several other Brahms works, including Kertész's highly regarded recordings of the two serenades. Sadly, it is out of print, but worth finding.

41. JOHANNES BRAHMS

String Sextet in B-flat (op. 18), String Sextet in G (op. 36), Quintet for Piano and Strings in F minor (op. 34), Quintet for Strings in F (op. 88), Quintet for Strings in G (op. 111), and Quintet for Clarinet and Strings (op. 115)

THE AMADEUS QUARTET

(Deutsche Grammophon 419 875-2, three CDs)

Cecil Aronowitz, violist (in the string sextets and string quintets); William Pleeth, cellist (in the sextets); Christoph Eschenbach, pianist; Karl Leister, clarinetist.

Recorded 1966–1968

Brahms's symphonies and concertos have found a perpetual home in the concert and recording repertories of the world's great orchestras, but although his chamber works enjoy considerable stature, they are less widely traveled. The problem, certainly for the works in this collection, is similar to the one that plagues Mozart's E-flat Divertimento: most are works for nonstandard ensembles. Although each has a string quartet at its heart, the quartet-plus-guest(s) format is transitory almost by definition, and rarely allows for the intense rehearsal and polishing that a touring quartet can lavish on its core repertory.

Still, there is a countervailing force—an urge to collaborate, on the part of soloists as well as quartets—that has helped keep some of the great nineteenth-century chamber repertory alive, and has fostered an enormous body of modern works for ensembles of every description. In many respects, though, the Amadeus Quartet and its guests on these recordings were well ahead of the curve.

The Amadeus, a British ensemble in which all but the cellist were originally Austrian, was founded in 1947 and quickly established itself as one of the most eloquent postwar European quartets, with a glowing tone and a sense of proportion that were particularly effective in the classic Viennese repertory. The guests for the sextets—the cellist William Pleeth and the violist Cecil Aronowitz—both led busy lives in London, Aronowitz mostly as a chamber player (he was a member of the Melos Ensemble and several other groups), and Pleeth as a soloist and in chamber music. They were such frequent guests of the Amadeus for quintets and sextets that one could almost say they were adjunct members. Karl Leister, the principal clarinetist of the Berlin Philharmonic from 1959 to 1993, took advantage of—and to some extent, abetted—the growing interest in the clarinet as a solo instrument with frequent chamber appearances outside his orchestra. Christoph Eschenbach is a distinguished conductor these days, and currently the music director of the Philadelphia Orchestra. But when he made this recording of the F minor Piano Quintet in 1968, he was a promising young German pianist who had won several European competitions and had made his London debut only two years earlier. He has always had a passion for ensemble music-making: his piano duet with Justus Frantz produced some durable Mozart and Schubert recordings, and after he turned his attention to conducting in 1973, he made a point of playing chamber music with the musicians in the orchestras he directed.

The works here cover the breadth of Brahms's life and stylistic evolution, from 1860, when he was in his late twenties and completed the Sextet in B-flat (op. 18), to 1891, when he reconsidered a planned retirement to compose the Clarinet Quintet (op. 115), one of his most exquisitely crafted scores. These are works that, the constriction of their timbral worlds notwithstanding, cover as vast an expanse of musical ideas as his symphonies and show a side of Brahms's musical innovation that is overshadowed by the symphonies' grand sweep.

In the B-flat major Sextet, we find Brahms looking back to Haydn, Mozart, Beethoven, and Schubert for formal and textural models, at a time when the prevailing wind in the Austro-German compositional world was blowing in the direction of the "music of the future," propounded by Liszt and Wagner. But if one can point to the Beethoven and Schubert influence in the tuneful opening movement, and to Haydn in the graceful Scherzo, the work's high point—a set of variations on an elegant, bittersweet theme—seems to glance back to baroque forms, phrasing, and ornamentation. Even in various transcriptions, from Brahms's own piano four-hand arrangement to the two-guitar version that Julian Bream and John Williams recorded in 1978, the Theme and Variations is as profoundly beautiful as it is inventive.

The F minor Piano Quintet (op. 34), completed in 1866, was started six years earlier as a string quintet with a second cello line, following Schubert's model. Not satisfied with it in that form, Brahms reworked the piece for two pianos, a version that still exists (as op. 34b). Clearly there were aspects of this music that appealed to him in both string and keyboard sonorities, and the Piano Quintet was the logical format in which those worlds could be joined. As in the First Sextet, Brahms kept the language of Beethoven and Schubert in sight, but he was moving more decisively toward a gestural world of his own, including a fresh approach to thematic development that left the theme's contours in place but manipulated its color and emotional weight. He undertakes some daring harmonic experimentation as well: the finale begins and ends in C-sharp minor, a key so distant from F minor that the movement seems at first to be from an entirely different work, but ultimately matches the rest of the score in spirit.

Between the conception and completion of the Piano Quintet, Brahms wrote a second string sextet, the G major work (op. 36), completed in 1865, and a decisive move toward the mature Brahmsian style. Its opening is oddly dark for the key, and there are some fabulous touches. The work's first sound is a two-note repeated cello figure, a slowed-down trill of sorts. As the arching first theme enters, the slow trill continues. In the Amadeus Quartet version, the trill is played quietly in the background with the theme ringing out clearly, a logical enough approach, although there are others that create different and equally transfixing effects. A wonderful period-instrument recording by L'Archibudelli (Sony Classical) balances the cello figure and the melody more closely, creating an eerie atmosphere. Either way, the two-note figure has a life of its own: the upper voices soon play a harmonically more interesting, downward spiraling version of it.

Barely two minutes into the work, dawn breaks. But Brahms being Brahms, the rest of the movement is by no means pure sunshine: the mobile trill figure and the questioning opening theme return. As always, Brahms's music embraces and mirrors life's ambiguities. The other movements also bear his hallmarks, including the barest hint of a gypsy accent in the Scherzo and the vital Presto giocoso.

The two string quintets—no. 1 in F major (op. 88), composed in 1882, and no. 2 in G major (op. 111), composed in 1890—are mature works, full of energy and confidence, but also the tension between melancholy and brightness. With each, Brahms continues to examine his lifelong fascinations. His passion for Bach's counterpoint, for example, drives the finale of the F major work; and the influence of gypsy music, a factor in so many Brahms scores, enlivens the finale of the G major score, which ends with that most popular of Hungarian gypsy dances, a lively czardas.

The G major Quintet might have been Brahms's last large work—that was his intention at the time—had he not been impressed by the virtuosity of Richard Mühlfeld, the principal clarinetist of the Meiningen orchestra. Brahms was so taken with Mühlfeld's work that in addition to the quintet, composed in the summer of 1891, he wrote him a Clarinet Trio (op. 114) and two sonatas (op. 120), his last major works.

There is precedent for this in the history of the clarinet, an instrument more typically found in an orchestra chair than in the solo spotlight: Mozart and Weber met clarinetists whose abilities inspired each composer to write truly magnificent pieces for it. Brahms, in fact, heard Mühlfeld perform the Mozart Clarinet Quintet and the Weber Concerto, and he rose to the challenge of providing the instrument with a work that could sit beside them. His quintet, a seductively melodic work from start to finish, is often ruminative and nostalgic, as befits an autumnal score, but parts of the third movement are quite playful. What this work offers is the emotional weight of his symphonies, without the heft.

All the performances in this set are exemplary, and they are recorded with an ambience that magnifies the warmth of the ensemble's tone without soaking it in false reverberation. Of the lot, the Clarinet Quintet is the clear standout. The dialogue between Leister and the quartet has a persuasive vitality, and Leister's tone is consistently rounded and supple. Most important, he makes the clarinet line sing, without using a great deal of vibrato, and without overcooking the already steamy music that Brahms gave him.

42. BEDŘICH SMETANA

Má Vlast (My Country)

CZECH PHILHARMONIC ORCHESTRA,
RAFAEL KUBELIK, CONDUCTING
(Supraphon 11 1208-2 031)

Recorded 1990

The wars of the twentieth century contributed to a view of nationalism as an essentially negative force—divisive by nature, lethal when pursued to its logical (or perhaps illogical) extreme. But nationalism has also been an important force in the history of composition, particularly in the nineteenth and early twentieth centuries, when composers all over Europe, and in the Americas as well, felt the need to step away from the Germanic, Gallic, and Italianate models that had been so influential over the previous few centuries, and to establish new musical dialects that would not only speak specifically to the history and cultural experience of their own people, but would also help make that experience comprehensible and attractive to listeners from other cultures.

Bedřich Smetana (1824–1884) devoted himself to the creation of a Czech musical idiom, and although his principal concern was opera—he wrote eight of them between 1863 and 1882—this cycle of six tone poems, depicting scenes from Czech history and the physical beauty of the country itself, has proven to be his most powerful and enduring score. The concept occurred to him during the composition of his fourth opera, *Libuse,* in 1872. But its composition was fitful. With another opera to write (*The Two Widows* of 1873), he laid the cycle aside, and when he took it up again in 1874, it was against the backdrop of health problems, not the least of which was blocked hearing, an ailment he first noticed during the summer of that year. By October he was completely deaf.

Yet he threw himself into the project, completing the first tone poem, "Vyšehrad," by November, with the second, "Vlatava" (better known in English as "The Moldau") in mid-December, and the third, "Šárka," by the end of February 1875. A hiatus of several months followed, and in October 1875, he wrote what he considered, at the time, the cycle's finale, "Z Českých Luhů a Hájů" (From Bohemian Fields and Groves). In 1878, after the first four tone poems were performed to some acclaim, he decided to add two more, "Tábor" and "Blaník," and to dedicate the entire cycle to the city of Prague.

The first of these pieces, "Vyšehrad," describes the high rock that overlooks Prague and was the site of the ancient castle from which the first Bohemian princes ruled. "Vlatava" describes the river for which it is named, following its course from its origin as a pair of woodland brooks, through the countryside and into the city, then past the majestic Vyšehrad and into the Elbe. It is often heard on its own, and it stands up nicely; but it is even better in context. Its principal theme bears a resemblance to the Israeli national anthem, "Hatikva," and was long thought to have been based on a Czech folk song. But Brian Large, in his authoritative *Smetana* (1970), established that the melody is actually a Swedish folk song that Smetana must have heard between 1856 and 1863, when he taught and conducted in Göteborg.

"Šárka," the shortest of these works, is the only one that tells a story, and it does so in a series of brilliantly orchestrated episodes. Its title character is a Bohemian Amazon who has sworn vengeance against all men because of the infidelity of her lover, and who leads a rebellion of women. Ctirad, a soldier, leads his army to quell this uprising, but he is unable to resist Šárka's beauty. She holds Ctirad under her spell, drugs him and his soldiers, and calls on her army of women to massacre them all. After the violence of "Šárka," "Z Českých Luhů a Hájů" offers some pastoral respite, complete with rejoicing country folk.

The last two pieces deal specifically with Jan Hus, the Czech Protestant reformer who was martyred in 1415, and his followers, the Hussites, who for Smetana were more important as a symbol of nationalistic heroism than for their religious beliefs. "Tábor" is named after the medieval town where Hus's followers were based, and it uses the Hussite chorale, "Ye Who Are God's Warriors," to depict the steadfastness with which the Hussites fought for their cause. The chorale is also heard in "Blaník," the closing work, which is named for the mountain into which the Hussite soldiers retreated after their defeat in 1452. Like the figure of Merlin in the English Arthurian legends, the soldiers of Tábor are believed to watch over the country from Blaník, ready to come to its aid in its darkest hour. Smetana presents a vision of their reappearance in the triumphal march that closes the piece, and the cycle.

Although "The Moldau" has traveled widely, the complete *Má Vlast* has remained largely the turf of Czech conductors. There are several classic recordings, starting with a magnificent 1929 traversal by Václav Talich and the Czech Philharmonic that made its way to CD (Koch Legacy) in a very good transfer from original 78 rpm discs in 1990. Like many performances from its time, it has some interpretive touches—an elegant string portamento, for example, and rubato phrasing that creates unusual emphases—that fell out of style in later years, but which now make the performance all the more interesting. In more recent times, Václav Neumann made several fine recordings of the set, including one with the Czech Philharmonic (Supraphon) and one with the Gewandhaus Orchestra of Leipzig (Teldec).

The one I have chosen, though, is the last of several recordings by Rafael Kubelik—his last performance of any work, in fact.

Kubelik was a highly esteemed conductor who had a troubled career. The son of the great turn-of-the-century violinist Jan Kubelik and a Hungarian countess, Marion Szell, he studied the violin with his father, but became interested in conducting at the Prague Conservatory and made his debut, at age nineteen, with the Czech Philharmonic. The following year, he toured the United States with his father, both as his piano accompanist and as a conductor, and in 1937, when he was twenty-three, he became Talich's assistant at the Czech Philharmonic, eventually succeeding him. He remained in Czechoslovakia during World War II, but said that he refused to speak German as a form of protest. When the war ended, he conducted *Má Vlast* to celebrate Czechoslovakia's liberation.

But the celebration was short-lived: when the Nazis were succeeded by the Communists, Kubelik left the country, saying that he could not face life under another tyrannical regime. Upon his departure in 1948, he vowed that he would not return until the Communists fell from power. He moved to London, where he quickly established his reputation with important productions of Mozart, Berlioz, and Janáček operas at Glyndebourne and Covent Garden. Then in 1950, he was appointed music director of the Chicago Symphony. The experience was disastrous: Kubelik's plan to renovate the orchestra by replacing twenty-two players ran into immediate opposition, and Claudia Cassidy, Chicago's most powerful music critic at the time, quickly became his implacable foe.

When he returned to London in 1954, he was appointed music director of Covent Garden—but there ran afoul of patriotic sentiment, particularly that of Sir Thomas Beecham, who objected to a foreigner directing Britain's premier opera company. Kubelik's offer to resign was declined, but when his contract ended in 1958, he did not renew it, and apart from a five-month tenure as music director of the Metropolitan Opera, he spent the rest of his life as a freelance conductor—a capacity in which he was greatly admired.

Among his many treasurable recordings is a 1971 account of *Má Vlast* with the Boston Symphony, a performance that many collectors regard as the best version on disc. Still, this 1990 concert recording matches the spirit and energy of the 1971 version, and captures a truly special moment. Kubelik, suffering from severe arthritis, had retired from conducting in 1985, but when the Communist government was toppled in Václav Havel's Velvet Revolution, he was invited to return, after forty-two years in exile, to open the 1990 Prague Spring Festival. He could not refuse. His old orchestra, the Czech Philharmonic, rose to the occasion as well, and its performance captures the electricity of the occasion. Kubelik then resumed his retirement, and died in 1996, at age eighty-two.

Conductor Rafael Kubelik conducting *Má Vlast*

Bedřich Smetana

43. MODEST MUSSORGSKY

Songs

SERGEI LEIFERKUS, BARITONE; SEMION SKIGIN, PIANIST
(Conifer Classics 75605 51229 2)

Includes Songs and Dances of Death, The Nursery, The Puppet Show, Forgotten, The Seminarist, Darling Savishna, The He-Goat, *and* Mephistopheles' Song of the Flea.

Recorded 1993

In his lifetime, Modest Mussorgsky (1839–1881) was considered of little account outside a small circle of composers in Russia. Born to a wealthy family and groomed for a military career, he proved a talented pianist as a child and was composing by the early 1850s. Although he studied briefly with Mily Balakirev, his training in composition was sketchy. Fired with ideas for musical projects, and counting on his family's financial resources, he resigned his commission in the tsar's personal regiment in 1858, after only two years.

But when the emancipation of the serfs in 1861 left the family stripped of its wealth, he was forced to become a civil servant. He was taken for a dilettante by many established musicians, and by the end of his life, at the age of forty-two, he was a lonely, impoverished alcoholic whose major works were left unfinished, unorchestrated, or in other forms of disarray.

There were a few among Mussorgsky's colleagues who recognized and admired his vision of a new Russian music, rooted in folk and church traditions, and closely bound to the rhythms and inherent musicality of the Russian language. Chief among his supporters was Nikolai Rimsky-Korsakov, who devoted himself to completing and revamping Mussorgsky's operas, and editing many of his other works—an effort that in great measure won Mussorgsky a posthumous reputation. History has favored his belief in Mussorgsky's music, the full wealth of which has come into focus only in recent decades.

Mussorgsky's songs are an essential key to his vision, and this collection by the Russian baritone Sergei Leiferkus—the first of four volumes devoted to Mussorgsky—shows something of their variety. Its twin centerpieces are two very different cycles. *The Nursery,* set to Mussorgsky's own texts, offers a child's-eye view of a day of mischief and irritating the nanny. And one of Mussorgsky's greatest works, *Songs and Dances of Death,* with texts by Arseny Golenishchev-Kutuzov, depicts Death lulling a baby to permanent sleep, seducing a young girl, snatching a drunken peasant caught in a blizzard, and appearing as a field marshall before the dead soldiers arrayed on a battlefield.

Leiferkus produces a rich sound and has the flexibility to tender both the childish, light touch required for *The Nursery* and the gravity demanded by the *Songs and Dances.* A dozen other songs are included as well, among them "Mephistopheles' Song of the Flea"— probably the most famous of Mussorgsky's songs, and given a lively, sardonic account here—and "Forgotten," a ballad about the death of a soldier that matches the spirit of the *Songs and Dances of Death* (and also has a text by Golenishchev-Kutuzov).

I chose this first volume of Leiferkus's series partly on interpretive grounds, but also for its concision: it brings together the greatest of Mussorgsky's songs on a single disc, and in good, up-to-date sound. Anyone seeking a more expansive view of this repertory, though, should seek the extraordinary recordings made between 1951 and 1957 by the great Bulgarian bass Boris Christoff (EMI, reissued on three CDs). Christoff's rich sound and interpretive intensity animate Mussorgsky's vocal writing brilliantly, and some of the works (including the *Songs and Dances of Death*) are presented in orchestral versions. Astonishingly, both the Leiferkus and Christoff recordings are out of print as of this writing, although I have found both listed by used-recordings vendors on the Internet, and I would be surprised if they didn't return to the active catalog at some point.

There is another attractive alternative currently available: *Songs and Dances of Death,* by the mezzo-soprano Marjana Lipovšek, with the pianist Graham Johnson. I prefer the weight and coloration of men's voices in this music—particularly in the *Songs and Dances*— but nothing in the songs inherently requires that. Lipovšek is a good judge of when the music needs breadth and when it needs subtlety, and her performances are attractive and persuasive. Her program includes the title work, "The Nursery," "Sunless" (another moving cycle on poetry by Golenishchev-Kutuzov), "Hebrew Song" (a setting of lines from Song of Songs), "Hopak," and "Mephistopheles' Song of the Flea" (Sony Classical, 1994).

44. MODEST MUSSORGSKY

Pictures at an Exhibition (Ravel orchestration), *Khovanshchina* Prelude (Shostakovich orchestration), *Night on the Bare Mountain* (Rimsky-Korsakov orchestration), and *Sorochintsky Fair* Gopak (Liadov orchestration)

VIENNA PHILHARMONIC, VALERY GERGIEV, CONDUCTING
(Philips 289 468 526-2)

Recorded 2000

By all rights, Modest Mussorgsky's principal claims to fame should be his grandly scaled operas, *Boris Godunov* and *Khovanshchina*, and his beautifully characterized songs, and now that more singers fluent in Russian are freely roaming the post-Soviet world, these works are likely to take their rightful place in the repertory. For the moment, though, the vast majority of classical music listeners associate Mussorgsky most closely with *Pictures at an Exhibition*, a work that is in many ways uncharacteristic of this composer of dramatic vocal music. Moreover, the version most people know is not the score as Mussorgsky wrote it—that is, as a solo piano suite—but the one on this recording, in which *Pictures* is filtered through the orchestral prism of Maurice Ravel.

Still, if an extended instrumental work was a rarity among Mussorgsky's output, it could be argued that *Pictures* follows an almost dramatic plan. Mussorgsky composed it in June 1874, after attending a memorial exhibition of paintings, sketches, and architectural drawings by his friend Viktor Hartmann, who had died the previous year at age thirty-nine, and in it he fully captures the experience of walking through a large, varied show.

The musical rendering of each picture is packed with atmosphere and detail. We meet the threatening "Gnome" of the first picture, then pass a mist-enshrouded "Old Castle" and, in "Bydlo," a depiction of a lumbering, off-kilter oxcart. Near the end of the work, this dark atmosphere returns, magnified, in the depiction of a Roman sepulcher, in "Catacombs," and in the fanciful, densely chromatic "Hut on Fowls' Legs." In between, we eavesdrop on quarreling and noisemaking of all kinds: Parisian children, in "Tuileries," women in the marketplace of "Limoges," chirping chickens in "Ballet of the Chicks in Their Shells," and the debating "Samuel Goldenberg and Schmuyle," one wealthy, the other poor, from a shtetl near Warsaw.

Having found supremely inventive ways to bring Hartmann's pictures to life, Mussorgsky added some nonpictorial rumination in the form of "Cum mortuis in lingua mortua" (With the Dead in a Dead Language), after "Catacombs," and, of course, in the "Promenade" movements, which separate the pictures and serve as a musical frame that evolves through the work, finally appearing as the basis of the spectacular finale, "The Great Gate of Kiev."

Mussorgsky's piano original captures all of this vividly, but Ravel's 1922 orchestration expands its dimensions immeasurably. Nor did he limit himself to merely applying coloration to the piano score: among the many effective reconsiderations is the dynamic pacing of "Bydlo." In the piano version, we stumble suddenly onto the oxcart: it arrives at full volume. Ravel begins the movement quietly, gradually increasing the volume as the cart wheels into view. And however powerful a pianist may be, there is no competing with the full-orchestra version of "The Great Gate."

Back in the LP days, a popular *Pictures* disc on the Columbia/Odyssey label let listeners have it both ways: Side One offered George Szell's performance with the Cleveland Orchestra, and Side Two included a 1958 concert recording by the great Russian pianist Sviatoslav Richter. Both recordings have been reissued on CD—separately rather than together, alas—and they both stand up nicely, as do old favorites by Leonard Bernstein and the New York Philharmonic (Sony, 1958) and Vladimir Horowitz, playing his own idiosyncratic edition of the piano score (RCA, 1947).

The account that blows away the competition, though, is a fairly recent concert recording by Valery Gergiev and the Vienna Philharmonic. No doubt the adrenaline of the moment contributed to the fire and excitement in the playing, but anyone familiar with Gergiev's studio recordings knows that it isn't just that. Gergiev, who has been the artistic director of the Maryinsky Theater in St. Petersburg (home of the Kirov Opera and Ballet) since 1988, and principal guest conductor at the Metropolitan Opera since 1997, seems to possess limitless energy, as well as a thorough command of the gestural language that drives Russian music. His use of extreme dynamics, carefully weighted balances, and tempos that suit the atmosphere evoked in each "picture" yield a vital, three-dimensional performance.

The fillers benefit from these qualities, too, particularly *Night on the Bare Mountain,* which in this hard-driven performance terrifies.

45. PETER ILYICH TCHAIKOVSKY

Symphonies: no. 4 in F minor (op. 36), no. 5 in E minor (op. 64), and no. 6 in B minor, *Pathétique* (op. 74)

LENINGRAD PHILHARMONIC ORCHESTRA,
EVGENY MRAVINSKY, CONDUCTING
(Deutsche Grammophon 419 745-2; two CDs)

Recorded 1960

Great recordings of the three last symphonies by Peter Ilyich Tchaikovsky (1840–1893) are plentiful, as one might imagine. These big virtuosic scores, full of graphic and varied instrumental coloration, dramatic gestures, and sweeping, irresistible melodies, offer ample opportunity for conductors to project a larger-than-life emotionalism and for orchestras to show off the beauty and power of their sound.

But as densely packed as the Tchaikovsky bins are with performances by the stars of the moment, these brisk, vital 1960 recordings by the great Russian conductor Evgeny Mravinsky continue to outshine them. Mravinsky, who died in 1988, spent his entire career in the Soviet Union, and was known in the West mainly through a handful of recordings that showed him to be a supreme interpreter of Russian music, particularly of Tchaikovsky and Dmitri Shostakovich.

The brilliant sound he drew from the orchestra may have had something to do with his demand for as many as ten rehearsals, even for standard repertory works, a requirement that the Soviet authorities willingly met. It is worth noting, too, that some of the best among the current Russian conductors—Valery Gergiev, Yuri Temirkanov, and Mariss Jansons, as well as the great German conductor Kurt Sanderling—were Mravinsky's students or conducting assistants.

As Tchaikovsky's most deeply personal works, these three symphonies offer Mravinsky and his Leningrad orchestra grand canvases on which to make their mark. Each reflects something of Tchaikovsky's psychological state at the time he composed it. More broadly, each can be understood as describing a battle between the individual spirit and the forces of Fate—a battle that is expressed and resolved differently in each work.

He began work on the Fourth in April or May 1877, around the same time he began a correspondence with Antonina Milykova, one of his pupils, which led to their disastrous marriage that July. The official story, put out by Tchaikovsky's brother, Modest, was that Tchaikovsky entered into the marriage because Antonina threatened to commit suicide if he refused. Recent scholarship has cast doubt on that, arguing that Tchaikovsky's motivation was partly financial (Antonina was expecting an inheritance) and partly because he believed that even if marriage did not alter his own sexual inclination, it would undercut gossip about it. He had told Antonina that the relationship would be platonic, and she assured him that she would not reveal his homosexuality. Tchaikovsky was unable to maintain the charade for more than two months; they separated, but never divorced.

Tchaikovsky must have had misgivings even as he was contemplating this arrangement, and to an extent they can be discerned in the "program" for the Fourth Symphony that he sent to his patroness, Nadezhda von Meck. In it, he describes the theme of the first movement as representing Fate as "an ominous power which hinders our striving after happiness." The second, too, is melancholy, but the spectacular pizzicato writing in the Scherzo represented, Tchaikovsky wrote, "fleeting ideas like those which run through our minds when we have had a glass of wine." The finale, which begins with a grand crash of brass and percussion and a furious descending string figure, has a divided focus: Fate is back to stake its claim, but there is also a spirited folksiness in the movement's themes that suggests an ability to escape Fate's clutches for the moment.

When Tchaikovsky began work on the Fifth, in 1888, he believed that inspiration had fled him. Yet by August he had completed the work, which boasts a distinct musical motto—again, widely perceived as representing Fate—that undergoes great transformations in color, tempo, and shape as it courses through the score. This symphony is less ambiguous than the Fourth: in the triumphant finale, Fate is mastered at last, transforming the work's minor tonality into major. Tchaikovsky may not have seen himself as the protagonist here, though. In the current edition of *The New Grove Dictionary of Music and Musicians,* Roland John Wiley shows that the work's thematic motto came from a Russian Orthodox Easter hymn, "Christ is Risen." Still, the thoroughly sensuous French horn solo in the second movement and the lilting character of the third, a waltz, suggest that a secular reading is not out of the question.

That optimism fled Tchaikovsky by the time he set to work on the Sixth Symphony, in 1892. "While composing it in my mind," he wrote in one of his letters, "I frequently wept." The work, which he gave the title *Pathétique,* evokes a restless, troubled soul. Its central movements, a lovely waltz movement and a gossamer, almost Mendelssohnian Allegro molto vivace, offer a few moments of light (usually tempered); but the larger first and last movements—both downcast Adagios—tell the real story.

The finale, in fact, was radical: instead of ending in the expected blaze of closing chords, the movement fades away—the individual, this time, succumbs to Fate. Tchaikovsky knew that this departure would cause displeasure, and when he conducted the premiere, on October 28, 1893, the reaction was unenthusiastic. A few days after the performance, he took ill, and on November 6 he died, possibly a suicide.

What is extraordinary about Mravinsky's readings is his ability to touch the emotional depths that Tchaikovsky's scores lay bare without making them seem cloying or sentimental. Fate is fought in all-out battles here. Instead of lingering on Tchaikovsky's melodies, Mravinsky takes uncommonly fast tempos, sweeping away visions of a glum Tchaikovsky in favor of one whose depressions are punctuated with episodes of frenzied determination. His players follow that vision, supplying incisive brass playing and a magnificently dark-hued string sound.

46. NIKOLAI RIMSKY-KORSAKOV

Scheherazade

ALEXANDER BORODIN

Symphony no. 2 in B minor

ROYAL CONCERTGEBOUW ORCHESTRA OF AMSTERDAM, KIRIL KONDRASHIN, CONDUCTING

(Philips 464 735-2)

Recorded 1979–1980

Nikolai Rimsky-Korsakov (1844–1908) was the most accomplished orchestral composer in the circle of self-taught Russian nationalists known collectively as "The Five," the others being Mily Balakirev (the leader of the group), Modest Mussorgsky, Cesar Cui, and Alexander Borodin. Alone among them, he was offered (and accepted) a post at the then-new St. Petersburg Conservatory—an institution that

"The Five" had, until then, unanimously opposed. Judging from his self-effacing letters and memoir, Rimsky-Korsakov regarded himself unworthy of this distinction, and upon taking up his professorial duties, he also sought ways to improve his own skills. He also frequently put those skills at the service of his colleagues, completing and orchestrating Mussorgsky's opera *Khovanshchina* and his showpiece *Night on the Bare Mountain* after that composer's death, and fully orchestrating Borodin's *Prince Igor.*

Among Rimsky-Korsakov's own works, the orchestral suite *Scheherazade,* composed in 1888—around the time he was occupied with Borodin's opera—is an especially dazzling example of his ability to translate visual and literary imagery into purely musical textures. It reflects, as well, the musical side of Russia's encounters with the Islamic world in the nineteenth century—something one also sees in, for example, Balakirev's virtuoso piano piece, "Islamey." Rimsky-Korsakov based his alluring work on stories from *A Thousand and One Nights,* the famous collection of Arabian tales, and he set the scene in a descriptive paragraph at the head of the published score:

"The Sultan Shahriar, convinced of the falseness and inconsistency of all women, had sworn an oath to put to death each of his wives after the first night. However, Sultana Scheherazade saved her life by arousing his interest in the tales she told during 1001 nights. Driven by curiosity, the Sultan postponed her execution from day to day, and at last abandoned his sanguine design. Scheherazade told miraculous stories to the Sultan. For her tales she borrowed verses from the poets and words from folk-songs, combining fairy tales with adventure."

The original published score also included titles for each of the movements: "The Sea and Sinbad's Ship" opens the work, followed by "The Story of the Kalendar Prince"—the Kalendars being storytellers—and "The Young Prince and the Young Princess," an evocative musical love scene, and finally a compound set of adventures, "The Festival of Baghdad—The Sea—The Ship Goes to Pieces on a Rock Surmounted by a Bronze Warrior."

Rimsky-Korsakov later withdrew these titles, although they continue to be used, quite understandably. And in the *Chronicles of My Musical Life,* written in his last years, he cautioned listeners against associating the movements with specific story lines, or assigning characterizations to musical motifs within the work. That said, he admitted that the sweetly winding, Eastern-tinged melody for solo violin that connects the movements is meant to represent Scheherazade herself, and the heavy brass theme represents the sultan. Their interaction can be tracked through the piece: listen to the way the sultan's music softens at the end of the third movement, after Scheherazade has narrated the love story of the young prince and princess.

The Russian conductor Kiril Kondrashin was an eloquent interpreter of the Russian repertory, and was known in the West for many years mainly through recordings—particularly a series of deeply felt Shostakovich symphonies—although he was periodically allowed to tour outside the Soviet Union. One particularly famous visit occurred in 1958, when he came to New York to conduct the concerts that marked the pianist Van Cliburn's celebratory return after winning the first Tchaikovsky Competition. Twenty years later, though, he was feeling artistically constrained in the Soviet Union, and used a visit to the Netherlands as an opportunity to defect. The Soviets immediately declared him a nonperson and withdrew all his recordings, but he seemed set to thrive in the Netherlands, where he was given a guest conducting post at the Concertgebouw Orchestra in 1979. That year he recorded this beautifully paced and almost cinematic *Scheherazade,* a reading distinguished by the shapely solo violin playing of the orchestra's concertmaster, Hermann Krebbers. Alas, his career in the West was cut short by a heart attack in 1981.

Kondrashin's *Scheherazade* has had several CD incarnations, the latest filled out with a concert performance of the Symphony no. 2 by Borodin (1833–1887), recorded in June 1980. There are echoes of *Prince Igor* here, perhaps not surprisingly, since both works were on Borodin's desk simultaneously over a long period. Borodin began the symphony in 1869 and didn't finish it until 1876, taking it up again for some final tinkering in 1886. In the end, it was left to Rimsky-Korsakov, as his posthumous editor, to supply the dynamic markings—minor touches, perhaps, but crucial guides for an interpreter. But this symphony is fully Borodin's, and it has a vitality and assertiveness, in Kondrashin's reading, that speak well for this composer's imaginative use of distinctively Russian themes and coloration.

47. EDVARD GRIEG

Holberg Suite (op. 40), *Two Elegiac Melodies*
(op. 34), *Peer Gynt* Suite no. 1 (op. 46) and Suite
no. 2 (op. 55), and "Evening in the Mountains"
and "At the Cradle" from *Lyric Pieces*
(op. 68, nos. 4 and 5)

ACADEMY OF ST. MARTIN-IN-THE-FIELDS,
SIR NEVILLE MARRINER, CONDUCTING
(Hänssler Classic 98.995)

Recorded 1994

Edvard Grieg (1843–1907), Norway's most famous composer—indeed, the most renowned composer of his day throughout Scandinavia—was actually of Scottish descent and had strong ties with Britain: his great-grandfather had emigrated to Norway less than a century before the composer's birth, and both his father and grandfather served as British consul in Bergen. Grieg himself entertained thoughts of a religious life, but he also studied music as a child, and was talented enough that the Norwegian violinist Ole Bull, hearing the fifteen-year-old Grieg play the piano, urged his parents to send him to the Leipzig Conservatory to polish his skills.

He hated it there, largely because he considered his teachers rigidly pedantic, yet there were compensations: he became familiar with the works of Schumann, an important influence, and even heard Clara Schumann play her husband's Piano Concerto at the Gewandhaus. It was also in Leipzig that he published his first collections of piano pieces and songs, but upon his return to Bergen in 1862, he still felt insufficiently trained, and set out for Copenhagen to study with Niels Gade, then the leading light of Scandinavian music, and a composer who had known both Schumann and Mendelssohn.

It was during another visit to Copenhagen, in 1864, that Grieg met Rikard Nordraak, a twenty-two-year-old composer intent on establishing a distinctly Norwegian musical style. The times were certainly right for it: musical nationalism was finding its life force within the passionate currents of romanticism, and it was in the air everywhere in Europe.

Nordraak fired Grieg with enthusiasm for the project, but did not live to see it to fruition: he died in 1866, at age twenty-three, leaving it to Grieg to prove that a Norwegian symphonic school, spiced with the country's folk melodies and evocations of its atmosphere, could have an international appeal. That isn't to say that Grieg's music never evoked other realms: on this disc, for example, the "Arab Dance" from the second *Peer Gynt* Suite draws on Turkish musical conventions (or at least, Turkish music as heard through European ears), and the dances of the *Holberg* Suite show him glancing in the direction of eighteenth-century France.

What the works on this disc best demonstrate is the most picturesque and seductive side of Grieg's music. Grieg met the Norwegian playwright Henrik Ibsen in 1866, not long before Ibsen completed *Peer Gynt,* his portrait of a scamp who some have interpreted as a satirical look at the Norwegian character, but which Ibsen himself described as a fantasy. But it wasn't until 1874, when Ibsen was contemplating a significant revision for performances in Christiana (now Oslo), that he asked Grieg to contribute an incidental score. Grieg expected it to be an easy job—an entr'acte here, some background scoring there. But Ibsen's ideas about the music were quite ambitious—something that should not have surprised Grieg, actually, because the letter inviting him to join the project (the text of which is included in the notes for this recording) presents the playwright's musical ideas in considerable detail.

At any rate, Grieg devoted much of the following year to *Peer Gynt,* complaining about it all the while. What he produced, though, was a magnificent new component to Ibsen's play—one that actually became better known around the world than the play itself, thanks to some expansive character pieces that stand beautifully on their own in the pair of suites that Grieg later compiled. Familiarity and perhaps some overuse in foreign contexts (cartoon soundtracks, for example!) may have made pieces like "Morning" and "Hall of the Mountain King" sound clichéd today, but they should be heard on their own terms. Sir Neville Marriner's readings are sumptuous and well-defined and the best of them—the elegant, bittersweet beauty of "Solveig's Song" in the instrumental version, at the end of Suite no. 2, for example—are impossible to resist.

If the suites aren't enough for you, in fact, Marriner and company, with the Ambrosian Singers and the soprano Lucia Popp, recorded a larger selection of the *Peer Gynt* music, including the vocal versions of the "Arab Dance," "Solveig's Song," and "Solveig's Cradle Song" in 1983 (EMI Classics). The attractions of that performance are many, but you would miss the lovely *Elegiac Melodies,* the excerpts from the *Lyric Pieces,* and, most crucially, the *Holberg* Suite, which is as great a draw here as the *Peer Gynt* music.

The suite was composed in 1884 to commemorate the bicentennial of Ludvig Holberg, a Norwegian-Danish playwright, and is properly called "Fra Holbergs Tid" (From Holberg's Time)—which explains its use of baroque dance forms. Grieg composed it for the piano, but quickly saw its implications, and produced the version for string orchestra heard here. Even more than the piano edition, which is now a rarity, the string version makes it clear that Grieg's use of the Gavotte, Musette, and Rigaudon notwithstanding, this is not an antiquarian exercise. Grieg's harmonic language and sense of texture are richly romantic, as are the dramatic gestures that crop up within the first ninety seconds of the opening Prelude.

The piece is also an outstanding test of a string orchestra's suppleness, and the strings of the Academy of St. Martin-in-the-Fields, always a strong component of this popular chamber orchestra, are heard to superb effect both in music that caresses, like the Sarabande and the Air, and in movements that demand fleetness and vigor, like the Prelude and the Rigaudon.

48. LUDWIG VAN BEETHOVEN AND CÉSAR FRANCK

Music from Saratoga: Beethoven and Franck

ITZHAK PERLMAN, VIOLINIST; MARTHA ARGERICH, PIANIST

(EMI 5 56815 2)

Includes Ludwig Van Beethoven's Kreutzer *Sonata for Piano and Violin no. 9 in A (op. 47) and César Franck's Violin Sonata in A.*

Recorded 1998

Beethoven gets top billing in the track listing, and the *Kreutzer* Sonata is unquestionably the greater work. But my principal reason for selecting this recording is for its meltingly supple account of the Violin Sonata by César Franck (1822–1890), a delicious piece that is not only Franck's most enduring score, but also one of the handful of great violin sonatas from the twilight of romanticism.

That isn't to say that the Beethoven performance is lacking by any measure. Both these works were recorded live at the Saratoga Performing Arts Center, in upstate New York, during a recital in July 1998, and the recording captures Itzhak Perlman at his most fiery and least cautious—qualities that were not typical of his playing at that point in his career, but which appear to have been brought out in his collaboration with the mercurial pianist Martha Argerich, whose work virtually always has a daring edge.

Actually, while each work requires a measure of dramatic flair from both the violinist and the pianist, these sonatas are otherwise polar opposites. The Beethoven is a muscular score in the "heroic" or "revolutionary" style that Beethoven was exploring at the time he composed it, in 1802–1803, although there seems not to have been a program of any sort attached to it. It takes its name from Rudolphe Kreutzer, a violinist in the entourage of the French ambassador to Vienna, to whom Beethoven dedicated the work when he published it in 1805. It is often said that Beethoven didn't write the work for Kreutzer, but for another virtuoso, the black, London-based violinist

George Polgreen Bridgetower. But even that isn't quite right. Beethoven had sketched the first two movements and completed the finale in 1802. He met Bridgetower when the violinist visited Vienna in the spring of 1803, and he finished the work in time for a concert that he and Bridgetower gave together that May. Eventually, Bridgetower and Beethoven had a falling-out; hence the dedication to Kreutzer, who reportedly regarded it as "unintelligible," and never played it.

The sonata opens with a grand declaration for solo violin, immediately mirrored by the piano. A short seesawing dialogue between the two instruments tumbles into a vigorous Presto in which both instruments vie for the spotlight, sometimes engaging in a concerto-like battle, sometimes in a graceful dialogue. The central variations sketch a more decorous give-and-take, but the finale returns to the more combative style of the opening movement—a point Argerich emphasizes here by making the piano's single opening chord into an explosion, a kind of pianistic cannon shot.

More introspective feelings drive the Franck. Where the Beethoven is outgoing and given to grand proclamation, the Franck is a stream of decidedly more intimate ideas. Its themes are supremely lyrical, and even when the music reaches its most heated moments—in the churning second movement, for example, or at the peak of the finale—it seems driven by private musings and rhapsodies, on which the listener is eavesdropping.

Even on purely technical grounds, though, the work is full of fascinating details. One is the comparative independence of the violin and piano lines. Through most of the work, the violin and piano have their own distinctive themes. They explore them with each other's support, and in dialogue, and there are passages where the themes seem to dovetail. But the two instruments rarely repeat each other's music, a notable exception being in the canonic opening of the finale, where such literal repetition is required by the form.

Franck's organ works, his Symphony in D, and his piano quintet all have their moments of irresistible lushness, but none compares to this sonata for sheer melodic invention. The reason can undoubtedly be traced to the great Belgian violinist and composer Eugène Ysaÿe to whom the work is dedicated. Ysaÿe was renowned for exactly the kind of creamy tone and dramatic performance this work demands.

That sound, or at least a shadow of it, pours through the crackle on the recordings he made between 1912 and 1919, when he was in his sixties and early seventies, but perhaps a better indication of his capabilities is his own music, which includes six ingenious and exacting sonatas for unaccompanied violin.

Knowing Ysaÿe's style is a key to understanding Franck's, at least in this work, and Perlman is unquestionably attuned to it. His tone is big and pure, but also perfectly focused, and he accepts every invitation to interpretive lavishness that Franck extends. The violin's opening discourse in the first movement, for example, is exquisitely shaped, with touches of portamento—a graceful sliding between notes— combining with careful modulations of tone color and dynamics to capture the line's passions. Perlman uses these effects throughout the work, but never to excess. And Argerich, at her temperamental best, matches his impulses move for move.

Slight allowances must be made for the circumstances of the recording: EMI includes a small amount of applause at the start of the disc and after each sonata, and an occasional cough from the audience threatens to break the spell. But it doesn't matter: both works benefit considerably from the electricity inherent in a live performance, a quality too often dissipated in the studio.

49. ANTONÍN DVOŘÁK

Symphony no. 9 in E minor (op. 95), *Carnival* Overture (op. 92), and Slavonic Dances, nos. 1 and 3 (op. 46)

NEW YORK PHILHARMONIC,
LEONARD BERNSTEIN, CONDUCTING
(Sony Classical SMK 60563)
Recorded 1962–1965

In 1892, Antonín Dvořák (1841–1904) came to New York City at the invitation of Jeanette M. Thurber, who had founded the National

Conservatory of Music of America in 1885, and had the idea of inviting one of Europe's preeminent composers to join its faculty. The appointment was for two years, and required Dvořák to teach a composition class six hours per week and to lead four hours of student orchestra rehearsals. He would also preside over ten concerts of his music, four in New York, six in other American cities. And he would have four months of vacation a year, all for an annual salary of $15,000—some thirty times his salary at the Prague Conservatory, and the equivalent of about $250,000 today.

What Dvořák also provided, during his two-year stay, were works that he hoped would be object lessons for American composers intent on finding their own national voice. In both his String Quartet no. 12 in F (op. 96), now called the *American* Quartet, and in his Symphony no. 9 in E minor (op. 95), which Dvořák himself called *From the New World,* the composer wrote American works using exactly the same methods he might use if he were writing a work to express the Czech spirit: he listened to folk melodies—particularly spirituals, and secondarily American Indian music—and created themes for his new works, not so much by quoting those melodies directly as by writing new ones that mirrored their character.

What emerged, actually, is not so much a template for American music as a hybrid: both the quartet and the symphony, their folk themes notwithstanding, fit snugly among the works that surround them in the Dvořák canon, and without much of a shift in perspective, they are as identifiably Czech as American. What that tells us is not necessarily that the works failed to achieve their goal—the Ninth Symphony was hailed as a masterpiece and recognized as having a strongly American character by critics who covered both its public rehearsal and its premiere by the New York Philharmonic in December 1893—but that Dvořák's personal style is so identifiable that it comes through even when he was intent on incorporating what to him were exotic elements.

In an interview published in the *New York Herald* a few days before the premiere of the Ninth Symphony, in fact, Dvořák said specifically that although spirituals and American Indian music captured his attention from the time he reached America, "I have not actually used any of the melodies. I have simply written original themes embodying the peculiarities of the music, and, using these themes as subjects, have developed them with all the resources of modern rhythms, harmony, counterpoint and orchestral color."

On close study, Dvořák's claim not to have quoted existing melodies directly crumbles a bit. The opening lines of the spiritual "Swing Low, Sweet Chariot" can be heard in the first movement, although Dvořák quickly melds those lines to a theme of his own. But a supposed second spiritual quotation—the lovely English horn theme of the second movement—is actually an original melody of Dvořák's; it became known as a spiritual only later, when a text, "Goin' Home," was affixed to it by William Arms Fisher, a student of Dvořák's.

Dvořák also noted, in the interview, that both the second and third movements were sketches for an opera or cantata that he was considering, based on Longfellow's "Hiawatha." He never completed that dramatic setting. But the degree to which sections of the Ninth—and possibly more of the score than Dvořák mentioned in the interview—work as a "Hiawatha" tone poem has been demonstrated by the musicologist Michael Beckerman. Speaking at a festival built around the Ninth, and staged by the Brooklyn Philharmonic in 1994, Beckerman showed that in addition to the acknowledged connections in the second and third movements, the finale of the Ninth perfectly matched (right down to the rhythmic cadence) the section of the Longfellow poem that describes Hiawatha's pursuit of Pau-Puk-Keewis. That may be stretching the connection, though, and certainly the most crucial aspect of the finale is its reminiscences of all the major themes of the three preceding movements.

There are some magnificent interpretations to choose from on disc. I've long admired the nobility of István Kertész's London Symphony Orchestra recording (Decca, both separately and as part of his traversal of all nine Dvořák symphonies). There is also great warmth—and an illuminating variety of ways in which the balance between Czech and American elements are calibrated—in the classic readings by Fritz Reiner and the Chicago Symphony (RCA), George Szell and the Cleveland Orchestra (Sony Classical), and Rafael Kubelik and the Vienna Philharmonic (Decca).

But by far the most thrilling recording of this symphony on disc is this 1962 performance by Leonard Bernstein and the New York

Philharmonic—a spectacular example of Bernstein at his freest and most spirited, and a fine illustration of how those qualities made Bernstein such a compelling performer. Bernstein begins by taking the introductory Adagio at an unusually slow pace, elongating notes and emphasizing its melancholy, ruminative character. But the orchestral blasts that help usher the listener into the Allegro molto—the first movement proper—are solid and exhilarating, and they continue to be so as the movement unfolds, briskly and joyfully.

That sense of contrast prefigures the one that occurs between the second movement, a Largo, and the Scherzo that follows it. The Largo is graceful, shapely, and dark; the Scherzo absolutely dances, and in fact, Bernstein emphasizes the Bohemian folk dance qualities of certain episodes in a way that no one else has done as vividly.

Still, the real heart of the performance is the Largo. Bernstein is not content simply to beat time here: both the English horn melody and the orchestral support are carefully and beautifully sculpted, and thoroughly songlike, and as the movement progresses, the Philharmonic's strings and winds play with a heart-stopping transparency.

Composer Antonin Dvořák

Bernstein's tempos throughout are remarkably fluid: in the first and last movements especially, he adjusts the pace—sometimes within a phrase—to match his admittedly speculative interpretation of Dvořák's emotional pulse. His shifts, and the changes in emphasis that sometimes accompany them, can strike listeners of a literalist bent as either excessive or downright odd, but go with them: their logic becomes apparent.

The other works—the *Carnival* Overture, recorded in 1965, and the Slavonic Dances, nos. 1 and 3, from 1963, are pure energy, both Bernstein and the Philharmonic at their best.

50. CAMILLE SAINT-SAËNS

Symphony no. 3 (op. 78)

PAUL DUKAS

The Sorcerer's Apprentice

SIMON PRESTON, ORGANIST; BERLIN PHILHARMONIC,
JAMES LEVINE, CONDUCTING
(Deutsche Grammophon 419 617-2)

Recorded 1986

For those of us who came of age at a time when rationalism was a highly prized quality in music—meaning, in practical terms, that early music and contemporary music were valued more highly than the purely emotional outbursts of late romanticism—the music of Camille Saint-Saëns (1835–1921) has always been something of a guilty pleasure. Obviously, that attitude demands reconsideration now. Most of us, after all, long ago came to terms with Anton Bruckner and Gustav Mahler, the most intensely emotional composers of the age; yet Saint-Saëns has retained the image of being decorative but not really serious, a purveyor of frothy, caloric music beneath a thin veneer of neo-classical elegance.

His Symphony no. 3—popularly known as the *Organ* Symphony because of the organ part that dominates its finale—deserves better standing. For that matter, so does Saint-Saëns himself. A true polymath, he was born in Paris, began his piano studies at age three, and made his formal debut playing Beethoven and Mozart concertos—from memory, and with his own cadenza in the Mozart—when he was ten. His composition studies were under way well before he entered the Paris Conservatoire in 1848. But he was equally passionate about his studies in the natural sciences, literature, religion, languages, and the visual arts. He published articles on several of these topics, as well as music criticism and scholarly studies of Renaissance music.

Early in his career, Saint-Saëns's talents won the attention and support of Hector Berlioz, Gioacchino Rossini, Charles Gounod, and Franz Liszt. He was passionate about the music of other composers, most notably Wagner, and defended them against more conservative opinion to the contrary. Yet, at the start of World War I, he argued for a ban on German music, Wagner's especially.

Saint-Saëns composed prolifically: in addition to his most famous opera, *Samson et Dalila,* he wrote a dozen others, as well as incidental music, chamber works, dozens of choral settings, both sacred and secular, a rich catalog of songs, and a long list of orchestral works that includes the popular *Danse macabre,* five piano concertos, two cello concertos, and two violin concertos. He maintained an active performing life as both a pianist and a conductor. His last piano recital, in 1921, commemorated the seventy-fifth anniversary of his youthful debut; he died in Algiers a few months later.

It was for a guest conducting appearance in 1886 with the Royal Philharmonic Society of London that Saint-Saëns was commissioned to write the *Organ* Symphony. Saint-Saëns's themes here have a Schubertian lilt, but they are developed as a series of thematic transformations, a mode of musical development that was widely associated with Liszt, who had died that year, and to whose memory the work is dedicated. Saint-Saëns scored the work for a huge orchestra, augmented not only by the organ but by piano four-hands. He cast it in two large movements, mainly to keep the focus on the thematic development, rather than on changes of tempo and texture. Still, each movement is easily divisible in half, and most CD versions (including this one) present the symphony as if it were in four movements, with track breaks at the Poco adagio second half of the first movement, and at the Maestoso second half of the second movement. That's okay: it makes it easy for listeners in need of a quick visceral thrill to hit the start of the Maestoso and catch that burst of organ sound and rippling piano figures within the lush orchestral texture that Saint-Saëns calls for.

James Levine's reading of the work boasts extraordinary transparency of texture. In the first movement, the wind and brass detailing has a definition I haven't heard on any other recording of the work, and although some might find this a clinical quality, the Berlin players address their lines with zest and precision. It is a quality that suits the finale as well: rarely does the piano writing sparkle as it does here.

Levine's tempos are generally brisk, and they create electricity in both halves of the second movement, with a big, rich-hued organ sound from Simon Preston and sharp-edged brass punctuation in the Maestoso. Levine also allows an occasional swoop from the strings as a nod to the romanticism at the heart of this streamlined, modern performance. Filling out the disc is a fully characterized, dramatic account of *The Sorcerer's Apprentice,* the popular showpiece by Saint-Saëns's younger compatriot, Paul Dukas (1865–1935).

The competition among recordings of the *Organ* Symphony is tough, though not huge. I am also very partial to the 1959 recording by Charles Munch and the Boston Symphony, with Berj Zamkochian on the organ (RCA Victor). Part of RCA's legendary Living Stereo series, it deserves the quaint legend "A Hi-Fi Spectacular!" emblazoned on its original cover, and on that of the latest reissue (which is filled out with 1956 recordings of Debussy's *La Mer* and Ibert's *Escales*). And while its orchestral sound lacks the bright illumination of Levine's, the organ sound on this recording has a floor-shaking heft that the DG disc does not quite match.

Notable, too, is a very fine 1964 recording by Georges Prêtre and the Orchestre de la Société des Concerts du Conservatoire, with the composer Maurice Duruflé as the organist (EMI). Prêtre's approach is the polar opposite of Levine's: his orchestral sound is smooth and velvety and his tempos are more relaxed. He makes a good case for this view, supported by muscular, spirited playing by Duruflé. That disc also includes Saint-Saëns's evocative *Carnival of the Animals,* with Alexis Weissenberg and Aldo Ciccolini as the duo-pianists, and Francis Poulenc's *Model Animals.*

51. GIUSEPPE VERDI

Requiem and *Four Sacred Pieces*

PHILHARMONIA ORCHESTRA AND CHORUS,
CARLO MARIA GIULINI, CONDUCTING
(EMI Classics 7243 567560 2; two CDs)

Elisabeth Schwarzkopf, soprano; Christa Ludwig, mezzo-soprano; Nicolai Gedda, tenor; Nicolai Ghiaurov, bass; Janet Baker, mezzo-soprano (in the Four Sacred Pieces).

Recorded 1963–1964

Because Giuseppe Verdi (1813–1901) devoted himself primarily to the opera stage, most of his music falls outside the purview of this book. But among his comparatively few nonoperatic scores are these two intensely emotional sacred works—pieces that, for me, embody the greatest and most expressive music he composed. Both, actually, were written in periods when, for various reasons, Verdi had put opera aside. The Requiem, composed in memory of the Italian nationalist poet Alessandro Manzoni, was completed in 1874, early in the long hiatus between *Aida* (1871) and *Otello* (1887). The *Four Sacred Pieces* were completed in 1898, five years after the premiere of Verdi's last and greatest opera, *Falstaff.*

The Requiem had its genesis in a plan Verdi proposed after Gioacchino Rossini's death in 1868. His idea was to invite Italy's best composers to compose sections of a Requiem, which would be performed on the first anniversary of Rossini's death. The project was scrapped, but not before Verdi completed his contribution, a thoroughly dramatic Libera Me.

When Manzoni died in 1873, Verdi again proposed an anniversary Requiem, although this time not a collaborative one. The Libera Me became its closing section. Verdi considered Rossini and Manzoni to be the peaks of Italian culture during his lifetime, and Manzoni's death, in particular, touched him deeply. His proposal of a Requiem in each case, despite the fact that he was not especially religious, is not surprising: one need not be pious to have thoughts about death and the prospect of a continuing life of the spirit, and for Verdi the Requiem was the format in which to explore those feelings.

Nor should it be surprising that he did so on his own musical terms—which is to say, with theatrical gestures and in operatic proportions. Someone listening to the Libera Me without focusing on the text could be forgiven for presuming that it is an operatic excerpt. The Lacrymosa section of the Dies Irae is based on music Verdi originally composed for *Don Carlo,* and in different circumstances, the Ingemisco would be a tenor show-stopper.

Verdi appears to have had an interesting insight into the Requiem: that by its nature, it describes something incomparably more dramatic than the stories of misplaced love that fill the opera stage. He responded with a score of unusual opulence, and if the solo vocal lines often have operatic contours, the choral writing is far more expansive than anything in Verdi's operatic canon. And for sheer visceral power, hardly anything in Verdi's operatic output matches the explosive writing— complete with bass drum thwacks—that punctuates the Dies Irae.

The earliest of the *Four Sacred Pieces*—the Ave Maria and the Laudi alla Vergine Maria—were composed in 1880 and 1890, between *Otello* and *Falstaff,* and were revised for their inclusion in this valedictory collection. There are glancingly operatic passages in these works, too, but for the most part Verdi seems to have felt liberated from the demands of the stage and free of stylistic constraints; his choral writing, which ranges from sublimely gentle to grandly scaled and robust, reaches backward to plainchant, and, in its surprisingly adventurous, chromatic passages, forward into the twentieth century. The effect is both poignant and powerful.

The immediate temptation is to reach for a recording, new or old, that allows one to revel in the sheer sonic grandeur of these works, and there are several worthy contenders. But there is a level of musicality in this 1964 Carlo Maria Giulini recording that has not been matched lately, and if there are places where it shows its age—in the form of tape hiss or slightly muddied textures—that seems a reasonable trade-off. (Having said that, the orchestral and choral sound here is generally fine, and the dynamics are still broad enough to blow you across the room in the Dies Irae and the Te Deum.)

Giulini does nothing to tone down the Requiem's operatic accent, nor does his excellent cast of singers—Elisabeth Schwarzkopf, Christa Ludwig, Nicolai Gedda, and Nicolai Ghiaurov, all top-drawer opera stars of the day, and in extremely good form. But as a countervailing force, Giulini and his singers bring an extra measure of elegance to the passages in which Verdi moved away from the contours of an operatic line, and where the quality of emotion required is decidedly nonoperatic. The choir, too, consistently wins admiration: in both the Requiem and the *Four Sacred Pieces,* it has the flexibility to produce both the silken pianissimo and the ferocious, full-throttle sound that Verdi demands.

Other favorites among Verdi Requiem recordings are Sir Georg Solti's broad-boned reading with the Vienna Philharmonic and the Vienna State Opera Chorus, in which Luciano Pavarotti, Joan Sutherland, Marilyn Horne, and Martti Talvela are all captured in their prime (Decca, 1968). The performance doesn't have the heart of Giulini's, but it has at least as much muscle, and in sonic terms it has the edge. It includes, however, the Requiem only, not the *Four Sacred Pieces.*

Sir John Eliot Gardiner, with a solid if less consistently starry group of soloists (Luba Orgonasova, Anne Sofie von Otter, Luca Canonici, and Alastair Miles), takes a very different approach. Using a period-instrument band, the Orchestre Révolutionnaire et Romantique, and the Monteverdi Choir, which is best known for its work in earlier music, he offers an educated guess at Verdi's balance and tempo preferences, and—the scholarly overlay notwithstanding—gives an electrifying performance, capped by a ravishing traversal of the *Four Sacred Pieces* (Philips, 1992).

52. GABRIEL FAURÉ

Requiem (1893 version, op. 48); *Cantique de Jean Racine* (op. 11); Messe Basse; *Tantum Ergo* (op. 65, no. 2); and *Ave Verum Corpus* (op. 65, no. 1)

ENGLISH CHAMBER ORCHESTRA,
MATTHEW BEST, CONDUCTING
(Hyperion CDA66292)

Mary Seers and Isabelle Poulenard, sopranos; Michael George, baritone; Corydon Singers; John Scott, organist.

Recorded 1987–1989

Given the large number of fine recordings of Gabriel Fauré's Requiem by famous conductors and soloists, this recording by Matthew Best may seem an unusual choice. But most of the starry recordings use the final version of the Requiem, completed in 1900; Best's uses an earlier, more lightly scored version that, for me, gets much closer to what Fauré had in mind when he composed this serene, sweetly melodic setting of the Requiem Mass.

Fauré (1845–1924) began work on the score in 1887, when he was choirmaster at the Madeleine, in Paris. He approached the task with ideas that had much in common with those that Brahms enshrined in his German Requiem, which was completed nineteen years earlier; indeed Fauré's attitude toward death informed the overall tenderness of the Requiem, which is in some ways a Gallic analogue of the Brahms. Like Brahms, Fauré had reservations about the traditional Requiem text, but although he made alterations to it, he did not go as far as Brahms, who jettisoned the Latin text completely in favor of scriptural passages, in German.

Specifically, Fauré agreed with Brahms that the Requiem should not focus on the fear of God's wrath. As he explained it, he regarded death, rather, as a "happy deliverance, an aspiration towards happiness above." So the Dies Irae movement that is the dramatic centerpiece of many Requiem settings is reduced, in the Fauré, to a brief passing section during the Libera Me. That placement itself is mean-ingful: the Dies Irae speaks of the final judgment as a "day of wrath," but the Libera Me asks for deliverance and eternal rest.

The first version of the Requiem included five of the eventual seven movements, and was performed at a funeral in 1888. But Fauré con-tinued to tinker with the score. He composed the Offertoire in 1889, and revived a setting of the Libera Me that he had written in 1877. Both these movements—as well as an expanded scoring that added trumpet, horn, violin, and bassoon parts—were featured in a perfor-mance in 1893. This edition of the score constitutes the second ver-sion of the Requiem, the one heard on the Best recording.

The third edition, which includes the same movements but with a further broadening of the orchestration, was undertaken for the work's first publication, in 1900. There is, however, circumstantial evi-dence that Fauré did not prepare this heftier orchestration himself, but delegated it to his student, Jean Roger-Ducasse. Presumably, he would have approved the results, but even so, one could make a case that the second version represents the most authentic edition of the piece—more complete than the original, but not as weighty as the final one.

It also includes some lovely touches that were written out of the 1900 version. Near the end of the Introit and Kyrie, a kettledrum adds empha-sis that was stripped from the final scoring. In the 1893 Sanctus, a solo violin weaves through the movement, an octave higher than the massed strings of the 1900 edition, and far more affecting. Filigree and wind doublings that thicken the textures of the final version are not heard in the 1893 score, so details that are usually buried emerge clearly.

Best and his assembled forces take the work at the brisk pace that Fauré intended, and his soloists—Mary Seers in the meltingly beauti-ful Pie Jesu, and Michael George in the Libera Me—give appropri-ately supple performances.

The performance here, originally released in a pairing with the Duruflé Requiem, has been reissued with some of Best's other Fauré recordings. The principal attraction among the other works is the magnificently tuneful *Cantique de Jean Racine,* a work for choir and organ that Fauré composed during his student years, in 1865. As in the Requiem, the Corydon Singers produce a lush, velvety sound that serves Fauré's melodic gift perfectly. There's also the attractive Messe

Basse, undertaken in 1881 and completed in 1906, and two motets (*Ave Verum Corpus* and *Tantum Ergo*) from 1894.

There is another recording of the 1893 version worth hearing. John Rutter, who has done considerable research into the evolution of the piece, made the first recording of this edition in 1985. Leading the Cambridge Singers and the City of London Sinfonia, with Carolyn Ashton and Stephen Varcoe as the vocal soloists, Rutter gets a sound that is nearly as angelic as that of Best's Corydon Singers. Like the Best recording, Rutter's performance has been reissued with recordings of Fauré's other sacred works (Collegium).

And finally, having argued the case for the 1893 version of the score, let me point out a favorite among the many recordings of the 1900 edition: Sir David Willcocks's 1967 account with the all-male Choir of King's College, Cambridge, and the New Philharmonia Orchestra (EMI Classics). Among the many attractions of this reading is the Pie Jesu, sung with great purity of tone by Robert Chilcott, a boy treble. The filler on that recording is the lilting Pavane (op. 50).

53. GUSTAV MAHLER

Symphony no. 4 in G

JUDITH RASKIN, SOPRANO; CLEVELAND ORCHESTRA,
GEORGE SZELL, CONDUCTING

Lieder eines fahrenden Gesellen
(Songs of a Wayfarer)

FREDERICA VON STADE, MEZZO-SOPRANO; LONDON
PHILHARMONIC ORCHESTRA, ANDREW DAVIS, CONDUCTING
(Sony Essential Classics SBK 46536)

Recorded 1965, 1978

It would not be quite right to say that Gustav Mahler (1860–1911) was the last great symphonist, since Jean Sibelius, Carl Nielsen, and

Dmitri Shostakovich followed him, as did Sir Edward Elgar, Ralph Vaughan Williams, and several American composers, including William Schuman, Roy Harris, and Leonard Bernstein. Lately the Finnish composer Einojuhani Rautavaara has also reinvigorated the symphony. What one can say, though, is that Mahler was for all practical purposes the last in a long line of great Austro-German symphonists, and that his music is the culmination of a tradition that had thrived since the middle of the eighteenth century, when Haydn, Mozart, and their contemporaries transformed the sinfonia from a curtain-raiser at the opera house (or for oratorios) into a form with formal and expressive ambitions of its own.

Its evolution was quick: the distance from early to late Haydn is vast, as is the distance from early to late Mozart. Beethoven took the form even farther afield, puzzling his audiences with works in which single movements were the length of whole Mozart symphonies. But Mahler stretched the symphony to its breaking point, expanding not only its duration, but also the heft of the required performing forces, and perhaps most crucially, the sheer emotional scope a listener could expect in such a work. For Mahler, the symphony was a form into which he could pour out his thoughts about destiny and mortality—or nature and creation—or in which he could work through his anguish at everything from his tenuous marriage to his increasingly poor health.

He had his champions in his day, among them Leopold Stokowski, who introduced several of Mahler's works to American audiences; the Dutch conductor Willem Mengelberg, who Mahler considered the greatest of his interpreters; and Bruno Walter, whose pioneering 1938 recording of the Ninth is a landmark in the history of Mahler on disc, as are the recordings he made between the late 1940s and early 1960s.

Of course, Mahler was a conductor himself (among his handful of posts were directorships of opera houses and orchestras in Kassel, Prague, Budapest, Leipzig, Hamburg, Vienna, and New York; he was the music director of the New York Philharmonic at the time of his death), and his understanding of the orchestra and its capabilities was phenomenal.

After his death, however, Mahler's star dimmed, and for several decades his works were rarities in the concert hall, let alone on disc. Although conductors like Walter continued to perform Mahler, it took until the 1960s for many others to rediscover the blend of power and sensuousness that his music offers, and to come to terms with the technical demands of large-scale works that require the agility to move quickly between thunderous choral and orchestral climaxes and passages couched in intense, heavenly pianissimos. When George Szell made this recording of the Fourth—still one of the most eloquent Mahler performances on disc—there were only a few recordings of the work to be found; now there are dozens.

Audiences, too, needed time to meet Mahler on his own terms. The decades between his death in 1911 and the revival that began in the 1960s—and which required another twenty years before Mahler's works were nearly as commonplace in the concert hall as Beethoven's—were a time when modern sensibilities rejected Mahler's ultraromanticism as overblown, ponderous, and self-indulgent. It was the opposite of Igor Stravinsky's or Pierre Boulez's extreme rationalism, on the one hand, and of the equally modern fascination with scaled-down, vibrato-less performances of Renaissance and baroque music on the other.

In the context of Mahler's full symphonic canon, the Fourth Symphony is actually relatively light. The entire work runs under an hour: of Mahler's symphonies, only the First is similarly brief. And after the Second and Third, which dealt with the resurrection of the soul and the creation of the universe, the Fourth offers a comparatively joyous, naïve view of Heaven, seen through a child's eyes (by way of a text from *Des Knaben Wunderhorn,* a collection of German folk poetry published in the early nineteenth century, from which Mahler drew for other works as well).

Mahler may have been drawn to this collection in part because the status of its component works as folk poetry gave him the freedom to do some literary reconstruction—something he could not have done with, say, the poetry of Goethe. That said, masterpiece status never daunted Mahler when he thought a work needed retouching. As a conductor, he regularly led his own reorchestrations of works by Bach, Beethoven, and others regarded (even in Mahler's day) as untouchable. His versions of these scores (among them the Beethoven Ninth Symphony and a collection of movements from the Bach Orchestral Suites) have been recorded in recent years and offer an illuminating look at Mahler's coloristic imagination, as applied to otherwise familiar music.

Of course, his own works also provide an ample view. The Fourth Symphony was composed in 1899 and 1900, but it has musical links with an 1892 song, "Wir geniessen die himmlischen Freuden" (We Enjoy Heaven's Delights), which was inspired by one of the *Knaben Wunderhorn* poems, "Der Himmel hängt voll Geigen" (Heaven is Full of Fiddles). It also shares some musical material with another of Mahler's *Wunderhorn* settings, "Es sungen drei Engel" (Three Angels Sang), which was used in the fifth movement of the gargantuan Third Symphony—and, indeed, Mahler considered using "Wir geniessen" as the basis of that work's finale, but decided in the end to hold it back for the Fourth.

Mahler's description of his intentions here, as quoted in Willi Reich's 1958 compilation, *Gustav Mahler in His Own Words—In the Words of His Friends,* is quite direct:

"In the three first movements, there reigns the serenity of a higher realm, a realm strange to us, oddly frightening, even terrifying. In the finale, the child, which in its previous existence already belonged to this higher realm, tells us what it all means." About this last movement, he added that he envisioned "a heaven of undifferentiated blue, which is much harder to suggest than changing, contrasting hues." As in the early movements, Mahler finds a measure of terror within this beauty, "just as on the most beautiful day, when the woods are drenched in sunlight, one is often suddenly gripped by a panic fear." (That alone tells us a lot about Mahler's worldview, and explains much of what one hears in his later symphonies.)

Mahler translates this vision wholesale into music. He opens with a chirping flute figure, supported by sleigh bells, a gesture that returns to demarcate structural elements of the opening movement, and is echoed, in altered form, later in the work as well. The second movement, or much of it, has the character of a relaxed Viennese country dance; yet there is a darker side, a jaunty fiddle figure, introduced at the very start, which Mahler said represented "Death the Fiddler." The third movement is an Adagio of sublime beauty, the longest movement here at over twenty minutes. But the centerpiece is the finale, which begins with a gently innocent clarinet theme that anticipates the opening of the soprano line and becomes the natural focus of the movement, although the return of the symphony's opening figure between several of the verses helps give the work a sense of cyclical completion.

Szell's recording, an ear-opener in its day, presents an interpretive vision that respects the sweep of Mahler's structure as well as the composer's impulse toward a blossoming, organic flow of rhythms. This last aspect is brought to life by the suppleness of Szell's conducting—not only an ebb and flow in dynamics, but also a truly expressive rubato that is executed with extraordinary precision by the Cleveland players.

The first two movements convey the spirit of the dance, as well as the dark shadows that are never far from Mahler, and the Adagio is breathtaking in both the time-expanding serenity of its beginning and end, and the passionate, high-anxiety episodes that erupt along the way. And in the finale, Judith Raskin sings the evocative text with all the childlike innocence and ecstasy it demands.

I generally dislike discs that bring together disparate performances—recordings by different conductors and orchestras—but Sony's compilation here is quite pleasing. Filling out the disc is a 1978 account of the *Lieder eines fahrenden Gesellen*. Mahler wrote this cycle between 1883 and 1885, the two years he spent conducting opera and symphonic concerts in Kassel. After an unhappy romance with one of the sopranos, Johanna Richter, Mahler wrote a cycle of six love poems, four of which are included in this work. Though a much shorter composition, there is a clear connection with Schubert's *Winterreise*—particularly in the final song, which recalls some of the imagery of the Schubert cycle, including the nocturnal departure and the linden tree. Frederica von Stade, at her youthful best in this recording, evokes the sense of worldweariness and disappointment already captured so persuasively by a twenty-five-year-old composer who would spend much of his life transforming those emotions into sound.

54. GUSTAV MAHLER

Symphony no. 9

BERLIN PHILHARMONIC,
LEONARD BERNSTEIN, CONDUCTING
(Deutsche Grammophon 435 378-2)

Recorded 1979

If the Fourth Symphony offers a vision of Heaven, the vast sonic canvas of the Ninth offers a look at life and death in the here and now, with extremes of elation and despair transformed into musical topography. Put more grandly, it is about mortality and the vain struggle to defeat it. It is confessional music, music of existential anguish, as much of Mahler's symphonic canon is.

Because that canon's range of gestures is so extreme, it lends itself to some peculiar exegesis. Read enough essays on Mahler's music and you'll encounter theories, advanced seriously, suggesting that Mahler's symphonies embody prophecies of the two world wars, racial strife, and other calamities that have befallen the world since his death in 1911. (Those particular prophecies are cited in a scholarly essay published in the score of the Sixth Symphony.) It is as if the music's tragic scope is too great to be merely autobiographical.

But Mahler had reason to think autobiographically in the grandest terms. The Ninth was started in 1908 and completed in 1909, a period immediately following a number of personal tragedies, among them the death of his daughter from scarlet fever and diphtheria; his resignation, under pressure, from the directorship of the Vienna Opera; and the discovery of a valve defect in his heart. Added to all this was a measure of despair about the deteriorating relationship with his wife, Alma, although it was not until after the work was finished, and Mahler was sketching his Tenth Symphony, that he discovered that Alma had begun conducting an affair with the architect Walter Gropius (whom she married after Mahler's death).

There is a degree to which Mahler's last three big works—the orchestral song cycle *Das Lied von der Erde,* and the Ninth and Tenth

---

Symphonies—can be seen as a trilogy, with *Das Lied* recalling the joys of youth, but also seesawing between vibrancy and intense pessimism; the Ninth fighting off the specter of death during its first three movements, and then succumbing to gradual but inevitable dissolution in the extraordinary closing Adagio; and the Tenth (which he completed sketching but did not live to orchestrate) conveying an acceptance of fate.

Mahler's symphonies are susceptible to several seemingly contradictory interpretive approaches. One school of thought that seems to be gaining currency is to set Mahler's emotionalism to one side, and to focus instead on the structural beauty and ingenuity of the music— on Mahler's artistic insight, in other words, rather than the heart on his sleeve. The music's emotional weight will, in any case, emerge naturally from a committed, well-played performance.

But while it can work—Pierre Boulez, Klaus Tennstedt, and Simon Rattle have made fine, even spectacular Mahler recordings in this style—there is something to be said for the more traditional approach. This was Leonard Bernstein's métier: Mahler's emotionalism dovetailed perfectly with his own extroverted and equally emotive conducting style, and that confluence served both Bernstein and Mahler well when Bernstein began his campaign to restore Mahler to the repertory during the 1960s.

His complete traversals of the Mahler symphony cycle, filled out with vocal works, for both Sony Classical (recorded in the 1960s and 1970s) and Deutsche Grammophon (recorded in the 1970s and 1980s) should be heard by anyone wishing to be drawn into Mahler's world. The earlier set has more fully attained classic status—it was, for many listeners, an introduction to Mahler and an impetus to trace the Mahler tradition back through the recordings of Bruno Walter and Willem Mengelberg.

But the Deutsche Grammophon recordings are not merely sonic upgrades. Bernstein continually reconsidered these works, searching for new ways to illuminate what he called the "yin-yang" of Mahler— the embrace of both life and death in his works. The solutions he arrived at in the 1980s include more expansive tempos in slow movements—which he had the technique to sustain without letting the music become diffuse—and sharper, more overtly temperamental shaping of brisker movements like the Rondo-Burleske of the Ninth.

Even in his early recordings, Bernstein was able to make Mahler's music thunder, and dance, and scream defiantly, and collapse in exhaustion; the later accounts magnify those effects. There may be a technical reason, apart from Bernstein's own growth: by the time he made his second cycle, Bernstein was recording exclusively in concert, a process that he believed yielded more electrifying results than the start-and-stop techniques of studio recordings. (His concession to the need for perfection on recordings was editing between takes of multiple performances, and recording the endings of works during rehearsals in order to have the performances followed by silence rather than applause.)

As it happened, Deutsche Grammophon issued two live recordings

Composer Gustav Mahler

of the Ninth: a 1985 version with the Royal Concertgebouw Orchestra of Amsterdam, and this Berlin recording, taped in 1979 but not released until 1992, two years after Bernstein's death. The Amsterdam version has many glories, including a finale that is truly wrenching. But I find the Berlin version, Bernstein's only recording with this orchestra, preferable for its tautness and precision, which in some cases—in the finale, for example—are the products of his notably zestier tempos. Both convey the sense of crisis and sheer physical breakdown that Mahler wrote into these pages. The Berlin version, though, adds a greater sense of urgency.

55. JEAN SIBELIUS

Symphony no. 2 (op. 43)

ROYAL PHILHARMONIC,
SIR JOHN BARBIROLLI, CONDUCTING
(Chesky CD-3)

Recorded 1962

The wave of musical nationalism that crested throughout Europe in the nineteenth century came late to Finland, but when it came, it played an important part in the drive to establish Finland itself as an independent nation with a culture of its own. Finland had been ruled by Sweden from the twelfth century until the early nineteenth century, and thereafter was an autonomous province of Russia. Culturally, the country was bifurcated, with the elite class speaking Swedish and the rustics speaking Finnish.

Jean Sibelius (1865–1957) was born into a Swedish-speaking family, but he began learning Finnish in the 1870s. He immersed himself in it more fully in the 1890s, when he became engaged to Aino Järnefelt, whose family was vehemently pro-Finnish and involved in the movement to make Finnish the country's official language. There were early detours, however: having studied composition in Helsinki with the composer Ferruccio Busoni, he left Finland for studies in Berlin in 1889, and Vienna from 1890 to 1891.

Away from home, Sibelius immersed himself in Finnish folklore, particularly the Kalevala, Finland's great national poem, which embodied everything from the story of creation to the exploits of ancient gods and heroes. By the time he was ready to return, he had sketched out plans to transform some of this into a distinctively Finnish music. What would be Finnish about it was its sound and spirit: he had no desire to weave folk melodies into his works—although folk music greatly interested him, and he studied it seriously—but to draw his themes from the same collective unconscious that gave those melodies their character.

In the nearly four decades that followed, he would attain that goal fully. His seven symphonies, violin concerto, and tone poems became the heart of a Finnish style that has continued to thrive.

Sibelius began work on the Second Symphony during a visit to Italy in February 1901, and he completed it in Finland eleven months later. When it was new, tensions were running high between Finland and Russia, and between political factions within Finland itself, and it wasn't long after its premiere that the Second was adopted as a musical declaration of Finnish nationalism. It's easy to see why. To glance at just two examples, the tense theme that makes its way speedily through the full range of strings can easily be heard as evoking turmoil, and the grandly stated theme of the finale, presented in the strings with its fantastic wind and brass punctuation and heard with blazing brass support in the work's closing pages, can be heard as a triumphant hymn of Finnish unity.

But the composer himself discouraged such programmatic notions, and his diary from the 1901 Italian visit suggests that the idea that inspired the Second Symphony's genesis was something else entirely: he describes a dream about the scene from the legend of Don Juan in which the Stone Guest arrives, and Sibelius—as the Don—realizes that the Guest is Death. On the back of the page is a musical sketch for what became the principal theme of the Second Symphony's slow movement. Later during the compositional process, he associated the same movement alternately with Christian imagery and with Dante's *Divine Comedy*.

Given all that, listeners can make their own associations with relative impunity. I tend to hear this music in the context of Sibelius's vaunted love of nature, full of string writing that evokes an icy shimmer and bluish, wintry hues, as well as a more robust, full orchestra scoring that creates windswept panoramas and distant thunder.

Curiously, Sibelius's music found some of its most enthusiastic champions in England, among conductors with no links to Finland whatsoever—among them Sir Thomas Beecham, Sir John Barbirolli, and Sir Colin Davis. He has had American champions as well, most notably Leonard Bernstein and Lorin Maazel.

All of them made superb Sibelius recordings that have turned generations on to the composer's work. But this account of the Second Symphony by Sir John Barbirolli has a fluidity of balances and tempos that helps reveal the full grandeur of the score. Barbirolli's relationship with the work and its composer go way back; he recorded it no fewer than four times, starting with a New York Philharmonic performance in 1940, then one with the Hallé Orchestra, in England, in 1952. This recording, originally for RCA, was his third, and he returned to the work in 1966 for another recording with the Hallé.

The principal strength of Barbirolli's Royal Philharmonic performance is a flexibility that allows for both nuance and raw power, two qualities necessary to bring out the almost visceral beauty of this work. The orchestra responds with perfect unanimity, and the recording itself, now more than forty years old, sounds magnificent, thanks to careful mastering by Chesky, a label that was started in the mid-1980s, and made its name by restoring to the active catalog a number of long-unavailable RCA recordings that were sought by collectors, but that RCA didn't consider worth the effort.

Interestingly, another label specializing in historical restoration, Dutton Laboratories, has Barbirolli's 1940 New York Philharmonic recording of the Second, along with the 1946 account of the Sibelius Violin Concerto, with the French violinist Ginette Neveu as the soloist, and Walter Süsskind leading the Philharmonia Orchestra. These were 78 rpm mono recordings, but Dutton's CD transfers bring a great deal of sonic breadth out of these antique discs. The Second Symphony performance is a bit more energetic and rough-hewn than the 1962 version, but it captures the start of Barbirolli's evolving relationship with the work—as well as a sense of the New York Philharmonic's sound during his time as its music director.

The Violin Concerto is a treat as well: Neveu was twenty-seven years old and a rising star when she made this recording, and her performance captures the aching passion and lyricism that have made this 1905 work one of the most widely loved twentieth-century concertos. Tragically, she was killed in a plane crash en route to an American tour in 1949.

56. LEOŠ JANÁČEK

String Quartet no. 1, *The Kreutzer Sonata;* and String Quartet no. 2, *Intimate Letters*

ALBAN BERG

Lyric Suite

JUILLIARD STRING QUARTET
(Sony Classical SK 66840)

Recorded 1995

Leoš Janáček (1854–1928) was Dvořák's successor as the great Czech composer of his age, and just as Dvořák claimed a place for the Czech style in the international chamber and symphonic repertories, Janáček focused his efforts principally on opera, writing a string of remarkably original works that have been performed with increasing frequency in recent decades. But Janáček was also one of the great individualists of early-twentieth-century orchestral and chamber music, a colorful composer who participated in the era's decisive drift away from the constrictions of tonality and conventional structure, yet adhered to none of the major stylistic schools.

The relatively homogenous textures of the quartets may do less justice to Janáček's sense of color than the orchestral Sinfonietta and *Taras Bulba,* the *Glagolitic* Mass, or some of the mixed-timbre chamber pieces. Nevertheless, these are irresistibly passionate scores, and in them, Janáček brings his operatic sensibilities to bear in fighting the homogeneity of the format.

Moreover, the Juilliard Quartet brought the two works together with Alban Berg's *Lyric Suite* in a touch of brilliant programming rare in the world of classical recordings. The three works share an interesting and unusual bond. Taken at face value—that is, for their musical qualities alone—all three are ear-grabbing, powerful, innovative pieces. Yet each also has a secret subtext that became clear years after the works were composed and first performed, when the composers' letters and annotated scores came to light.

Janáček's first quartet, composed in 1923, was inspired by "The Kreutzer Sonata," Tolstoy's short story about an unhappy marriage, but instead of offering a musical condensation of the narrative, Janáček focuses on the story's dark psychological mood. Both harmonically and in his use of recurring episodes of harsh, fleet *sul ponticello* playing—an eerie effect accomplished by bowing close to the bridge—Janáček's tense score conveys the desperation in Tolstoy's story in the most gripping way. Janáček, working at a white-hot pace, completed the work in less than a month.

The subtext? Since 1917, Janáček had been in love with Kamila Stösslová, the young, unhappily married wife of an antiques dealer whom Janáček and his own wife met during a vacation that year. The two couples cultivated a friendship during Janáček's final decade, but Janáček also pursued a correspondence of his own with Kamila, of which some seven hundred letters survive to document the considerable effect she had on his creative life. Fantasy visions of Kamila lay behind the role of the seductive gypsy in *The Diary of One Who Disappeared,* as well as the heroines of operas as diverse (and generally tragic) as *Kát'a Kabanová, The Cunning Little Vixen,* and *The Makropolos Affair.* And when he read Tolstoy's "Kreutzer Sonata," he imagined her in that context as well.

This was, to a great extent, a one-sided love affair, an aging composer's ardor for a woman who was nearly forty years his junior, and who was able, for a decade, to keep the relationship from becoming too complicated. In the spring of 1927, that changed, at least to the extent that, during a series of woodland walks, the relationship between Janáček and Kamila grew more intense. Even so, it had its limits: Janáček described their connection as entirely spiritual, and it was still some time before they actually kissed for the first time.

Nevertheless, in January 1928 Janáček resolved to celebrate their relationship in a new string quartet, which he at first called *Love Letters,* but eventually changed to the slightly more reserved *Intimate Letters.* Janáček's letters give two explanations of the work. To Kamila, he wrote that "our life is going to be in it," starting with "my impression when I saw you for the first time." To his friend, the writer and editor Max Brod, he described the work as a declaration that Kamila had been his principal inspiration, but added that "we both look to clearing ourselves of the charge of a relationship other than our purely spiritual one."

Like the first quartet, *Intimate Letters* was completed in a matter of weeks, and it burns with all the intensity that Janáček promised. And yet, the vigorous, at times even frenzied, last movement ends with a mysterious inconclusiveness, on a chord that the ear expects to resolve, but which merely hangs in the air.

Alban Berg and his music will be discussed more fully later, but his six-movement *Lyric Suite,* composed in 1925, is every bit as fiery as the two Janáček works, for what turns out to be a similar reason. For more than fifty years, the work was revered as an early example of the expressivity that Berg was able to impose on works composed using the twelve-tone method pioneered by his teacher, Arnold Schoenberg. Listeners admired certain structural niceties—the fact that each movement quotes the one before it, with the sixth also pointing back to the first, for example, or the alternation of fast and slow movements that pull in opposite directions, with the fast movements increasing in speed and intensity from the Allegretto gioviale opening movement to the penultimate Presto delirando, while the slow movements ratchet down from an Andante amoroso second movement to the Largo desolato finale.

Those titles suggested that Berg had a program in mind, but it was not clear exactly what it was until 1976, when the composer George Perle discovered Berg's annotated score, a document that provided a complete key. The work, it turns out, is a record of a love affair between Berg and Hanna Fuchs-Robettin during the 1920s. Both Berg and his paramour were married, and the affair was doomed, a circumstance documented in the pained finale. But the work also portrays Berg's excitement at their meeting, in the opening Allegretto gioviale, and their mutual expression of love (in the Allegro mistoerioso—Trio estatico). He also transformed their initials into a thematic figure—A B-flat B F, using the German nomenclature in which B is B-flat and H is B.

The Juilliard Quartet was a year shy of its fiftieth anniversary when it made this disc, although at the time the only remaining player from the original lineup was the first violinist, Robert Mann (who retired in 1997). Its sound, at this time, was rich and rounded in the middle and lower registers, offset at times by a sometimes strident edge at the top. That sound suits these pieces, which are about passion—complete with its dangers and disappointments—rather than unmitigated beauty. More to the point, the Juilliard players bring to these performances a depth of experience that yields truly wrenching interpretations.

The influence this ensemble has had on chamber music performance standards cannot be overstated. Vigorous and at times even aggressive when the music invites that quality (as sections of these three pieces do), the Juilliard's performances have always shown that the conveying of explosive emotion is not at all incompatible with ensemble precision. And because the group teaches at the New York conservatory for which it is named, several generations of quartets—from the Tokyo to the Emerson and beyond—have adopted the Juilliard's streamlined approach. The Juilliard's discography is vast, and although Sony Classical has not kept its greatest discs in print, the group's recordings of the quartets by Beethoven, Schubert, Brahms, Debussy, and Elliott Carter, among others, are worth seeking out.

57. CLAUDE DEBUSSY

La Mer, Jeux, Le Martyre de Saint Sébastien
(orchestral fragments), *Prélude à l'après-midi d'un*
faune, Images, Nocturnes, **and** *Printemps*

MONTREAL SYMPHONY ORCHESTRA,
CHARLES DUTOIT, CONDUCTING

(Decca 460 217, two CDs)

Recorded 1988, 1989, 1994

It's probably no wonder that Claude Debussy (1862–1918) always hated hearing his music described as impressionistic. The first documented use of the term was in a letter from the judges at the Institut des Beaux Arts, responding to *Printemps,* a two-movement symphonic suite he composed in 1887 during his two-year stay in Italy as a winner of the Prix de Rome. They hated the work, and cautioned him to avoid "this vague impressionism, which is one of the most dangerous enemies of truth in works of art."

There was a more philosophical reason, as well. At the time it became current as a way to describe Debussy's work, impressionism referred to a school of French painting that included Monet, Manet, Renoir, Cézanne, and Degas—and even in that application, its use was at first pejorative. But Debussy's nonmusical interests brought him closer to the symbolist poets than to the impressionist painters, and if his work had to bear a label, he undoubtedly would have preferred one in that spirit.

Like all such labels, impressionism is shorthand, and whatever Debussy's objections, it is useful: it places his music in historical perspective and concisely describes music that is awash in painterly chromaticism and largely liberated from the strictures of classical form. But a label is also a crude tool, and one has to look beyond it to hear the exceptions as well as the rules implicit in its definition. Works like *La Mer* and the *Prélude à l'après-midi d'un faune,* for example, are often adduced as impressionistic masterpieces, but they can also be heard in a very different way—not as the musical equivalent of the hazy pointillism of impressionistic art, but as works with subtle gradations of color and texture that yield an almost photographic clarity. This is, of course, exactly the opposite of impressionism, as the term is commonly understood.

The Swiss conductor Charles Dutoit made a specialty of French music during his years as music director of the Montreal Symphony, and he made dozens of superb recordings with that orchestra in a tenure that lasted from 1977 to 2002, when they parted ways in a public clash of temperament, ego, and power (on both sides) that left everyone, including listeners, on the losing end. So it goes in the supposedly placid classical music world.

These recordings from better days are among Dutoit's finest, and they offer a good overview of the Debussy orchestral canon, including the unjustly maligned *Printemps,* a minor but charming work. Debussy was quoted as saying, "I have made mysterious nature my religion," and one can hear that reverence for the natural world in Dutoit's readings of these precisely nuanced pieces. The *Prélude à l'après-midi d'un faune* (1894) mythologizes nature somewhat, suggesting the fantasies of a faun, falling asleep on a hot afternoon after chasing nymphs and naiads.

The three *Nocturnes* (1897–1899) are more abstract studies of the play of light in the sky—on clouds, on dust, and as a backdrop to the song of the Sirens. And the masterpiece of Debussy's nature series, the three-movement *La Mer* (1905), is as vivid an evocation of the ocean's grandeur as you will hear in music. Dutoit's performance has the power and shimmer to make Debussy's seascape seem three-dimensional and, as in all of these readings, he offers that photographic sharpness that makes one reconsider the parameters of impressionism.

Not all the pieces are nature works, of course. The heart of *Images* (1906–1912) is *Ibéria,* a set of three snapshots of Spain, complete with flamenco rhythms and the atmosphere of the Mediterranean night, all filtered through Debussy's idiosyncratic harmonic prism. Included as well are two late-stage works—the ballet *Jeux* (1913), and sections of Debussy's incidental score for *Le Martyre de Saint Sébastien,* a play by the Italian poet and novelist Gabriele D'Annunzio that was controversial in its day for its linkage of Christian,

Composer Claude Debussy

pagan, and erotic imagery, and because Saint Sebastian was portrayed by a female dancer (Ida Rubinstein, who commissioned the work). D'Annunzio protested that, peculiar as parts of his play were, it sprung from deeply felt religious feelings, and Debussy's music—often haunting, sometimes devotional, sometimes ecstatic—testifies on the playwright's behalf.

58. CLAUDE DEBUSSY

Preludes, Books I and II

PAUL JACOBS, PIANIST
(Nonesuch 9 73031-2, two CDs)

Recorded 1978

For most listeners, the aural image that comes most immediately to mind when impressionism is mentioned is of a rich orchestral fabric, harmonically ambiguous, full of the shimmer, sweep, and pastel coloration of strings, harp, and winds, all carefully balanced in the service of a textured, naturalistic depiction or an uncanny evocation of atmosphere. But the orchestral palette was hardly necessary to Debussy: some of his most enduringly pictorial works are for the solo piano.

These twenty-four preludes—twelve each in Book I (1910) and Book II (1913)—cover a vast expanse of descriptive ground, from the "sad, icy, limitless landscape" (to use Debussy's own words) of *Des pas sur la neige* (Footprints in the Snow) and the Gothic grandeur of *La Cathédrale engloutie* (The Sunken Cathedral) to the sweet innocence of *La Fille aux cheveux de lin* (The Girl with the Flaxen Hair), the picaresque *General Lavine—Eccentric,* and the dazzling *Feux d'artifice* (Fireworks).

These pieces make heavy demands on a pianist's technique and imagination. Technically, their textures seem to require more than ten fingers, and if that is to a large extent an illusion of Debussy's language, it takes great speed and agility to produce it. It also calls for imagination. Debussy's titles, as well as some of the descriptive language in the scores themselves, are meant to suggest interpretive goals for a pianist.

There is a caveat: Debussy inscribed his titles at the ends of his pieces, rather than at the top, a move that has led more than a few commentators to wonder whether he wanted the music to be locked to these images, or, as Paul Jacobs has suggested, whether the music inspired the titles rather than the reverse. That may be the case for some of these pieces—*La Fille aux cheveux de lin,* for example. But it's difficult to imagine that he didn't begin writing *Ondine* (his portrait of a water sprite), or *Hommage à S. Pickwick Esq. P.P.M. P.C.* (a portrait of an English gentleman, with its opening quotation from *God Save the King*), without those specific images in mind.

For the many listeners who regard Walter Gieseking's 1953–1954 EMI recordings as the supreme readings of these pieces, Jacobs may seem a peculiar choice. Gieseking's performances are incomparable, and they should be heard. But what I admire in the Jacobs recordings is a flexibility in both tempo and rhythm that lets these familiar pieces stake out fresh ground, and a carefully calibrated balance between the music's Gallic coolness and the joy of adventurous exploration. Jacobs had a wonderful ear for Debussy's coloration and textural weight. While there is great delicacy in some of his readings—*Les sons et les parfums tournent dans l'air du soir* (Sounds and Perfume Swirl in the Evening Air) and *La Cathédrale engloutie* are good examples—often his playing has an almost orchestral power.

Jacobs was born in New York in 1930, studied at the Juilliard School, and might have fallen into a conventional soloist's career. But the mainstream romantic repertory didn't excite him as much as contemporary and baroque music. He pursued these specialties in Europe from 1951 to 1960; in fact, he was the first to perform Arnold Schoenberg's complete piano music (works he later recorded) in Paris. When he returned to New York, he became the pianist and harpsichordist of the New York Philharmonic, and was an important presence in New York's musical life, both as a cultural gadfly and as an eloquent champion of new works.

Jacobs died at age fifty-three in 1983, one of the first prominent musicians to die of AIDS. Other pianists have, of course, taken up the new music banner, but for listeners who knew Jacobs's work with the Philharmonic and various new music ensembles—and also as a recitalist—his presence is still missed.

He did, however, leave behind a series of superb recordings on the Nonesuch label, including more Debussy (the Etudes, *Estampes,* and *Images*), the complete Schoenberg piano music, and chamber and solo works by Elliott Carter. A compilation of concert performances from the 1970s, released in 2001 by Arbiter, a label that specializes in historical recordings, includes illuminating accounts of works by Ferruccio Busoni, Manuel de Falla, and Maurice Ravel, as well as a performance of a Chaconne by Chambonnières played on the harpsichord, and an incendiary account of Beethoven's *Waldstein* Sonata.

59. MAURICE RAVEL

The Orchestral Works

NEW YORK PHILHARMONIC AND CLEVELAND ORCHESTRA,
PIERRE BOULEZ, CONDUCTING
(Sony Classical SM3K 45842, three CDs)

Includes Menuet Antique; La Valse; Daphnis et Chloé *(complete ballet);* Shéhérazade: *Ouverture de Féerie;* Valses Nobles et Sentimentales; Ma Mère L'Oye *(complete ballet);* Fanfare pour L'Eventail de Jeanne; Le Tombeau de Couperin; Une Barque sur l'Océan; Bolero; Rapsodie Espagnole; Alborada del Gracioso; *Concerto for the Left Hand;* Pavane pour une Infante Défunte. *Philippe Entrement, pianist (Concerto for the Left Hand); Camerata Singers* (Daphnis et Chloé); *New York Philharmonic (*Menuet Antique *through* Bolero), *and Cleveland Orchestra (*Rapsodie Espagnole *through* Pavane pour une Infante Défunte), *Pierre Boulez, conducting.*

Recorded 1972–1983

The forces of historical concision have swept Debussy and his younger compatriot, Maurice Ravel (1875–1937), into the same stylistic corner, where they have become the twin pillars of impressionism. And there are works in which their commonalities are undeniable: Ravel's *Daphnis et Chloé* and *Une Barque sur l'Océan,* for example, certainly breathe the same air as Debussy's carefully shaded, assertively pictorial orchestral scores. But each had a distinct musical personality, and the musical interests that animated their work pushed their scores in different directions.

Ravel's works are a virtual catalog of his varied musical interests; in fact, just about the only one not represented in this set is jazz, the influence of which can be felt in some of his chamber music (the Violin Sonata, for example) and in the Piano Concerto in G, the one significant orchestral work not included here. Still, the collection affords a fairly comprehensive overview of what Ravel had on his mind.

There is, for example, his love for the musical past, which he studied assiduously, and which informed works like the graceful *Menuet Antique*, the sweetly turned *Pavane pour une Infante Défunte* (Pavane for a Dead Princess) and especially *Le Tombeau de Couperin*, a baroque suite in modern harmonic garb. Each of these pieces is rooted in the rhythms and structures of seventeenth-century dance movements, and in that regard they edge toward another of Ravel's interests— dance itself. Several of the pieces here—including the two most colorful works in the set, *Daphnis et Chloé* and *Ma Mère L'Oye* (Mother Goose)—were written for the ballet stage.

But whether for the stage or the concert hall, the idea of movement inspired Ravel. Witness *La Valse*, an evocation of the Viennese waltz, in all its swirling grandeur, as well as the *Valses Nobles et Sentimentales*, another, more variegated examination of the same dance, and of course *Bolero*, a work commissioned by the dancer Ida Rubinstein, and driven by the insistent rhythm of the flamenco dance.

Bolero points to yet another of Ravel's consistent points of reference: Spain. The fact that his mother was Basque gave Ravel a connection to Spain, and he had others, including his friendship with the Spanish pianist Ricardo Viñes. Oddly, he did not visit Spain until 1924, some seventeen years after he wrote the *Rapsodie Espagnole*, his first important orchestral score. Here, and in *Alborada del Gracioso*— originally written for piano in 1905, and later orchestrated—he drew on distinctly Iberian rhythms and melodies, and imitated the sound of the guitar, creating an effect that even the great Spanish nationalist composer, Manuel de Falla, described as having a subtle authenticity.

Ravel's Spanish works also reflect an attraction to a Mediterranean exoticism, of which one hears another hint in the *Shéhérazade*

Overture, a surviving fragment of an opera Ravel began and abandoned in 1898 (unrelated to the alluring song cycle he composed less than a decade later under the same title).

Ravel explored orchestration as an art entirely separate from composition. *Bolero,* after all, would be almost nothing but a repeating, proto-minimalist rhythmic figure if not for Ravel's methodical introduction of every sonority a modern orchestra is capable of producing, presented in a logical, gradually expanding sequence. And quite a few of the pieces here—*Pavane pour une Infante Défunte, Alborado del Gracioso, Une Barque sur l'Océan,* the *Valses Nobles et Sentimentales,* and the *Tombeau de Couperin*—began life as solo piano works. They remain quite appealing in that form, but in every case, Ravel's mastery of orchestral timbre makes them into grander, more three-dimensional works.

Pierre Boulez's appreciation of that aspect of Ravel, and his feeling for the composer's varied concerns, made his recordings some of the most brilliantly characterized interpretations of the late twentieth century. It is difficult, in fact, to reconcile the reputation for cold braininess that haunted Boulez during his tenure as music director of the New York Philharmonic with the lushness, warmth, and energy of—to cite one notable example—his reading of *La Valse.*

The centerpiece of this set, though, is his account of *Daphnis et Chloé.* Composed for Sergei Diaghilev's Ballets Russes in 1910, the work is a tale of shepherds, nymphs, marauding pirates, and the ancient god Pan, based on a pastoral story by the Greek poet Longus. Ravel gave it some of his most tantalizingly picturesque music—indeed, some of the most purely sensuous music in all of the classical repertory. Boulez, with the New York Philharmonic and the Camerata Singers, registers every movement, shudder, and sigh that Ravel and the choreographer Mikhail Fokine hoped to suggest, and the transfer to CD has benefited this classic recording enormously in matters of clarity, timbre, and dynamic heft.

60. ERIK SATIE

L'Oeuvre pour Piano (The Piano Works)

ALDO CICCOLINI, PIANIST

(EMI Classics, 7243 574534 2 4, five CDs)

Recorded 1966–1971

or

Oeuvres pour Piano (Piano Works)

ALDO CICCOLINI, PIANIST

(EMI Classics CDZB 67282 2, two CDs)

Recorded 1966–1971

The Italian-born, Paris-based pianist Aldo Ciccolini has had a distinguished career as an interpreter of both the French impressionists and the great nineteenth-century Viennese composers, but his best-known and most durably endearing recordings are the series of LPs he devoted to the music of Erik Satie (1866–1925). EMI has reissued the set on CD both in its complete form and in a two-disc survey (note the fine distinction in the French title) that covers many of the highlights. I have listed both sets above; the specific pieces noted below are included in both editions.

Satie was one of music's true original spirits, a composer who stood to the side of every serious school of thought about music current in his day, and wrote what pleased him, rules and stylistic conventions notwithstanding. To a great extent, what pleased Satie was simplicity: much of his music is about stripping away complexity and letting a harmonic, melodic, or rhythmic idea sing out directly. He is unquestionably an odd duck among the composers in this book, yet he is also emblematic both of his time and place—Paris in the years surrounding World War I—and of the lighter, more iconoclastic spirit of the avant-garde. It is no accident that John Cage, one of the greatest musical provocateurs of the mid-twentieth century, declared Satie central to the history of twentieth-century music.

He had a slow start. As a student at the Paris Conservatoire in the mid-1880s, he was described as incomparably lazy, a gifted pianist who rarely bothered to practice. His teacher, Georges Mathias, called him "worthless." Satie's friend and collaborator on songs and theater pieces, the poet Contamine de Latour, asserted that the young composer remained at the Conservatoire only because his student status reduced his compulsory military service to one year from five, and Satie managed to shorten even that term by deliberately contracting bronchitis.

When he set out on his career, in 1887, he quickly settled into Paris's bohemian life, spending much of his time in cabarets, including the Chat Noir, where he conducted an ensemble that accompanied shadow theater, and the Auberge de Clou, where he worked as a pianist and met Claude Debussy, with whom he maintained a quarter-century friendship. Some of the works he composed at this time—including his most famous piano pieces, the sweetly lilting *Gymnopédies*—are sober, direct, and slightly melancholy, with the simplest harmonies supporting their graceful melodies.

The early 1890s, though, found Satie exploring new terrain: under the influence of Joséphin Péladan, he became interested in religious mysticism, and became the resident composer for the Rosicrucian Salons over which Péladan presided. Among the works this involvement yielded are *Le Fils des Étoiles* and the *Première pensée et sonneries de la Rose+Croix*, in which he pursued a peculiar form of harmonic stasis built largely on repeated, tolling chords. It is fairly dour by Satie's standards, but he did not linger long in this byway: he broke with Péladan and, for two years, was the founder and sole member of his own religion, the Église Métropolitaine d'Art de Jésus Conducteur.

At any rate, he was back on track as a composer. The *Gnossiennes*, composed between 1890 and 1897, have all the charm of the *Gymnopédies* and something more—an exotic melodic accent that gives them a Middle Eastern flavor. There is also something of this exoticism in the *Trois Mouvements en forme de poire*—"Three Movements in the Shape of a Pear," for piano four hands (double-tracked by Ciccolini here)—which was published in 1903, but includes music from the 1890s as well as material based on the café songs that he played to support himself.

A turning point came in 1905, when Satie reconsidered his misspent youth and enrolled at the Schola Cantorum to study counterpoint with Albert Roussel and composition with Vincent d'Indy. Yet, if his technique improved, the spirit of his music was largely unchanged—indeed, he continued to write short works, as he always had, under titles that were whimsical or just peculiar.

Works of this period include the humorous *Croquis et Agaceries d'un gros bonhomme en bois* (Teasing Sketches of a Fat Man Made of Wood), *Peccadilles importunes* (Inconvenient Trifles), the playfully aphoristic *Sports et divertissements* (Sports and Diversions), and *Embryons desséchés* (Dessicated Embryos), the last a rather lively work given its title.

Satie became an almost respectable figure in the Parisian musical world after Ravel and Debussy began performing his music, in 1911, but his later piano works were as full of surprises as ever. The *Sonatine bureaucratique* of 1917, for example, is a delightful parody of the classical-era sonatina (such as those by Clementi that every piano student learns); by contrast, *La Belle Excentrique,* composed in 1922, captures the energy and accents of the popular music hall.

Ciccolini revisited these works in the 1980s, recording the full set again. The remakes, available on five separate EMI CDs, are lovely and deserve acknowledgment; but they don't always have the magical lilt that Ciccolini brought to his earlier accounts, and it may even be that the clinical clarity of early digital sound yielded a less suitably mysterious atmosphere than the analog recordings.

The older performances have retained their vibrancy all these decades later, and sonically, EMI's transfers do them full justice. These discs won an audience for Satie in the 1960s and 1970s, when his music had long been eclipsed. Now the pianists who grew up hearing those albums are including Satie in their programs, although he remains a minority concern: his work actually turns up most frequently on series devoted to contemporary music, validating Cage's observation about Satie's place in the musical cosmos.

61. MANUEL DE FALLA

El Sombrero de Tres Picos, Interludio y Danza
from *La Vida Breve,* and *El Amor Brujo*

L'ORCHESTRE DE LA SUISSE ROMANDE,
ERNEST ANSERMET, CONDUCTING
(Decca 289 466 991-2)

Recorded 1955, 1961

There are two ways to look at the current of Spanish musical nationalism that blossomed around the turn of the twentieth century. One is that it was a late manifestation of the wave of romantic nationalism that swept over Europe all through the nineteenth century; the other is that the wave never really reached Spain at all—that the Spanish national school was actually a natural outgrowth of a peculiar brand of musical isolationism peculiar to the Iberian peninsula. Either way, Manuel de Falla (1876–1946) was in the vanguard of Spanish composers—others included Isaac Albéniz and Enrique Granados—whose works thoroughly embodied Spain's unique musical accent, and who were fondly adopted by the European mainstream.

To get to the heart of Falla, one has to understand the characteristics of Spanish music and what shaped it. Because of its position at the western edge of the Mediterranean, Spain was an outpost for virtually every civilization that navigated, explored, and traded in the region, from the Phoenicians, Greeks, Romans, and Visigoths, to the North African Moors and the gypsies. Each of these cultures brought influences that mingled with those of their predecessors, but the influence of the Moors and the gypsies was particularly decisive.

The Moors invaded Spain in 711 and established Islam and Arabic culture as an important element in Spain's history. The Spanish Christians battled them for centuries and eventually pushed them out of the peninsula, yet Moorish influence continued to shape Spanish architecture, the Spanish language (Spanish words beginning with the letters "al" generally have Arabic roots), and Spanish music, which retained the plaintive, modal quality of Arabic music. Gypsy music was a later addition to Spain's musical culture, and although it is generally brighter and more exuberant than the Arabic component, its modal accent was complementary and contributed to a mixture not found elsewhere in Europe.

The musical amalgam in which these influences can be heard at their purest is flamenco, which combines soulful vocal melodies, a set of established dance rhythms, and distinctive timbres—guitars, tambourines, the modally inflected voice, and percussive dance. It is flamenco's melodic shapes and sharply defined rhythms that classically trained composers searching for an authentic Spanish voice drew upon, and they made it part of an entirely new blend, the fresh elements being orchestral instrumentation as well as themes and structures that took a more urbane notice of developments elsewhere in Europe.

One problem Falla faced during his early years in Madrid was a paucity of resources. Spain's orchestral culture at the time was underdeveloped, and although Falla was a good pianist, he was not a virtuoso. Between 1900 and 1904 he tried writing zarzuela, a Spanish form of operetta that relied on stock characters but drew on the popular flamenco vocabulary. But his attempts were unsuccessful, and in 1907 he moved to Paris, where he remained for seven years.

During that time, he absorbed a great deal of French musical culture, which augmented but did not displace his own musical style. The French, for their part, were enamored of Spanish music, as Ravel's various Spanish works, Debussy's *Ibéria* (from his piano work *Images*), and, for that matter, Georges Bizet's *Carmen*, which was composed a year before Falla's birth, all suggest.

And indeed, France and Spain are intertwined in Falla's major works. His opera, *La Vida Breve* (The Short Life), represented on this disc by an evocative interlude and dance, was composed in Spain in 1905, but was not produced until 1913, when it had its premiere in Nice. *El Amor Brujo* (Love, the Magician), similarly, was composed in 1914 and 1915, after Falla reestablished himself in Madrid, but it was revised several times before the final version had its premiere in Paris in 1925. The work, drawing on gypsy legends, tells the story of Candela, a young gypsy girl, and her lover, Carmelo, who together perform an exorcism to prevent Candela's dead lover from haunting her. It includes some of Falla's most durable flamenco-inflected music, including the *Canción del Amor Dolido* (Song of Suffering Love) and the *Danza Ritual del Fuego* (Ritual Fire Dance).

While Falla was in France, the Russian impresario Sergei Diaghilev heard some of his music, and persuaded him to compose for his Ballets Russes. Falla had already composed a piece that he thought would do, with a bit of expansion. That was *El Sombrero de Tres Picos* (The Three-Cornered Hat)—a comedy in which the old magistrate of a small town falls in love with the miller's beautiful wife, but is humiliated as he tries to win her. Here, too, several of the vivid dances from the score are frequently heard on their own—and often in classical guitar arrangements, which thoroughly suit their spirit.

When the work had its premiere, in London in 1919, the performance was led by Ernest Ansermet, the young Swiss conductor who had been on the Ballets Russes' podium since 1916, when he was introduced to Sergei Diaghilev by Igor Stravinsky. Ansermet formed his Orchestre de la Suisse Romande in 1918, and shaped it into a magnificent radio and recording ensemble, with which he made dozens of discs that remain classics for their blend of structural elegance and coloristic vividness. It was in music that most required that balance that Ansermet was revered: in addition to Falla, his finest recordings were the early Stravinsky ballets, the music of Debussy and Ravel, and pictorially lush scores like Rimsky-Korsakov's *Scheherazade*.

Ansermet's real strength was his ability to find and expose the depths of brightly colored works that many of his colleagues treated more superficially. By the time he made these recordings—*El Amor Brujo* in 1955, the others in 1961—Ansermet knew their twists and turns intimately, and he was able to point up both the Iberian vitality of Falla's dances and vocal pieces, and the cosmopolitan wit of his orchestration. These remain among the most sizzling accounts of this music on record. They are graced, as well, by the thoroughly stylish vocal contributions of Teresa Berganza in *El Sombrero de Tres Picos,* and Marina de Gabarain in *El Amor Brujo.*

Composer Manuel de Falla

62. RICHARD STRAUSS

Tone Poems

STAATSKAPELLE DRESDEN,

BERLIN PHILHARMONIC,

KARL BÖHM, CONDUCTING

(Deutsche Grammophon 463 190-2, three CDs)

Includes An Alpine *Symphony,* Don Juan, Rosenkavalier *Waltzes,* Also Sprach Zarathustra, *Festival Prelude,* Till Eulenspiegel's Merry Pranks, *"Dance of the Seven Veils" from* Salome, Ein Heldenleben, *and* Death and Transfiguration.

Recorded 1957–1972

Richard Strauss (1864–1949) straddled the nineteenth and twentieth centuries, but he was molded by the earlier era. Although some of his later works—the opera *Capriccio,* for example—reflect an interest in the neoclassicism swirling through mid-twentieth century music, he never abandoned tonality or the quest for orchestrational lushness, and never dabbled in any of the more experimental styles and techniques of the time. But as an authentic extension of romanticism (as opposed to neoromanticism) well into the twentieth century, he was one of Europe's most famous and admired composers for most of his life.

He came of age in a world dominated, musically, by Brahms and Wagner, with Wagner as the more decisive influence, particularly in the tone poems, which share the Wagnerian goal of making both deep emotion and aspects of plot and character palpable through music. But where each of these composers' contemporary partisans tended to line up in vehement opposition to one another, Strauss admired and drew important elements of his style from both. It was characteristic, in fact, for Strauss to embrace values that others considered antithetical. His tone poems and many of his other works, for example, are programmatic and representational; yet he was not opposed to the concept of "absolute" music—that is, music driven by form and other purely musical values, rather than by external notions or imagery.

Strauss composed prolifically, producing chamber works, songs, orchestral music, and operas, and his legacy has fared generally well. Several of his operas—most notably *Salome, Elektra,* and *Der Rosenkavalier*—have been centerpieces of the canon since their premieres. And his tone poems, composed mostly around the turn of the century, have remained enduringly popular.

One could argue that the tone poem genre includes everything from Vivaldi's *Four Seasons* and Beethoven's *Pastoral* Symphony (his denial that it is representational notwithstanding) to Liszt's symphonic poems. They have always found a receptive public. And why not? As intellectually engaging or challenging as abstract music can be, there is something to be said for hearing a composer use an orchestra, or its component sections, to mimic the sounds of nature, the cacophony of a battle, or even a fairly complex plot line, all the while maintaining a sense of musical structure and integrity.

Strauss perfected that art in these pieces, which present a fantastic gallery of characters, including the picaresque prankster of *Till Eulenspiegel,* the hero of *Ein Heldenleben,* and of course, Don Juan, all distinctly drawn, and woven into contexts that are sometimes fairly simple tableaux (as in *Don Juan*), sometimes more complex *(Till Eulenspiegel's Merry Pranks),* and sometimes embody expressions of philosophical ideals (*Also Sprach Zarathustra* and, to a great extent, *Ein Heldenleben*). *Death and Transfiguration* reaches higher still: in this work, lasting nearly twenty-five minutes, Strauss meant to, as he put it, "represent the dying moments of a man who has striven for the highest ideal goals." And in *Also Sprach Zarathustra,* inspired by Friedrich Nietsche's portrayal of a "superman," Strauss used competing tonalities of C and B to symbolize the tension between Nature and Man.

Because their scene-painting, storytelling, or philosophical conceits are painted so vividly, these works have become textbook studies in orchestration, as well as virtuoso display pieces for conductors, orchestras, and high-fidelity sound systems. The recordings in this set are by no means the latest word in spectacular fidelity; some are in mono. But they capture the orchestra's sound honestly. Karl Böhm's credentials in this music are impeccable: he was friendly with Strauss during the composer's late years, and during his own long career, he was an uncommonly perceptive interpreter of Strauss's operas and orchestral works.

Böhm's luminous performance of *Death and Transfiguration*, recorded at a Salzburg concert in 1972, is probably the highlight of the set. But in the other works, too, he conveys both the broad strokes and the nuances in perfectly weighted gestures. This economically priced set (the three CDs cost just slightly more than a single top-priced disc) includes the painterly and bracing *Alpine* Symphony, the lovely waltzes from *Der Rosenkavalier,* the steamy "Dance of the Seven Veils" from *Salome,* and one trifle, the Festival Prelude, a bombastic, celebratory work composed for the opening of the Konzerthaus in Vienna.

Given their popularity as showpieces, the Strauss tone poems have been recorded frequently, and often with distinction. Strauss himself made several recordings, some of which—versions of *Don Juan, Till Eulenspiegel's Merry Pranks,* and the neoclassical *Bourgeois Gentilhomme* Suite from 1929 and 1930—were reissued on Pearl, a label that specializes in historical recordings. The briefly available *Legendary Strauss Recordings* (RCA) is worth seeking for its interpretations recorded between 1934 and 1941 by Willem Mengelberg, Leopold Stokowski, Sir Thomas Beecham, Serge Koussevitzky, and Frederick Stock.

Also among the greatest Strauss performances are Fritz Reiner's recordings with the Chicago Symphony Orchestra, all available on midprice CD reissues (RCA Victor, 1950s and early 1960s). Don't let their vintage put you off: these were models of the art of orchestral recording in their day, and they sound fresher, more powerful, and more lifelike than many more recent digital recordings.

63. ARNOLD SCHOENBERG

Suite (op. 29), *Verklärte Nacht* (op. 4), and Three Pieces for Chamber Orchestra

MEMBERS OF THE ENSEMBLE INTERCONTEMPORAIN,
PIERRE BOULEZ, CONDUCTING

(Sony SMK 48465)

Recorded 1982–1983

Half composer, half lightning rod, Arnold Schoenberg (1874–1951) is unquestionably one of the most important figures in the history of twentieth-century music, not only for the body of works he created, but as the focal point of a central (and therefore often ferocious) debate about the nature of musical language in the modern era. For many listeners who consider melodic and harmonic beauty to be absolute values, Schoenberg is a devil who seduced composers away from the universally comprehensible musical grammar that had evolved since medieval times, and who replaced both the grand sweep of melody and the warm lushness of nineteenth-century harmony with cragginess and dissonance. For others, he was a liberator who saved music from wallowing in a dead end of manipulative emotionality and harmonic stagnation.

Schoenberg came to this position honestly. Born and raised in Vienna, he learned the violin as a child, and taught himself the cello, but his family's financial circumstances precluded formal musical studies. His only lessons in composition were with Alexander von Zemlinsky, a friend who was three years older, but who had attended the Vienna Conservatory and composed in a rich, Brahmsian style. Schoenberg's early works—including the stunningly beautiful *Verklärte Nacht,* composed in 1899—owed something to Brahms, as well as to Strauss's tone poems and Wagner's sweeping chromaticism.

Not long into the first decade of the twentieth century, though, Schoenberg became convinced that tonality—the system of harmonic relationships within and between musical keys that had been central to musical syntax for the previous 600 years—had reached its expressive zenith in the works of Wagner, Liszt, and Mahler, and perhaps in his own *Gurrelieder,* a mammoth work for a huge orchestra, with chorus and soloists, that he completed in 1901. Schoenberg was not alone in this belief. The French impressionists had also concluded that a way around the conventions of tonality was necessary, and the language they pioneered was one solution. Like Liszt and Wagner, but with a different accent and different techniques, the French composers had pushed chromaticism to its limits, using it not simply to create variety by momentarily escaping the confines of specific keys, but rather, to create pictures in sound.

In both its French and German versions, this use of chromaticism to paint pictures or, in Mahler's case, to convey emotional states, loosened music from its traditional moorings in tonality, a hierarchical system in which the notes of the scale are weighted in importance by their relationship to the root note of the key. Ultimately, their experiments rendered the notion of a key center almost irrelevant. But it wasn't until Schoenberg that the cord was decisively cut.

Schoenberg was not especially interested in pictorialism; his hope was that skirting the rules of tonality would yield fresh thematic material, as well as an entirely novel harmonic world. His first response was to write works so densely chromatic that it was impossible to describe them as being in a particular key. Then, around 1920, he took the next logical step, jettisoning tonality entirely, in favor of a system in which the twelve notes of the octave (that is, the seven notes of the scale, plus all the intervening sharps and flats) were treated equally. Just as composers once chose a key and used its notes to create themes, they would now begin, in Schoenberg's system, by devising a "tone row" using all twelve notes. The row would be the basic building block of a composition.

It wasn't as limiting as it sounds. Once the row was established, the composer could use half of it to form a theme, saving the other half to be introduced later as a countertheme. Several rows could be used in a single work. And although notes could not be repeated in constructing the row itself, they could be repeated in, say, the statement of a theme based on the row. Moreover, a backward (or "retrograde") version of the row could be used. A related yet entirely different row (called an inversion) could be derived by inverting the intervals between each note of the original row. And yet another row could be created by doing both those things (making it a retrograde inversion).

Because the tone row was also called a series, Schoenberg's method came to be known as serialism, and it had broader implications that other composers (including Pierre Boulez, who conducts the recording at hand) explored more fully: if the pitches of the scale could be organized as a series, so could other elements of music. One could, for example, create a series of note durations, dynamics, or even approaches to tone color and expression. These could be governed in much the same way as the series of pitches.

Even this simplified explanation may seem abstruse, but it's important to note that in the hands of an inspired composer (Schoenberg not least among them), these techniques can yield powerful, moving music, and now several decades on, some serial works have found their way into the repertory. Among the youngest generation of composers, who have no stake in the stylistic battles of their predecessors, serial techniques have become simply one of many available tools, useful for a particular sound or effect within works that are rooted in one or more different esthetics.

In the middle and late decades of the twentieth century, though, many composers who were drawn to serialism were as enamored of its science as its art, and very deliberately used its techniques to create music that sounded entirely unlike that of earlier times. It wasn't meant, necessarily, to be irritating; the composers themselves were inured to the dissonance and angularity it yielded, and relished it. But for a significant part of the classical music audience, it was too great a leap, and that audience laid its discontent with a large body of modern music at Schoenberg's doorstep, not entirely fairly.

This disc offers three glimpses of Schoenberg, each at a different point in his journey. The earliest of these pieces, *Verklärte Nacht* (*Transfigured Night*), was inspired by a haunting poem by Richard Dehmel in which a woman confesses to her beloved that she is pregnant with another man's child, and he responds that through the power of their love, the child will become his. Commentators hold different views about whether the Dehmel poem was merely a jumping-off point for a thoroughly abstract piece of music, or whether Schoenberg was seeking to capture, within the texture of a string sextet, the pictorial spirit of a Strauss tone poem, or even the intensity of a Wagnerian scene.

I lean toward the latter view, for although this twenty-nine-minute work is surely not a line-by-line musical translation of the poem, its two distinct sections mirror the scene's emotional structure: the first half of the piece is steeped in Wagnerian anxiety, and, while the second half is by no means without its moments of high drama, its character is brighter, more hopeful. The strings of the Ensemble Inter-Contemporain, whose day-to-day work takes them through thornier, less openly emotional scores, revel in this moment of Schoenbergian romanticism.

Of course, on its more typical turf, the group plays with an illuminating warmth. The Three Pieces for Chamber Orchestra were composed in 1910, when Schoenberg was experimenting with the notion that musical ideas could be expressed directly, completely, and concisely, without the need of tonality or the conventional structural model that included an exposition of the basic ideas, followed by a development, or expansion on them. This phase was brief in Schoenberg's work, and its products were sparse: the first two of the Three Pieces clock in at 0'55" and 0'36" in this performance; the third, which is actually an unfinished fragment, runs 0'45". Given that the set is scored for a dozen instruments, including string quartet, bass, harmonium, winds, and brass—the setup alone would take several times longer than the performance—it seems likely that Schoenberg intended a somewhat larger collection but abandoned the project. It was not published in his lifetime.

The Suite (op. 29), composed between 1924 and 1926, and scored for two clarinets, bass clarinet, violin, viola, cello, and piano, is brash and forceful and exerts an irresistible draw, particularly in as lively and precise a performance as the Ensemble InterContemporain players provide. One gets the sense that at least part of Schoenberg's agenda here was showing that twelve-tone works need not seem entirely alien: the work is cast in four very traditional movements, beginning with a three-part Overture, in which one hears hints of a ländler (a traditional Austrian country dance), and followed by a vigorous, spiky movement called "Tanzschritte" (Dance Steps), as well as a Theme and Variations movement, in which a traditional (and tonal) theme lies at the heart of the twelve-tone variations and, of all things, a Gigue, the typical finale of a baroque dance suite.

64. IGOR STRAVINSKY

Petrushka and *Le Sacre du Printemps*

COLUMBIA SYMPHONY ORCHESTRA,
IGOR STRAVINSKY, CONDUCTING

(Sony Classical MK 42433)

Recorded 1960

or

Le Sacre du Printemps and *L'Oiseau de Feu* Suite

COLUMBIA SYMPHONY ORCHESTRA,
IGOR STRAVINSKY, CONDUCTING

(Sony Classical SS 89062—SACD format)

Recorded 1960, 1967

Without question, Igor Stravinsky (1882–1971) was a central force in twentieth-century music, yet judging from the comparatively constricted list of his works that are regularly performed or recorded, one could get the impression that his reputation rests on three early ballets—*L'Oiseau de Feu* (*The Firebird*), *Petrushka,* and *Le Sacre du Printemps* (*The Rite of Spring*). A longer study of his work list shows that not to be an entirely fair assessment: works like *L'Histoire du Soldat,* the Duo Concertante, the *Dumbarton Oaks* Concerto, the Symphony of Psalms, *Les Noces, Apollon Musagète, Pulcinella,* and Stravinsky's great opera, *The Rake's Progress,* have all made their impact, and enjoy occasional revivals, as do some of Stravinsky's other scores.

But there is no denying that the trilogy of early ballets—and particularly *The Rite of Spring,* with its brutally hammered, dissonant chords and its swirling energy—made the greatest impact on the way both composers and listeners came to perceive modern music. To this day, one hears freshly minted works that borrow patches of rhythm and color from *Rite.* And thanks to Walt Disney's including a truncated version of it in the original *Fantasia,* wedded to visions of dinosaurs—the work's actual subject, the dance of a sacrificial virgin in an ancient, pagan rite, would not have made ideal family viewing— it was probably the first twentieth-century score that had a wide following among children as well as adults.

One odd trait that makes Stravinsky emblematic of his restless time is the fact that, successful as this early style was, he jettisoned it fairly quickly. During his long career, he touched on virtually every current in twentieth-century composition, from the celebration of a nationalistic mythology in those early ballets, to a more cosmopolitan experimentalism in the 1920s, neoclassicism in the 1930s, serialism in the 1950s, and a synthesis of modern styles in his last years. He did not invent any of these styles, in the sense that Schoenberg can be said to have invented serialism; but once he adopted them, he was able, to varying degrees, to give them a personal twist, something to make his music stand out as a distinctively Stravinskian shaping of the style at hand.

His early style, which spawned the ballets, was an outgrowth of the Russian musical nationalism espoused by Rimsky-Korsakov, who was an early mentor, with Alexander Glazunov and Peter Tchaikovsky as important models. Stravinsky, in fact, retained his fondness for Tchaikovsky throughout his life, a preference that may have seemed odd to listeners who regarded Stravinsky's brash, unsentimental style to be the polar opposite of Tchaikovsky's. But the impulse toward a distinctive, identifiable Russianness was a strong force in Stravinsky's early works, and Tchaikovsky embodied that.

There was a degree to which he found useful material in Rimsky-Korsakov's music, especially his use of lavish orchestrational techniques to suggest a magical atmosphere in his late operas. But Stravinsky's harmonic and rhythmic imagination was freer than Rimsky-Korsakov's, and his eagerness to bend rules and conventions pointed to paths his predecessors had not explored. What interested him, at this point, was evoking the contemporary Russian spirit in terms that would appeal to modernists elsewhere in Europe—particularly Paris, which, handily, was obsessed with things Russian.

Sergei Diaghilev and his Ballets Russes were already entrenched in the Parisian dance world, and it was through Diaghilev and his choreographer, Mikhail Fokine, that Stravinsky made his grand splash with *The Firebird* in 1910. The story is that of Prince Ivan who, wandering in the enchanted garden of the sorcerer Kashchey, captures the Firebird, and releases her in exchange for one of her feathers. The prince is entertained by thirteen enchanted princesses, who are required to return to Kashchey's castle at sunrise. He follows them, and in an encounter with Kashchey, remembers the Firebird's magic feather, which he waves in the air, summoning the Firebird, who casts a series of spells and tells the prince that he can destroy Kashchey by breaking the egg that represents his soul.

Stravinsky stole a page from Rimsky-Korsakov here, using chromaticism to evoke Kashchey's world, and music rooted in Russian folk song to evoke the prince. Still, Stravinsky's thumbprint is clear in the edgy harmonies and knife-sharp rhythms of the work. He continued this balance of the traditional and the exploratory in *Petrushka*, his 1911 follow-up for Diaghilev and Fokine. As in *The Firebird*, folk song and a chromatically enhanced sense of the magical propel a story set at the Shrovetide Fair in St. Petersburg, where the characters in a puppet theater—a ballerina, a Blackamoor, and Petrushka—come to life and enact a tragic love triangle that ends in Petrushka's death, capped with a bi-tonal coda in which Petrushka's ghost taunts the onlookers.

Firebird and *Petrushka* were immediate successes. *The Rite of Spring*, at least according to legend, had a somewhat more controversial birth in 1913. Stravinsky's collaborators were Nicolai Roerich, a painter with an abiding passion for archaeology and ethnography, and Vaslav Nijinsky, the great choreographer and dancer. *The Rite* is an enactment of an ancient springtime ritual (or at least, Roerich's, Nijinsky's, and Stravinsky's notion of one) in which a chosen virgin dances herself to death as an offering to the gods. There are folk influences here—the opening bassoon melody, for example, is said to be based on a Lithuanian folk song—but for the most part Stravinsky cut his links with the past in this work, focusing instead on jagged, irregular rhythms and harmonic brusqueness. He was, in effect, using the latest ideas of musical modernity to project the power of primitive ritual.

The immediate result was a riot at the Théâtre des Champs-Elysées on the night of the premiere, May 29, 1913. The exact cause of this disturbance has been debated for decades: the idea that the music was simply too much for the audience to take in, though an appealing myth, is probably not the whole story. Stravinsky, after all, had captured the Parisian public's collective heart in his previous two works, and the shouting is said to have started before listeners can have heard much to find objectionable.

It's possible that the demonstration was aimed partly at Nijinsky, whose choreography for Debussy's *Jeux* had displeased Diaghilev's audiences only two weeks earlier. Other factors have been mentioned as well: *The New Grove Dictionary of Music and Musicians* includes unseasonable heat, a high percentage of tourists in the audience, and the fact that the "open cinema–like design of the new theater tended to encourage a certain social fractiousness" among the circumstances, and notes that subsequent performances, including an open rehearsal the following day, went on without incident. Still, the riot is part of the work's lore, and the contours of the music, even today, seem to promote the idea that it did not go down easily.

Stravinsky, conducting the work on this recording, made nearly a half century later, brings out every bit of its ferocious, elemental power, but also does wonders with nuance. The brilliance of the scoring, especially in the winds and brass, is highlighted as well.

I have included two couplings for Stravinsky's 1960 recording of *The Rite*. It is available on a conventional CD with a bright-hued, wonderfully sardonic account of *Petrushka*. It has also been issued in the new SACD "Super-Audio" format—a high-resolution system that, at least in this case, requires a special SACD player. Many companies are now making hybrid SACDs, which can also be played on standard CD or DVD players, and Sony Classical may eventually follow suit, as its pop music arm has with a series of Bob Dylan recordings in the

Composer Igor Stravinsky

summer of 2003. Keep an eye out for this one: the improved definition of the SACD makes Stravinsky's reading of *The Rite* sound even more powerful.

It is astonishing, though, that Sony does not, as this is written, have a concise two-CD set that brings together all three of these works (and which would allow for the composer's 1961 recording of the full *Firebird* instead of the suite). Stravinsky recorded prodigiously for Sony's corporate predecessor, CBS Masterworks, and in the early 1980s the label brought together most of his stereo recordings in a huge boxed LP edition. Sony reissued that set on twenty-two CDs in 1991, but that extremely important box is no longer available, and most of its contents are unavailable individually. That, as much as anything, is a reflection of the scandalous state of the classical record industry today.

65. IGOR STRAVINSKY

The Mono Years

IGOR STRAVINSKY, CONDUCTING
(Sony Classical MH2K 63325, two CDs)

Includes Le Baiser de la Fée, *Symphony in C (plus a rehearsal fragment),* Pulcinella, L'Histoire du Soldat *Suite; Octet for Wind Instruments. The Cleveland Orchestra (everything through* Pulcinella) *and a chamber ensemble. Igor Stravinsky, conducting.*

Recorded 1952–1955

Long out-of-print on LP, and not available on CD until 1998, these vintage recordings come from a brief transitional period in the history of recording, when the process had progressed from direct-cut 78 rpm discs, to recording sessions captured on tape and released on LPs, but before stereo recordings were commercially introduced. Stravinsky eventually rerecorded these pieces in stereo, and as the remakes became the standard entries in the Stravinsky discography, the mono recordings faded from view. Collectors have always prized them, though.

For one thing, the great majority of Stravinsky's stereo recordings were made with the Columbia Symphony Orchestra, a superb ensemble that was contracted by the record label for session work, and often included top-flight musicians. But it wasn't an orchestra that worked together week in and week out. For these mono recordings, Stravinsky leads the Cleveland Orchestra, then in the early years of its relationship with George Szell, and sounding magnificent. The sound here is extremely fine, and the beneficiary of a careful transfer from the master tapes.

The set is also appealing as a compilation of some of Stravinsky's most inviting works beyond the Sergei Diaghilev ballets. A few of these works, in fact, illuminate an important aspect of Stravinsky's artistic persona: that of the expert pilferer who could spot a useful musical idea at fifty paces, and could then transform it into a work that bore his unquestionable stylistic thumbprint.

In the case of *Pulcinella,* completed in 1920, the basic material is a handful of eighteenth-century pieces, mostly by the Italian composer Giovanni Battista Pergolesi. The raw materials were handed to Stravinsky by Diaghilev and the choreographer Leonid Massine, who hoped that he would put together a pastiche along the lines of Ottorino Respighi's Rossini-based "Boutique Fantasque," for a production with set designs by Pablo Picasso. But Stravinsky did more than cobble the music into a dance suite. Setting aside the turbulent style that rocked *The Rite of Spring,* he deconstructed these baroque pieces. Although he kept the spotlight on their essential mechanisms—their often sprightly rhythms, their structural symmetries, and their elegantly ornamented melodies—he refracted these elements through his modernist prism, painting a purely Stravinskian layer of orchestrational touches and imaginative expansions onto the original scores.

Pulcinella is most frequently heard by way of the orchestral suite that Stravinsky drew from it, and while that makes amusing listening, the full work presented here is a far grander conception, not only because it includes vocal music not represented in the suite, but also—

and more crucially—because the suite strips away some of the most assertive of Stravinsky's orchestrations, focusing on the work's neo-classical aura at the expense of its neoromantic elements.

Le Baiser de la Fée (The Fairy's Kiss), composed in 1928, had a genesis similar to that of *Pulcinella*. When Stravinsky was commissioned to write a ballet for the dancer Ida Rubinstein, the stage director Alexandre Benois proposed a Tchaikovsky montage, and suggested that Stravinsky use some of Tchaikovsky's piano music as its basis. Stravinsky was plainly happy to indulge his lifelong love of Tchaikovsky, but that isn't to say that he approached the materials gingerly: where he orchestrated the pieces, he did so with a complete command of Tchaikovsky's sense of color, yet veered off into his own sound world regularly enough to keep the work from being mistaken for a mere arrangement. He also added fresh music of his own, mostly but not entirely in a convincingly Tchaikovskian style.

L'Histoire du Soldat, a 1918 dramatic piece with a spoken text by Charles-Ferdinand Ramuz, is a Faustian tale in which a soldier, returning to his home village, encounters a suave devil who persuades him to sell his soul (represented by his rustic violin) in exchange for wealth and power. It's a great story, although not everyone agrees: the author Kurt Vonnegut found it unconscionable that Stravinsky, at the end of World War I, set a quaint morality tale instead of an essay on the horrors of war, and so wrote a libretto of his own, about the trial of Private Eddie Slovik, the American soldier executed for desertion during World War II. It missed the point entirely, and did violence to a work in which the music and the original text fit together snugly.

Still, the music stands nicely on its own, without any text at all, and Stravinsky arranged several instrumental suites based on this material. One could even argue that the narration inevitably distracts the ear from the musical joys of this acerbic, tuneful, and thoroughly inventive score, with its quirky marches and its tilt toward popular music by way of a Tango and a Ragtime movement. Stravinsky here performs the ten-movement chamber suite.

Along with these theater pieces, the set includes two of Stravinsky's abstract scores. The Symphony in C, composed in 1940, is a broad-boned neoclassical work for a Beethoven-scale orchestra, in which

Stravinsky applied his rhythmic sensibilities and thematic angularity to Haydnesque structural models. The Octet, composed in 1922 and 1923, and revised in 1952, is a trim piece, also neoclassical in spirit and expression, and tinged with the sardonic accent that was a central hallmark of Stravinsky's style throughout his long career.

66. REYNALDO HAHN

La Belle Époque: The Songs of Reynaldo Hahn

SUSAN GRAHAM, MEZZO-SOPRANO;
ROGER VIGNOLES, PIANIST
(Sony Classical SK 60168)

Recorded 1998

When it is performed in the right spirit and with the right nuance, early-twentieth-century French art song creates a universe of its own, unlike anything else in the vocal literature. Naturally, it shares elements of the harmonic and melodic vocabulary of French instrumental music of the time: like these impressionistic works, it relies on a suaveness that makes it sound urbane, even when it is at its most unabashedly pictorial. The heart of the form lies in the relationship between the poetic text and the notes that convey and support it, and while one can, of course, say the same of German, Italian, and English songs, there is something about French poetry—its attitude as well as its sound—that yields especially alluring vocal lines. And the piano accompaniment in French songs typically matches the sheer sensuality of the vocal writing.

Francis Poulenc, Henri Duparc, Maurice Ravel, and Gabriel Fauré all wrote magnificent songs and cycles; for that matter, one can hear the roots of the modern French song style as far back as Hector Berlioz, in *Les Nuits d'Été*. Yet for me, the most seductive composer

---

of French song was an outsider of sorts. Reynaldo Hahn's settings have all the qualities that give French song of this era its unique character, yet he was not French, except by training. Born in Venezuela, Hahn (1874–1947) moved to Paris with his family at age four and, when he was eleven, entered the Paris Conservatoire, where he studied with Jules Massenet. He took French nationality in 1909.

He moved in interesting circles: Paul Verlaine was present when Hahn's early settings of his poetry were performed, and the composer's closest friends in Paris were Sarah Bernhardt and Marcel Proust. In addition to his songs, he wrote piano works, chamber music, a ballet, and several operas, including *Ciboulette,* which was a Parisian favorite early in the twentieth century, and *Le Marchande de Venise,* a version of Shakespeare's *Merchant of Venice* in which Hahn, who was part-Jewish, replaced Shylock's "pound of flesh" speech with an aria that expresses Shylock's fury at centuries of persecution. Because of his Jewish ancestry, Hahn's music was banned during the Nazi occupation of France, and the composer spent most of the war in hiding. After the war, he became director of the Paris Opera.

Hahn's songs were, admittedly, conservative: compared with the somewhat more spare, direct settings of Claude Debussy and younger composers, Hahn's music can seem a throwback to the lush Parisian salon style of the turn of the century—where, after all, he flourished as a young composer. But writing this music off on those grounds won't do: the twenty-four selections Susan Graham has included on this disc show the breadth of Hahn's expressive palette. Their variety runs from bright, celebratory pieces (the ebullient "Le Printemps" and "Fêtes galantes," for example) to explosions of passion ("Dans la nuit" and "Mai"), but Hahn's real métier was delicious melancholy— the quality that animates "Fumée," in which the singer likens her life to a fleeting puff of cigarette smoke, or "L'Énamourée," sung to the still-felt presence of a dead lover. And in song after song—"Tyndaris," "L'Heure exquise," "Quand la nuit n'est pas étoilée," "Nocturne"— Hahn's sense of how to turn a melody and when to modulate into an unexpected key makes these short works utterly transfixing.

Graham was in her early thirties and at the start of a flourishing opera career when she made this album, one of her first recordings. She was introduced to Hahn's songs by Roger Vignoles, the pianist here, and she saw the music's expressive possibilities immediately: she later described the encounter with Hahn as "love at first sing." The match between repertory and performer could not be better. Graham's honeyed mezzo-soprano, dark and dusky enough to suit the mood of the most heartfelt of these songs, is also flexible enough to persuasively convey the more light-spirited ones. More crucially, she has the musical intelligence necessary to bring the emotional core of each song vividly to life, mainly through phrasing that has a way of seeming surprising and inevitable at the same time. After Graham's gently wistful account of "Si mes vers avaient des ailes," which closes the disc, you will find yourself sitting in silence wondering what hit you.

67. AGUSTÍN BARRIOS

From the Jungles of Paraguay:
John Williams Plays Barrios

JOHN WILLIAMS, GUITARIST
(Sony Classical SK 64396)

Includes Vals no. 3, Preludio in C minor, Cueca, Maxixa, La Catedral, Julia Florida, *Vals no. 4,* Una Limosna por el Amor de Dios, *Mazurka appassionata,* Las Abejas, Medallon Antiguo, *Chôro de Saudade, Aire de Zamba,* Aconquija, *Preludio in G minor,* Sueño en la Floresta, Villancico de Navidad.

Recorded 1994

The conventional wisdom holds that establishing the guitar as a serious concert instrument was the accomplishment solely of Andrés Segovia, who transcribed works by Bach and other antique composers, begged new works from the composers of his time, and toured the world performing this repertory with an evangelical zeal from the 1920s until shortly before his death in 1987. But although Segovia's energetic crusade unquestionably created an audience for the guitar among listeners who had previously regarded it mainly as a folk instrument, there was actually a thriving guitar world long before he played his first recital.

In Segovia's native Spain, for example, there was a circle of virtuoso players who were students of the guitarist-composer Francisco Tárrega, some of whom—Miguel Llobet and Emilio Pujol, for example—made recordings that capture a refined, technically polished style years before Segovia cut his first discs. There was also a culture of virtuoso guitar music, in Spain, France, and Austria, that dated back to a circle of prolific composer-players in the early nineteenth century. And although the guitar as we now know it—like the piano and most other instruments—evolved in the early nineteenth century, its earlier iterations included a baroque precursor with a narrow body and double strings, and the Spanish vihuela, also a narrow-body instrument. Each had an estimable repertory that can be played on the modern guitar—as can music written for the lute, more a cousin to the guitar than an ancestor.

The concert guitar thrived outside Europe as well, particularly in Latin America, where the tradition of the guitarist-composer continued into the twentieth century. Probably the greatest and most inventive of these musicians was Agustín Barrios (1885–1944), a composer whose music is to the guitar what Chopin's is to the piano. Many of his works are short dance movements (including waltzes and mazurkas) and colorful, harmonically adventurous character pieces. But there are also extended multipart essays. *La Catedral,* surely his most popular work, begins with a melancholy Bachian prelude, moves on to a sober but almost impressionistic movement marked Andante religioso, and concludes with a brisk, rippling fantasy. *Sueño en la Floresta* (Dream in the Woodland) is a brilliant tremolo study full of unusual harmonic changes. Both those qualities are also heard in his last known work, *Una Limosna por el Amor de Dios* (An Offering for the Love of God).

Barrios was a magnificent eccentric. Although surviving information about his family background doesn't quite bear out his claim to have been descended from Guaraní Indian chiefs, he grew up in a part of Paraguay where the Guaraní influence was strong, and he embraced its traditions. Starting in around 1930, he listed his name on concert posters as Chief Nitsuga Mangoré—Nitsuga is Agustín backwards; Mangoré is a Guaraní name—and performed in full Indian dress, including a plumed headband.

He also adopted a measure of poetic Guaraní mysticism. In his autobiographical *Profesión de Fe,* he wrote: "Tupã, the Supreme Spirit and protector of my race, found me one day in the middle of a verdant copse enraptured while in the contemplating of Nature. 'Take this mysterious box,' he said, 'and unveil its secrets.' And confining within it all the songs of the birds and the mournful sighs of plants, he left it in my hands. Obeying Tupã's command, I took [the box] to my heart and passed many moons at the edge of a spring. And one night Yacy, our Moon Mother, reflected in the crystalline liquid, feeling the sadness of my Indian soul, gave me six silver moonbeams so that with them I might unmask the secrets of the box. And the miracle took place: from the depths of the box emerged a marvelous symphony of all the virgin voices of our America!"

Behind this peculiar veneer, though, was a supremely gifted musician who made about three dozen 78 rpm discs, starting in 1913. About half of these were briefly available on LP, released by the specialist El Maestro label in the early 1980s, and they show Barrios to have had a formidable technique, a beautifully mellow sound, and a soulful interpretive style.

Of course, one could gather as much from his music, which was virtually unknown until the mid-1970s, when the musicologist Richard Stover began investigating Barrios's life and work, and publishing performing editions of his scores. It was also around then that the Australian-born, London-based guitarist John Williams (no relation to the film composer of the same name) began championing his works. In 1977, Williams released *John Williams Plays the Music of Barrios,* a varied collection of fifteen pieces that showed the range of Barrios's compositional interests and the richness of his imagination. That disc—or all but one piece (the Chôro de Saudade)—has been reissued on a budget-priced CD, *Latin American Guitar Music* (Sony Classical), and is worth hearing, not only for the Barrios performances, but for the inclusion of a 1978 recording of the epic Theme and Variations with a Fugue on "Folia de España" by the Mexican composer Manuel Ponce.

But in 1994 Williams had another look at Barrios, and the result is this disc, a collection for which he rerecorded the best pieces from the 1977 album, as well as several others not represented there. Williams's perspective on this music had not changed dramatically, but the changes are telling: where the 1977 performances are charmingly straightforward, Williams's 1994 versions are suppler and more carefully nuanced, with a great deal more of the rhythmic fluidity that was central to the performance style of Barrios's time (and not only among guitarists). In sonic terms as well, the 1977 recording was recorded fairly dry and close; the 1994 recording sets Williams in an opulent acoustic that gives his sound a lovely bloom.

Williams was a student of Segovia's, but his style and musical interests proved quite different. Like the great English guitarist and lutenist Julian Bream—whose spectacular series of recordings for RCA are, unfortunately, mostly out of print—Williams was interested in contemporary composers outside the parochial and largely Spanish contingent that wrote music for Segovia. Where Segovia played in a romantic style that prized lyricism over all else, Williams developed a remarkably crisp technique and a streamlined, modern sound. With Bream, he set the standard for modern guitar performance.

Williams also recorded what I consider one of greatest guitar LPs ever made, an album that, alas, has never been transferred to CD (although a few selections from it have turned up on compilations). Called *Virtuoso Variations for Guitar* (CBS Masterworks), it brings together seven technique-bending variation sets, among them the Bach Chaconne, the Paganini Caprice no. 24, works by Fernando Sor and Mauro Giuliani, two of the great nineteenth-century composer-guitarists, and dance movements, also in variation form, by the Elizabethan lutenists John Dowland and Daniel Batchelar.

Guitarist John Williams

68. SIR EDWARD ELGAR AND RALPH VAUGHAN WILLIAMS

English String Music

SINFONIA OF LONDON,
SIR JOHN BARBIROLLI, CONDUCTING
(EMI Classics 567264-2)

Includes Sir Edward Elgar's Introduction and Allegro *(op. 47),* Serenade in E minor *(op. 20),* Elegy *(op. 58), and* Sospiri *(op. 70); Ralph Vaughan Williams's* Fantasia on a Theme by Thomas Tallis *and* Fantasia on Greensleeves. *Allegri String Quartet (Introduction and Allegro); New Philharmonia Orchestra (Elegy and* Sospiri).*

Recorded 1963–1966

Both Sir Edward Elgar (1857–1934) and Ralph Vaughan Williams (1872–1958) wrote grander, more exalted works than the ones compiled here. In Elgar's case, there are three symphonies, concertos for the violin and the cello, grand oratorios like *The Dream of Gerontius* and *The Kingdom,* and of course the *Enigma* Variations; and from Vaughan Williams, there are nine great symphonies as well as chamber works and song settings, any of which arguably deserves a place in this list.

Sometimes, though, it's a performance of smaller works that makes the most direct and consistent appeal. Most of this disc is a classic 1963 collection of lushly scored works for string orchestra by these two great English composers; Elgar's brief Elegy and *Sospiri,* recorded three years later and added for the CD reissue, are a welcome bonus. *Sospiri,* in particular, was composed in 1914, possibly as a forlorn response to the start of World War I, and is an uncommonly beautiful work.

But then, all of these are—that's the point of them. Elgar's Introduction and Allegro, composed in 1905, grabs a listener by the lapels with a plangent, full-power burst of string sound and then melts into a two-tiered texture, with a string quartet set against the orchestra.

Elgar's lyricism, aided here by the hint of a Welsh folk song, takes over the Introduction and builds gradually to a broad-boned climax before giving way to the energetic counterpoint of the Allegro.

The Serenade, composed a dozen years earlier, has a Tchaikov-skian lilt, as well as the same sense of a string orchestra's potential heft that would later enliven the Introduction and Allegro. More important, a sense of its Victorian roots seems to pour out of it, in self-consciously elegant themes that soar through all three move-ments, and the comfortably plush harmonies—no tricks, no innova-tions, just a seductive warmth and a sense of depth from the highest to lowest string lines.

The two Vaughan Williams pieces share the opulence of the Elgar works, but little else: where Elgar conceived of his pieces as expres-sions of conservative modernity, speaking of their own time in their own terms, Vaughan Williams, in his fantasias, looks back to an ear-lier English golden age—that of the Tudors, in the sixteenth century. "Greensleeves" is a tune virtually everyone knows, although in this setting—a 1934 adaptation of music from *Sir John in Love,* Vaughan Williams's 1928 opera based on Shakespeare's *Merry Wives of Windsor*—he moves quite far afield in his exploration of the melody's implications, and he weaves in a second, uncredited folk tune, "Lovely Joan."

The *Fantasia on a Theme by Thomas Tallis,* composed in 1910 (and revised in 1919), is based on a hymn that Tallis contributed to a psalter in 1567, and which Vaughan Williams discovered when he was editing and arranging pieces for *The English Hymnal,* in 1906. The simple melody made an important impact on Vaughan Williams: he orchestrated the work for double string orchestra, with the second orchestra meant to be set at a distance from the first. That arrange-ment allows for both antiphonal interplay between the two string bodies, and a truly sumptuous sound when they join forces. The piece, apart from becoming immensely popular, was a watershed for Vaughan Williams: his approach to string scoring through the rest of his canon can be traced to techniques he developed here.

Sir John Barbirolli had a profound connection with all this music, and in a long recording career—he made his first discs in 1911 and his last in 1970, the year he died—he made eloquent recordings of works by both these composers, and other English pastoralists as well (most notably Frederick Delius). In the works at hand, both he and his ensembles understood the purely visceral appeal that Elgar's and Vaughan Williams's string scoring can have, and they basically let it rip, producing a sound that is rich and enveloping without diving fully into an un-Victorian sensuality. EMI's production adds to the allure: the stereo image underscores the music's textural wealth and, given that the earliest of these recordings is more than four decades old, the timbres and ambience are remarkably true to life.

69. SERGEI RACHMANINOFF

Concerto no. 3 in D minor for Piano and Orchestra (op. 30)

SERGEI PROKOFIEV

Concerto no. 3 in C major for Piano and Orchestra (op. 26)

VAN CLIBURN, PIANIST
(RCA Red Seal 6209-2-RC)

Symphony of the Air, Kiril Kondrashin, conducting; Chicago Symphony Orchestra, Walter Hendl, conducting.

Recorded 1958, 1960

This disc offers a glimpse of two traditions of the classical music world, both endangered or perhaps already extinct. One is of the tradition of the composer who was also a virtuoso instrumentalist, as both Rachmaninoff and Prokofiev were. The other is the tradition of the musical career launched by a competition victory, in which Van Cliburn holds a fairly unique place.

The composer-virtuoso was the norm through most of Western

musical history, going back at least to Renaissance times, and thriving—if somewhat weakened—into the twentieth century, when the decidedly modern concept of specialization forced musicians to choose between composing and interpreting. Naturally, there are exceptions that prove the rule. Leonard Bernstein was equally eloquent as a conductor and a composer, as are Pierre Boulez and Lukas Foss. Bernstein, Foss, and Benjamin Britten were also fine pianists who regularly performed other composers' music. Several minimalist composers perform as well, but usually only their own works, and those who do describe their technique as functional rather than virtuosic.

Sergei Rachmaninoff (1873–1943) and Sergei Prokofiev (1891–1953) were from a world in which composers devoted much of their time to (and earned much of their livelihood by) touring as performers. Like Mozart and Beethoven, they were highly regarded as pianists, and they generally wrote their piano concertos for their own use. Both of the works on this disc, in fact, were composed for American tours. Rachmaninoff gave the premiere of his Third Concerto in 1909 with the New York Symphony Orchestra, Walter Damrosch conducting; a few months later, he returned to play the work with the rival New York Philharmonic, under the baton of Gustav Mahler, another great composer-performer. (The two orchestras eventually merged, to form today's New York Philharmonic.) The Prokofiev Third is a bit more complicated: sections date back to 1911, but it coalesced into the concerto we know today in 1921, when the composer played its premiere with Frederick Stock and the Chicago Symphony.

Although they sit together well here, they are very different works. The Rachmaninoff, though perhaps a bit less popular than his Second Concerto, has always struck me as the most seductive of his works for piano and orchestra. Its opening theme has a sweet, instantly memorable quality that calls to mind the simplicity of a folk song, or perhaps the rhythmic and melodic plainness of an old Russian church chant. Rachmaninoff was aware that early listeners ascribed the theme to one or the other, and he denied them both, saying that it "simply wrote itself," and that his hope was "to 'sing' the melody at the piano, as a singer would sing it."

It sings, and so do the rest of the themes that hold this beautiful score together. But there is also another necessary component: virtuosity.

There is ample detail to test a pianist's technique and imagination, the latter serving to keep the splashiest writing from seeming merely showy. The joy of this work is its balance of brilliant technical display and limpid lyricism.

Prokofiev's music is typically more tart than Rachmaninoff's, but his Third Concerto opens with a deceptively dreamy passage for orchestra, from which the sizzling solo piano line emerges at full-throttle, and hurtles toward a pounding chordal section. A touch of the Soviet modernist character that defines some of Prokofiev's music—mechanistic rhythms, torrential floods of notes—makes its way into the piece as well. And yet another side of Prokofiev peeks through in the central movement, a Theme and Variations based on a neoclassical motif akin in spirit to the music of the composer's *Classical* Symphony of 1917. That light touch doesn't last long: soon enough the rhythmic angularity returns, along with the demand for fingers of steel. But as in the Rachmaninoff, a lyrical undercurrent runs through the piece as well.

These are among Van Cliburn's best recordings, made soon after the lanky Texan returned to the United States from his triumph at the Tchaikovsky Competition in Moscow in April 1958. Competitions have always been a double-edged sword in music: as far back as Claude Debussy, musicians railed against them as unnatural and antiartistic. The case against them is simple enough: an interpretation cannot be measured objectively in the way that, say, a high jump can. And because a performer is likely to connect, or not, with every member of a jury in a different way, the award of a competition's top prize is invariably a matter of compromise. Nevertheless, competitions are part of the Darwinian mechanism of the concert world. Young musicians continue to enter them in the hope that a victory will put them in the spotlight long enough to launch their careers.

That's how it worked for Cliburn, the biggest competition winner ever, for reasons that are partly extramusical. Having won a prestigious international competition held in Moscow, where the repertory was largely Russian and the favorites were Russian pianists—and all this at the height of the Cold War—Cliburn became an instant hero at age twenty-three, not only in America, but in Russia and Europe as well. Upon his return to the United States, he was greeted with a ticker-tape parade, household-name status, and an instant career with all the concerts, recordings, and television appearances a young musician could want.

The problem was, Cliburn discovered that he didn't really want all that. He toured for nearly two decades, and made a string of recordings that range from a powerfully etched account of Samuel Barber's Sonata and some very beautiful Chopin and Liszt, to more frivolous collections of encore favorites. But celebrity and the demand to keep his repertory fresh wore on him, and by the late 1970s, he essentially retired to Fort Worth, Texas, venturing out only occasionally to play the Tchaikovsky First Concerto or one of the two on this disc with a handful of orchestras.

His main concern, since 1977, has been the Van Cliburn International Piano Competition, which he established with the aim of doing for young pianists what the Tchaikovsky Competition had done for him. It hasn't particularly worked: without the freak political

Pianist Van Cliburn in a ticker-tape parade after winning first prize in the 1958 International Tchaikovsky Competition

dimension that made Cliburn famous well beyond the normal precincts of the classical music world, the winners of his competition have found that their victories yield only a tiny career boost. This is the great irony of Van Cliburn: the eager young players who come to Fort Worth every four years would do anything for the opportunities Cliburn had. But Cliburn—the only pianist to truly emerge from a competition with instant fame, and probably the only one who ever will—didn't really want it.

Nevertheless, these recordings capture Cliburn at the absolute height of his technical and interpretive powers, and at a time when the prospect of a concert career still excited him. The Rachmaninoff, in fact, was recorded at a Carnegie Hall concert with the great Russian conductor Kiril Kondrashin, just a few weeks after his victory in Moscow, and the electricity in the performance is palpable. The Prokofiev was recorded with the orchestra that gave it its premiere, just over two years later. In both, Cliburn's playing is focused and controlled, and he produces a range of sound that runs from lush beauty, in the Rachmaninoff, to sparkling and more sharp-edged in the Prokofiev.

70. EDGARD VARÈSE

Ionisation, Amériques, and Arcana

THE NEW YORK PHILHARMONIC,
PIERRE BOULEZ, CONDUCTING

Offrandes, Octandre, Intégrales, and Density 21.5

ENSEMBLE INTERCONTEMPORAIN,
PIERRE BOULEZ, CONDUCTING
(Sony Classical SK 45844)

Lawrence Beauregard, flutist in Density 21.5; *Rachel Yakar, soprano in* Offrandes.

Recorded 1977, 1984

Edgard Varèse

Edgard Varèse's relationship to the musical mainstream of the early twentieth century was nearly akin to Carlo Gesualdo's place in the compositional world of the late Renaissance and early baroque. Both composers stood apart from the major stylistic battles of their times, and each developed an idiosyncratically dissonant personal language. Like Gesualdo, Varèse (1883–1965) had his champions during his lifetime, but his music was more fully prized by the musicians of later generations. For all their noisy assertiveness, Varèse's works touch something in listeners' psyches.

Born in Paris and raised in Turin, Varèse returned to Paris when he was twenty to study at the Schola Cantorum (where his teachers included Albert Roussel and Vincent d'Indy) and later at the Conservatoire (where he worked with Charles-Marie Widor). A brief sojourn in Berlin, where Richard Strauss arranged for performances of his early scores, brought him into contact with Schoenberg's early music, which he brought back to Paris with him when he returned in 1913. Unfortunately, he left most of his own early works in a Berlin warehouse, where they were destroyed in a fire.

He arrived in the United States in 1915, and in addition to composing, he conducted and organized societies for the promotion of new music, among them the International Composers Guild, which flourished from 1921 to 1927, and the Pan American Association of Composers, which took up the cause from 1928 to 1934. Between 1928 and the end of his life, Varèse spent extended periods in New York and Paris, undertaking major projects and trying to find sponsors to underwrite a laboratory where he could explore his blossoming interest in electronic sound, and develop his idiosyncratic ideas about composition.

That he was never able to establish his dream laboratory was a source of great frustration for Varèse, but his music shows that outlandish sounds were by no means beyond his grasp, regardless of the financial or technical impediments he faced. His first published orchestral work, *Amériques* (1918–1922), uses a large orchestra with eleven percussionists. Its placid opening is scored for alto flute, set against a percussion texture; but the work grows quickly, with seemingly free-floating thematic fragments set against blocks of carefully organized and orchestrated material and grand waves of sound. The urban and the exotic—heard, for example, in the recurring use of both a siren and a lion's roar (a string-operated percussion instrument that creates a sound like the one it is named for)—are juxtaposed, as are explosive percussion figures and eerily focused string lines.

The work's title might suggest that it is a Frenchman's portrait of America, but Varèse meant the title more broadly, as an emblem of the new, "symbolic of discoveries—new worlds on earth, in the sky or in the minds of men." That, in a way, could describe several of the pieces here. *Arcana* (1925), also scored for large orchestra, and played with pointed vigor by the New York Philharmonic, combined Varèse's interest in constantly shifting texture with an insistent drive—sometimes rhythmic, sometimes merely a matter of atmosphere—that goes beyond the energy of *Amériques*.

Ionisation (1930–1931) is a compact work for thirteen percussionists, who play forty instruments. Rhythms alternately interlock and compete, and textures of every sort mingle freely: hard-edged and soft sounds are set against one another, as are rattles and gongs, and sounds of wood, steel, and drumskin. A pair of sirens weave through the texture, giving Varèse's organized structures a touch of the chaos of the urban life that so thoroughly enthralled him.

Pierre Boulez, probably France's most influential composer in the second half of the twentieth century, and an increasingly eloquent conductor, succeeded Leonard Bernstein as music director of the New York Philharmonic in 1971, and led the orchestra until 1977. It was a comparatively unhappy time: the Philharmonic audience was suspicious of Boulez's adventures in new music, and generally found him a chilly interpreter of the Germanic mainstream repertory. There was, in truth, no way a listener would have guessed, back then, that he would become a magnificent Mahler conductor in the mid-1990s. Still, Boulez made some splendid recordings with the Philharmonic, and this Varèse disc remains one of the landmarks.

For the CD reissue, Sony has added a handful of recordings that Boulez made later with his own Parisian new-music band, the Ensemble InterContemporain. Included is Varèse's most lyrical piece—but one not without its gymnastic moments—*Density 21.5* (1936), for solo flute; the intensely moody vocal setting, *Offrandes* (1921); *Octandre* (1923), a three-movement chamber score (for winds, brass, and double-bass) that is as shimmeringly changeable as *Amériques,* and ends with a brightly dissonant, celebratory brass fanfare; and *Intégrales* (1924), for winds, brass, bass, and seventeen percussion instruments.

Boulez's other Varèse recordings are worth exploring as well. With the Ensemble InterContemporain, he has recorded vivid accounts of *Déserts, Ecuatorial,* and *Hyperprism* on a disc that also includes a New York Philharmonic recording of Elliott Carter's Symphony for Three Orchestras (Sony Classical); and in 1995, as part of a growing association with the Chicago Symphony, he remade *Amériques, Arcana, Ionisation,* and *Déserts* (Deutsche Grammophon). The Chicago versions are in some ways more sharply defined than the older Philharmonic recordings; but each has its attractions and the more expansive program on the Sony disc gives it the edge.

71. CHARLES IVES

Three Places in New England (Orchestral Set no. 1) and Orchestral Set no. 2

CARL RUGGLES

Sun-Treader and *Men and Mountains*

RUTH CRAWFORD SEEGER

Andante for Strings

THE CLEVELAND ORCHESTRA AND CHORUS,
CHRISTOPH VON DOHNÁNYI, CONDUCTING
(Decca 289 443 776-2)

Recorded 1993–1994

Half a century after his death, it remains difficult to keep Charles Ives (1874–1954) and his music in anything like a realistic perspective.

One is hard-pressed to endorse the stark declaration in *The New Grove Dictionary of Music and Musicians* that Ives "is regarded as the leading American composer of art music of the 20th century," a claim even his most vehement advocates would admit is too sweeping. He was *a* leading composer, certainly, and perhaps *the* leading American composer of the *early* twentieth century, but in a pantheon so heavily populated with composers who flourished after 1925, it's difficult to accord him absolute primacy.

By the same token, the contention of Ives detractors that he was an amateur and a charlatan is equally unsupportable. He was by no means untrained. Ives's father was a professional musician, and Ives gravitated toward music early, studying the piano and organ (he spent fourteen years of his youth as a church organist) and playing drums in one of his father's bands, which performed one of his early marches when he was thirteen. His father was apparently open-minded about the harmonic experiments Ives began fairly early on, inspired—or so the lore goes—by sitting on a hill and hearing two marching bands, at different points in a parade, playing in clashing keys. At Yale, as a student of Horatio Parker, he expanded his horizons and continued to experiment.

Upon his graduation in 1898, Ives moved to New York and began a thirty-year career in the insurance business. But if he became a Sunday composer, music was where his heart was, and judging from his manifestoes on the subject (most notably his *Essays before a Sonata*), he regarded it as a means of communication that had crucial philosophical, political, and social components. He was keen to establish a rugged American style, distinct from that of Europe by way of its adventurous approach to harmony, and concerned with American issues—which could mean anything from American vernacular music (hymns, marches, and popular tunes) to expounding musically on American holidays, places, or thinkers and writers (Emerson, for example).

The two Orchestral Sets touch on some of these concerns. The first and better known of the two, *Three Places in New England*, composed between 1903 and 1911, but not performed until 1931, begins with *The "St. Gaudens" in Boston Common,* a harmonically hazy, warm-hued tribute to the Fifty-fourth Massachusetts Volunteer

Infantry, the first black Union Army regiment to fight in the Civil War—a topic that would have been close to Ives's heart, given his father's service in the same war and his family's history as abolitionists. The second sketch, *Putnam's Camp, Redding, Connecticut,* looks back at the Revolutionary War in typically Ivesian terms, with snippets of marches—from "Yankee Doodle" to an anachronistic John Philip Sousa quotation—swirling together in incompatible keys. And the masterly *Housatonic at Stockbridge,* one of Ives's greatest scores, uses competing sonorities, rhythms, and thematic material to portray the currents within the large, slow-moving river, as well as the variety of sights and sounds on its shores.

The Orchestral Set no. 2 (1912–1915) continues along similar lines, opening with the harmonically murky (but also sparkling, thanks to the percussion) *Elegy to Our Forefathers,* and then moving through *The Rockstrewn Hills Join in the People's Outdoor Meeting,* a vigorous mélange of ragtime fragments and fractured hymns joined in characteristically Ivesian chaos, and the moving finale, *From Hanover Square North . . . ,* a response to news of the sinking of the *Lusitania* by a German U-boat in 1915.

American music has generally left European conductors a bit puzzled, and many who have made an effort to come to terms with it—Kurt Masur and Riccardo Muti, for example—have been unable to fully convey its heartbeat, let alone its spirit. Christoph von Dohnányi, the German conductor who led the Cleveland Orchestra from 1984 to 2002, was an exception, and although his discography is weighted toward Germanic romanticism, it also includes, besides this nicely packed and beautifully played collection of American works, a powerful reading of Edgard Varèse's *Amériques.*

Dohnányi and his players bring a useful clarity and precision to these six character pieces. Above all, they show that Ives's weird harmonic juxtapositions are not merely thumb-in-the-eye pranksterism, but carefully weighed gestures that make an emotional and visceral point.

He is equally persuasive in the Ruggles and Crawford Seeger works, which are composed in quite a different spirit. Carl Ruggles (1876–1971), like Ives, with whom he was friendly, was a crusty New Englander. He studied at Harvard with John Knowles Paine, who, like

Ives's teacher, Horatio Parker, was one of the most respected American composers of the day. But Ruggles won greater success as a watercolorist than as a composer, and he actually wrote very little music: the conductor Michael Tilson Thomas recorded Ruggles's complete published works for CBS Masterworks (now Sony Classical) in the early 1980s, and the entire set fit on two LPs that have never been transferred to CD.

But if Ruggles's musical catalog was small, it was extraordinarily concentrated, not least because he worked and reworked his scores throughout his life. His affinity with Ives and his penchant for skirting the expectations of European harmonic models notwithstanding, Ruggles adhered to more conventional notions of form, and to an almost romantic sound world. *Sun-Treader* (1931), a grandly scaled paean to the heroic spirit of creativity, is his greatest work, and Dohnányi's shaping of its arching lines, as well as his balancing of its conflicting currents of neoromanticism and dissonant modernism, conveys the full scope of this score's monumental character.

Men and Mountains, started, finished, and reconsidered various times between 1920 and 1936, is much smaller in scale and ambition, but also suppler, with moments of wrenching delicacy nestled between statements that strive for the titanic.

Ruth Crawford Seeger's link to this program is through Ruggles, a close friend of the Seeger family, which also included her husband, the composer and musicologist Charles Seeger, and their children, the folksingers Pete, Mike, and Peggy Seeger. Crawford Seeger (1901–1953) had been a student of her husband, and of Alban Berg in Vienna, and is represented here by a string orchestra arrangement of the Andante from the work for which she is best known, her String Quartet (1931–1933). It is a beautiful, haunting work, built of waves of slowly overlapping, sustained lines that crash into a surprising climax.

72. GEORGE GERSHWIN

Rhapsody in Blue and *An American in Paris*

FERDE GROFÉ

Grand Canyon Suite

COLUMBIA SYMPHONY ORCHESTRA AND NEW YORK
PHILHARMONIC, LEONARD BERNSTEIN, CONDUCTING,
AND PIANIST IN THE *RHAPSODY*

(Sony Classical MK 42264)

Recorded 1959, 1964

As a composer of everything from popular songs and Broadway musi-
cals to piano concertos and a work of operatic ambition, George
Gershwin (1898–1937) was one of a handful of early-twentieth-
century composers who saw no point in maintaining a gulf between
popular culture and high art. It was an issue that was hotly debated,
often along age lines, with older classical musicians decrying the influence of jazz in modern musical life, while their younger colleagues
saw no problem. The rhythms, after all, were fascinatin'.

Gershwin was grounded in both worlds: he began studying the
classical repertory, as a pianist, when he was twelve, but when he took
his first job, at fifteen, it was as a song salesman for the Jerome H.
Remick Company, a Tin Pan Alley song publisher. At seventeen, he
worked as a rehearsal pianist during the preparation of a Broadway
show by Jerome Kern; and at twenty, he had songs in a handful of
shows, as well as a full show of his own, *La La Lucille*. Yet all the
while he was studying composition and counterpoint formally with
the composer Edward Kilenyi.

Gershwin's music has proven as suited to all worlds as Gershwin
himself. Take a song like "Summertime," one of the show-stoppers in
Gershwin's opera, *Porgy and Bess*. A standard in just about any musical

genre, you can hear it in its original operatic form, or in jazz transformations by Ella Fitzgerald, Louis Armstrong, and probably three-quarters of the jazz singers who have ever spent time on stage. There is even a sizzling, bluesy rock version by Janis Joplin with Big Brother and the Holding Company. In every one of these treatments, the song seems entirely at home.

The *Rhapsody in Blue,* Gershwin's most famous work for the classical concert hall, and one of the few crossover works to become thoroughly entrenched in the international repertory, almost wasn't written. Gershwin had spoken vaguely with the jazz bandleader Paul Whiteman about writing a concerto for jazz piano and orchestra, but did not believe they had agreed upon such specifics as a deadline or a performance date. But in January 1924, Whiteman announced that the work would have its premiere at a concert on February 12. Gershwin didn't think so: his principal concern at the moment was finishing the score for another Broadway musical, *Sweet Little Devil.* But Whiteman persuaded Gershwin that if he could produce a piano score, Ferde Grofé (1892–1972), Whiteman's own orchestrator, would fill out the instrumentation.

As it turned out, Gershwin was able to produce the piece fairly quickly, largely during a train trip to Boston, and in his rough score, he gave Grofé a sense of the coloration he had in mind by annotating particular themes and passages with the names of players in Whiteman's band. When the piece was played, Olin Downes, the *New York Times* critic, wrote that it "shows an extraordinary talent," but went on to lacerate it for a list of sins ascribed to Gershwin's technical immaturity. He noted, though, that the piece offered some of the most original music on Whiteman's program, and that the audience responded to it with tumultuous applause—as, indeed, audiences continued to do as Gershwin performed it over the next several months, and as they do today when the performance has the requisite swing.

In recent years, several musicians have felt the need to reimagine *Rhapsody in Blue,* and a couple—the jazz pianist Marcus Roberts (Sony Classical) and the classical pianist Fazil Say (Warner Classics), for example—have infused their readings with a free-spirited, improvisatory sensibility. The beauty of this performance by Leonard Bernstein, though, is that it finds its freedoms fully in the context of Gershwin's score.

Bernstein was a capable and enthusiastic jazz pianist, and he and Gershwin were certainly kindred spirits. Bernstein, too, wrote for the theater as well as the concert hall, and he had an abiding passion for popular music of all kinds. In his frequent televised talks on music—which ranged from Young People's Concerts to the Norton Lectures at Harvard University—he regularly quoted from jazz and rock songs while explaining the classics, and one never had the sense that he was pandering. It should be no surprise that his account of the *Rhapsody* is in many ways the most eloquent and supple to be found on disc.

There are passages in his reading that are notably more ruminative than one typically hears, as well as some daredevil zestiness. But Bernstein's interpretive choices are consistently persuasive, not least because the work as a whole is performed with the same polish and care that Bernstein brought to more conventional European classics.

The two companion works here are painterly scores in the old tradition of representational music. Gershwin's *An American in Paris,* composed during a European visit in 1928, evokes the urban landscape of its time: one hears the bustle of modern street life, including the honking horns of Parisian traffic, and if it sounds quaint when compared with the more raucous portraits of city life composed by Edgard Varèse around the same time, it makes its case with a good balance of urbanity and excitement, qualities that Bernstein's performance preserves.

Grofé's most famous work, the *Grand Canyon Suite,* was a fixture of symphonic pops concerts for many years, but has largely fallen from favor. One can see why: movements like "On the Trail," with its clip-clopping of pony hooves, sound downright corny now, and even the closing "Cloudburst" sounds clunky when compared with Beethoven's or Vivaldi's storms. Still, heard on its own terms—as a pictorial work by a talented if not always inspired composer of music with populist ambitions—there are some lovely touches, including the shadings of the "Sunrise" and "Sunset" movements, and the sweet-toned violin line, played by John Corigliano (the father of the composer) in "On the Trail."

73. AARON COPLAND

The Copland Collection—Orchestral and Ballet Works, 1936–1948

AARON COPLAND, CONDUCTING
(Sony Classical SM3K 46559, three CDs)

Includes El Salón México, An Outdoor Overture, Billy the Kid *(Orchestral Suite)*, Quiet City, John Henry, Our Town, Las Agachadas, Fanfare for the Common Man, Rodeo (Four Dance Episodes), Music for Movies, Appalachian Spring *(Suite)*, Letter from Home, Danzón Cubano, Lincoln Portrait, *Symphony no. 3, and Concerto for Clarinet, Strings, Harp and Piano. Henry Fonda, narrator; Benny Goodman, clarinetist; New Philharmonia Orchestra, London Symphony Orchestra, New England Conservatory Chorus, Columbia Symphony Strings, Aaron Copland, conducting.*

Recorded 1963 to 1976

From the mid-1950s into the 1970s, Columbia Masterworks, the predecessor of what is today Sony Classical, was directed by Goddard Lieberson, an extraordinary executive of a sort no longer found in the offices of the major record labels. A trained composer who also worked as a music critic and novelist, Lieberson recognized that one of the most important things a record label could do was to document the music of the age, ideally in recordings supervised—and, where applicable, performed—by the composers themselves. And indeed, two large projects that will always remain monuments to Lieberson (who died in 1977) were *Stravinsky Conducts Stravinsky* and *Copland Conducts Copland,* series that captured authoritative performances by two of the composing giants of the twentieth century who were also skilled conductors.

Sony has not yet transferred the complete Copland series to CD, but it included the most essential recordings in three boxed sets (of which this is the second volume) in 1990, the year Copland celebrated his ninetieth birthday. As the middle installment in a three-volume series, this set misses the seminal early works in which Copland was finding his way and establishing his style, and the later works—particularly the piano and chamber music—in which he expanded beyond the cheery tonality of his most popular pieces. But it does explore the peaks of Copland's "populist" period, when he adopted the idea—suggested by Dvořák in the 1890s, and proven effective by Stravinsky in his early ballets—of transforming folk themes into the basis of a new national style.

It is on account of these folk-tinged works that the Brooklyn-born, Paris-trained Copland (1900–1990) has become regarded as the father of American music, although Copland himself—a witty, gentle, and generous man—would have smiled and pointed out that he had many predecessors, stretching back to William Billings in the eighteenth century, the mid-nineteenth-century piano virtuoso and composer Louis Moreau Gottschalk, the long tradition of Arthur Farwell, Edward MacDowell, Horatio Parker, Scott Joplin, Charles Tomlinson Griffes, and, of course, the great Yankee individualists, Charles Ives and Carl Ruggles, all of whom straddle the nineteenth and twentieth centuries.

Still, Copland was the first native-born composer of unalloyed concert music to entrance the American public; and along with other composers of his generation, he was among the first to establish American music as an equal player with its European (and, more recently, Asian) counterparts in the global exchange of musical ideas. He also worked hard on behalf of Mexican and Latin American composers—in this set, his *El Salón México* (1933–1936), *Danzón Cubano* (1942), and *Las Agachadas* (1942) testify to his affection for their musical accents—and he wrote several books meant to explain music (particularly contemporary music) to both specialist and non-specialist listeners.

Among the most enduring items included in this collection are suites from Copland's picturesque ballet scores, *Billy the Kid* (1938–1939), *Rodeo* (1942), and *Appalachian Spring* (1945). The first, written for Lincoln Kirstein's Ballet Caravan, draws some of its raw material from cowboy songs—"Old Paint," "Git Along Little Dogies," and "The Old Chisolm Trail," among them—but Copland also creates his own representations of the prairie, a frontier town, card games and gun battles, and the capture and death of its hero. *Rodeo,* written for the dancer and choreographer Agnes de Mille, is in very much the same spirit: particularly vibrant is its closing "Hoe-Down." And the invitingly bittersweet *Appalachian Spring* Suite—which includes among its eight movements a set of lovely variations on the Shaker tune, "Simple Gifts"—remains Copland's most frequently played score.

But there are other crucial pieces here as well. In *Lincoln Portrait* (1942), Copland supports a narration drawn from Lincoln's great speeches—read here with distinction by Henry Fonda—with music that is in the thoroughly accessible style that Copland had by then established as quintessentially "American." Other pieces offer an urban counterpoint mirror image to the Western ballets. In *Quiet City* (1940), a muted, jazz-tinged trumpet line intertwines with a lyrical English horn solo to capture the atmosphere of a late, lonely night in 1940s New York. *Our Town* (1940) and *Music for Movies* (1942), both derived from film scores, conjure the earthy and the urbane, as the settings demand, and the rising brass theme of the stately *Fanfare for the Common Man* (1942) transcends issues of city versus country, and even specific nationality.

Copland revisited the *Fanfare* theme in his Third Symphony (1944–1946), a vital work that is beginning to be performed as frequently as it deserves. And closing the set is the alternately lyrical and fiery Clarinet Concerto (1947–1948) that Copland composed for Benny Goodman, who gives it a stunning reading.

That said, in the late 1990s, the clarinetist Charles Neidich located the original score of the concerto, and discovered that Goodman had persuaded Copland that the work would be more frequently performed if he lightened up on the high-flying runs that originally appeared at several crucial moments. Copland accepted Goodman's advice, which is reflected in the standard published edition, but Neidich has shown that the original version is both playable and exciting. His recording, with I Musici de Montréal, is included on *Composers in New York,* a disc that also includes works by Samuel Barber, William Schuman, and Morton Gould (Chandos).

There are numerous other Copland discs worth knowing. Leonard Bernstein recorded superb accounts of the great ballets (Sony Classical) and monumental performances of the Third Symphony (for both

Sony Classical and Deutsche Grammophon). Leonard Slatkin (on EMI Classics and RCA) and Michael Tilson Thomas (on Sony Classical and RCA) have made several fine, energetic, and thoroughly recommendable Copland discs as well. And of course, there are more installments of the *Copland Conducts Copland* series, including the other volumes of Sony Classical's Copland Collection—*Early Orchestral Works, 1922–1935* and *Orchestral Works, 1948–1971*—as well as separate discs (also on Sony), among them, one that offers the complete, beautifully expansive chamber version of *Appalachian Spring* and another with William Warfield's soulful rendering of *Old American Songs* (1950–1952).

74. SAMUEL BARBER

Adagio for Strings (op. 11), Overture to *The School for Scandal* (op. 5), *Second Essay for Orchestra* (op. 17), *Medea's Dance of Vengeance* (op. 23a), *Andromache's Farewell* (op. 39), and Intermezzo from *Vanessa* (op. 32)

MARTINA ARROYO, SOPRANO; NEW YORK PHILHARMONIC
AND COLUMBIA SYMPHONY ORCHESTRA,
THOMAS SCHIPPERS, CONDUCTING
(Sony Classical MHK 62837)

Includes Gian Carlo Menotti's Overture to Amelia al Ballo; *Alban Berg's Introduction to* Wozzeck; *Vincent d'Indy's Introduction to* Fervaal *(op. 40).*

Recorded 1960–1965

Samuel Barber (1910–1981) was one of the great American neoromantics, an original voice in the generation that also included Aaron Copland and William Schuman—and also, on the harmonically thornier side of the new-music street, Elliott Carter and Milton Babbitt. His

---

early career seemed charmed: he was born in West Chester, Pennsylvania, near Philadelphia, and began studying composition at the Curtis Institute when he was thirteen. Some early song settings won considerable acclaim, and by his early twenties he had won some important prizes—including the first of two Pulitzers, when he was twenty-five—and his works had been performed by the Philadelphia Orchestra and the New York Philharmonic.

His breakthrough, though, the Adagio for Strings—which was actually a breakaway movement from an early string quartet (op. 11)—was given a celebrated premiere by Arturo Toscanini and the NBC Symphony in 1938, and quickly became one of the most popular works in the growing canon of American symphonic scores. Barber's two *Essays for Orchestra* and his lilting setting of James Agee's *Knoxville: Summer of 1915* further cemented his reputation, and his first opera, *Vanessa,* both a popular and critical success when it was first heard in 1958, won Barber a second Pulitzer.

Barber continued to compile a varied catalog of symphonic, chamber, vocal, and piano works, and enjoyed an unbroken chain of successes—until 1966, when his *Antony and Cleopatra* opened the new Metropolitan Opera House at Lincoln Center. Hindered in part by a production that overtaxed the untried stage technology of the new house, the opera was poorly received. A 1975 revision fared considerably better; but the work's failure at the Met appeared to have broken Barber's spirit; he composed very little new music thereafter.

What he left, though, was an extraordinary and durable body of work, and this recording by Thomas Schippers offers some of the highlights. Barber composed the earliest of the works here, the *School for Scandal* Overture, when he was twenty-one, but the piece shows his mastery of the orchestra. Tempestuous, vital string writing is offset by the kind of sweetly lyrical themes (most notably an English horn solo, beautifully played here) that became a signature move for Barber.

That lyricism is explored further in the *Second Essay for Orchestra,* which begins with ruminative and invitingly mysterious wind writing and expands into a comprehensive and sometimes vehement exploration of the orchestra's full resources. A similar slate of qualities animates *Medea's Dance of Vengeance,* a work from 1955 in which Barber's lyricism is tempered by a neoclassical edge that, while never as acerbic as Stravinsky's neoclassicism, shows traces of Stravinsky's influence.

The Adagio, of course, is ubiquitous, and it has been given some mawkish readings over the years, as well as some that go out of their way to avoid sentimentality by speeding the music along. Schippers steers a sensible middle course: his reading clocks in at just over nine minutes—two minutes longer than the recording by Charles Munch, which seems to be the speed king for Barber Adagios. But there is a tautness in Schippers's account that touches on the music's emotionality without wallowing in it, and the New York Philharmonic string sound is seductively lush.

That lushness buoys Schippers's account of the Intermezzo from *Vanessa* as well. And there is a glimpse of Barber's sense of drama in *Andromache's Farewell,* a work based on a scene from Euripides' *Trojan Women.* In this twelve-minute scene—Barber's contribution to the New York Philharmonic's first season at Lincoln Center—the solo soprano and the orchestra are equal partners in conveying Andromache's torment in the moments before her son, Astyanax, is hurled by the Greeks over the battlements of Troy. The vocal writing is full of fireworks, and Martina Arroyo—who made this recording with Schippers soon after the premiere, in 1963—gives a performance that will send shivers up your spine. Yet there is more to the work than that. Barber stopped short of writing what would have been obvious—a searing mad scene—and instead let Andromache retain her regal dignity. It was that kind of choice that makes his music so cherishable.

The heart of this CD reissue from Sony Classical's Masterworks Heritage series is an all-Barber album that Schippers made with the New York Philharmonic in 1965, but the label has also added two more of Schippers's classic Barber performances, as well as an overture by Barber's longtime friend Gian-Carlo Menotti, and operatic overtures by Alban Berg and Vincent d'Indy. Although the Barber is of particular interest here, the other works also reflect well on the artistry of Schippers, an eloquent conductor best remembered for his championship of American composers. He died of lung cancer at age forty-seven, in 1977.

Assembled during a brief window when Sony Classical had decided to package its deep catalog reissues with the care they deserve—a plan sadly abandoned after only a handful of releases in an effort to cut expenses—this album is not only a great sonic improvement on the original vinyl issues, but an aesthetic treat as well. Offered in a cardboard gatefold cover instead of a plastic jewel case, the CD is held in a sleeve that reproduces the inner liner of an old CBS Masterworks LP. The booklet, affixed to the inside front cover, includes lucid annotations, complete recording information, quite a few infrequently seen pictures of Schippers (including some from the recording sessions, with Barber and Menotti), and reproductions of the covers of the original LPs from which these recordings are drawn.

In the classical record world, and particularly in the CD era, packaging is often utilitarian and taken for granted. Releases like this show that it can be more than that.

75. KURT WEILL

Kleine Dreigroschenmusik, Mahagonny Songspiel, Happy End, Berliner Requiem, Pantomime I (from Der Protagonist), Vom Tod im Wald, and Violin Concerto

LONDON SINFONIETTA, DAVID ATHERTON, CONDUCTING

(Deutsche Grammophon 459 442, two CDs)

Mary Thomas and Meriel Dickinson, mezzo-sopranos; Philip Langridge and Ian Partridge, tenors; Benjamin Luxon, baritone; Michael Rippon, bass; Nona Liddell, violinist.

Recorded 1975

Few composers have had as strangely bifurcated a career as Kurt Weill (1900–1950). He spent his early years in Berlin, composing symphonic works, chamber pieces, and an amalgam of opera and jazz-tinged cabaret music that evokes its time and place more thoroughly than any other music of the era. But the era turned quickly: when the Nazis came to power, in 1933, the popular Weill was in their sights. Not only was he Jewish, but his penchant for drawing on jazz rhythms and timbres was regarded as an affront to Aryan culture. Moreover, he was an associate and collaborator of the leftist playwright Bertolt Brecht, most notably on *Die Dreigroschenoper (The Threepenny Opera)* in 1928 and *Aufstieg und Fall der Stadt Mahagonny (The Rise and Fall of the City of Mahagonny)* in 1930. And some of his works—even those he wrote with librettists other than Brecht, like *Die Bürgschaft,* in 1932, and *Der Silbersee,* in 1933—included material that was openly critical of totalitarian rule. As soon as the Nazis ordered his shows closed, Weill and his wife, the singer Lotte Lenya, fled to Paris.

They remained in Paris for two years, and it was there that Weill and Brecht undertook their last collaboration, *The Seven Deadly Sins.* Then, in 1935, Weill put Europe behind him entirely. He sailed to New York, turned his back on the works of his German youth, and insisted that the "W" in his name be pronounced in the English, rather than German, way. And musically, he first devoured American popular forms, making a study of everything from minstrel shows and railroad songs, to the works of George Gershwin, which he revered. He then devoted himself to the quintessential American form of the time, the Broadway musical, creating a string of hits that included *Street Scene, Lady in the Dark, Lost in the Stars,* and *One Touch of Venus.*

As a Broadway composer, Weill staked a place outside the classical music mainstream in which he was trained, but he attracted the notice of the concert world nevertheless: Aaron Copland, for one, cautioned listeners not to be fooled by what might at first seem banality in Weill's music. "It is a purposeful and meaningful banality if one can read between the lines, as it were, and sense the deep hidden tragedy in its carefree quality." Copland may have heard that tragedy as the echo of Weill's flight from the Nazis. But actually, its roots are deeper: you can also hear it within the scores on this compilation of his Berlin works.

At the time David Atherton made this set, Weill was something of a connoisseur's specialty. After his death in 1950, his works seemed to fade into obscurity. There were occasional revivals—Broadway stagings of *Threepenny Opera,* and an operatic staging of *Lost in the Stars,* for example—but a Weill Renaissance of sorts did not begin to gather steam until around 1980, when opera companies began revisiting works like *Mahagonny, The Threepenny Opera, Der Silbersee,* and even some of the Broadway works, like *Street Scene;* young ensembles began looking into the chamber and symphonic music; and a new breed of cabaret singers took up both the Berlin and New York repertory. Around the same time, Weill scholarship came of age with Kim Kowalke's in-depth study, *Kurt Weill in Europe,* and the establishment of the Kurt Weill Foundation, based in New York. The foundation has overseen the production of a complete edition of Weill's music and has encouraged performances of his works around the world.

The Atherton recording, made five years before the first wave of the Weill revival crested, was crucial in calling attention to these neglected works. The wedges in the door, clearly, were the suites from *Threepenny Opera* and *Mahagonny.* Everyone, even listeners who knew nothing about Weill, knew "Die Moritat vom Mackie Messer" (better known in English as "Mack the Knife") from *Threepenny Opera,* and "Alabama Song" from *Mahagonny.* They had, after all, been pop hits, for Bobby Darin and the Doors, respectively. But the suites, with their wind-heavy orchestrations, their sharp-edged rhythmic character, and their dark-tinged melodies, proved that those songs were just the tip of the iceberg.

And then there was the rest of the collection, three more Brecht collaborations—*Vom Tod im Wald* (Death in the Forest), from 1927, Weill's dissonant, sharp-edged setting of Brecht's poem about a Mississippi lynching; a set of songs from *Happy End* (1929), another theater piece; and the *Berliner Requiem* (also 1929), a wrenching, sardonic cantata for male voices. All are supported by what had by then become Weill's characteristic wind sound, as are a dance section from Weill's 1925 operatic collaboration with Georg Kaiser, *Der Protagonist,* and the Violin Concerto (1924), a magnificent piece that flirts with atonality—particularly in the solo line—but in which Weill's deep-rooted lyricism ultimately prevails.

The performances are beautifully and energetically played, but most important, they perfectly capture the accent and atmosphere of Berlin in the 1920s. The music itself provides those qualities to a great degree, but what Atherton and company bring to it is an informed sense of that time and sound—something that many of the recordings of this music made since 1975 have not been able to match.

76. ALBAN BERG

Violin Concerto

ANNE-SOPHIE MUTTER, VIOLINIST; CHICAGO SYMPHONY
ORCHESTRA, JAMES LEVINE, CONDUCTING
(Deutsche Grammophon 437 093-2)

Includes Wolfgang Rihm's Time Chant.

Recorded 1992

If Arnold Schoenberg was the founder of the Second Viennese School and the codifier of the twelve-tone language that became that school's principal engine, his two most important students, Anton Webern and Alban Berg, are equally central to the movement's history. And it was the music of Berg (1885–1935) that was embraced earliest by a public that found Schoenberg's experiments too harsh and Webern's aphoristic pieces too puzzling. Berg's Violin Concerto, in particular, struck a responsive chord with soloists, who in turn were able to sell it to a public that, for decades, was resistant to music of the Schoenberg circle.

Berg began his studies with Schoenberg in 1904, when he was nineteen, and when Schoenberg, then thirty, was still writing in the late romantic style of *Verklärte Nacht*. He was still on hand as Schoenberg's style evolved toward *Erwartung* and beyond. But if Schoenberg's influence was decisive, Berg was not quite a tabula rasa. By the time he began working with Schoenberg, he had composed some seventy songs, and he maintained literary associations that had an influence on his later songs and on his two operas, *Wozzeck* and *Lulu*.

The early works Berg composed under Schoenberg's tutelage—the Seven Early Songs (1905–1908) and the Piano Sonata (op. 1, completed in 1908)—were in a fully romantic style, but by 1910, when he completed his String Quartet (op. 3), Berg had moved away from the constraints of tonality. Success came to him fairly early, in the form of his first opera, *Wozzeck*. From the time of its first performance, in 1924, this grim tragedy was a hit with European audiences, and until it was banned by the Nazis, who considered atonality to be a debasement of German artistic values, performance fees for the work provided Berg with a comfortable income.

Berg approached twelve-tone composition more cautiously than either Schoenberg or Webern, often combining tone rows and their basic permutations with themes that were freely atonal (but not twelve-tone) or unabashedly lyrical. This is the approach he takes in the Violin Concerto, his last completed score. Commissioned to write the work by Louis Krasner, a young American violinist, Berg began work on the piece after the death of Manon Gropius—the eighteen-year-old daughter of Alma Mahler and Walter Gropius—in April 1935.

The concerto became a memorial to her (its dedication reads "To the memory of an angel"), and, for the occasion, Berg assembled an unusually gentle twelve-tone row, built of major and minor intervals and part of a whole-tone scale. By design, it sounds more conventionally lyrical than tone rows often do, and it allows Berg to slip into purely tonal harmony, as he does at several points.

The tender Andante and the lively Allegretto that make up the work's first half are a portrait of the young girl; the vigorous Allegro and the soulful Adagio in the second half evoke the tragedy of her untimely death. The heart of this emotional finale is a Bach chorale, "Es ist genug," the closing movement from Cantata no. 60—and a piece that not only grows naturally out of the twelve-tone row Berg constructed for the work, but also ends with a whole-tone scale. Krasner always insisted that this was pure coincidence; that Berg wanted to quote a Bach chorale, and took care to find the right one, but that he did not build his tone row with this one in mind. At any rate, the

Bach, as well as the shapely violin line that Berg winds around it, contributes to the spiritual quality of the work's final pages.

The concerto's deeply felt lyricism has been a lure for violinists, even those who rarely venture into the modern repertory. And quite a few have made recordings in which the solo line is couched with a sweetness that reflects Berg's inspiration and intentions. But this collaboration between Anne-Sophie Mutter and James Levine is a quantum leap in Berg interpretation. Mutter brings not only an uncommonly sweet sound to the solo line, but her nuanced phrasing creates its own kind of beauty. Levine, with the virtuosic Chicago Symphony Orchestra at hand, matches those impulses closely. In the closing section especially, there is no performance as haunting.

Mutter began her career as a teenager in the 1970s, and her early recordings of Vivaldi and Mendelssohn concertos made a strong impression. Her artistry has grown enormously since then, as has her stature both as a touring soloist and a recording violinist. Although she has kept her focus on the standard repertory—recent recording

Violinist Anne-Sophie Mutter

projects have included the Beethoven Sonatas and her second look at the Vivaldi *Four Seasons*—she has also used her clout in the service of new music, which she both commissions and records.

Time Chant is an example. Written for Mutter by the German composer Wolfgang Rihm (born in 1952), it was inspired partly by the violinist's ability to produce a beautifully modulated, floating tone even in the upper reaches of the violin's range, but also by the composer's own peculiar vision of time as fluid and forward moving, on the one hand, and elastic and expandable on the other. The illusion he strives to create in each of the two movements is of a moment in which time is suspended, and within which the violin—abetted by orchestral textures that are often static, but occasionally dynamic and even explosive—probes and explores both the moment's limits and its own. As in the Berg, Mutter produces an exquisite tone and finds coherence and expressivity within Rihm's unusual structure.

77. DMITRI SHOSTAKOVICH

Symphony no. 5 in D minor (op. 47) and Symphony no. 9 in E-flat major (op. 70)

NEW YORK PHILHARMONIC,
LEONARD BERNSTEIN, CONDUCTING
(Sony Classical SMK 61841)

Recorded 1959 and 1965

Arguably the greatest symphonist of the mid-twentieth century, Dmitri Shostakovich (1906–1975) was something of a throwback. At a time when composers around the world were seeking ways to abandon both the structural forms and the harmonic language that had driven Western music for more than two centuries, Shostakovich embraced those traditional elements and clung to them with a fierce tenacity. Yet if his sensibility and musical language were essentially romantic, his fifteen symphonies, with their tart harmonies and sharp evocations of psychic turmoil, are unmistakably of the twentieth century.

More specifically, they are of the twentieth century as Shosta-kovich experienced it: as a subject of the Soviet Union who came of age, artistically, during the Stalin era. He had the misfortune to be born at a time and place where the fortunes of creative artists were dangerously bound to the whims of the state (or its leader), and the fact that biographers continue to debate the degree to which he either accommodated or rebelled against the regime is a demonstration of the ambiguities of that atmosphere.

The Fifth Symphony, completed in 1937, came out of a particu-larly intense drama that could have scuttled Shostakovich's career. A child at the time of the Russian Revolution, Shostakovich found offi-cial encouragement early on, and he reciprocated with works like the Second and Third Symphonies, which include choral movements glo-rifying the Revolution. By the early 1930s, he was regarded both in and outside the Soviet Union as one of the country's most promising composers. When his 1934 opera, *Lady Macbeth of Mtsensk,* had its premiere, *Pravda* hailed it as a work that "could only have been writ-ten by a Soviet composer, brought up in the traditions of Soviet cul-ture," and in the two years that followed, it had some two hundred performances in the Soviet Union, as well as productions abroad.

Then, in January 1936, Stalin caught up with it, and was offended by the score's thorny idiom and the vivid sexuality of its libretto. *Pravda* duly published a denunciation entitled "Muddle instead of Music," in which Shostakovich was accused of "formalism" and writing "anti-people music" that, to the Soviet ear, was an "intention-ally ungainly, muddled flood of sounds." A few days later, after Stalin attended a Bolshoi performance of Shostakovich's ballet *Bright Stream,* a second attack was published. Shostakovich, barely thirty, was in disgrace and in despair.

When he completed his Fourth Symphony, a few months later, he had it rehearsed, but decided that its modernist leanings would likely result in another assault, and so put off its premiere. Instead, he began sketching the Fifth, a work that is more conservative harmonically, yet more emotionally direct and immensely more powerful. In its opening Moderato movement, the angular string themes create an impression of intense, inner searching, intruded upon by a sinister, grotesque march figure. The second movement, marked Allegretto, is a Scherzo and Trio, rich in dialogue between the strings, winds, and brass, with a few lighter moments. The dark aura of the first movement returns in the Largo, where it is explored more deeply and is built into a passionate climax that collapses into an unearthly serenity. The brash, brassy finale shatters that uneasy calm.

The symphony was an instant hit at its premiere in November 1937, and Soviet officialdom called it "a Soviet artist's reply to just criticism." But for Shostakovich, this was no act of contrition. In Solomon Volkov's *Testimony*, published in 1979 as Shostakovich's dictated memoirs (an assertion some scholars contest, although Shostakovich's son has said that the content rings true), the composer is quoted disputing the official description, describing the finale in particular as a parody of Soviet exultation. "It's as if someone were beating you with a stick and saying, 'your business is rejoicing,' and you rise, shaky, and go marching off, muttering, 'our business is rejoicing, our business is rejoicing.'"

In truth, musicians and listeners figured that out long before Volkov's book was published. This 1959 recording by Leonard Bernstein preceded the book by twenty years, and its account of the finale is an incisive combination of absolute brutality (in the opening brass figures, taken at a breakneck pace, and the desperately climbing string figures, whipped up by the percussion, near the ending) and pathos (in the slow central section, with its quietly swirling string figures and melancholy wind melodies).

Bernstein conducts with his heart on his sleeve, and so the aching introspection of the first and third movements of the Fifth Symphony, and the parodistic qualities of its Allegretto, are all shown in high relief.

Bernstein's electrifying performance—the first of the conductor's two recordings of the work, and the one that conveys the score's wrenching spirit with the greatest force and clarity—has been coupled on this CD with a fine performance of the Ninth Symphony (also the earlier of Bernstein's two), a work unusual in the Shostakovich canon for its comparative cheerfulness.

The Ninth Symphony was completed in 1945, and its opening pages, with their dancing flute lines, folkish brass figures, and energetic string writing, suggest that it may be a sigh of relief after the terrors and privations of the war years (experiences embodied in Shostakovich's Seventh and Eighth Symphonies). There is, of course, a long slow Moderato that could, in this postwar context, be seen as a tribute to the fallen; but it is followed by a bright-hued, dancing Presto, a short, quiet Largo, and a finale that attains the perkiness of the first movement, with a surprising touch of the vehemence of the Fifth.

Bernstein calibrates this changeable piece perfectly, and draws a crisp, clear-textured performance from the mid-1960s New York Philharmonic. The reading argues persuasively that this almost neoclassical detour in the Shostakovich canon deserves better than its status as a footnote among the composer's late symphonies.

78. DMITRI SHOSTAKOVICH

Concerto for Violin and Orchestra no. 1 in A minor (op. 77)

DAVID OISTRAKH, VIOLINIST; NEW YORK PHILHARMONIC, DIMITRI MITROPOULOS, CONDUCTING

Concerto for Cello and Orchestra no. 1 in E-flat (op. 107)

MSTISLAV ROSTROPOVICH, CELLIST; PHILADELPHIA ORCHESTRA, EUGENE ORMANDY, CONDUCTING

(Sony Classical MHK 63327)

Recorded 1956, 1959

This CD, from the same Masterworks Heritage series that yielded Thomas Schippers's Barber collection, is another great example of what a record label can do when its producers take the time to search the vaults for important recordings that have long been out of print. Both of the performances here were first recordings of important concertos by Shostakovich, played by the soloists for whom he composed them.

They were not originally released together: the Violin Concerto was recorded in New York in January 1956, during the legendary violinist David Oistrakh's triumphant tour of the United States. It was originally released on an LP with no other works. The Cello Concerto was recorded in Philadelphia in November 1959, a few days after Mstislav Rostropovich gave the work its American premiere. Shostakovich himself was present for both the premiere and the recording session. That LP included a coupling—the Shostakovich First Symphony, which has not been included on this CD.

The booklet for this 1998 reissue, though, captures the spirit of the time by including the original front cover artwork from both original albums, and the back cover of the Violin Concerto LP, as well as notes excerpted from both original liner essays, and photographs from the recording sessions.

The CD, which originally came in an LP-style cardboard sleeve (it has since been reformatted for a plastic jewel case), also devotes several pages to a fascinating tribute to the LP format on its fiftieth anniversary. It includes an essay about the invention of the 33 rpm disc, reproductions of early advertisements describing the system, and the famous photograph of Dr. Peter Goldmark, who is usually credited as the inventor of the format, holding a fifteen-inch stack of LPs beside the eight feet of 78 rpm discs required to hold the same amount of music. The tribute is a bit peculiar, coming fifteen years after the CD was introduced as the LP's replacement. It is the equivalent of including a tribute to the 78 rpm disc in an LP published in 1963 (that is, fifteen years after LPs began to push 78s out of the market). And in that regard, the tribute is actually a bit subversive: audiophiles, after all, continue to argue that the sound of an LP is superior to that of a CD.

If you're going to undertake a bit of subversion—even if it's corporate rather than political—a Shostakovich disc is a great place to do it. Shostakovich himself regarded many of his works as veiled protests against the Soviet regime, although many others were glorifications of the state that are now regarded either as shameless or self-preservational (or both), depending on one's level of sympathy for Shostakovich and the pressures he lived with.

Those pressures swirled around the creation of the Violin Concerto. Shostakovich began writing it in July 1947, after a visit to Prague for performances with Oistrakh, and he completed it in 1948. That was the year, however, of Stalin's second denunciation of "formalist" Soviet composers—Shostakovich, Nikolai Miaskovsky, and Sergei Prokofiev among them. Dismissed from his teaching positions, and blacklisted as a composer of concert works, he was forced to rehabilitate himself by writing garish, poster-quality scores for films glorifying Stalin, among them *The Unforgettable Year 1919* and *The Fall of Berlin.*

Under the circumstances, Shostakovich added the Violin Concerto to a collection that also included his Fourth and Fifth String Quartets, and the song cycle, "From Jewish Folk Poetry," all stored away as the composer awaited better times. The Violin Concerto would not have pleased Soviet officialdom: cast in four movements, it is in Shostakovich's characteristically acidic style, with movements that touch melancholy depths (parts of the opening Nocturne movement, as well as the dark Passacaglia, its brilliant cadenza notwithstanding) offset by movements of manic energy (the Scherzo and the hard-driven Burlesque finale). It wasn't until 1955—two years after Stalin's death—that Shostakovich let Oistrakh perform the score, and when he did, he replaced the original opus number (77) with a later one (99), meant to hide the fact that the piece was seven years old.

The history of the Cello Concerto is less complicated. The work itself is notably brighter and more immediately accessible than its violin counterpart, although it is not without its moments of pure Russian melancholy—the cello theme of the Moderato movement being a case in point.

Shostakovich first considered composing a concerto for Rostropovich after hearing him play Prokofiev's Symphony Concerto in 1952, but he did not get around to writing the work until the summer of 1959. To a degree, it adheres to classical models that Shostakovich had not used for some time: its lively opening movement essentially adopts the contours of sonata form—although Shostakovich himself described it as a "jocular march"—and the finale is a spirited Rondo, albeit with a decidedly Russian accent rather than a Viennese one. Between them is the Moderato and an extended, virtuosic cadenza.

Rostropovich is said to have astonished Shostakovich by learning and memorizing the work in a mere four days. But Shostakovich knew what Rostropovich was capable of, and he tailored the work to his considerable strengths. The cadenza, especially, probes his sumptuous, singing tone, his steel-clad technique, and his ear for shape and nuance. In return, Rostropovich fashioned the cello line into a thoroughly personal and irresistible drama.

Shostakovich knew Oistrakh's strengths, too, of course, and on these recordings both soloists put their hearts fully into the music Shostakovich gave them. Oistrakh had the tougher job, in the sense that the materials he had to work with have a sharper, more bitter edge. But that appears to have given him a sense of mission: bringing the turmoil encrypted in Shostakovich's work to the West, where the composer and his circumstances were still imperfectly understood.

79. BÉLA BARTÓK

The Six String Quartets

THE EMERSON STRING QUARTET
(Deutsche Grammophon 423 657, two CDs)

Recorded 1988

Béla Bartók's quartets—unconventional works for the most conventional of ensembles—are the centerpieces of his chamber music output, and for some listeners, the most important and personal works in his entire catalog. There seems to be something about the quartet as a musical medium that encourages composers to pour themselves fully into these works, and that leads listeners to hear them as particularly confessional. That isn't an iron-clad rule, of course: Haydn wrote some meaty, colorful pieces as well as some supremely courtly ones, but not many that seem to offer autobiographical insight. The same can be said of Mozart and even the earliest batch of Beethoven quartets. But from middle Beethoven on, the medium came to imply a weighty message. The cycles by Bartók and Shostakovich, to cite the two most prominent modern examples, are regarded not merely as musical works, but as testimonies to the composers' inner turmoil, creatively, personally, and politically.

Bartók (1881–1945) was drawn to the quartet and the expressive opportunities it offered throughout his life, and what we know today as his First Quartet, composed in 1908, was actually preceded by three youthful attempts dating back to 1896 and 1898. The six mature works take him from a world of post-Wagnerian chromaticism— sometimes tinged with hints of the folk music that he collected on field trips in the Hungarian and Romanian countryside with his colleague Zoltán Kodály—through a period of increasing harmonic and rhythmic complexity, toward an intensely melancholy conclusion in 1939, on the eve of World War II. At the time of Bartók's death, there were plans—and a formal commission—for a seventh quartet.

Audiences are used to Bartók's language these days, but it is easy to see why these works were considered difficult in the composer's lifetime, and for a couple of decades thereafter. Bartók's harmonic language covers a broad range that extends to some harsh dissonances, and although the perspective of time (and other music) has helped listeners understand that dissonance, in all its variety, can be—and, in fact, always has been—an expressive tool, it seemed provocative when these works were new.

Similarly, the percussive aspect of Bartók's string writing undoubtedly bruised some sensibilities. Listeners could deal with a piano being pounded on: there was a long tradition of that, reaching into the nineteenth century, when improvements in piano construction made it possible for the instrument to withstand the occasional beating. But quartet playing had been more genteel.

In addition, Bartók imported some unusual and decidedly exotic rhythms into this Austro-German form, including an interestingly off-kilter Bulgarian dance figure in the Scherzo of the Quartet no. 5 (1934). And he was quite precise in his demands on matters of string color, noting whether he wanted the musicians to play with extreme vibrato or none at all, and making extensive use of effects ranging from portamento (sliding) and pizzicato (plucking rather than bowing the strings) to sul ponticello (playing on the bridge, to create an eerie, glassine sound) and sul tastiera (using the bow on the fingerboard).

However this sounds to listeners now, the works remain a handful for performers. But they seem to hold no terrors for the Emerson String Quartet, a group that was formed in 1976 when its members were fresh out of the Juilliard School. These players—Eugene Drucker and Philip Setzer, violinists (they alternate in the first and second chairs); Lawrence Dutton, violist; and David Finckel, cellist—included the Bartók Quartets in their repertory from the start. They first presented the complete cycle in 1979, when they had been performing professionally for only three seasons, and in 1981, the year the musical world was celebrating the Bartók centenary, the Emersons made a tremendous splash by playing all six works in a single concert at Alice Tully Hall.

These recordings were made eight years after that marathon, as the Emerson was preparing to repeat it at Carnegie Hall. They are, for starters, models of technical assurance: even in the densest and most vigorous writing, these players perform with complete unity of purpose and exemplary ensemble precision. To get a sense of their achievement, listen to the Quartet no. 5, with its intricate rhythms, its extremes of lyricism and brashness, its unusual sliding effects, its use of quarter tones in surreal moments of distantly remembered music of childlike innocence, and the sheer, unrelenting energy of its finale. In all six of these works, the Emersons offer everything in the right measure, including a sense of each piece as a distinct landmark along Bartók's compositional path.

80. BÉLA BARTÓK

Concerto for Orchestra; *Music for Strings, Percussion, and Celesta;* and *Hungarian Sketches*

CHICAGO SYMPHONY ORCHESTRA,
FRITZ REINER, CONDUCTING
(RCA 09026-61504-2)

Recorded 1955, 1958

As one of the great twentieth-century orchestral showpieces—a work that focuses on the timbres and capabilities of every department of an orchestra in a way that is substantial rather than merely dazzling— Béla Bartók's Concerto for Orchestra has been recorded dozens of times since its premiere in 1944. And in the early years of digital recording and compact discs, the work's broad dynamics and the constant shifting of focus among the various orchestral timbres made it a hot item for both conductors and record companies. But few recordings of the work match this 1955 account by Fritz Reiner and the Chicago Symphony, either for interpretive insight or for the sheer warmth, richness, and naturalness of the recorded orchestral sound.

Reiner was one of three Hungarian conductors, all born and trained in Budapest, who took over American orchestras and transformed them into world-class instruments. In Philadelphia, Eugene Ormandy built on the lush sound that Leopold Stokowski had developed, and created an orchestra renowned for its enveloping string tone. George Szell took up the reins of the Cleveland Orchestra in 1946, and made it one of the world's tautest, most disciplined ensembles, ideal in the classical and early romantic repertory. And Reiner, after stints in Cincinnati and Pittsburgh, took on the Chicago Symphony in 1953 and made it a highly polished, flexible ensemble with a solid brass section that was later given an even brighter sheen by one of his successors— another Hungarian—Sir Georg Solti.

One element of Reiner's style that was legendary was his almost microscopic beat—a wiggle of the finger rather than the broad sweep of the baton. Still, his musicians clearly knew what he wanted: the Concerto for Orchestra was recorded only two years into his tenure, but his mastery of the score and his command of the ensemble allow him to find unusual balances and intricacies that catch the ear without interrupting the work's thrust, and the performance is tight and precise. Those qualities also inform an invigorating performance of the *Music for Strings, Percussion, and Celesta,* and the sweetly folk-inspired *Hungarian Sketches,* both recorded three years later.

Reiner and Bartók had known each other for nearly four decades when the Concerto for Orchestra was written, and although Reiner did not commission it or conduct the premiere, he had a hand in the process. Bartók was seven years Reiner's senior, but when they first met in 1905, they were both students of the pianist István Thomán at the Budapest Academy. When Bartók joined the faculty, Reiner became his student, and when Reiner graduated in 1909, it was Bartók who signed his diploma.

Reiner, having made his way to the United States in the early 1920s, was in a position to help Bartók emigrate in 1940, and to find gainful and creative employment once he arrived. Already ill, and virtually unknown to American audiences, Bartók was living a hand-to-mouth existence in New York when Reiner and the Hungarian violinist Joseph Szigeti prevailed upon Serge Koussevitzky, the conductor of the Boston Symphony Orchestra, to commission a work from him. That was the genesis of the Concerto for Orchestra: Bartók composed it in eight weeks at a private sanitorium at Saranac Lake, in the Adirondacks, between August and October 1943. Koussevitzky was thrilled with it: after conducting its premiere in December 1944, he told Bartók that he considered it "the best orchestral piece of the last 25 years."

The five-movement Concerto for Orchestra is a vigorous piece, perhaps surprisingly so, given the pressures on the ailing, expatriate composer. Themes with a Hungarian folk flavor propel the opening of the first, third, and fourth movements, of which the third is a soulful, elegiac Andante non troppo. In the fourth, an Intermezzo, the folklike theme is interrupted by a twisted parody of the Viennese march that Shostakovich used to represent the advancing German forces in his *Leningrad* Symphony in 1941. Bartók has his brass and percussion respond to this march with rude, jeering noises. The second movement is light-spirited, with ample attention focused on combinations of winds. The final movement includes a perpetual motion for strings, with a beautifully worked-out fugue that leads to a blazingly triumphant brass coda.

Bartók provided a sense of what the score is all about. "The general mood of the work represents, apart from the jesting second movement, a gradual transition from the sternness of the first movement and the lugubrious death-song of the third, to the life-assertion of the last one."

The *Music for Strings, Percussion, and Celesta* was composed in 1936 as a tenth-anniversary work for the Chamber Orchestra of Basel, but if its textures are necessarily more compact, it is in some ways a precursor of the Concerto for Orchestra. Its layout is interesting: the orchestra is divided into three groups; two are independent string bodies, and the third includes piano, celesta, harp, xylophone, and timpani. The work begins with a melancholy fugue for strings, but its second movement, an Allegro, if still dark-hued, is brisk and propulsive. A xylophone and timpani introduce the Adagio, prefiguring the side drum opening of the second movement of the Concerto for Orchestra. And the high-energy finale whirls its way through a folklike dance, with strings and harp sometimes evoking the cymbalom (a Hungarian dulcimer), interrupted only briefly for a hint of the ruminative writing heard earlier in the work.

Reiner offers a glimpse of Bartók's lighter side as well, by way of the *Hungarian Sketches,* a 1931 suite of spicy but straightforward orchestral pieces, inspired by Hungarian folk melodies and originally written for the piano between 1908 and 1911.

81. KARL AMADEUS HARTMANN

Concerto Funèbre; Symphony no. 4; and Chamber Concerto

ISABELLE FAUST, VIOLINIST; PAUL MEYER, CLARINETIST;
PETERSEN QUARTET; MUNICH CHAMBER ORCHESTRA,
CHRISTOPH POPPEN, CONDUCTING
(ECM New Series 1720)

Recorded 1999

Here are three deeply moving works by a composer whose music deserves to be more widely known. Karl Amadeus Hartmann (1905–1963) was born in Munich and studied at the Academy of Music there, with some additional private studies with Anton Webern in 1941 and 1942. His works began to attract attention in the 1920s, both on their musical merits and because they embodied a vibrant current of social criticism.

His politics were decidedly to the left; in fact, among the authors whose writings he used in works that decried the materialism of the age (and the influence of the United States in that regard) were Karl Marx and Johannes Becher. He was hardly alone among artists and intellectuals in this regard: many American composers of the time would not have disagreed with him. Of course, such views were the antithesis of the rising force of fascism. "The categorization of art as political or non-political, engaged or disengaged, seems to be somewhat superfluous," he wrote at the time, "for no artist, unless wishing himself as written off to nihilism, can sidestep his commitment to humanity."

The scores on this recording by Christoph Poppen and the Munich Chamber Orchestra come from a later, more troubled age, but they are all informed by those same sentiments. When the Nazis came to power in 1933, Hartmann chose to remain in Germany, but in a form of internal exile. He refused to have his works performed in his homeland. He did, however, continue to compose, and he was able to spirit his scores out of Germany for performances in Geneva and elsewhere.

In his works of this time, he made his feelings about the Nazi regime clear, either directly—in his titles or in his choice of texts for vocal works—or more obliquely, through musical quotations from works, composers, or styles that the Nazis found objectionable.

To take a few examples from the disc at hand, several of the principal clarinet themes in the Chamber Concerto (1930–1935) are couched in the accents of klezmer, an Eastern European Jewish dance music. The *Concerto Funèbre* (1938, revised 1959) uses melodies associated with the Czech nationalism of Bedřich Smetana, as well as a Russian revolutionary song. Those references—to say nothing of the mournful, angry character of the work as a whole—were anathema to ideologues like Joseph Goebbels, whose pronouncements about what Nazi art should and should not embody were employed by Hartmann as a kind of subversive road map.

After World War II, Hartmann presided over Musica Viva, a series that presented works by composers banned by the Nazis, and encouraged the creation of new German music. He also revised many of the works he had composed during the war years. In some cases he removed specific anti-Nazi references (which had already served their purpose), but he sharpened the tensions and passions that the works embody. Other works were pulled apart and reconfigured to present more focused settings for the thoughts that had originally inspired them.

The Symphony no. 4 was one of the latter: although it was completed in 1947, much of its material comes from a symphony for string orchestra and soprano, composed in 1938. The finale, an Andante appassionato movement rooted in the twelve-tone style that Hartmann undoubtedly studied with Webern, shows how moving and eloquent twelve-tone writing can be.

The Symphony and the *Concerto Funèbre* are wrenching, intensely soulful works, with strong currents of tragedy and searing anger—elements that Poppen and his young Munich ensemble tap into fully in their recording. The Chamber Concerto is a slightly lighter work, with some shapely, comparatively carefree melodies in a clarinet line that floats freely above the more turbulent string writing. Perhaps Poppen put it at the end of the disc as a way of closing on a brighter note. But even this piece is unlikely to be mistaken for cheerful entertainment.

That is not to say that this recording is a document of depression and hopelessness. Just the opposite: even as these works' rich string textures and tightly wound themes capture the despair that Hartmann felt, the music also conveys a sense that a person of conscience can stand against the forces of a dark age, and come through victorious, if also scarred.

82. OLIVIER MESSIAEN

Quatuor pour le Fin du Temps
(Quartet for the End of Time)

TASHI: PETER SERKIN, PIANIST; IDA KAVAFIAN,
VIOLINIST; RICHARD STOLTZMAN, CLARINETIST;
FRED SHERRY, CELLIST
(RCA Gold Seal 7835-2-RG)

Recorded 1975

In the early 1970s, a group of musicians mostly in their twenties (the oldest was thirty) banded together to play a few concerts of works for the odd combination of violin, clarinet, cello, and piano, or smaller groupings of those instruments. The best known of these players was Peter Serkin, whose father, Rudolf Serkin, was one of the most revered pianists of the time; but the others—the cellist Fred Sherry, the violinist Ida Kavafian, and the clarinetist Richard Stoltzman—were all beginning to establish careers as soloists and chamber players, and each has since earned a measure of prominence.

Although their original idea was just to play some concerts, not to start a band, they worked together well, and their spirited performances won them an enthusiastic and mostly young following. They adopted the name Tashi—a Tibetan word meaning "good fortune," and also the name of Peter Serkin's dog—and jumped into the national spotlight with an unusual performance in New York in January 1976. The venue was the Bottom Line, a Greenwich Village club that mostly presents rock and folk music. But the young, casually dressed members of Tashi seduced the club's audience with the work that was quickly becoming its signature piece—Messiaen's luminous, harmonically prickly vision of the Apocalypse, composed in a prisoner-of-war camp during World War II.

Olivier Messiaen (1908–1992), one of France's most influential twentieth-century composers, developed an unusually expressive style that drew on everything from birdsong and Balinese dance rhythms to more conventionally Western chromaticism and serial techniques. He composed prolifically, contributing more than 250 works to virtually every genre, from solo piano music and songs to chamber music, symphony, and opera. His use of color and texture was extraordinary and often picturesque, but at the core of all his music is a deep current of Roman Catholic mysticism, which his harmonic and gestural language is meant to explore, symbolize, celebrate, and convey.

Messiaen began composing when he was seven years old, and when he was eleven, he entered the Paris Conservatoire, where his teachers included the composer Paul Dukas and the organist Marcel Dupré. When he completed his studies, in 1930, he became the principal organist at La Trinité, in Paris, a post he held until the 1970s. He also began teaching at the École Normal de Musique, in 1936, and was beginning to win some recognition as a composer, having established the Jeune France composers' circle, with André Jolivet, Daniel Lesur, and Yves Baudrier.

When World War II broke out, in 1939, Messiaen was conscripted into the French Army. Captured by the Germans in May 1940, he was sent to Stalag 8A, a prisoner-of-war camp in Görlitz, Silesia, and it was there—inspired by a passage from chapter 10 of the Revelation of Saint John—that he composed this remarkable quartet, which became his most frequently performed work. The unusual instrumental combination reflected what was available to him, in terms of both instruments and players. The premiere took place on January 15, 1941, with Messiaen at the piano, Henri Akoka on the clarinet, Jean LeBoulaire on the violin, Etienne Pasquier on the cello, and five thousand fellow prisoners in the audience.

Messiaen wrote a set of beautifully descriptive program notes to accompany the work, indicating what he had in mind for each of its eight movements, and they are included with the Tashi recording. Just by way of example—to convey something of the flavor of Messiaen's writing—here is his note for *Abîme des Oiseaux* (Abyss of the Birds), a movement for solo clarinet lasting nearly eight minutes: "The abyss is Time, with its sadnesses and tediums. The birds are the opposite of Time; they are our desire for light, for stars, for rainbows and for jubilant outpourings of song!"

All told, the work offers stylized glimpses of both apocalyptic terror and the sublime, transcendant qualities of salvation in the postapocalyptic world to come. Tashi's performance benefits from the group's youthful energy, but also from the sense that the players had a deeply felt response to Messiaen's spiritual tableaux. Nearly three decades after its release, the playing still has a freshness—and, more to the point, a searing intensity—that brings this peculiar vision to life.

It is also Tashi at its best. The group continued for years with a changing roster that reflected anything from the works at hand to the availability and interest of the members. Early on, it abandoned the informality of its Bottom Line performance and became a more conventional chamber ensemble, albeit one with a special interest in new music. It went on to make plenty of recordings, many of them excellent. But this is the disc that most fully captures the spirit of adventure that the band represented in its early days.

83. HEITOR VILLA-LOBOS

Bachianas Brasileiras, nos. 1, 2, 5, and 9

VICTORIA DE LOS ANGELES, SOPRANO (IN NO. 5);
ORCHESTRE NATIONAL DE LA RADIODIFFUSION
FRANÇAISE, HEITOR VILLA-LOBOS, CONDUCTING
(EMI Classics 66964-2)

Recorded 1956–1958

It's difficult not to have a soft spot for the music of Heitor Villa-Lobos (1887–1959), the first Brazilian composer to achieve international prominence, and still the country's best-known composer of concert music. His copious output covers a vast range of styles, from the almost purely folkloric to sophisticated 1920s modernism, but at heart, his goal was the same as Edvard Grieg's, Jean Sibelius's, Bedřich Smetana's, Nikolai Rimsky-Korsakov's, and Sir Edward Elgar's: he wanted to write music that would unequivocally express the spirit of his country.

Villa-Lobos keyed into that spirit in a very direct way. A self-taught musician, he learned the cello from his father, and supported himself, as a teenager, by playing in theaters, hotels, and movie houses. He also learned to play the guitar, and around the turn of the century he immersed himself in the vivid street music of his native Rio de Janeiro. He was particularly fond of chôros, a kind of dance music typically performed by a band, in which the players were free to improvise around a work's rhythms and harmonies, much as jazz players do.

It was also a form in transition: composers like Ernesto Nazareth (whom Villa-Lobos knew from his days as a cinema musician) typically blended the harmonic moves of the chôros with such European dances as waltzes and polkas, creating hybrids that influenced Villa-Lobos and other composers interested in exploring both musical streams. Another important influence was the regional folk music Villa-Lobos heard during trips around Brazil between 1905 and 1913.

By 1915, Villa-Lobos had a growing portfolio of compositions, and that November he presented a concert devoted to his works—a performance that, thanks largely to the brickbats hurled by Rio's conservative critics, established him as the most promising voice of new Brazilian music. Visits to the country by Arthur Rubinstein and Darius Milhaud, in 1918, helped expand his horizons, not the least by bringing him news of the latest musical developments in Europe, including the ascendant star of Igor Stravinsky. And in 1923, he decided to explore this musical world for himself. He toured briefly around Europe before settling in Paris, where he mingled with composers as diverse as Stravinsky, Maurice Ravel, Manuel de Falla, and Edgard Varèse, and where he established his own credentials as a composer to be taken seriously before sailing back to Brazil in 1930.

Villa-Lobos undertook the *Bachianas Brasileiras* series—nine works bear that title—soon after his return. As the title suggests, the works are meant as an homage to J. S. Bach, whom Villa-Lobos described as "a kind of universal folkloric source, rich and profound," and a composer whose music spoke to listeners of every country and culture. Villa-Lobos's plan was to weave together elements familiar from Bach with purely Brazilian musical strains, although there are long stretches in these pieces—and certainly in the four included on this disc—where a listener might strain to hear clear evidence of either musical partner.

Still, Villa-Lobos arranged the works as baroque suites, of a sort, with comparatively formal names usually paired with more evocative titles in Portuguese or, in some cases, the names of Brazilian popular dances (the Modinha and the Embolada, for example). Villa-Lobos did not use Bach's dance forms, although in some of the works he includes an Aria that is a rough equivalent of a Bach slow movement. A few of the works include formal Fugue movements, as clear a nod to Bach as can be found anywhere.

The four *Bachianas Brasileiras* included in this set, recorded under the composer's baton in the 1950s, are quite varied in style and structure. The best-known—indeed, probably the most widely known of any of Villa-Lobos's compositions apart from his guitar music—is no. 5, a two-movement work for soprano and eight cellos. The first movement, an Aria composed in 1938, is mostly vocalise, and is an exquisitely haunting melody. When Villa-Lobos gets around to setting Manoel Bandeira's poetry, at the center of the movement, the text is more declaimed than sung, but it has a sultry quality that is difficult to resist—and in any case, the vocalise returns to finish the movement. Victoria de los Angeles brings a small but lovely sound to the song, and ample character and power to the more outgoing second movement, Dança (Martelo), which Villa-Lobos added in 1945.

The other three works, if not as immediately seductive as no. 5, paint an inviting picture of at least one corner of Villa-Lobos's output, and will grow on you. The opening movement of no. 1, composed in 1930, begins with a distinctively Brazilian rhythm, over which a soaring, Grieg-like melody takes flight. The second movement taps into the cello's tendency toward the lugubrious, and the finale, a robust Fugue, is built on a theme similar to that of Bach's Passacaglia in C minor, but phrased in a jazzier, more rhythmically insistent style.

Bachianas Brasileiras no. 2 (1930) has a quality that we now think of as cinematic, although the age of lavish film scores was actually still some years in the future when Villa-Lobos composed it. A tenor saxophone, in its first movement, is meant to portray one of Rio's free spirits. Its second movement, "O Canto da Nossa Terra" (Song of Our Land), runs the gamut from sweetly plaintive string melodies to dramatic, dark-hued writing for saxophone, trombone, and pizzicato strings, intended to suggest the black magic of Brazil's voodoo cults. The core of the third movement is a folk song, presented in a loosely sliding trombone line, with lush string support. But the real showpiece here is the finale, a Toccata, "O Trenzinho do Caipira" (The Little Train of Caipira), a magnificent tone poem that follows a train through the countryside, until it grinds to a halt at its destination. The shaking of rattles and the scratchy rasping of guiros provide the engine noise; the winds are its whistle, and the strings, piano, winds, and percussion describe the short but eventful ride.

The final entry in the set, no. 9 (1945), is straightforward and retrospective: the opening Prelúdio begins with a melody rooted in plainchant—rhythmically square and unharmonized, with a droning C sustained beneath it. One of Villa-Lobos's strengths was morphing themes, and in this case, the plainchant melts into rich, Elgarian string writing. A weighty but vigorous fugue brings no. 9, and the full set, to an end.

Villa-Lobos appears not to have been as fastidious a conductor as some other composers, but he was able to convey the spirit of these pieces to this French radio orchestra, which plays the music with both energy and, where offered the opportunity, a highly caloric romanticism.

In truth, as much as I admire de los Angeles's reading, if the only installment of the *Bachianas Brasileiras* set you are interested in is the opening Aria from no. 5, I would suggest another recording instead (or as well)—the 1945 performance by the Brazilian soprano Bidu Sayão, also with Villa-Lobos conducting. Her version has a bigger sound and greater suppleness than de los Angeles's, and it was re-issued recently as part of a magnificent overview of Sayão's career, with songs and arias by Charles Gounod, Jules Massenet, Reynaldo Hahn, Henri Duparc, Claude Debussy, Maurice Ravel, Charles Koechlin, and Ernest Moret, as well as Ernani Braga's settings of eight Brazilian folk songs (Sony Classical).

Composer Heitor Villa-Lobos with the traditional Brazilian instrument the xucalho

84. BENJAMIN BRITTEN

War Requiem (op. 66)

GALINA VISHNEVSKAYA, SOPRANO; PETER PEARS, TENOR;
DIETRICH FISCHER-DIESKAU, BARITONE; SIMON PRESTON,
ORGANIST; MELOS ENSEMBLE; HIGHGATE SCHOOL CHOIR;
BACH CHOIR; LONDON SYMPHONY ORCHESTRA
AND CHORUS, BENJAMIN BRITTEN, CONDUCTING
(Decca 414 383-2; two CDs)

Recorded 1963

Benjamin Britten's eloquent music conveys much about this enigmatic man and his humanistic concerns, but it is also emblematic of the great dilemma composers faced throughout the twentieth century: that of finding a fresh musical language without breaking with the great traditions and forms, or—in completely practical terms—the listeners who regard those forms as the basis of musical communication. Britten (1913–1976) was interested in certain avant-garde musical trends, and his approach to orchestration and tone color were unquestionably influenced by modern notions of sound, as was his use of dissonance, angularity, Asian musical elements, and even serial techniques. Yet in a more elemental way, Britten's music remained firmly tethered to the language of romanticism and the nineteenth-century aesthetic in which rich textures and sweeping lyricism were absolute values.

As a consequence, Britten rarely figures on lists of twentieth-century trailblazers. The compensation was that long before his death in 1976, many of his works had found a place in the standard repertory—among them, the operas *Peter Grimes* and *Billy Budd*, a handful of orchestral works, including *The Young Person's Guide to the Orchestra* and the *Simple Symphony,* the *Nocturnal* for guitar, the *Ceremony of Carols,* and this searing *War Requiem.*

Britten was a pacifist, and among the concerns that occupied him throughout his life were the horrors of war and the importance of working for peace and reconciliation. The *War Requiem* is his principal statement on those subjects. Composed for the dedication of the

---

new Coventry Cathedral in 1962—the old one having been destroyed in a German bombing raid twenty years earlier—the work juxtaposes the traditional Requiem text, sung in Latin, with battlefield poetry by Wilfrid Owen, an English poet and soldier who died in World War I, sung in English.

The contrast between the texts is magnified by the arrangement of the performing forces. The tenor and baritone soloists, who sing the Owen texts (mostly), represent an English soldier and a German soldier, and for the premiere—and for this recording—the English tenor, Peter Pears, and the German baritone, Dietrich Fischer-Dieskau, sang those parts. The music Britten gave them is essentially lyrical, yet with an urgency that mirrors the battlefield imagery of Owen's poetry. The soprano and the choruses are the celebrants of the Requiem Mass, but if their formal, ancient texts are detached from the stark imagery that the tenor and baritone offer, their music is often more sharp-edged and turbulent, and is supported by emotionally charged orchestral scoring. The boys' choir, which sings sections of the Requiem text, is placed at a distance from the other performers, and represents a level of innocence and purity, which prevail at the work's end.

Britten's hope was that the Russian soprano Galina Vishnevskaya would sing the premiere, representing another nation that suffered greatly during World War II. Her inclusion was also meant to further expand the notion of reconciliation, which could apply not only to the war that took place between 1939 and 1945, but also to the Cold War then under way. At the last minute, the Soviet authorities decided not to permit her to attend, and for the premiere, her English colleague Heather Harper took over. But nearly a year later, Britten conducted the work again at the Royal Albert Hall, in London, and this time Vishnevskaya was on hand, as were Pears and Fischer-Dieskau. This recording was made a week before that performance. The work was an immediate hit, and in its first five months on the market, the recording sold 200,000 copies, an extraordinary sale for a contemporary work.

The technical details of the sessions were overseen by John Culshaw, the legendary producer who, a few years earlier, presided over the first stereo recording of Wagner's *Ring* cycle, conducted by Sir Georg Solti. The *War Requiem* was also notable for its production values, most notably the placement of the work's large forces in the stereo picture. Decca's method was to record directly to a stereo master—a practice that was lauded at the time, since the live sound mixing saved a tape generation and yielded superior sound when the results were pressed on a vinyl LP. Now, as record labels revisit their master tapes in order to produce 5.1 Surround mixes for DVD-Audio and SACD, there is reason to regret Decca's procedure—but who knew?

For many years, Britten's own recording of this chilling work had the field to itself, and even now, as the competition grows, few performances match this one's intensity. Pears and Fischer-Dieskau paint their contributions with a dignified, Everyman quality, and if the Russian soprano Galina Vishnevskaya has an occasionally abrasive moment, even that adds something to the charged quality of the performance, as do other occasional rough edges.

The conductors of more recent recordings have prized smoothness a bit more than Britten did. One alternative in which this works to the music's advantage is Robert Shaw's account with the Atlanta Symphony Orchestra and Chorus, the soprano Lorna Haywood, the tenor Anthony Rolfe-Johnson, and the baritone Benjamin Luxon (Telarc, 1988). Shaw preferred a silkier, more heavenly choral sound than Britten, but that isn't to say that he demurred on the work's power. The brass, organ, and percussion textures are especially vibrant, and the orchestra's strings have an appealing transparency.

85. BENJAMIN BRITTEN

The Young Person's Guide to the Orchestra (op. 34), Simple Symphony (op. 4), and Variations on a Theme of Frank Bridge (op. 10)

LONDON SYMPHONY ORCHESTRA, ENGLISH CHAMBER
ORCHESTRA, BENJAMIN BRITTEN, CONDUCTING

(Decca 289 417 509-2)

Recorded 1963–1968

If the *War Requiem* shows a particularly forceful side of Britten—and illustrates the extent to which he drew upon, and carefully balanced, both a modernist acerbity and an antique sense of the devotional—the works on this compilation project the composer's gentler, more immediately accessible, persona.

The Young Person's Guide to the Orchestra is often paired on disc with Sergei Prokofiev's *Peter and the Wolf,* mainly because both works move their spotlights through each section of the orchestra, letting attentive listeners of all ages hear what the various strings, winds, brass, and percussion instruments can do. Both works include texts that tell which instruments are about to be heard; but where the text is virtually inextricable from the Prokofiev, it is optional in the Britten. Most performances present the *Guide* without the text, as does the composer's 1964 recording.

Actually, this work is far more than a didactic tour of the orchestra, and its title should not be regarded as a limitation: Britten might as easily have called the piece "Purcelliana" or something to that effect. Composed in 1945, the year the musical world was commemorating the 250th anniversary of Henry Purcell's death, the *Guide* begins with a robust, full orchestra rendering of a hornpipe from Purcell's *Abdelazar, or The Moor's Revenge.* The focus on the different instrumental groups, and the individual players within them, takes place in the context of a wonderfully inventive and virtuosic set of variations, with a fugue thrown in for good measure.

The *Simple Symphony,* though composed in the winter of 1933–

1934, when Britten was entering his twenties, is based on pieces he composed about a decade earlier, between the ages of ten and thirteen. Its movement titles—"Boisterous Bourrée," "Playful Pizzicato," "Sentimental Saraband," and "Frolicsome Finale"—reflect the innocence at the music's heart. But there is nothing childish about this score. Britten's themes are beautifully crafted and memorable, and his harmonizations are often seductively lush. Given those qualities, along with the music's varied string timbres and articulations—from long, winding lines to speedy pizzicato figures—it has become a repertory staple for string orchestras eager to show off the flexibility and richness of their sound.

Less frequently heard are the more ambitious and wide-ranging *Variations on a Theme of Frank Bridge,* composed in 1937, and also scored for string orchestra. Frank Bridge was Britten's teacher, and it was from Bridge's *Idyll no. 2* for string quartet, composed in 1906, that Britten drew the theme for this work, which was part tribute and part declaration of independence.

In a way, this score has elements that link it to both the *Simple Symphony* and the *Young Person's Guide.* Like the *Guide,* it is a variation set that includes a fugue as part of its finale, and although it is written for a string ensemble rather than a full orchestra, it explores and tests a wide range of techniques and sound combinations. And like the *Simple Symphony,* it balances jauntiness with wistfulness, occasionally using old forms—courtly dances, marches, and Italian arias—as models.

Still, its expressive range exceeds that of both works and even in the lighter variations, this is a deeply passionate score. Composed soon after the death of Britten's mother, and at a time when he was beginning to discover his own homosexuality, the work is framed by a series of troubled, chromatic movements. A plaintive Adagio throws the work into darkness immediately after its introduction and the first statement of the Bridge theme. The final three movements are a "Funeral March," which recaptures the mood of the Adagio; the Elgartinged "Chant," and a fugue that leads into a Mahleresque finale. The inner variations, by contrast, are bright and vital—momentary distractions, perhaps, from the troubles of the outer sections.

All these pieces have been recorded many times, and given the generally fine state of orchestral playing these days, there are many superb versions out there. Britten's own recordings benefit from his authoritative, vigorous readings as well as the superb playing of the London Symphony in the *Guide* and the English Chamber Orchestra in the string works.

86. WITOLD LUTOSŁAWSKI

Symphonic Variations, Symphony no. 1, *Musique Funèbre,* Symphony no. 2, Concerto for Orchestra, *Jeux Vénitiens, Livre pour Orchestre,* and *Mi-Parti*

POLISH RADIO SYMPHONY ORCHESTRA,
WITOLD LUTOSŁAWSKI, CONDUCTING

(EMI Classics 5 73833 2, two CDs)

Recorded 1976–1977

Chopin and baroque "alla Polacca" dance steps notwithstanding, Poland did not play a significant role in the development of the musical mainstream through the nineteenth century. But in the twentieth century—and particularly since the post-Stalin thaw of the 1950s—several generations of Polish composers have been writing imaginative, individualistic works that have made a strong impact internationally.

Witold Lutosławski (1913–1994) was one of the architects of the contemporary Polish musical world, and his works continue to hold a place in the modern canon. Lutosławski's music has everything—long-lined lyricism and inventive structures, a harmonic language that ranges from comfortable lushness to pungent acidity, and a daring and exploratory use of tone clusters, quarter-tone writing, colorful instrumental effects, and even a measure of improvisation, within precisely defined limits.

Lutosławski was also an accomplished conductor, as one can hear in this mid-'70s compilation, which presents his own vital performances of some of his most important works up to that point, in a conveniently compact overview. It is not comprehensive: Lutosławski's 1970 Cello Concerto, as well as the Third and Fourth Symphonies, the Partita, the Piano Concerto, and the works in the "Chain" series are also crucial among his contributions to the repertory.

What this collection shows, however, is the clear development of Lutosławski's style. The *Symphonic Variations* (1936–1938), one of his earliest surviving works, comes from just after his student years at the Warsaw Conservatory. Its theme has a folk character, and its initial presentation bears a hint of Shostakovich's tartness. But Lutosławski quickly goes his own way, filling the nine-minute score with rugged rhythmic counterpoint and textural interplay. Probably its most striking feature, though, is its sheer energy, an element Lutosławski was always able to summon in his bright, variegated scoring.

World War II broke out not long after this work's premiere, in 1939, and Lutosławski joined the Polish Army as a radio communications officer. He was arrested by the Nazis early in the war, but escaped and returned to Warsaw, where he and the composer Andrzej Panufnik organized underground concerts of music the Nazis had banned.

After the war, he reasoned that there was no point writing sophisticated concert music for a devastated country, so he devoted himself to educational works and arrangements of folk music. In 1947, he completed his First Symphony, a work he had started in 1941. Like the *Symphonic Variations,* it is full of ear-catching combinations of instrumental color and unusual rhythmic and melodic turns. But when it had its premiere in 1948, the Communist government declared it formalistic and banned it. Lutosławski again turned to writing children's music, and took the opportunity to develop what he called his "sound language."

Lutosławski was not as spooked as Shostakovich by the threat of government interference, but his next works were a bit more easygoing. The Concerto for Orchestra (1950–1954), which draws on folk melodies, also has a remarkably strong profile, and makes as direct an appeal as Bartók's work of the same title. It has remained one of Lutosławski's most popular works, although he has described it as marginal. (Listening to his vivid performance, one doesn't get the feeling that this was his opinion when he made this recording.)

Musique Funèbre (1954–1958), by contrast, was stealth avant-gardism: although its rich string texture recalls Bartók, to whom it is a tribute, it uses serial techniques. And by the time of the irresistibly tactile *Jeux Vénitiens* (1960–1961), any pressure to write conventional music that Lutosławski may have felt had clearly dissipated. Here, Lutosławski began experimenting with John Cage's "chance" techniques, which leave certain elements of a work to serendipity, or at least, to the performer's discretion. But Lutosławski did not trust "chance" operations entirely. He imposed strict rules and parameters, and often provided pitches, leaving only the rhythms to be supplied by the musicians.

The Second Symphony (1965–1967) was wilder still: its two movements are explosions of controlled cacophony, within which points of melodic or textural focus continually emerge and disappear. And in *Livre pour Orchestre* (1968), he experimented with sliding string sounds and quarter-tone pitches—that is, pitches centered in the space between the half-step pitches of adjacent black and white piano keys. A sense of mystery pervades the work; yet against its otherworldly harmonic fabric, and between its scampering figures, brass fanfares give the piece a sense of being rooted. *Mi-Parti* (1975–1976),

Composer Witold Lutosławski

a fairly new work when Lutosławski made these recordings, pursues a similar agenda—sliding figures and gauzy backdrops prevail—but with a greatly expanded palette.

These last few works leave thoroughly contradictory impressions. Sections of them sound as though the players are rampaging through the score, creating sound effects and slabs of color and texture with complete abandon. But it is clear that this is an illusion—that, in fact, there is an acute discipline at work, both on the compositional level and in the music's execution.

87. LEONARD BERNSTEIN

Candide Overture; Symphonic Dances from *West Side Story;* Symphonic Suite from *On the Waterfront;* and *Fancy Free*

NEW YORK PHILHARMONIC,
LEONARD BERNSTEIN, CONDUCTING
(Sony Classical SMK 63085)

Recorded 1960–1963

In his lifetime, Leonard Bernstein (1918–1990) was admired primarily for his eloquence as a conductor, both on the podium and as a persuasive, open-minded advocate for music of all kinds, who conveyed his infectious enthusiasms to a generation of listeners who grew up watching his televised *Young People's Concerts* in the 1950s and 1960s. It was only secondarily that he was known as a composer—and at that, his "serious" symphonic works never quite enjoyed the renown that his theater and film music did. History may yet redress that: Bernstein's three symphonies, and works like the beautiful *Chichester Psalms* and the quasi-violin concerto, *Symposium,* continue to turn up on concert programs and occasionally on new recordings.

The more popular works, though, have settled comfortably into the canon of contemporary American music, and if they aren't freighted with the philosophical heft that supports many modern works (including some of Bernstein's symphonic scores), there is no question that they have earned their place. This compilation of Bernstein's early 1960s recordings, remastered in pristine sound quality, goes a long way toward explaining why—and, along the way, showing something of Bernstein's range, even in this particular corner of his catalog.

Candide (1956) plays in both theaters and opera houses these days, but its melody-packed and effervescent Overture has a life of its own. It is one of Bernstein's most distinctive calling cards: for anyone who saw him conduct, this work's glittery ebullience brings to mind that side of his public persona. Indeed, the most memorable part of a memorial concert presented at Carnegie Hall after Bernstein's death was a virtuosic, conductorless account of this work by members of the New York Philharmonic and several other orchestras with which Bernstein was associated.

West Side Story (1957) was of course Bernstein's biggest hit, both in the theater and in the great film version with Natalie Wood and Richard Beymer. Bernstein did not conduct the original Broadway cast recording or the soundtrack album, both of which are classics, and when he revisited the score late in life—with a cast headed by the opera stars Kiri Te Kanawa and José Carreras (Deutsche Grammophon, 1984), the results were mixed. What this disc offers is the set of Symphonic Dances that Bernstein assembled (in orchestrations by Sid Ramin and Irwin Kostal) for concert use.

As the title suggests, the main vocal themes are offered instrumentally, and the best of them—for example, the hauntingly beautiful "Somewhere"—are included among the suite's nine short movements. So is the 1950s New York atmosphere of the work, basically an updating of *Romeo and Juliet* with Tony and Maria as the star-crossed lovers, and gangs of Anglos (the Jets) and Puerto Ricans (the Sharks) as the Montagues and Capulets. Bernstein's stylistic omnivorousness served this drama perfectly: the Jets' themes have a jazzy tinge, and the Sharks' music leans on Latin rhythms. There are also moments when both are combined: at the center of the suite (the fifth of the nine movements), the melody of "Maria"—the graceful love song that is Tony's central moment—is set to a cha-cha beat.

Suggesting atmosphere—and specifically, the atmosphere of New York—came naturally to Bernstein. *West Side Story* shows that from one side; another, somewhat bleaker view is presented in the evocatively dark-hued music he contributed to *On the Waterfront* (1954), Elia Kazan's film about a man's rebellion against the corrupt union leaders who controlled the longshoremen in New York harbor. Heard on its own in the Symphonic Suite included here, the music gets quickly to the heart of the film, capturing the violence that runs through the story, as well as the blossoming romance between Terry Malloy and Edie (the characters played by Marlon Brando and Eva Marie Saint) that makes it possible for Terry to turn against the union boss, Johnny Friendly. This work's sharp edges and disquieting dissonances give it a weight and sobriety that make it more at home in the serious concert hall than as part of a symphonic pops program.

Fancy Free, Bernstein's 1944 ballet about three sailors on shore leave in New York—a piece later reworked as the musical (and film)

Composer Leonard Bernstein

On the Town—offers yet another perspective on New York, or at least New York as it was during World War II. Like *West Side Story*, this score is an amalgam of symphonic and jazz styles that tie it firmly to its time and place. But the violent sides of both *West Side Story* and *On the Waterfront* are absent here. Instead, this is bright, youthful music, innocent and fun, but sophisticated as well.

88. BERNARD HERRMANN

The Film Scores

LOS ANGELES PHILHARMONIC,
ESA-PEKKA SALONEN, CONDUCTING
(Sony Classical SK 62700)

Includes The Man Who Knew Too Much: *Prelude*; Psycho: *A Suite for Strings*; Marnie: *Suite*, North by Northwest: *Overture*; Vertigo: *Suite*; Torn Curtain; Fahrenheit 451: *Suite for Strings, Harps, and Percussion*; *and* Taxi Driver: *A Night-Piece for Orchestra*.

Recorded 1996

Film music has an ambiguous standing in the classical music world, and deserves greater respect than it has traditionally been accorded. That isn't to say it hasn't had its champions in classics circles. Over the years, several labels, including RCA Red Seal, Decca, and Nonesuch, have devoted series within their classical lines (short-lived ones, but still) to fresh recordings of film scores that had attained classic status. And most classical music review magazines have sections devoted to soundtracks, in which the music is treated as seriously as the symphonic concert music elsewhere in the publication.

There is, of course, no reason it shouldn't be. Although the viewers sitting in the reflected glow of the silver screen are principally occupied with the story, acting, and scenery before them, the music—both the short cues and the longer underscoring—plays a crucial role in establishing the emotional temperature of a character or a scene. A film composer has to have the concert composer's standard arsenal— a grasp of harmony and orchestration, and a fertile imagination. But the job requires a certified skill above and beyond that: an ability to produce music to tightly specified lengths (which often change during the editing).

A part of that supplementary skill is at least a minor suspension of the traditional compositional ego: the reason Arnold Schoenberg never became a film composer wasn't that he considered film music below him—he very much wanted to write for Hollywood—or even that Hollywood found his music impenetrable. It was that when he told studio moguls that he insisted on maintaining complete control of his work and how it was to be used in a film, the discussions ended.

Bernard Herrmann (1911–1975) was neither egoless nor lacking a personal artistic outlook. He developed the latter when, as a young man, he befriended the iconoclastic Charles Ives, and inherited Ives's notion (Beethoven's too, if it comes to that) that an artist need not be bound by rules. And as for ego, while he had no illusions about having the last word about how his music is heard in a film, he had his limits: when his score for *The Magnificent Ambersons* was mangled, in 1942, he withdrew his name from the credits. And his lack of success as composer of concert works and opera (he considered his operatic version of *Wuthering Heights* his masterpiece) was a source of tremendous annoyance.

Still, Herrmann understood how the film world worked, and he was able to write extraordinary music within its constraints. Born in New York, he studied conducting and composition at New York University and the Juilliard School, but also absorbed a great deal about the niceties of orchestration by studying scores on his own in the New York Public Library. In his early twenties, he became an assistant conductor on CBS radio, and by 1936 he began composing incidental music for radio dramas.

Among the weekly programs Herrmann wrote music for were *The Mercury Theater on the Air* and the *Campbell Playhouse,* both directed by Orson Welles. And when Welles made *Citizen Kane,* he invited Herrmann to compose the music. That was his first film score, and the start of an enormously productive career that included scores for *The*

Day the Earth Stood Still, Journey to the Center of the Earth, The Seventh Voyage of Sinbad, Jason and the Argonauts, The Devil and Daniel Webster, and *Jane Eyre.*

In these works, Herrmann developed a style in which texture and short signature melodic and rhythmic figures were central—a distinct change from the long-lined lyricism of predecessors like Max Steiner and Wolfgang Erich Korngold. This made his music perfect, at least for a time, for the thrillers that Alfred Hitchcock was making, and indeed, Hitchcock's films seemed to bring out the best in Herrmann. Most (but not all) of Esa-Pekka Salonen's disc is devoted to Herrmann's Hitchcock music, including many of the truly famous bits—the violent, stabbing violins that accompany the shower scene in *Psycho,* for example.

But there is plenty more to keep an ear on. Also in *Psycho,* the driving music—Janet Leigh's escape in a rainstorm with her boss's money in the trunk of her car—is full of pounding figures that suggest tension and fear, the sense of being chased, even though no one is chasing her. Leigh's first moments in Anthony Perkins's hotel (a section called "The Madhouse") are underscored with gently foreboding music that leads, in this suite, directly into the shower scene. The music evolves from there: by the time one reaches the section labeled "The Cellar," Herrmann's string writing has grown more menacingly nimble; yet the finale, heard on its own, brings the music back to the gentle eeriness of "The Madhouse," and understandably so.

Herrmann toyed with allusions to the standard canon when he saw the need. In the "Scène d'Amour," from *Vertigo,* he makes an overt allusion to the "Liebestod" in Wagner's *Tristan und Isolde.* There are sections in *Psycho* (the suite movement called "The Water") that recall Manuel de Falla, both in musical contours and orchestrations, and in one of the two non-Hitchcock scores here, *Fahrenheit 451,* Herrmann uses lush strings and harps in an allusion to the music of Gabriel Fauré. But these are passing touches. Herrmann's music, overall, is decidedly his own, and there were times when he was positively visionary: the *North by Northwest* music, and even parts of the Prelude to the *Psycho* suite, use figuration of the sort that that Philip Glass would incorporate into his style in the 1970s and later.

Included on this disc, as well, is a short suite from *Torn Curtain,* the score that ended Herrmann's relationship with Hitchcock. It was 1966, and Hitchcock wanted a score that was in tune with the times. That didn't interest Herrmann, who thought he could maintain Hitchcock's interest by writing music in his own style, but for a bizarre ensemble that included twelve flutes, sixteen French horns, nine trombones, two tubas, and a cello- and bass-heavy string section. Hitchcock heard very little of the music before dismissing Herrmann, who went on to other things, including the dream-turned-nightmare score for François Truffaut's *Fahrenheit 451* and the uncharacteristically blues-tinged music for Martin Scorsese's *Taxi Driver*—a score Herrmann completed the day he died. Suites from both are included here.

Herrmann himself conducted recordings of several discs' worth of his film music for Decca, and some of them were reissued on CD, briefly, in the mid-1990s. Those are great performances, full of the vigor and tension that this music needs. But in at least one regard, Esa-Pekka Salonen's performance surpasses them: the British orchestras that Herrmann led—the London Philharmonic and the National Philharmonic—play the music as if they were hired for an afternoon's session work, and were eager to get on to the next gig. That is, it's entirely competent and efficient, but it doesn't compare to the edge-of-the-seat energy and textural clarity that Salonen's Los Angeles players bring to the music.

It could be that the Los Angeles musicians found the local history in these scores exciting, but I think it's more than that. Ever since he took over this orchestra in 1991, Salonen has transformed it into a lively force in the American concert world, and the excitement he has created around the ensemble can be heard in its musicmaking. Born in Finland in 1958, and a talented composer, Salonen has been drawn to contemporary music from the early days of his career. His first recordings to win wide attention were authoritative readings of works by Olivier Messiaen and Witold Lutosławski, and he has since gone on to make estimable Stravinsky, Nielsen, Debussy, and Ligeti discs.

In the case of the Herrmann works, the films from which the scores are drawn are clearly a part of his cultural consciousness, and in his performances one hears a determination to let Herrmann's music speak for itself—but also, to evoke something of the missing visual component.

89. MILTON BABBITT

Three Compositions, Duet, Semi-Simple Variations, Partitions, Post-Partitions, Tableaux, Reflections for Piano and Synthesized Tape, *Canonical Form,* and *Lagniappe*

ROBERT TAUB, PIANIST

(Harmonia Mundi USA 905160)

Recorded 1985

One can easily list the opposites of Milton Babbitt's music. Where romanticism is rooted, at least in part, in a kind of magnified emotionality, Babbitt's work is supremely rational in both structure and content, to the point where he has argued that every note in a musical work should be so completely justified that changing so much as a tone color or a dynamic marking would put the score's structure asunder. And where minimalism, among contemporary styles, strove for a harmonically stripped-down, rhythmically direct music, Babbitt created pieces that are thoroughly, and purposefully, complex. To make the point, he has referred to himself as a maximalist.

Although he said it as a succinct and humorous way of distancing his music from that of the minimalists, the term is apt. As a young man, Babbitt (who was born in 1916) was attracted to jazz and theater music, and in the mid-1940s, he actually wrote a musical, *Fabulous Voyage,* in the then-current theatrical style. But he was also writing concert works that used the serial techniques that had been pioneered by Arnold Schoenberg. By the end of the 1940s, he had expanded on Schoenberg's idea of creating themes by arranging the twelve tones of the scale into strictly defined tone rows. Babbitt decided that if tones could be organized in that way, other compositional parameters, like dynamics and timbre, could be, too. This "total serialism" was enthusiastically taken up by Pierre Boulez, Luigi Nono, and other serial composers.

To casual listeners, this approach yielded music that was angular, dissonant, and altogether too brainy. Such complaints didn't bother

Babbitt: in a 1958 article in *High Fidelity,* called "Who Cares If You Listen?"—an editor's title, to which Babbitt strenuously objected—Babbitt wrote: "The time has passed when the normally well-educated man without special preparation could understand the most advanced work in, for example, mathematics, philosophy and physics. Advanced music, to the extent that it reflects the knowledge and originality of the informed composer, scarcely can be expected to appear more intelligible than these arts and sciences to the person whose musical education usually has been even less extensive than his background in other fields."

I think Babbitt was wrong there. A better approach is the one offered in a set of program notes by the composer Charles Wuorinen, whose music is similarly cerebral. After explaining at some length the structure and relationships within one of his works about to have its premiere, Wuorinen added that it wasn't necessary for listeners to know or understand any of this—all they had to do was sit back and listen.

Not long after Robert Taub released this extraordinary collection, I had the occasion to put Wuorinen's advice into practice. At a recital in which Taub played several of these works, I listened at first with the scores in hand, laboring through Babbitt's complex notation and trying to focus not only on how what I was hearing was represented on the page, but also on the details of how the score fulfilled the various goals Babbitt described in his notes. After a few pieces, though, I realized that I was worrying about the music rather than listening to it. I closed the score, settled in, and listened. And it quickly became clear that this music, heard without technical or analytical baggage, had the freedom, spirit, and soaring quality that one hears in a great improvisation by a jazz pianist—particularly a player like Cecil Taylor, whose brand of jazz is harmonically and rhythmically advanced.

That impression, of course, was thoroughly dependent upon the performer's having the technique and imagination to project it, and that, in turn, underscores the importance, for composers like Babbitt, of having interpreters like Taub, who was a student of Babbitt's at Princeton, and not only understands thoroughly what the composer is getting at, but has the pianistic wherewithal to give those ideas a voice. Taub does not have a conventionally starry career, along the lines of a Maurizio Pollini or a Vladimir Ashkenazy. But in many ways he is second to none: his Beethoven and Schumann performances are as refreshing and illuminating as his Babbitt.

Babbitt's piano music is not the most famous corner of his catalog. Perhaps more emblematic are works like *Philomel* (1964), for soprano and electronic tape, or *All Set* (1957), for jazz ensemble. But the works here, composed between 1947 and 1985 (the most recent, *Lagniappe,* was written specifically for the recording) offer a superb overview of the creative path Babbitt has traveled. The earliest works, *Three Compositions* (1947–1948), *Duet* (1956), and *Semi-Simple Variations* (1956), are elegantly transparent, given how densely packed they are: *Duet,* for example, lasts a mere thirty-six seconds, but has the character of a Bach two-part invention, and the *Semi-Simple Variations* offer five views of a simple theme in only a minute and a quarter.

Textural clarity remains a central concern in *Partitions* (1957) and *Post-Partitions* (1966), but here Babbitt has replaced the counterpoint of the earlier works with more densely harmonized passages and more vivid leaps into the piano's highest register. *Tableaux* (1973) ranges even more widely over the keyboard, and adds to the mix a demand for a virtuosic dexterity. The most famous of the works here, *Reflections* (1974), uses a synthesizer track that sounds quaint now, but which creates a variegated, pointillistic fabric within which the piano line darts nimbly. When Taub toured with this work in Asia, he was stopped by Chinese authorities who suspected that the synthesizer track was encoded espionage. He was able to convince them otherwise by performing the piece for them. *Canonical Form* (1983), like *Lagniappe,* was written for Taub, and restores the contrapuntal concerns of the early works with the grander sense of texture and sonority Babbitt developed in the 1970s.

90. JOHN CORIGLIANO

Richard Stoltzman: The Essential Clarinet

RICHARD STOLTZMAN, CLARINETIST; LONDON
SYMPHONY ORCHESTRA, LAWRENCE LEIGHTON-SMITH,
CONDUCTING

(RCA Red Seal 09026-61360-2)

Includes John Corigliano's Concerto for Clarinet and Orchestra; Aaron Copland's Concerto for Clarinet, Strings, Harp, and Piano; Igor Stravinsky's Ebony Concerto; *Leonard Bernstein's* Prelude, Fugue, and Riffs; *Stoltzman conducts Woody Herman's Thundering Herd in the Stravinsky*

Recorded 1987

John Corigliano's colorfully scored, technically demanding Clarinet Concerto is the principal draw here, but the disc also stands as a great overview of the modern repertory for clarinet and orchestra—and also as a showcase for Richard Stoltzman, a clarinetist whose discography has tilted toward crossover projects in recent years, but who established his bona fides as an eloquent advocate of new music and a lively interpreter of the standard canon, both as a member of the chamber group Tashi and on his own.

Corigliano, born in New York in 1938, studied composition with Otto Luening (at Columbia University) and Vittorio Giannini (at the Manhattan School of Music), and overcame a few obstacles in his path to becoming a composer. One was not having mastered an instrument: although he has a sufficiently formidable piano technique to negotiate the thickets of his scores during interviews, he was never a public performer, and when asked what instrument he plays, he has been known to answer, "My stereo." A second obstacle was the objection of his father, also called John Corigliano, who was the concertmaster of the New York Philharmonic from 1943 to 1966, and had seen the difficulty that contemporary composers face in both making a living and finding an appreciative audience.

Edging into a musical career by way of jobs at Columbia Records and at two New York radio stations (WQXR and WBAI), and by undertaking orchestrations for pop recordings (most notably *Naked Carmen,* a rock version of the Bizet opera), he made his first compositional splash with a violin sonata that, in 1964, impressed a competition jury at the Spoleto Festival. The jury included Samuel Barber, Walter Piston, and Gian-Carlo Menotti, and with the prize on his resumé, commissions began coming in. By the late 1970s, several of Corigliano's bigger works—a piano concerto, an oboe concerto, and a setting of Dylan Thomas's *Poem in October*—had appeared on recordings, establishing Corigliano as a composer with a fresh voice that was filtered through an eclectic, accessibly neoromantic style.

Actually, the neoromantic label does not describe Corigliano's music adequately. Corigliano prizes melody, but is as likely to write a spiky, angular tune as a gently lyrical one. His approach to harmony is essentially tonal, but he uses patches of dissonance and even twelve-tone rows when they suit his expressive needs. He draws on world music as well, and although he has been known to quote from past masters—his Fantasia on an Ostinato, for example, uses a theme from the Beethoven Seventh Symphony as a starting point—his pieces are not rewrites of the nineteenth century.

The Clarinet Concerto, commissioned by the New York Philharmonic for its principal clarinetist, Stanley Drucker, and first performed at the end of 1977, with Leonard Bernstein conducting, was a turning point for Corigliano, if only in the sense that it allowed him to focus his expressive powers on a large-scale work for musicians he had known all his life. The notion that the piece was for an ensemble Corigliano considered family defined its parameters. Corigliano wanted every player on the orchestra's roster to be in the performance, and several elements flow from that particular decision. For example, instead of crowding all those players on the stage, Corigliano assigned wind and brass groups to perform from positions in the balconies, creating a surround-sound effect in the piece's wild finale. That, in turn, called to mind the antiphonal brass music of Gabrieli, which Corigliano quotes in that final movement. Closer to home, the central slow movement, an Elegy, is a memorial to the composer's father, and includes a singing solo violin line in addition to the solo clarinet.

The work was an immediate hit, and within a few seasons it was performed again by the Philharmonic and by orchestras all over the United States, both with their own principal clarinetists and with Stoltzman, who was just starting to establish his touring career. As showpieces go, a clarinetist could hardly want more: the solo line uses the full range of the instrument and virtually every effect and timbral nuance that can be summoned on it. Stoltzman seems to share with Corigliano an enjoyment of extremes: the Mahlerian Elegy is passionate and songful, a perfect contrast to the athleticism of the outer movements.

The other works in this collection are all products of the 1940s, a time when many composers recognized jazz as an American lingua franca, and sought ways to incorporate its rhythms, melodic shapes, and harmonic syntax into their music. The clarinet, which was largely buried in the orchestra but had a life of its own in jazz, invited this approach, as did the availability of soloists like Benny Goodman, who, although primarily a jazz player, was adept at classical performance as well. Goodman's own recording of the Copland Clarinet Concerto (1947–1948), with the composer conducting, is included elsewhere in these pages, but Stoltzman's reading has some lilting turns of phrase that make it a worthy rival.

Bernstein's *Prelude, Fugue, and Riffs* (1949) was composed for Goodman as well, and is a more overtly jazzy score cut from the same fabric as parts of *West Side Story*. Stravinsky's *Ebony* Concerto (1945), written after the composer heard a concert by Woody Herman, is hardly a concerto at all: the solo clarinet line peeks through now and then, but mostly this is an ensemble piece, for winds and brass, with Latin-accented percussion touches and occasional punctuation by a guitar and a piano. In a nicely authentic touch, Stoltzman convened Herman's band for this recording, which has a ragtag edge that seems suited to the work's spirit.

91. STEVE REICH

Early Works

STEVE REICH AND RUSSELL HARTENBERGER, CLAPPING;
NURIT TILLES AND EDMUND NIEMANN, PIANISTS

(Nonesuch 79169 2)

Includes It's Gonna Rain, Come Out, Piano Phase, *and* Clapping Music.
Recorded 1965–1987

Steve Reich, born in New York in 1936, is a founder of a compositional movement that has not only proven important in the development of modern music, but also has found an enormous popular following—something virtually unprecedented in the musical history of the twentieth century. That Reich and his like-minded colleagues (Philip Glass, Terry Riley, and LaMonte Young, among the founders) have long sought to distance themselves from the label applied to that movement—*minimalism*—is worth bearing in mind, if only for its similarity to Debussy's loathing for the term *impressionism*.

That said, the early minimalists are often spoken of as if they thought and worked as a single musical organism. Actually, for all the interplay among them in the late 1960s, and for all their shared love of repetition as a means of propulsion, these composers had styles that were not only very different from one another's, but were also immediately identifiable. Reich's training included both conventional composition work (with Hall Overton, William Bergsma, Vincent Persichetti, Darius Milhaud, and Luciano Berio) and time spent in Ghana studying traditional African drumming techniques. Not surprisingly, in his music, rhythmic patterns are central.

This collection captures the first steps in the evolution of Reich's style, and of his particular corner of minimalism. Reich has moved miles from these pieces—now his works are complex multimedia scores for instrumental ensemble and voices, with video by his wife, Beryl Korot. Yet there are elements from these early works that he periodically revisits. In any case, these old scores stand up well all these decades later, and within them, one can still hear the excitement of discovery.

The two earliest works are tape pieces, and it was while he was making the first, *It's Gonna Rain* (1965), that Reich accidentally stumbled upon "phasing," a principle that drove his work for years. Having made a recording of Brother Walter, a black Pentecostal preacher in San Francisco, Reich set about making the recording into an electronic piece. While preparing a series of tape loops—short lengths of recording tape with their ends spliced together so that they play continuously—Reich discovered that if two identical loops began in unison, but moved at slightly different speeds, interesting patterns would be created as the two loops continued to move farther out of phase. Moreover, he discovered, if the loops continue playing, they will eventually move back into phase, so that they are once again in unison.

That process was the first part of *It's Gonna Rain*. In the second part, Reich began with a longer pair of loops, and then added second, third, and fourth pairs to create an expanded, rhythmically contrapuntal texture. In the second piece, *Come Out* (1966), he used similar procedures on a section of an interview with Daniel Hamm, a nineteen-year-old who was arrested (and later acquitted) during the Harlem riots of 1964. The patterns Hamm's voice creates as the loops go out of phase—like those created by Brother Walter's oratory—are hypnotic.

Reich took up the use of taped voices again in later works, most notably *Different Trains* (1988), a work for tape and string quartet, in which the memories of American train porters and European Holocaust survivors are juxtaposed. But after *Come Out*, he decided to apply his phasing technique to instrumental music. Two identical tapes moving out of sync, of course, was mainly a mechanical issue: all one needed was a pair of tape machines operating at slightly different speeds (although Reich undoubtedly manipulated the rate at which the phase changes occurred). Making the process work with instruments and live musicians meant forcing the phase displacement by having one of the players either drop or add a beat (or part of one) at prescribed intervals, so that the two identical lines moved apart incrementally but audibly.

Reich's first experiment with this process was *Piano Phase* (1967), in which two pianists (here the exceptional Nurit Tilles and Edmund

Niemann, who perform together under the name Double Edge) are given short melodic figures that move out of phase just as the taped voices did. The principal difference in effect is that the piano, more dramatically than the voices, leaves tones and overtones hanging in the air as the melodic figures move on, and creates a layer of phantom harmonies. The effect, at first, is like a slight tape echo; by the middle of the twenty-minute piece, the textural web is so thick that it's difficult to believe one is hearing only two pianos.

Clapping Music (1972) examines the process yet again, from a purely rhythmic perspective, and in a way that anyone can try. Two musicians begin by clapping a fairly simple rhythmic pattern in unison, and then gradually move out of phase and then back toward a unison finale. The performance here, by Reich and Russ Hartenberger, a longtime member of Reich's ensemble, lasts only 4:39, and of course, it's just clapping. But at its height, the phasing process yields patterns that are surprisingly intricate.

92. STEVE REICH

Tehillim

SCHÖNBERG ENSEMBLE WITH PERCUSSION GROUP
THE HAGUE, REINBERT DE LEEUW, CONDUCTING

Three Movements

LONDON SYMPHONY ORCHESTRA,
MICHAEL TILSON THOMAS, CONDUCTING
(Nonesuch 79295 2)

Recorded 1992–1993

Tehillim (1981) was a turning point for Steve Reich, and it remains one of his most thoroughly satisfying works. From the mid-1960s until he began work on this score in 1980, he had avoided writing for singers. Having started out with a series of works in which his con-

---

cern was a psychoacoustical issue—how interesting patterns are created when identical rhythmic or melodic lines gradually move out of phase—he spent most of the 1970s moving beyond that in a series of chamber works in which repeated figuration expanded into grand contrapuntal textures. The question of setting texts had interested him for some time, but he was unable to find a way into the process that was consistent with his established style.

His problem, as he saw it, was that if he were to set an English text—which was his first inclination—the melodic and rhythmic shapes of the vocal line would be dictated by the text and its meaning, a point that limited his own rhythmic and melodic prerogatives. He came to terms with that problem once he realized that by repeating words or parts of words, he could maintain control over both melody and rhythm. This led to the composition of *The Desert Music* (1984), a gripping setting of poetry by William Carlos Williams. For *Tehillim,* though, he found a different solution, one that occurred to him in the mid-1970s, when he was becoming reconnected with Judaism, and spent some time studying the traditional Hebrew cantillation tropes used in the reading of sacred texts.

Reich realized that by setting Hebrew Psalm texts (*tehillim* is Hebrew for psalms), he could sidestep his linguistic concerns partly because most of the audience would be listening to the sung texts more for their sound than for their meaning, and partly because the Hebrew psalm texts that he chose (excerpts from Psalms 19, 24, 18, and 150) actually suited the kinds of metrical shapes that had become part of his stylistic thumbprint.

The decision to move ahead with this project liberated Reich in other ways, too. Instead of the dense textures he had been building toward in his most ambitious works to this point (*Music for 18 Musicians,* for example), he wrote for a more transparent band, with percussion in the foreground and winds either doubling the vocal lines or supporting them with slowly moving chord sequences. At the same time, he increased his use of chromaticism in the supporting ensemble music, which moves between simple consonance and patches of more enigmatic harmony.

Naturally, certain hallmarks of Reich's style remain front and center. Sharply defined rhythms, and repetition, for example, continue to propel the music. Sometimes the rhythms flow naturally from the texts; often, the combination of text, rhythm, and the percussion underlay creates an exotically ritualistic atmosphere.

Reich oversaw his own recording of the work with his ensemble, Steve Reich and Musicians, conducted by George Manahan (ECM, 1981), and that performance stands up well. But there is something to be said for letting a work settle into a performance tradition before recording it, and this 1993 version by the Dutch conductor Reinbert de Leeuw, leading the Schönberg Ensemble with the support of Percussion Group The Hague, has the edge in brightness and fluidity.

It also offers a second work, which the ECM original does not. That piece, *Three Movements* (1986), is an alternately lyrical and vigorous orchestral score in which Reich expands on techniques he explored in *The Desert Music* and *Sextet* (1985). The London Symphony Orchestra, conducted by Michael Tilson Thomas, plays the work with a timbral astringency that suits Reich's language and calls to mind the sound of his own ensemble.

For listeners interested in exploring Reich's music more thoroughly, the performances on this disc, as well as those on *Early Works* and virtually every major piece Reich composed through the mid-1990s, are included in *Works 1965–1995,* a comprehensive boxed set (Nonesuch).

93. PHILIP GLASS

Music in Twelve Parts

PHILIP GLASS ENSEMBLE,
MICHAEL RIESMAN, CONDUCTING
(Nonesuch 79324 2; three CDs)

Recorded 1993

Although he came to resent the label minimalism, Philip Glass helped found the compositional school bearing that name in the late 1960s, when he and other young composers rebelled against the complexities and harmonic abrasiveness of the twelve-tone and serial music that were the dominant new-music styles of the time. Glass, who was born in Baltimore in 1937, had been trained in those styles at the Juilliard School, although classmates later remembered him as veering toward more consonant music even then. And his post-Juilliard studies with Darius Milhaud, in Aspen, or Nadia Boulanger, in Paris, would not have involved the rigors of serial technique.

While Glass was in Paris to study with Boulanger, from 1964 to 1966, he signed on as an assistant to the sitar virtuoso Ravi Shankar, who was in Paris to write a score for the film *Chappaqua,* and it was during his work with Shankar that Glass had a musical epiphany. In the Indian classical music tradition, complexity tends to be rhythmic, not harmonic, and musical ideas unfold slowly and inexorably. When Glass returned to New York, he began incorporating those ideas into his style, and he assembled a group—the Philip Glass Ensemble—to perform the pieces he was writing.

In its earliest incarnation, the Philip Glass Ensemble included whatever musicians dropped in for rehearsals and performances. But it soon coalesced around a pair of wheezy electric organs, reed instruments, and vocalists (usually sopranos). The singers, typically, were given solfege syllables (do, re, mi, etc.) or number sequences to sing, rather than conventional texts. And both the singers and instrumentalists worked their way through pieces in which Glass explored what became the central minimalist paradox: using repetition, or the appearance of stasis, to move a work forward.

In Glass's case, that involved what he called "additive process." To explain it simply, imagine the musicians repeating a musical figure a prescribed number of times and then extending the figure by adding a note (or several). With this as a basic template, all kinds of permutations are possible. Glass also adopted an extremely stripped-down language. His themes were built on repeating intervals—a minor third, for example, was a favorite—or fragments of major and minor scales; his rhythms tended to be straightforward, even metronomic. Still, in Glass's early works, additive process and a kind of rough-hewn counterpoint transformed these elements into more complex and involving textures, and each piece examined these materials from a new angle.

Music in Twelve Parts (1971–1974), a set of twelve connected works lasting about three and a half hours, is a grand summation of all this, and a look at what would come next. But that was not Glass's original intent for this score: when he completed what is now Part I, he gave it the title *Music in Twelve Parts* because its component keyboard, wind, and voice lines added up to twelve lines of music. When a friend of the composer's heard the piece and asked what the other eleven parts would be like, he decided to expand the project.

The first eight parts look at different rhythmic or harmonic issues that Glass had been investigating in his music. In Part I, for example, the subject is the interval of a fifth. Each of the instruments plays a steadily moving line, but at any point in the movement, at least one of the instruments is playing an F-sharp and another is playing a C-sharp (together, a fifth), creating the illusion of a drone running through the work. Other movements look at different intervals, or at how harmonically unbalanced chords find resolutions.

As it turns out, by Part VIII, Glass had essentially completed his summation, having revisited all the major techniques he had used until then. So in Part IX and Part X he explores different forms of ornamentation, and in Part XI and Part XII, he abandons what had until that point been an esthetic based on harmonic stasis, and modulates freely and actively from key to key. Part XII even includes something that had been anathema to Glass—and is presented here as a joke—a twelve-tone row, in the bass line.

Glass and his ensemble recorded the work for Virgin in the early 1970s, although only Part I and Part II were issued on LP; it took until 1989 for the label to issue the rest of the set. This version, recorded in 1993, is in some cases brisker and in some cases more expansive than the original, but overall it is more tightly played and better recorded. In either version, the score stands as a monument to a crucial, experimental period in late-twentieth-century American music. Glass's work has become more monumental in both character and texture, but *Music in Twelve Parts* explains a lot about this music's roots.

94. PHILIP GLASS

Koyaanisqatsi

ALBERT DE RUITER, BASS; PHILIP GLASS ENSEMBLE,
WESTERN WIND VOCAL ENSEMBLE
(Nonesuch 79506-2)

Also available on DVD (MGM 1003766).

Recorded 1998

Godfrey Reggio's series of film meditations on the generally unwholesome state of civilization, and the world at large, seems to have had a decisive appeal to Philip Glass, both philosophically and artistically, for he has provided scores for all of them—the full-length *Koyaanisqatsi* (1982), *Powaqqatsi* (1997), and *Naqoyqatsi* (2002), as well as the short films, *Anima Mundi* (1991) and *Evidence* (1995). Each of these works has its salient points, and the distance from *Koyaanisqatsi* to *Naqoyqatsi* is considerable. Yet in many ways *Koyaanisqatsi* is the most powerful of the group, and it remains one of the highlights in a large and still growing catalog of works.

By the time he completed *Koyaanisqatsi*, Glass had been arguing for some time that his work should no longer be regarded as minimalist—that since his first opera, *Einstein on the Beach* (1976), or at the very least, since its fully orchestrated successor, *Satyagraha* (1980), both his compositional goals and the textures of his music had gone far beyond the stripped-down simplicity that the label implied. *Koyaanisqatsi* offers further support for that argument. Colorfully scored for a large ensemble of orchestral instruments, electronic keyboards, and singers, it unfolds with a drama and vividness that are at times almost Wagnerian in their romantic spirit.

Koyaanisqatsi takes its name from a Hopi word meaning "crazy life," "life in turmoil," "life disintegrating," "life out of balance," and "a state of life that calls for another way of living," a set of definitions that aptly summarize the view of contemporary Western society that Reggio presents here, and in the other installments of his "qatsi" series. Like its successors, *Koyaanisqatsi* has no characters, no dialogue, and no narration, only a balletic flow of images, often sped-up or slowed-down, and matched to Glass's score.

Among the images are grand natural vistas—majestic deserts, beautiful cloud formations—as well as scenes of our crowded, busy, mechanized, polluted civilization. More often than not, the juxtapositions of nature's and mankind's realms leave civilization looking decadent, depressing, or ludicrous. Yet what saves the film from being an unambiguous flat-earther polemic is that some of the high-tech imagery is actually quite beautiful. Traffic patterns, filmed from the air, at night, and sped-up, create rivers of red and white light. The glass towers of an urban center reflect the clouds and changing light over the course of a day. Even a scene of pure destruction—the demolition of the Pruit Igoe housing project—has a certain melancholy grace in the context that Glass's score creates.

The score itself is quite varied. The opening section ("Koyaanisqatsi") is almost ritualistic: the film's title is intoned in a sepulchral groan by the bass Albert de Ruiter, to the accompaniment of an almost Bachian organ figure. Those moves are mirrored in the final movement ("Prophecies"). The movements in between include an essay in choral polyphony ("Vessels"), a movement for winding strings, sharp-edged brass, and stabs of textless choral sound ("Pruit Igoe"), and a long movement steeped in relentless, ecstatic energy in the style of Glass's earlier ensemble works ("The Grid").

When the film was released, Glass cut the eighty-seven-minute score in half to accommodate the limitations of the original LP (Antilles, 1982). In many ways, that original disc holds up nicely, but this version, Glass's 1998 remake for Nonesuch, is far better. Many of the original performers (including de Ruiter) are on this version, too, and nearly all of the deleted music has been restored. As vital as the original recording is, the new one unfolds more smoothly and with an even greater bite—the product, no doubt, of Glass's having frequently performed the score in concert, with and without the film.

Of course, you can have it both ways: the film is available on DVD, with the complete original soundtrack remixed for 5.1 Surround Sound, and the picture looking great.

Composer Philip Glass

This is unquestionably the best way to take in this work. And it allows a listener to ponder the philosophical intricacies of watching a broadside about the depredations of Western civilization, captured in a work that could not have been created without an ample consumption of resources (from film stock and chemicals to the gasoline used to transport the film crews around the country, to say nothing of the aerial shots) and played in a high-tech home audiovisual system.

95. JOHN ADAMS

Shaker Loops (1978, revised 1983)

ORCHESTRA OF ST. LUKE'S,
JOHN ADAMS, CONDUCTING

Violin Concerto (1993)

GIDON KREMER, VIOLINIST; LONDON SYMPHONY
ORCHESTRA, KENT NAGANO, CONDUCTING
(Nonesuch 79360)

Recorded 1988, 1994

When John Adams cruised onto record collectors' radar screens, with the 1981 release of an LP bringing together *Shaker Loops,* in its string septet version, and *Phrygian Gates,* a grandly exploratory solo piano work, it became clear even to doubters that minimalism would have legs. The style, established in New York during the late 1960s by Philip Glass, Steve Reich, Terry Riley, LaMonte Young, and others, had evolved considerably since then, moving from chamber-scale experiments to works for larger forces and even, in Glass's case, operas. But the style's influence among composers was slight: most new minimalist works were still by composers in the style's founding circle. And although minimalism had built a large and enthusiastic following, mostly among younger listeners, it was dismissed as a passing trend by the musical establishment.

All that began to change with the arrival of Adams, the first important outsider to crash the minimalist party. He was ten years younger than Glass, Reich, and company, and he came from an entirely different milieu. Born in New Hampshire in 1947, he studied composition at Harvard with Leon Kirchner, a composer whose emotional, rigorously structured music had little in common with minimalism's abstraction and simplicity. After completing his studies, Adams moved to California, where he briefly dabbled in atonal music and electronic tape pieces, as well as experiments with chance music, influenced by the works and philosophy of John Cage. By the late 1970s, he began to be drawn to the minimalist approach of building large-scale works from short, repeated musical figures.

Adams, though, brought a few important new elements to the style. For one thing, while the East Coast minimalists were writing largely for their own ensembles, which tended to lean heavily either on percussion (as Steve Reich and Musicians did) or on electronic keyboards and reeds (like the Philip Glass Ensemble), Adams wrote for conventional chamber groups and soloists.

Adams's first works also embraced free chromaticism, something rarely encountered in the minimalist palette at that time. It was, after all, partly in response to the extreme chromaticism of Schoenberg and the serialists that minimalism began, so in its early years, minimalists kept their harmonic language simple, and largely confined to major and minor chords and scale figures derived from them. Minimalism had also rejected the emotional overlay that had characterized romantic music, and that was another quality that Adams was exploring.

Even on its first release, *Shaker Loops* impressed listeners as a fresh, vital amalgam of minimalism and neoromanticism. The piece makes full use of minimalism's motivating rhythmic processes; yet it sheds the harmonic and expressive limitations that the style's founders had imposed on it. Adams recognized it as a pivotal work in the development of his own style. Having originally scored it for three violins, he reworked it for string quartet and string septet before producing what he regarded as the final string orchestra version—heard here, under the composer's direction—in 1983. The expansion magnifies the music's incipient romanticism, and Adams projects both the score's energy (listen to the irresistibly driven first movement) and a sense of mystery (in the slow, hazy second movement, for example) that is bound into the work's origin. That origin is in the composer's memories of the remnants of a Shaker village not far from where Adams grew up in New Hampshire. To an extent, *Shaker Loops* is meant to evoke what Adams imagined as the ecstatic state that members of this religious sect reached during their services.

There is also a musical pun in the title: in Renaissance terminology, trills were called shakes, and were executed as quickly repeated notes. A version of that effect opens the work. The second part of the title refers to the music's construction. Its four connected movements are built of short, repeating motifs, written so that they end on notes that connect easily to the notes on which they begin—hence the term *loops,* an allusion to the continuously cycling tape loops used by electronic music composers of the 1950s and 1960s.

Because the "loops" in the Adams work are of unequal lengths, the relationships between the musical lines are in constant flux, and new juxtapositions and structures emerge as the players continue repeating their figures. For further variety, the conductor signals changes in each instrumental part.

Of course, it isn't necessary to know how the piece works to be won over by its invigorating rhythms and seductive textures. But composition is often about posing and then solving puzzles, and there is a satisfaction in understanding the solutions, even if the principal appeal of a work is visceral.

Adams made good on the promise that this early work showed, and his catalog of works—now fairly sizeable—is packed with fascinating adventures, along with one or two wrong turns. Not least among his attributes is a stylistic catholicity that has led him to revisit classic forms as well as various pop styles, sometimes underpinned by an enlivening sense of humor.

The second work on this disc, the Violin Concerto, was composed in 1993, and catches Adams in a very different phase of his career. There are moments that, heard in isolation, could be described as minimalist, but for the most part this concerto has a decidedly non-minimalist angularity. Sometimes the lines are blurred: Adams himself has likened the motoric energy in the closing Toccare movement to that of *Shaker Loops,* yet a listener encountering it without knowing its authorship would probably hear it as a virtuosic twentieth-century Toccata. Gidon Kremer plays the concerto's long, fluid solo lines with warmth and heart, and revels in the demands of the work's faster, more energetic writing. And with the support of equally vigorous orchestral playing, led by Kent Nagano, Kremer makes the case for this as a substantial addition to the concerto repertory.

There are comparatively few alternative recordings of these pieces, but the original septet recording of *Shaker Loops* is available on CD, now coupled with *Light over Water,* an appealing work for synthesizers and brass (New Albion). And anyone drawn to Adams's music would do well to investigate *Earbox,* a handsomely packaged ten-CD overview of his works (Nonesuch, 1998).

96. GREGORIO PANIAGUA

La Folia

ATRIUM MUSICAE DE MADRID
(Harmonia Mundi 901050)
Recorded 1980–1981

This delightfully idiosyncratic recording by Gregorio Paniagua and his Atrium Musicae de Madrid was ear-opening when it was released in 1982, and it continues to delight more than two decades later. Paniagua's premise is musicological: noting that composers of virtually every nationality and era since the late fifteenth century have based works and variation sets on the elegantly simple melody and chord progression known as *La Folia* or *Folias de España,* he compiled a broad compendium of *Folias*-based works.

But he didn't stop there. Instead of presenting the pieces derived from this antique dance form in a dry, didactic program, neatly arranged by country and period, Paniagua wove some thirty-five examples into a vast suite that hops freely through time and space, with new twists and variations to keep things lively.

A setting by the seventeenth-century Spanish composer Gaspar Sanz, arranged here for guitar, flute, violin, and castanets, for example, melts into a fifteenth-century setting, played on the dulcimer. That gives way to a set of harpsichord variations published in 1648 by the Flemish composer Jacob van Eyck, which leads, in turn, to a freewheeling country fiddle performance of a piece from John Playford's *English Dancing Master* of 1651. That country dance, however, is overlaid with twentieth-century sound effects and improvisations.

Renaissance settings for crumhorns, Indian raga versions, contemporary harmonizations, and bits of jazz all waft through Paniagua's compendium. So do recordings of Parisian public transport, the sound of Paniagua starting his Land Rover, and a few exploding champagne corks. If this sounds a bit madcap, don't let that put you off. As an overview of the way *La Folia* has been used, this is as instructive as it is entertaining—and one shouldn't shortchange the value of the latter in an undertaking of this kind.

It is also difficult not to be amazed by the flexibility of the six musicians who make up Atrium Musicae. Technically, the group is a period-instrument ensemble, and a fine one, judging by the polished, atmospheric performances of the fifteenth- and sixteenth-century items. But these performers are equally adept at the other styles represented here, and each plays a sizeable list of instruments, ancient and modern, conventional and exotic.

The group has taken a similar approach to other old dance forms—the Tarantella and the Villancico—and has also turned its inventive attentions to ancient Greek music and the music of Spain during the years of Arab dominance, all for Harmonia Mundi.

97. ARVO PÄRT

Tabula Rasa

STUTTGART STATE ORCHESTRA, DENNIS RUSSELL DAVIES,
CONDUCTING; LITHUANIAN CHAMBER ORCHESTRA,
SAULUS SONDECKIS, CONDUCTING

(ECM New Series 817 764)

Includes Fratres *(Violin and Piano version),* Cantus in Memory of Benjamin Britten, Fratres *(Cello Ensemble version), and* Tabula Rasa. *Gidon Kremer and Tatiana Grindenko, violinists; Keith Jarrett and Alfred Schnittke, pianists; the Twelve Cellists of the Berlin Philharmonic; Stuttgart State Orchestra, Dennis Russell Davies, conducting; Lithuanian Chamber Orchestra, Saulus Sondeckis, conducting.*

Recorded 1977, 1983, 1984

This recording introduced many American listeners to Arvo Pärt, an Estonian composer who was born in 1935, and although his music has been recorded plentifully since its release in 1984 on the enterprising ECM label, it retains a special place in the Pärt discography.

One of its selling points is the eclectic roster of performers who banded together in the cause of a composer who was little known at the time. Gidon Kremer had, only a few years earlier, established himself as one of the great violinists of his generation, but also as something of an iconoclast with a fascination for new music. Keith Jarrett was a star jazz pianist, whose multidisc albums of improvisatory music had helped establish ECM as a force in the jazz world—and who later made interesting recordings of Bach's *Goldberg* Variations, the Shostakovich Preludes and Fugues, and other classical works. Dennis Russell Davies had already proved his bona fides as a pioneering new-music conductor, having founded the American Composers Orchestra about a decade earlier. And Alfred Schnittke, an innovative composer who was also championed by Kremer, makes a cameo appearance playing the prepared piano (that is, a piano that has had objects placed among its strings to produce unusual timbres).

The initial impression that this music left was that Pärt was a minimalist—and indeed, all the hallmarks are there: the music is tonal, accessible, and driven by repetition and gradual change. But as more of Pärt's music was heard, it became apparent that the truth was more complicated. Although some of his techniques are decidedly minimalist, his music also draws on the long tradition of sacred music, with elements of plainsong, Russian Orthodox chant, and harmonizations from medieval and Renaissance church music mingling in his textures.

Antiquity and modernism, in other words, sit side by side in Pärt's works. And it soon emerged that he was not alone. Other composers working mostly in Eastern Europe—Sofia Gubaidulina (from Russia), Giya Kancheli (from Georgia), and Henryk Górecki (from Poland) are the best known—shared this breadth of interests and influences. Each has established a distinctive style, but they and Pärt are often grouped together, along with the English composer John Tavener and the Japanese composer Somei Satoh, in what is sometimes called the Mystical school of contemporary composition.

Pärt came to this style soon after he turned forty, having first composed in the neoclassic style that was in vogue with Soviet composers during his youth (Prokofiev was a model) and later in a style that used serial techniques, and earned him official censure. In 1968, he had a change of heart, and devoted himself to the study of chant and simple counterpoint, composing very little until 1976, when he reemerged with his new quasi-minimalist style. These pieces were no more popular with Soviet officialdom than his serial works, and they were frowned upon by academics as well. But convinced that this was the path he wanted to take, Pärt emigrated to Vienna in 1980, and moved from there to Berlin.

Since then, Pärt has composed mostly choral works, usually with sacred texts. But the works on this recording, all composed in 1977, remain among his most enduring (not to mention popular) scores. His own description of his style in these pieces is "tintinnabulation," because, as he has explained, the tones of the triad, on which he leans heavily, evoke the ringing of bells.

In the works on this recording, the term can be taken literally, as well: *Cantus in Memory of Benjamin Britten,* a threnody composed as a response to the British composer's death at the end of 1976, begins and ends with the tolling of a bell, the body of the work being a descending scale figure in an ethereal string texture. In the cello ensemble version of *Fratres* (1977), a bell sound is evoked by a low-note pizzicato. And in *Tabula Rasa* (1977), the sound of a prepared piano contributes an appropriate jangling at times.

Still, the bell effects are hardly the most striking aspects of the performances. *Tabula Rasa,* for two solo violins and orchestra, is an intense meditation built around a repeating melancholy figure that is offered with different textural densities every time it is heard. The effect, over the work's twenty-six-minute duration, is magical, and it is not surprising that listeners over the years have described this music as "celestial" or "angelic."

Pärt wrote several versions of *Fratres,* two of which are included here. These two are so different as to be almost separate works, despite the fact that they are both based on the same repeating chord progression. Interestingly, the versions here are presented in the reverse of the logical order: the one for cello ensemble is the core of the work—that is, the essential chord progression, which evolves through its repetitions without additional adornment. In the version for violin and piano that opens the CD, that deliciously gloomy chordal unity is supplanted by flights of virtuosic fiddle writing. Kremer plays this music with great energy, but also with an austere tone, as if to preserve the score's spiritual sobriety amid its overt display.

Other versions of *Fratres*—for strings and percussion; violin, strings, and percussion; wind octet and percussion; eight cellos; string quartet; and cello and piano—are included, along with the *Cantus in Memory of Benjamin Britten,* and a couple of short string works that aren't included here, *Summa* (1978) and *Festina Lente* (1988), can be heard on a fine recording by the Belgian orchestra I Fiamminghi (Telarc, 1994).

98. HENRYK GÓRECKI

Symphony no. 3 (op. 36)

DAWN UPSHAW, SOPRANO; LONDON SINFONIETTA,
DAVID ZINMAN, CONDUCTING

(Nonesuch 79288-2)

Recorded 1991

Every now and then a freakish hit seizes the imagination not only of classical record buyers, but also of record collectors who usually avoid the classics, but are for some reason drawn to a particular release. Some of these are easily explained: when Luciano Pavarotti, Placido Domingo, and José Carreras put professional rivalries aside to team up as the Three Tenors, anyone even vaguely interested in opera or singing paid attention. But the hits of the 1990s were decidedly odd: a collection of Gregorian plainsong sailed up the charts when it was reissued under the title *Chant.* Hildegard of Bingen was briefly in vogue as well, although attempts to buff her up with electronic sounds thankfully failed.

Perhaps the strangest out-of-the-blue hit, though, was this recording of the elegiac Symphony no. 3 by the Polish composer Henryk Górecki (born in 1933). It was released in the spring of 1992, but took until the end of the year to take off. By the following February, *Music Week,* the British equivalent of *Billboard,* moved the disc from its classical to its pop chart, where it was listed in the top 10. In the United States, *Billboard* continued to list it on its classical chart, but it remained in the top 25 for nearly forty weeks, and according to Nonesuch, the label that issued it, it was selling on the order of ten thousand copies a day, a hefty amount for a classical recording of any kind, let alone a serious work by a living composer—at that, a symphony in three slow movements, with the subtitle, *Symphony of Sorrowful Songs,* and vocal texts sung in Polish.

Górecki was not widely known outside Poland at the time. In his early years—from 1959 to around 1970—he was an avant-gardist, concerned with juxtapositions of sound masses of different volume and intensity. But by the mid-1970s, he had gravitated toward a style that used elements of minimalism and lush neoromanticism, but wasn't quite either. Both those elements rub shoulders in this symphony, which was composed in 1976. Other composers, mostly in Eastern Europe and the Soviet Union, were exploring similar ideas, and their work eventually coalesced as what we now think of as the Mystical school. And that may have been its appeal in 1992: it actually made sense in the context of the *Chant* and Hildegard vogues.

Still, the work was not new to recordings; in fact, there were three recordings on the market by the time David Zinman and Dawn Upshaw recorded their version, which is by far the best in terms of orchestral and vocal sound, as well as vocal expressivity. It had even made a film appearance. In 1986, it was used in the soundtrack of the Gérard Depardieu film *Police,* and when Erato released the recording used in the film—one by Ernst Bour, who had conducted the work's premiere—it put the name of the film and a production photo on the cover, giving scant information about Górecki and the work.

But the music made an impact that was greatly magnified when the Zinman-Upshaw version was released six years later. Its opening movement begins with a bass ostinato that crawls around the bottom of the orchestra, sounding almost like a tape playing at half speed. Cellos and violas enter after a time, and as Górecki makes his way upward in the orchestration, layer by layer, the music builds in intensity and plaintiveness. The movement's structure is palindromic: after its climax, it makes its way back down to the depths. Between the climb and the descent, though, is the first of the three soprano settings, this one drawn from a fifteenth-century lamentation that Górecki found at a Polish monastery.

The text of the middle movement is a brief prayer that had been scrawled on the wall of a basement cell in the Gestapo's headquarters in Zakopane by an eighteen-year-old girl held prisoner there. The orchestral music supporting this setting is dense and mysterious, and the vocal line begins almost listlessly and low in the soprano range, a prayer whispered from the brink of death. But Górecki gives the soprano a slowly rising line, and then lets her range freely and sweetly through the movement, a symbolic triumph of this young prisoner's spirit.

The finale, maintaining the character of the second movement, is a setting of a Polish folk song, sung by a mother searching for a son who may have been killed in an uprising. It is the most varied of the movements, although it rings its changes with a minimalist deliberation, resting for nearly eight minutes on a repeating rocking figure before moving to a section in which the massed violins principally repeat a single note as the harmony changes beneath them, and the soprano line hovers gracefully above.

A significant attraction here is Dawn Upshaw, an American soprano whose recital programs have always shown range and depth, and who has an ability to shape a phrase eloquently in, it appears, any language. She sings this music with a profound feeling for the texts, both what lies immediately within them and the broader historical contexts that they suggest. There is also the sheer beauty of her voice, which is supported firmly by the rich sound that Zinman gets from the London Sinfonietta, an orchestra with ample experience in new music of all kinds.

99. EINOJUHANI RAUTAVAARA

Symphony no. 7, *Angel of Light;* and *Annunciations* (Concerto for Organ Brass Group and Symphonic Wind Orchestra)

KARI JUSSILA, ORGANIST; HELSINKI PHILHARMONIC ORCHESTRA, LEIF SEGERSTAM, CONDUCTING

(Ondine ODE 869-2)

Recorded 1995

If Jean Sibelius established an internationally embraced Finnish symphonic school virtually ex nihilo, the generations that followed him continued to bear the standard. Today, some of the most widely admired new music is pouring forth from Helsinki and environs. In the mid-1970s, two powerful operas, Aulis Sallinen's *The Horseman* and Joonas Kokkonen's *The Last Temptations,* caught the attention of the opera world, and since then a wave of symphonic and chamber works by Kaija Saariaho, Magnus Lindberg, and Esa-Pekka Salonen have enlivened concert programs in Europe and the United States. Each of these composers has a distinctive style, and one could do justice to the current state of Finnish music—so long as one didn't claim to be showing its totality—by choosing works by any of them.

Still, the contemporary Finn whose works I have found most consistently magical is Einojuhani Rautavaara, an imaginative and prolific composer who was born in Helsinki in 1928. Rautavaara studied musicology and composition in Helsinki, and caught the ear of Sibelius, who helped arrange for a Koussevitzky Foundation scholarship that brought him to New York and Tanglewood, in 1955 and 1956, for studies with Aaron Copland, Roger Sessions, and Vincent Persichetti. Thereafter, he continued his studies in Italy and Germany.

From the start, his musical language was fairly eclectic. The influences of Finnish folk song, neoclassicism, a grand romantic sweep, and, most strikingly, a sense of the sacred and the otherwordly mingle freely. He has used both serial techniques and pure tonality, but a combination of the two is more typical. Taped sound, quasi-medieval harmonies, and jazz allusions have found their way into his works as well, yet for all that, the music never sounds like an indecisive hodgepodge.

The Symphony no. 7 was composed in 1994 on a commission from the Bloomington Symphony Orchestra, in Indiana. Subtitled *Angel of Light,* it is one of several works with titles that evoke angelic imagery (others include *Angels and Visitations,* from 1978; *Angel of Dusk,* a 1980 double-bass concerto; and *Playgrounds for Angels,* a 1981 brass work), although Rautavaara has cautioned listeners against too picturesque an interpretation of these titles. The works, he has said, are not meant to be programmatic. Instead, they tap into a mystical current that runs through many of Rautavaara's scores, and that seems to lift his music into a realm beyond the normal mechanics of symphonic music-making. At his best—and there are moments of this in the Seventh—he seems able to make the distinctions between wind, string, and even percussion writing blur into a continuum.

Surrendering to this effect is probably the way to go, but focusing at least briefly on the mechanics is rewarding as well. The opening movement is marked Tranquilo, although it doesn't remain so for long. Hazy string textures give way to themes that are alternately mournful or, in the case of the gracefully harmonized flute writing, almost rhapsodic. A hymn melody emerges, and seems intent on growing into an epic climax, with brass and percussion fully unleashed; but that impulse is cut short, suppressed by more ruminative string and wind writing, flecked with glimmers of glockenspiel and vibraphone.

The second movement begins more energetically, with lightly dissonant wind and brass bursts, and touches of quasi-military snare drums as well as wood sticks and other more tactile percussion. Rautavaara doesn't let the music linger: texture and mood are constantly reshuffled, and the interplay of melodic ideas and shifting colors keeps the movement on edge until its final moment, when a slow variation on the hymn theme from the first movement is countered by short trumpet bursts and ominous orchestral rumbling. The movement fades gently into its successor, which is marked Come un sogno (Like a Dream), and couched in truly ethereal string writing with a gentle harp underpinning. This time, the lush string bed remains a constant through most of the movement, with other textures—and another hint of the hymn theme—shifting position above and around it. As in the first movement, fiery figures are engulfed in serenity almost as soon as they emerge.

The finale begins with an idiosyncratically angular trumpet figure, echoed in the strings, which then go their own serene, dark-hued way, punctuated by echoing trumpet figures. One hears the ghosts of Sibelius and Ralph Vaughan Williams in the broad, string-heavy chord masses and modal harmonic progressions, as well as in the evocation, by strings, winds, and percussion, of the howling northern wind. More than any of the other movements, this is where an analysis of Rautavaara's themes and orchestration breaks down: the hymn melody is explored in further variations; there is an extensive stream of wind arpeggiations that, if heard entirely on their own, might evoke Philip Glass; and the rich string writing builds to an inexorable climax, followed by an equally surprising slow fade to silence. Yet the effect of the whole is vastly greater than the sum of these details.

The companion piece here, *Annunciations,* is a kaleidoscopic organ concerto composed in 1976–1977 for an organ festival in Stockholm. The solo organ line, sometimes thoroughly melded into the orchestral texture, emerges as a titanic, colorful, and entirely unbridled force. Both works seem to draw on the same well of mystical experience or, at least, mystical longing. In each, elements of a conventional religiosity (the hymn in the symphony, the sometimes processional organ writing in *Annunciations*) are surrounded and eventually overridden by a sense of greater grandeur and an intense, vigorous spirituality.

There are already several recordings of the symphony, each with a different and equally substantial Rautavaara work as a coupling. Leif Segerstam's carefully considered balances and ability to project the music's powerful atmosphere, rather than just its compositional deftness, gives his reading an edge on purely conceptual grounds, and the Helsinki Philharmonic Orchestra's playing is as warm and rich as one could want.

A version by Hannu Koivula, with the Royal Scottish National Orchestra (Naxos), offers joys of its own, including brisker tempos that yield a brighter, more vivid picture in certain passages, as well as a thematically related companion—*Angels and Visitations,* the first of Rautavaara's angel scores.

100. BRIGHT SHENG

H'un: In Memoriam 1966–1976

NEW YORK CHAMBER SYMPHONY,
GERARD SCHWARZ, CONDUCTING

The Stream Flows

LUCIA LIN, VIOLINIST

Three Chinese Love Songs

LISA SAFFER, SOPRANO; PAUL NEUBAUER, VIOLIST;
BRIGHT SHENG, PIANIST

My Song

PETER SERKIN, PIANIST
(New World Records 80407-2)

Recorded 1990–1991

One thing that keeps any musical language vital is its ability to absorb and be affected by new influences, and although one hears classical music described as a calcified tradition by people who either don't listen to much of it, or who are impatient with its rate of change, its history has been driven by the assimilation of diverse musical accents and ideas.

This is what ignited the various currents of romantic nationalism in the nineteenth century, when native folk forms were adopted by composers of concert works; and from a more internationalist point of view, it can be seen in the German and English adoption of distinctly French rhythmic figures (and specific dance forms) in baroque times, the Viennese fascination with Turkish sounds and rhythms in the late eighteenth and early nineteenth centuries, or French composers' interest in Spanish musical accents near the turn of the twentieth century. More recently, ideas borrowed from painting gave rise to impressionism, and young composers have drawn freely on the rhythms and timbres of jazz, rock, and other popular forms that appeal to them.

But good old-fashioned migration continues to play a crucial role. Since the late 1980s, some of the freshest music to turn up on contemporary music programs has been written by young composers who were born in China, began their musical training there, and emigrated to the United States for further study.

It is actually a fairly large group, and every season new names join the roster. In addition to Bright Sheng (born in 1955), the most accomplished and frequently performed of the group include Tan Dun, Zhou Long, Chen Yi, Guo Wenjing, Ge-Gan Ru, and, most recently, Huang Ruo. Each has developed a distinct style, but what animates most of their works is a clear sense that East and West can indeed meet, in the context of contemporary musical language. The best of their works fuse traditional Chinese timbres, rhythms, and folk melodies with up-to-date Western notions of harmony and orchestration. The resulting blend is not a matter of mere exoticism, but rather an enriching admixture that creates a searching cross-cultural dialogue.

Sheng's *H'un: In Memoriam 1966–1976,* a stark and often terrifying memoir of the Cultural Revolution, which the composer lived through, was the first of this composer's works to make an impact in the United States, and it provides a bracing glimpse of some of the issues in that dialogue. Sheng was born in Shanghai, and was drawn to the Western music he heard in his father's record collection. He began learning the piano at age five. The Cultural Revolution interrupted those studies. When his family's piano and record collection were confiscated, Sheng practiced on the pianos in his junior high school, and when he graduated, he was able to avoid being assigned to agricultural work by auditioning for a job as an accompanist to a folk ensemble in Chinhua Province, near Tibet. Sheng made a careful study of Chinese traditional music during those years. But he retained his interest in Western music as well, and when the Cultural Revolution ended, he enrolled at the Shanghai Conservatory, where he earned a composition degree.

When he came to New York in 1982, to continue his studies at Queens College and Columbia University, he had a vague idea that he could find his own compositional voice by combining elements of

Western and Chinese music. But he was not sure how it could be done, and most of his teachers advised him to choose one style and stick with it. So he put his background in Chinese music aside until the late 1980s, when he began studying with Leonard Bernstein. Bernstein, in his typically emphatic way, told Sheng that "everything is fusion," and pointed to folk music sources in Brahms, Shostakovich, and Stravinsky, as well as his own pop music borrowings.

With Bernstein's encouragement, Sheng reclaimed his musical heritage while composing *H'un,* which means "lacerations," in 1987, the year he became an American citizen. The twenty-one-minute work is an exorcism of sorts: its atmosphere is dark and hazy, its harmonic language bristles with tension, and its themes are sometimes strained, sometimes stifled. Sheng's orchestra is augmented with Chinese percussion instruments, and is deployed with a fascinating flexibility. Nothing remains static as the work unfolds: one hears wind lines that range from screaming bursts of angularity to slow-moving, sepulchral explorations of the deep bass range; both sighs and insistently searching figures from the strings; flecks of Chinese metallic percussion; and insistent pounding figures of various weights and intensity. Even when that intensity lets up momentarily, and an eerie flute solo floats over the strings, hopelessness and foreboding continue to hang in the air. *H'un* is not particularly dissonant music, but the discomfort of the age it describes is palpable.

The other works on this recording are somewhat lighter in spirit, but have an intensity of their own. *The Stream Flows,* from 1990, for unaccompanied violin, is in two movements, the first based on a Chinese song from which the work takes its name, and the second on a folk dance. The violin is perfectly suited to this adaptation: using bent pitches and microtones (the notes between the notes of the Western scale), Sheng begins the opening movement by evoking the melody's origins clearly, and then heads off in an increasingly complex direction of his own. The second movement, similarly, begins with the simple three-note melody and straightforward rhythm of the folk dance, but becomes a virtuosic exploration in which the folk elements periodically reassert themselves.

An earlier vocal version of *The Stream Flows* is included in the *Three Chinese Love Songs,* composed in 1987. Here the vocal line honors the traditional sources, while the accompanying viola and piano provide a free-ranging commentary. And *My Song*, a four-movement suite from 1988, has a spiky quality reminiscent of Bartók, but with hints of Chinese melodies where Bartók would have included Hungarian country dances.

Composer Bright Sheng

Another 100: More Albums You Should Own, or at Least Know About

Think of this list as supplementary rather than secondary: any of these recordings might have made its way into the main section of the book. The fact that they didn't is more a function of having to limit my list to one hundred than an indication of any deficiency in these works or performances.

1. *AN ENGLISH LADYMASS:* Thirteenth- and fourteenth-century chant and polyphony. Anonymous 4. (Harmonia Mundi HMU 907080)

2. GUILLAUME DUFAY: Gloria ad modum tubae, *Se la face ay pale* (chanson), and Missa *Se le face ay pale.* Early Music Consort of London, David Munrow, conducting. (Virgin Classics 62183-2)

3. JOHANNES OCKEGHEM: Requiem and Missa *Mi-Mi.* Hilliard Ensemble, Paul Hillier, conducting. (EMI Classics 61219-2)

4. GREGORIO ALLEGRI: Miserere; WILLIAM MUNDY: Vox Patris Caelestis; GIOVANNI PIERLUIGI DA PALESTRINA: Missa

Papae Marcelli. The Tallis Scholars, Peter Phillips, conducting. (Gimell CDGIM 339)

5. ANTIPHONAL MUSIC OF GABRIELI AND FRESCOBALDI: Philadelphia Brass Ensemble, Cleveland Brass Ensemble, and Chicago Brass Ensemble (in Gabrieli); E. Power Biggs, organist; Boston Brass Ensemble, Richard Burgin, conducting (in Frescobaldi). (Sony Classical 62353)

6. WILLIAM BYRD: Mass for Three Voices, Mass for Four Voices, and Mass for Five Voices. Pro Arte Singers, Paul Hillier, conducting. (Harmonia Mundi HMU 907223)

7. JOHN DOWLAND: *Complete Lute Music.* Paul O'Dette, lutenist. (Harmonia Mundi 2907160.164, five CDs)

8. *INSPIRED BY BACH.* JOHANN SEBASTIAN BACH: Six Suites for Unaccompanied Cello (BWV 1017-12). Yo-Yo Ma, cellist. (Sony Classical, 63203-2, two CDs) [Ma's second traversal of the Suites, recorded 1994–1997]

9. JOHANN SEBASTIAN BACH: *The Art of Fugue* (BWV 1080). Fretwork. (Harmonia Mundi HMU 907296)

10. JOHANN SEBASTIAN BACH: Harpsichord Concertos in D minor (BWV 1052), E (BWV 1053), D (BWV 1054), A (BWV 1055), F minor (BWV 1056), F (BWV 1057), G minor (BWV 1058); and Triple Concerto in A minor (BWV 1044). Richard Egarr, harpsichordist (with Rachel Brown, flutist, and Andrew Manze, violinist, in BWV 1044). Academy of Ancient Music, Andrew Manze, conducting. (Harmonia Mundi 907283, two CDs)

11. GEORGE FRIDERIC HANDEL: Coronation Anthems: *Zadok the Priest* (HWV 258), *The King Shall Rejoice* (HWV 260), *My Heart Is Inditing* (HVW 261), and *Let Thy Hand Be Strengthened* (HWV 259). Choir of Westminster Abbey; The English Concert,

Trevor Pinnock, organist, Simon Preston, conducting. (Archiv 410 030-2)

12. GEORG PHILIPP TELEMANN: *Sinfonia Spirituosa* (TWV 44:1); Overture in D (TWV 55:D6); Concerto in C for Four Solo Violins (TWV 40:203); Concerto in A for Four Violins, Strings, and Continuo (TWV 54:A1); Concerto in G for Four Solo Violins (TWV 40:201); Concerto in A for Violin, Strings, and Continuo (*The Frogs*, TWV 51:A4); and Concerto in D for Four Solo Violins (TWV 40:202); Symphony in D (TWV Anh.50:1). Musica Antiqua Koln, Reinhard Goebel, conducting. (Archiv 471 492-2)

13. FRANZ JOSEPH HAYDN: *The Complete Piano Trios*. The Beaux Arts Trio. (Philips 454 098-2, nine CDs)

14. FRANZ JOSEPH HAYDN: Missa *in Tempore Belli* (Hob. XXII: 9), Missa *Sancti Bernardi von Offida* (Hob. XXII: 10), and Insanae et Vanae Curae. Joanne Lunn, soprano; Sara Mingardo, alto; Topi Lehtipuu, tenor; Brindley Sherratt, bass; Monteverdi Choir, English Baroque Soloists, Sir John Eliot Gardiner, conducting. (Philips B0000032-02)

15. WOLFGANG AMADEUS MOZART: Symphonies (complete). The Academy of Ancient Music, Christopher Hogwood and Jaap Schroeder, conducting. (L'Oiseau-Lyre 452 496-2, nineteen CDs)

16. LUDWIG VAN BEETHOVEN: The Five Piano Concertos and Triple Concerto. Leon Fleischer, pianist; The Cleveland Orchestra, George Szell, conducting (Piano Concertos); Isaac Stern, violinist; Eugene Istomin, pianist; Leonard Rose, cellist; Philadelphia Orchestra, Eugene Ormandy, conducting (Triple Concerto). (Sony Classical SB3K 48397, three CDs)

17. LUDWIG VAN BEETHOVEN: Piano Trio in D, *Ghost* (op. 70, no. 1); and Piano Trio in B-flat, *Archduke* (op. 97). The Beaux Arts Trio. (Philips 412 891-2).

18. LUDWIG VAN BEETHOVEN: *The String Quartets: The 1964–1970 Cycle*. The Juilliard String Quartet. (Sony Classical SB8K 87889, eight CDs)

19. FRANZ SCHUBERT: Symphonies (ten, complete). Academy of St. Martin-in-the-Fields, Sir Neville Marriner, conducting. (Philips 470 886-2, six CDs)

20. FRANZ SCHUBERT: Impromptus (ops. 90, 142). Murray Perahia, pianist. (Sony Classical MK 37291)

21. FRANZ SCHUBERT: *Trout* Quintet for Piano, Violin, Viola, Cello, and Bass (D. 667); and *Death and the Maiden* String Quartet in D minor (D. 810). Emil Gilels, pianist; Rainer Zepperitz, bassist; the Amadeus Quartet. (Deutsche Grammophon 449 746-2)

22. FELIX MENDELSSOHN: Octet in E-flat (op. 20) and Quintet in B-flat (op. 87). Academy Chamber Ensemble. (Philips 420 400-2)

23. FELIX MENDELSSOHN: *A Midsummer Night's Dream* (complete). Edith Wiens, soprano; Christiane Oertel, mezzo-soprano; Friedhelm Eberle, speaker; Leipzig Radio Choir; Leipzig Gewandhaus Orchestra, Kurt Masur, conducting. (Teldec 2292-46323)

24. HECTOR BERLIOZ: *Les Nuits d'Été* (op. 7); Arias from *La Damnation de Faust* (op. 24), *Benvenuto Cellini, Les Troyens,* and *Beatrice et Bénédict*. Susan Graham, mezzo-soprano; Orchestra of the Royal Opera House, John Nelson, conducting. (Sony Classical SK 62730)

25. HECTOR BERLIOZ: Requiem (op. 5) and *Symphonie Funèbre et Triomphale* (op. 15). Ronald Dowd, tenor; Wandsworth School Boys' Choir; London Symphony Orchestra and Chorus, Sir Colin Davis, conducting. (Philips 416 283-2, two CDs)

26. FRÉDÉRIC CHOPIN: The Nocturnes (ops. 9, 15, 27, 32, 37, 48, 55, 62, op. posth.). Garrick Ohlssohn, pianist. (Arabesque Z6653-2, two CDs)

27. FRÉDÉRIC CHOPIN: Concerto no. 2 for Piano and Orchestra in F minor (op. 11), *Grande Fantasia on Polish Airs* in A major (op. 13), and *Grande Polonaise Brillante* (op. 22). Emanuel Ax, piano; Orchestra of the Age of Enlightenment, Sir Charles Mackerras, conducting. (Sony Classical SK 63371)

28. FRÉDÉRIC CHOPIN: Sonatas for Piano, no. 1 in C minor (op. 4); no. 2 in B-flat minor, "Funeral March" (op. 34); no. 3 in B minor (op. 58); Etudes (ops. 10, 25); and Fantaisie in F minor (op. 49). Vladimir Ashkenazy, pianist. (Decca 466 250-2, two CDs)

29. ROBERT SCHUMANN: *Dichterliebe* (op. 48) and *Liederkreis* (op. 24). Matthias Goerne, baritone; Vladimir Ashkenazy, pianist. (Decca 458 265-2)

30. ROBERT SCHUMANN: Concerto for Piano and Orchestra in A minor (op. 54) and Quintet for Piano and Strings in E-flat (op. 44). Rudolf Serkin, pianist; the Budapest String Quartet; Philadelphia Orchestra, Eugene Ormandy, conducting. (Sony Classical MYK 37256)

31. NICCOLÒ PAGANINI: Twenty-four Caprices for Solo Violin. Itzhak Perlman, violinist. (EMI Classics 67257 2)

32. JOHANNES BRAHMS: Fantasies (op. 116), Piano Pieces (op. 119), and Sonata no. 2 in F-sharp minor (op. 2). Emanuel Ax, pianist. (Sony Classical SK 69284)

33. JOHANNES BRAHMS: Sonatas for Piano and Cello, no. 1 in E minor (op. 38) and no. 2 in F (op. 99). Mstislav Rostropovich, cellist; Rudolf Serkin, pianist. (Deutsche Grammophon 410 510-2)

34. EDVARD GRIEG: Concerto for Piano and Orchestra in A (op. 16), Piano Sonata in E minor (op. 7), *Poetic Tone Pictures* (op. 3), Album Leaves (op. 28), Agitato, and *Lyric Pieces* (ops. 43, 54, 65). Leif Ove Andsnes, pianist; Bergen Philharmonic Orchestra, Dmitri Kitayenko, conducting. (Virgin Classics 61745-2)

35. PETER ILYICH TCHAIKOVSKY: Violin Concerto in D (op. 35); JOHANN SEBASTIAN BACH: Violin Concerto no. 2 in E (BWV 1042) and Prelude in E (from BWV 1006); EUGÈNE YSAŸE: *Rêve d'enfant* (op. 14); FELIX MENDELSSOHN: *O, For the Wings of a Dove*; FRÉDÉRIC CHOPIN: *Nocturne in D-flat (op. 27, no. 2)*; PABLO DE SARASATE: *Zigeunerweisen* (op. 20). Mischa Elman, violinist; London Symphony Orchestra, Sir John Barbirolli, conducting; Marcel van Gool and Carroll Hollister, pianists. (Pearl GEMM CD 9388; recordings from 1929 to 1933)

36. ANTONÍN DVOŘÁK: Concerto for Cello and Orchestra in B minor (op. 104); PETER ILYICH TCHAIKOVSKY: *Variations on a Rococo Theme* (op. 33). Mstislav Rostropovich, cello; Berlin Philharmonic, Herbert von Karajan, conducting. (Deutsche Grammophon 413 81902)

37. ANTONÍN DVOŘÁK: Serenade in E (op. 22); Serenade in D minor (op. 44). Academy of St. Martin-in-the-Fields, Sir Neville Marriner, conducting. (Philips 400 020-2)

38. ANTON BRUCKNER: The Symphonies (no. 0, nos. 1–9). Chicago Symphony, Sir Georg Solti, conducting. (Decca 448 910, ten CDs)

39. MAX BRUCH: Concerto no. 1 for Violin and Orchestra in G minor, *Scottish Fantasy*; HENRI VIEUXTEMPS: Concerto no. 5 for Violin and Orchestra in A minor. Jascha Heifetz, violinist; New Symphony Orchestra of London, Sir Malcolm Sargent, conducting. (RCA 6214-2)

40. GUSTAV MAHLER: *Das Lied von der Erde* and "Rückert Lieder." Kathleen Ferrier, contralto; Julius Patzak, tenor; Vienna Philharmonic, Bruno Walter, conducting. (Decca 466 576-2)

41. GUSTAV MAHLER: *The Complete Symphonies*. Symphonies 1–9, Adagio from Symphony no. 10, additional live performances of Adagietto from Symphony no. 5 and Part I of Symphony no. 8, "Rückert Lieder," and "Kindertotenlieder." Lee Venora, Lucine Amara, Adele Addison, Reri Grist, Dame Gwyneth Jones, Erna Spoorenberg, sopranos; Jennie Tourel, Lili Chookasian, Dame Janet Baker, mezzo-sopranos; Gwenyth Annear, Norma Procter, Anna Reynolds, altos; Richard Tucker, John Mitchinson, tenors; Vladimir Ruzdjak, baritone; George London, Ezio Flagello, Donald McIntyre, bass-baritones; Hans Vollenweider, organist; Schola Cantorum New York; Columbus Boychoir; Juilliard Chorus; Collegiate Chorale; Transfiguration Boys Choir; Finchley Children's Music Group; Leeds Festival Chorus; Orpington Junior Singers; Highgate School Boys Chorus; New York Philharmonic; Israel Philharmonic; London Symphony Orchestra and Chorus, Leonard Bernstein, conducting. (Sony Classical SX12K 89499, twelve CDs)

42. CARL NIELSEN: Symphony no. 2, *The Four Temperaments;* and Symphony no. 4, *The Inextinguishable*. New York Philharmonic, Leonard Bernstein, conducting. (Sony Classical SMK 47597)

43. FREDERICK DELIUS: *On Hearing the First Cuckoo in Spring, Brigg Fair, Summer Night on the River, Irmelin* Prelude, Dance Rhapsody no. 2, *A Song before Sunrise,* and *Summer Evening*. Royal Philharmonic Orchestra, Sir Thomas Beecham, conducting. (EMI Classics 67553-2)

44. RALPH VAUGHAN WILLIAMS: *A Sea Symphony*. Sheila Armstrong, soprano; John Carol Case, baritone; London Philharmonic Orchestra and Choir, Sir Adrian Boult, conducting. (EMI Classics 764016-2)

45. SIR EDWARD ELGAR: Cello Concerto in E minor (op. 85) and *Sea Pictures* (op. 37). Jacqueline Du Pré, cellist; Dame Janet Baker, mezzo-soprano; London Symphony Orchestra, Sir John Barbirolli, conducting. (EMI Classics 56219)

46. ALEXANDER SCRIABIN: *The Complete Piano Sonatas.* Marc-André Hamelin, pianist. (Hyperion CDA67131/2, two CDs)

47. FERRUCCIO BUSONI: Concerto in C major for Piano and Orchestra (with Male Chorus), op. 39. Garrick Ohlssohn, pianist; the Cleveland Orchestra and Men's Chorus, Christoph von Dohnányi, conducting. (Telarc CD-82012, or CD-80207)

48. ISAAC ALBÉNIZ: *Iberia, Navarra, Suite Española, Pavana-Capricho, Tango, Rumores de la Caleta,* and *Puerta de Tierra.* Alicia de Larrocha, pianist. (EMI CDMB 64241, two CDs)

49. LEOŠ JANÁČEK: Sinfonietta, *Taras Bulba, Lachian Dances,* Suite for String Orchestra, *Mládi,* Capriccio, and Concertino. Vienna Philharmonic, Sir Charles Mackerras, conducting; London Philharmonic, François Huybrechts, conducting; Los Angeles Chamber Orchestra, Sir Neville Marriner, conducting; London Sinfonietta, David Atherton, conducting; Paul Crossley, pianist, and various chamber players. (Decca 448 255-2, two CDs)

50. JEAN SIBELIUS: Concerto for Violin and Orchestra in D minor (op. 47); KARL GOLDMARK: Concerto for Violin and Orchestra in A minor (op. 28). Joshua Bell, violinist; Los Angeles Philharmonic, Esa-Pekka Salonen, conducting. (Sony Classical SK 65949)

51. MARIE-JOSEPH CANTELOUBE: *Songs of the Auvergne;* HEITOR VILLA-LOBOS: *Bachianas Brasileiras* no. 5. Kiri Te Kanawa, soprano; English Chamber Orchestra, Jeffrey Tate, conducting; Lynn Harrell and Instrumental Ensemble in the Villa-Lobos. (Decca 444 995-2, two CDs)

52. GABRIEL FAURÉ: Quartets for Piano, Violin, Viola, and Cello, no. 1 in C minor (op. 15) and no. 2 in G minor (op. 45). Emanuel Ax, pianist; Isaac Stern, violinist; Jaime Laredo, violist; Yo-Yo Ma, cellist. (Sony Classical SK 48006)

53. CLAUDE DEBUSSY: String Quartet in G minor (op. 10) and String Quartet in F. Orlando String Quartet. (Philips 422 837-2)

54. MAURICE RAVEL: The Complete Piano Music. *Pavane pour une Infante Défunte, À la manière de Chabrier, À la manière de Borodine,* Sonatine, *Miroirs, Ma Mère L'Oye* (with Gaby Casadesus, pianist), Habanera (with Gaby Casadesus, pianist), *Jeux d'eau,* Prélude in A minor, *Menuet sur le nom d'Haydn, Berceuse sur le nom de Gabriel Fauré* (with Zino Francescatti, violinist), *Le Tombeau de Couperin, Valses Nobles et Sentimentales, Menuet Antique, Gaspard de la Nuit,* and Piano Concerto for the Left Hand (with the Philadelphia Orchestra, Eugene Ormandy, conducting). Robert Casadesus, pianist. (Sony Classical 63316)

55. OTTORINO RESPIGHI: *Fountains of Rome* and *Pines of Rome;* CLAUDE DEBUSSY: *La Mer.* Chicago Symphony Orchestra, Fritz Reiner, conducting. (RCA 68079-2)

56. GEORGE GERSHWIN: Piano Music and Songs. Joan Morris, mezzo-soprano; William Bolcom, pianist. (Nonesuch 79151)

57. SERGEI RACHMANINOFF: *Symphonic Dances* (op. 45) and *The Bells* (op. 35). Yelizaveta Shumskaya, soprano; Mikhail Dovenman, tenor; Alexei Bolshakov, baritone; Russian Republican Capelle; Moscow Philharmonic Orchestra, Kiril Kondrashin, conducting. (RCA 32046-2)

58. SERGEI RACHMANINOFF: Concerto for Piano and Orchestra no. 2 in C minor (op. 18), *Rhapsody on a Theme of Paganini* (op. 43), and Prelude in C-sharp minor (op. 3, no. 2). Arthur Rubinstein, pianist; Chicago Symphony Orchestra, Fritz Reiner, conducting. (RCA 63035-2)

---

59. BÉLA BARTÓK: Concerto no. 2 for Violin and Orchestra and Sonata for Solo Violin. Yehudi Menuhin, violinist; Philharmonia Orchestra, Wilhelm Furtwängler, conducting. (EMI Classics 69804-2)

60. *BENNY GOODMAN COLLECTOR'S EDITION.* BÉLA BARTÓK: *Contrasts;* LEONARD BERNSTEIN: *Prelude, Fugue, and Riffs;* AARON COPLAND: Clarinet Concerto; IGOR STRAVINSKY: *Ebony* Concerto; MORTON GOULD: *Derivations* for Clarinet and Band. Benny Goodman, clarinetist; Béla Bartók, pianist; Joseph Szigeti, violinist; Columbia Jazz Combo, Leonard Bernstein, Igor Stravinsky, Morton Gould, conducting; Columbia Symphony Orchestra, Aaron Copland, conducting. (Sony Classical MK 42227)

61. ARNOLD SCHOENBERG: *Gurrelieder.* Karita Mattila, soprano; Anne Sofie von Otter, mezzo-soprano; Thomas Moser, Philip Langridge, tenors; Thomas Quasthoff, bass-baritone; Berlin Philharmonic, Sir Simon Rattle, conducting. (EMI Classics 57303-2, two CDs)

62. ARNOLD SCHOENBERG: Choral Music, including *Friede auf Erden* (op. 13), *Kol Nidre* (op. 39), *Dreimal tausend Jahre* (op. 50a), *Psalm 150* (op. 50b), *A Survivor from Warsaw* (op. 46), and others. John Shirley-Quirk, Günther Reich, narrators; BBC Singers; BBC Chorus; BBC Symphony Orchestra; members of the London Sinfonietta; Pierre Boulez, conducting. (Sony Classical SK2 44571, two CDs)

63. ARNOLD SCHOENBERG: *Pierrot Lunaire* (op. 21, German and English versions) and *Herzgewächse* (op. 20). Lucy Shelton, soprano; Da Capo Chamber Players, Oliver Knussen, conducting. (Bridge BCD 9032)

64. ANTON WEBERN: *Complete Works.* Christiane Oelze, Françoise Pollet, sopranos; Mary Ann McCormick, mezzo-soprano; Gerald Finley, bass; Gidon Kremer, violinist; Clemens Hagen, cellist; Pierre-Laurent Aimard, Gianluca Cascioli, Oleg Maisenberg, Eric Schneider, Krystian Zimerman, pianists; BBC Singers; Emerson String

Quartet; Ensemble InterContemporain; Berlin Philharmonic, Pierre Boulez, conducting. (Deutsche Grammophon 457 637-2, six CDs)

65. CHARLES IVES: String Quartet no. 1, *From the Salvation Army;* and String Quartet no. 2; SAMUEL BARBER: String Quartet (op. 11). Emerson String Quartet. (Deutsche Grammophon 435 864-2)

66. SAMUEL BARBER: Adagio for Strings (op. 11), Overture to *The School for Scandal* (op. 5), *Essay for Orchestra* (op. 12), *Second Essay for Orchestra* (op. 17), *Third Essay* (op. 47), *Medea's Dance of Vengeance* (op. 23a), Concerto for Violin and Orchestra (op. 14), Cello Sonata (op. 6), Canzone (op. 38a), *Excursions* (op. 20), Nocturne (op. 33), *Summer Music* for Wind Quintet (op. 31), and *Souvenirs:* Pas de deux, Two-Step. Elmar Oliveira, violinist; Alan Stepansky, cellist; Israela Margalit, pianist; Principal Winds of the New York Philharmonic; St. Louis Symphony Orchestra, Leonard Slatkin, conducting. (EMI Classics 742872)

67. DMITRI SHOSTAKOVICH: Trio for Piano, Violin, and Cello no. 2 in E minor (op. 67); PETER ILYICH TCHAIKOVSKY: Trio for Piano, Violin, and Cello in A minor (op. 50); PETER KIESEWET-TER: *Tango Pathétique.* Martha Argerich, pianist; Gidon Kremer, violinist; Mischa Maisky, cellist. (Deutsche Grammophon 459 326-2; live recording 1998)

68. DMITRI SHOSTAKOVICH: Symphony no. 8 in C minor (op. 65). Leningrad Philharmonic, Evgeny Mravinsky, conducting. (Philips 422 442-2, live recording 1982)

69. SERGEI PROKOFIEV: Piano Sonatas, no. 7 (op. 83) and no. 8 (op. 84). Yefim Bronfman, pianist. (Sony Classical MK 44680)

70. SERGEI PROKOFIEV: *Lieutenant Kije* Suite (op. 60); ZOLTAN KODÁLY: *Háry János* Suite. Cleveland Orchestra, George Szell, conducting. (Sony Classical MYK 38527)

71. SERGEI PROKOFIEV: Violin Concertos, no. 1 in D (op. 19) and no. 2 in G minor (op. 63). Isaac Stern, violinist; Philadelphia Orchestra, Eugene Ormandy, conducting. (Sony Classical MYK 38525)

72. SERGEI PROKOFIEV: *Peter and the Wolf* (op. 67); CAMILLE SAINT-SAËNS: *Le Carnaval des Animaux;* BENJAMIN BRITTEN: *The Young Person's Guide to the Orchestra* (op. 34). Leonard Bernstein and Henry Chapin, narrators; New York Philharmonic, Leonard Bernstein, conducting. (Sony Classical SMK 60175)

73. JOAQUÍN RODRIGO: *Concierto de Aranjuez;* HEITOR VILLA-LOBOS: Concerto for Guitar and Orchestra, Preludes, Mazurka-Chôro from *Suite Populaire Brésilienne.* Julian Bream, guitarist; Monteverdi Orchestra, Sir John Eliot Gardiner, conducting; London Symphony Orchestra, André Previn, conducting. (RCA 6525-2)

74. *TEREZIN MUSIC ANTHOLOGY,* Vol. II. GIDEON KLEIN: Fantasie and Fugue; Sonata; Trio for Violin, Viola, and Cello; Two Madrigals; *Pvrní Hřich;* and Czech and Russian folk song arrangements. Members of the Group for New Music; Allan Sternfeld, pianist; soloists from the Prague Philharmonic Choir; Vladimir Dolzul, tenor; Pavel Kühn, conducting. (Koch International Classics 3-7230-2)

75. ARTHUR HONEGGER: Symphony no. 2 and Symphony no. 5 *(Di Tre Re);* DARIUS MILHAUD: *Suite Provençale* (op. 152) and *La Création du monde.* Boston Symphony Orchestra, Charles Munch, conducting. (RCA 60685-2)

76. FRANCIS POULENC: "Les Banalités," "Les Chansons Villageoises," "Les Fiançailles pour Rire," "Le Travail du Peintre," "Priez pour Paix," "La Souris," "Nuage," "Ce Doux Petit Visage," "Main Dominée par le Coeur," "Montparnasse," "Les Chemins de l'Amour— Valse Chantée," "À sa Guitare," "C," and "Fêtes Galantes." Nathalie Stutzmann, contralto; Inger Södergren, pianist. (RCA 63137-2)

77. ERICH WOLFGANG KORNGOLD: Music from the Films—*The Sea Hawk; The Private Lives of Elizabeth and Essex; Captain Blood; The Prince and the Pauper.* London Symphony Orchestra, André Previn, conducting. (Deutsche Grammophon 471 347-2)

78. HENRI DUTILLEUX: Symphony no. 2; *Métaboles;* and *Timbres, Espace, Mouvement.* Toronto Symphony Orchestra, Jukka-Pekka Saraste, conducting. (Finlandia 3984-25324-2)

79. LUCIANO BERIO: *Formazioni,* Folk Songs, and Sinfonia. Jard van Nes, mezzo-soprano; Electric Phoenix (vocal ensemble); Royal Concertgebouw Orchestra of Amsterdam, Riccardo Chailly, conducting. (Decca 425 832-2)

80. ELLIOTT CARTER: Sonata for Flute, Oboe, Cello, and Harpsichord; Sonata for Cello and Piano; and Double Concerto for Harpsichord and Piano. Joel Krosnick, Fred Sherry, cellists; Charles Kuskin, oboist; Harvey Sollberger, flutist; Gilbert Kalish, pianist; Paul Jacobs, harpsichordist; Contemporary Chamber Ensemble, Arthur Weisberg, conducting. (Nonesuch 79183)

81. ELLIOTT CARTER: *The Vocal Works (1975–1981): Three Poems of Robert Frost; A Mirror on Which to Dwell; Syringa;* and *In Sleep, In Thunder.* Patrick Mason, baritone; Christine Schadeberg, soprano; Katherine Ciesinski, mezzo-soprano; Jan Opalach, bass-baritone; Jon Garrison, tenor; Speculum Musicae; David Starobin, Donald Palma, William Purvis, and Robert Black, conductors. (Bridge BCD 9014)

82. LUKAS FOSS: *Time Cycle, Phorion,* and *Song of Songs.* Adele Addison, soprano; Jennie Tourel, mezzo-soprano; Columbia Symphony Orchestra, New York Philharmonic, Leonard Bernstein, conducting. (Sony Classical SMK 63164)

83. JOHN CAGE: Sonatas and Interludes. Aleck Karis, pianist. With "Composition in Retrospect," read by John Cage, 1982. (Bridge 9081 A/B, two CDs)

84. TORU TAKEMITSU: *Riverrun, Water-Ways, Rain Coming, Rain Spell,* and *Tree Line.* Paul Crossley, pianist; Sebastian Bell, flutist; Gareth Hulse, oboist; London Sinfonietta, Oliver Knussen, conducting. (Virgin Classics 59020-2)

85. GEORGE CRUMB: *Ancient Voices of Children* and *Music for a Summer Evening (Makrokosmos III).* Jan DeGaetani, mezzo-soprano; Michael Dash, boy soprano; The Contemporary Chamber Ensemble, Arthur Weisberg, conducting; Gilbert Kalish, James Freeman, pianists; Raymond DesRoches, Richard Fitz, percussionists. (Nonesuch 79149)

86. GEORGE CRUMB: *Black Angels;* THOMAS TALLIS: Spem in Alium; ISTVÁN MÁRTA: *Doom. A Sigh;* CHARLES IVES: *They Are There!—Fighting for the People's New Free World;* DMITRI SHOSTAKOVICH: Quartet no. 8. The Kronos Quartet. (Nonesuch 79242)

87. LOU HARRISON: *La Koro Sutro, Varied Trio,* and Suite for Violin and American Gamelan. David Abel, violinist; Julie Steinberg, pianist; William Winant, percussionist; Choir, Philip Brett, conducting; American Gamelan, John Bergamo, conducting. (New Albion NA 015)

88. TERRY RILEY: *In C.* Members of the Center of the Creative and Performing Arts in the State University of New York at Buffalo, Terry Riley, conducting. (Sony Classical MK 7178)

89. *MUSIC OF OUR TIME.* GYÖRGY LIGETI: *Atmospheres;* MORTON FELDMAN: *Out of Last Pieces;* EDISON DENISOV: *Crescendo e Diminuendo;* GUNTHER SCHULLER: *Triplum;* OLIVIER MESSIAEN: *Trois Petites Liturgies de la Présence Divine* and Improvisations by the orchestra. Paul Jacobs, pianist; John Canarina, ondes martinot; New York Philharmonic, Leonard Bernstein, conducting. (Sony Classical SMK 61845)

90. NED ROREM: Selected Songs. "The Waking"; "Root Cellar"; "My Papa's Waltz"; "I Strolled Across an Open Field"; "Memory"; "Orchids"; "The Serpent"; "Night Crow"; "Snake"; "Little Elegy"; "The Nightingale"; "Nantucket"; "Lullaby of the Woman of the Mountain"; "Love in a Life"; "What If Some Little Pain"; "Visits to St. Elizabeth's"; "Stopping by the Woods on a Snowy Evening"; "Spring"; "See How They Love Me"; "Now Sleeps the Crimson Petal"; "I Am Rose"; "Ask Me No More"; "Far-Far-Away"; "Early in the Morning"; "Alleluia"; "Such Beauty as Hurts to Behold"; "Sally's Smile"; "Youth, Day, Old Age and Night"; "O You Whom I Often and Silently Come"; "Full of Life Now"; "As Adam Early in the Morning"; and "Are You the New Person?" Carole Farley, soprano; Ned Rorem, pianist. (Naxos 8.559084)

91. STEVE REICH: *Drumming, Six Pianos,* and *Music for Mallet Instruments, Voices, and Organ.* Steve Reich and Musicians. (Deutsche Grammophon 427 428, two CDs)

92. WENDY CARLOS: *Sonic Seasonings, Aurora Borealis,* and *Midnight Sun.* Wendy Carlos, synthesist. (East Side Digital ESD 81372, two CDs)

93. PHILIP GLASS: *Songs from Liquid Days* (settings of lyrics by Laurie Anderson, David Byrne, Paul Simon, and Suzanne Vega). Bernard Fowler, Janice Pendarvis, Linda Ronstadt and the Roches, vocalists; the Kronos String Quartet; the Philip Glass Ensemble, Michael Riesman, conducting. (Sony Classical MK 39564)

94. LOUIS ANDRIESSEN: *De Tijd.* Schönberg Ensemble, Reinbert de Leeuw, conducting. (Nonesuch 79291)

95. PETERIS VASKS: *Musica Dolorosa,* Cantabile for String Orchestra, *Lauda, Voices,* and Symphony for String Orchestra. I Fiamminghi, Rudolf Werthen, conducting. (Telarc CD-80457)

96. JOAN TOWER: Violin Concerto, Flute Concerto, Piano Concerto, and Clarinet Concerto. Elmar Oliveira, violinist; Carol Wincenc,

flutist; Ursula Oppens, pianist; David Shifrin, clarinetist; Louisville Orchestra, Joseph Silverstein and Max Bragado-Darman, conducting. (D'Note Classics DND 1016)

97. AARON JAY KERNIS: *Colored Field, Musica Celestis,* and *Air.* Truls Mørk, cellist; Minnesota Orchestra, Eije Oue, conducting. (Virgin Classics 45464)

98. OSVALDO GOLIJOV: *Last Round* for Double String Quartet and Bass; *Lullaby and Doina* for Flute, Clarinet, Bass, and String Quartet; *Yiddishbuk: Inscriptions for String Quartet;* and *The Dreams and Prayers of Isaac the Blind,* for Clarinet and String Quartet. The St. Lawrence String Quartet, with Todd Palmer, clarinetist; Tara Helen O'Connor, flutist; Mark Dresser, bassist; and the Ying Quartet. (EMI Classics 57356-2)

99. THOMAS ADÈS: *Life Story.* Includes *Catch, Darknesse Visible, Still Sorrowing, Under Hamelin Hill, Five Eliot Landscapes, Traced Overhead,* and *Life Story.* Thomas Adès, pianist and organist; Valdine Anderson and Mary Carewe, sopranos; Lynsey Marsh, clarinetist; Anthony Marwood, violinist; Louise Hopkins, cellist; David Goode and Stephen Farr, organists. (EMI Classics 5 69699 2)

100. PETER SCHICKELE: *The Dreaded P.D.Q. Bach Collection: The Complete Vanguard Recordings,* Vol. 1. (Vanguard 159/62-2, four CDs)

Illustration Credits

Index

Academy of Ancient Music, 48
Academy of St. Martin-in-the-Fields, 153
Adams, John, 302–5
Addison, Adele, 86
Adès, Thomas, 336
Akoka, Henri, 266
Alban Berg Quartet, 105, 106, 107
Albéniz, Isaac, 196, 328
Aler, John, 38
Alldis, John, 70
Allegri, Gregorio, 321
Amadeus Quartet, 134, 135, 137
Ambrosian Singers, 155
Ameling, Elly, 101
American Composers Orchestra, 307
Andriessen, Louis, 335
Ansermet, Ernest, 196, 198
Antonini, Giovanni, 31
Argerich, Martha, 156, 158
Armstrong, Louis, 236
Aronowitz, Cecil, 134, 135
Arrau, Claudio, 124, 126
Arriaga, Juan Crisóstomo, 84–85
Arroyo, Martina, 241, 243
Arts Florissants, Les, 9, 10
Artusi, Giovanni Maria, 20, 21
Asawa, David, 17
Ashkenazy, Vladimir, 119, 288
Ashton, Carolyn, 170

Atherton, David, 244–47, 245–46
Atlanta Symphony Orchestra and Chorus, 127, 273
Atrium Musicae de Madrid, 305, 306
Auer, Leopold, 95
Augér, Arleen, 127, 129
Ax, Emanuel, 119

Babbitt, Milton, 241, 286
Bach, Carl Philipp Emanuel, 32
Bach, Johann Sebastian, 19, 29–42, 43, 49, 53, 54, 97, 115, 128, 172, 173, 220, 248–49, 268, 269, 288, 307, 322, 326
Bach Choir, 271
Bach Ensemble, 35
Bagby, Benjamin, 3
Baird, Julianne, 35, 37
Baker, Dame Janet, 101, 165
Balakirev, Mily, 143, 150, 151
Ballet Caravan, 239
Ballets Russes, 192, 198, 209
Bandeira, Manoel, 268
Barber, Samuel, 240, 241–44, 290, 331
Barbirolli, Sir John, 178, 180–81, 223–24
Barrios, Agustín, 217–20
Bartók, Béla, 76, 256–61, 277–78, 319, 330
Batchelar, Daniel, 220
Battle, Kathleen, 81
Baudrier, Yves, 265

BBC Symphony Orchestra, 70
Beauregard, Lawrence, 228
Beauséjour, Luc, 55
Becher, Johannes, 262
Beckerman, Michael, 160
Beecham, Sir Thomas, 51, 64–67, 141, 180, 201
Beethoven, Johann, 90
Beethoven, Ludwig van, 10, 39, 56, 68, 76, 77, 78, 85, 86–99, 115, 130, 131, 136, 156–58, 163, 171, 172, 184, 201, 237, 250, 257, 288, 290, 323–24
Bell, Donald, 86
Benois, Alexandre, 214
Berg, Alban, 108, 181, 183–84, 234, 241, 243, 247–50
Berganza, Teresa, 198
Bergsma, William, 292
Berio, Luciano, 292, 333
Berlin Philharmonic, 81, 92, 134, 135, 162, 175, 200
Berlioz, Hector, 72, 111–14, 115, 131, 141, 163, 215, 324
Bernhardt, Sarah, 216
Bernstein, Leonard, 39, 89, 91–92, 114, 147, 158, 160–62, 171, 175, 176–78, 225, 230, 235, 236–37, 240, 250, 252, 253, 279–82, 289, 290, 291, 318, 330
Best, Matthew, 168
Beyer, Franz, 72
Beymer, Richard, 280
Big Brother and the Holding Company, 236
Billings, William, 239
Biondi, Fabio, 58
Bizet, Georges, 197
Blochwitz, Hans Peter, 73
Bloomington Symphony Orchestra, 313
Boccherini, Luigi, 106
Böhm, Karl, 200, 202
Bolet, Jorge, 126
Bonney, Barbara, 73, 102
Borodin, Alexander, 150–52, 151, 152
Boston Baroque, 72
Boston Symphony Orchestra, 93, 142, 164
Bostridge, Ian, 45, 99, 102
Boulez, Pierre, 172, 176, 190, 192, 203, 205, 225, 228, 230, 231, 286
Bour, Ernst, 311
Brady, Nicholas, 27
Brahms, Johannes, 39, 93–96, 110, 127–38, 168, 184, 200, 203, 318, 325
Brandenburg Consort, 45
Brando, Marlon, 281
Bream, Julian, 136, 219
Brecht, Bertolt, 245, 246

Brendel, Alfred, 103, 104–5, 126
Bridge, Frank, 275
Bridgetower, George Polgreen, 156–57
Britten, Benjamin, 17, 61, 64, 225, 271–76, 274, 307, 332
Brod, Max, 183
Brooke, Gwydion, 64, 67
Brother Walter, 293
Browning, John, 55
Bruch, Max, 326
Bruckner, Anton, 162, 326
Brüggen, Frans, 92
Brymer, Jack, 64, 66
Bull, Ole, 153
Busnois, Antoine, 8
Busoni, Ferruccio, 95, 179, 190, 328
Byrd, William, 13, 15, 19, 39, 322

Cage, John, 193, 195, 278, 303, 333
Cambridge Singers, 170
Camerata Singers, 192
Canonici, Luca, 167
Canteloube, Marie-Joseph, 328
Capella Reial de Catalunya, La, 84
Carafa, Fabrizio, Duke of Andria, 10
Carlos, Steve, 335
Carlos, Wendy, 31, 335
Carmignola, Giuliano, 60
Caroline, Queen, 46
Carreras, José, 280, 310
Carter, Elliott, 184, 190, 231, 241, 333
Casals, Pablo, 106, 107
Case, Dr. John, 13
Cassidy, Claudia, 141
Chamber Orchestra of Basel, 261
Chambonnières, Jacques Champion de, 190
Chance, Michael, 19, 26, 45
Chapelle de Québec, La, 72
Chapelle Royale, La, 129
Chelsea Opera Group, 72
Chen Yi, 317
Chicago Symphony Orchestra, 93, 130, 132, 160, 202, 224, 225, 230, 247, 249, 259
Chilcott, Robert, 170
Choir of Christ Church Cathedral, Oxford, 48
Choir of King's College, Cambridge, 45, 170
Chopin, Frédéric, 97, 108, 117–20, 126, 276, 325, 326
Christian IV, King of Denmark, 13
Christie, William, 9, 12
Christoff, Boris, 144
Christophers, Harry, and the Sixteens, 48
Ciccolini, Aldo, 165, 193, 195

City of London Sinfonia, 170, 222
Clement, Franz, 94
Clementi, Muzio, 195
Cleobury, Stephen, 45
Clerks' Group, 7, 9
Cleveland Orchestra, 86, 87, 146, 160, 170, 174, 190, 212, 213, 233
Cleveland Orchestra and Chorus, 231
Cleveland Orchestra Choir, 86
Cliburn, Van, 152, 224–28
Cobham, Sir Henry, 13
Collegium Vocale, 129
Columbia Symphony Orchestra, 207, 213, 235, 241
Concert des Nations, Le, 83, 85
Concerto Vocale, 25
Consort of Musicke, The, 12, 14, 15, 26
Copland, Aaron, 238–41, 245, 289, 313, 330
Corigliano, John, 237, 289–91
Corydon Singers, 168, 169
Couperin, François, 54
Covey-Crump, Rogers, 26
Crabtree, Libby, 45
Crawford Seeger, Ruth, 231, 233, 234
Crumb, George, 334
Cui, Cesar, 150
Culshaw, John, 272
Curzon, Sir Clifford, 61, 62, 63–64
Cutting, Francis, 15, 17
Czech Philharmonic Orchestra, 138, 140, 141, 142

Damrosch, Walter, 225
Daniels, Charles, 26
Daniels, David, 17
D'Annunzio, Gabriele, 186
Dante, 179
da Palestrina, Giovanni Pierluigi, 321
Darin, Bobby, 246
d'Avalos, Maria, 10
Davies, Dennis Russell, 307
Davies, Ryland, 70
Davis, Andrew, 170
Davis, Sir Colin, 51–52, 70, 72–73, 77, 78, 80, 111, 112, 114, 180
Debussy, Claude, 108, 125, 164, 184, 185–90, 194, 197, 198, 210, 216, 226, 270, 285, 329
de Falla, Manuel, 190, 196–99, 268, 283
de Gabarain, Marina, 198
Dehmel, Richard, 205
de Latour, Contamine, 194
de Leeuw, Reinbert, 294, 296
Delius, Frederick, 224, 327

Deller, Alfred, 15, 17–19
Deller Consort, 5, 15
de los Angeles, Victoria, 267, 269
de Mille, Agnes, 240
Denisov, Edison, 334
Depardieu, Gérard, 311
de Ruiter, Albert, 299, 300
de Saraate, Pablo, 326
Desprez, Josquin, 7–9
d'Este, Leonore, 11
Diaghilev, Sergei, 192, 198, 209, 210, 213
Dickinson, Meriel, 244
d'Indy, Vincent, 195, 241, 243
Disney, Walt, 208
Domingo, Placido, 310
Donath, Helen, 70, 73
Dooley, Jeffrey, 35, 37
Doors, the, 246
Dorati, Antal, 80
Double Edge, 294
Dowland, John, 12–15, 23, 220, 322
Downes, Olin, 236
Drake, Julius, 99
Drucker, Eugene, 258
Drucker, Stanley, 290
Dudevant, Baroness Aurore (George Sand), 118
Dufay, Guillaume, 321
Dukas, Paul, 162–65, 265
Duparc, Henri, 215, 270
Dupré, Desmond, 15, 17
Dupré, Marcel, 265
Duruflé, Maurice, 165
Dutilleux, Henri, 333
Dutoit, Charles, 185, 186
Dutton, Lawrence, 258
Dvořák, Antonín, 77, 116, 158–62, 181, 239, 326
Dylan, Bob, 210–12

Elgar, Sir Edward, 171, 222–24, 328
Elliott, Paul, 26, 48
Elman, Mischa, 95
Emanuel, Carl Philipp, 53, 57
Emerson String Quartet, 74, 107, 256, 258
English Baroque Soloists, 38, 73, 83
English Chamber Orchestra, 61, 168, 274, 276
Ensemble Intercontemporain, 203, 206, 228, 230
Ensemble Organum, 4, 6
Eschenbach, Christoph, 134, 135
Esterházy princes, 74, 78
Europa Galante, 58, 59
Eybler, Joseph, 71

Farwell, Arthur, 239
Fauré, Gabriel, 168–70, 215, 283, 329
Faust, Isabelle, 262
Feltsman, Vladimir, 42
Finckel, David, 258
Finley, Gerald, 129
Fischer-Dieskau, Dietrich, 101, 103, 104, 105, 271, 272, 273
Fitzgerald, Ella, 236
Fleischer, Leon, 87
Fleming, Renée, 102
Florida, Julia, 217
Fokine, Mikhail, 192, 209
Fonda, Henry, 240
Fontes, Marquis de, 55
Forkel, Johann Nicholas, 32, 40
Forman, Milos, 70
Foss, Lukas, 225, 333
Franck, César, 156–58
Frantz, Justus, 135
Frederick II, king of Prussia, 10
Friedrich II, Elector, 36
Friedrich Wilhelm IV, king of Prussia, 116
Fuchs-Robettin, Hanna, 184
Furtwängler, Wilhelm, 91

Gabrieli, Giovanni, 290
Gade, Niels, 153
Gardiner, Sir John Eliot, 19, 21, 22, 38, 43–45, 73, 83, 167
Gedda, Nicolai, 165, 167
Ge-Gan Ru, 317
George, Michael, 26, 168, 169
George II, king of England, 43–44
Gergiev, Valery, 145, 147, 148
Gershwin, George, 235–37, 245, 329
Gesualdo, Carlo, 9–12, 23, 229
Gewandhaus Orchestra of Leipzig, 141
Ghiaurov, Nicolai, 165, 167
Giannini, Vittorio, 289
Giardino Armonico, Il, 29–32, 60
Gieseking, Walter, 189
Gilbert, Kenneth, 41
Giuliani, Mauro, 220
Giulini, Carlo Maria, 167
Glass, Philip, 283, 292, 296–302, 314, 335
Glazunov, Alexander, 208
Goebbels, Joseph, 263
Goerne, Matthias, 102
Goethe, Johann Wolfgang von, 101, 125
Goldberg, Johann Gottlieb, 40
Goldmark, Dr. Peter, 254
Golenishchev-Kutuzon, Arseny, 144, 145
Golijov, Osvaldo, 336
Goode, Richard, 96–99

Goodman, Benny, 240, 290, 330
Goosens, Eugene, 51
Górecki, Henryk, 308, 310–12
Gottschalk, Louis Moreau, 239
Gould, Glenn, 38–42, 61
Gould, Morton, 240, 330
Gould, Stephen Jay, 70
Gounod, Charles, 163, 270
Graham, Susan, 215, 216
Granados, Enrique, 196
Grant, Simon, 26
Gray, Cecil, 10
Greiter, Mattaeus, 9
Grieg, Edvard, 153–55, 326
Griffes, Charles Tomlinson, 239
Grindenko, Tatiana, 307
Gritton, Susan, 45
Grofé, Ferde, 235, 236, 237
Gropius, Manon, 248
Gropius, Walter, 175, 248
Grumiaux, Arthur, 34
Gubaidulina, Sofia, 308
Guo Wenjing, 317

Hagegård, Håkan, 102
Hahn, Reynaldo, 215–17, 270
Hallé Orchestra, 180
Hamm, Daniel, 293
Handel, George Frideric, 27, 43–52, 53, 57, 81, 82, 115, 128, 322–23
Hanover Court Orchestra, 95
Harper, Heather, 272
Harris, Roy, 171
Harrison, Lou, 334
Hartenberger, Russell, 292, 294
Hartmann, Karl Amadeus, 262–64
Hartmann, Viktor, 146
Havel, Václav, 142
Haydn, Franz Joseph, 39, 74–83, 85, 88, 89, 136, 171, 256–57, 323
Haywood, Lorna, 273
Heifetz, Jascha, 34, 93, 95, 96
Helsinki Philharmonic Orchestra, 312, 315
Hendl, Walter, 224
Henry VIII, king of England, 9
Herford, Henry, 45
Herman, Woody, 289, 291
Herreweghe, Philippe, 129
Herrmann, Bernard, 282–85
Heseltine, Philip (pen name Peter Warlock), 10
Highgate School Choir, 271
Hildegard of Bingen, 1–3, 310, 311
Hill, Martyn, 14
Hilliard Ensemble, 12

Hindemith, Paul, 39
Hitchcock, Alfred, 283, 285
Hobbson, Jane, 86
Hoffmeister, Frank, 35, 37
Hogwood, Christopher, 48, 50–51, 73
Holberg, Ludvig, 155
Honegger, Arthur, 332
Horne, Marilyn, 167
Horowitz, Vladimir, 55, 119, 126, 147
Hotter, Hans, 101
Hunt, Lorraine, 51
Hus, Jan, 140

Ibert, Jacques, 164
Ibsen, Henrik, 154
I Fiamminghi, 309
Il Giardino Armonico, 29–32, 60
International Composers Guild, 229
Isaac, Heinrich, 9
Ives, Charles, 231–33, 239, 283, 331, 334

Jacobs, Paul, 187–88
Jacobs, René, 23, 25
James I, King, 13
Janáček, Leoš, 141, 181–84, 328
Jan de Luxembourg, king of Bohemia, 4
Jansons, Mariss, 148
Järnefelt, Aino, 178
Jarrett, Keith, 42, 307
Jenkins, Neil, 26
Jennens, Charles, 46, 49
Joachim, Joseph, 95, 134
Jochum, Eugen, 134
John Alldis Choir, 70
Johnson, Graham, 144
Johnson, Robert, 15, 16, 17
Jolivet, André, 265
Joplin, Janis, 236
Joplin, Scott, 239
Juilliard String Quartet, 181, 182, 184
Jussila, Kari, 312

Kaiser, Georg, 246
Kancheli, Giya, 308
Karl Philip, prince of Schwarzenberg, 82
Kashkashian, Kim, 67, 69
Katims, Milton, 106–7
Kavafian, Ida, 264
Kazan, Elia, 281
Kern, Jerome, 235
Kernis, Aaron, Jay, 336
Kertész, István, 61, 64, 134, 160
Kiesewetter, Peter, 331
King, Andrew, 26
Kirchner, Leon, 303

Kirkby, Emma, 14, 26, 28, 48, 51, 73
Kirstein, Lincoln, 239
Kleiber, Carlos, 93
Klein, Gideon, 332
Kodály, Zoltán, 257, 331
Kodolfsky, Adolf, 53
Koechlin, Charles, 270
Koivula, Hannu, 315
Kokkonen, Joonas, 313
Kondrashin, Kiril, 150, 152, 224, 228
Koopman, Ton, 55
Korngold, Wolfgang Erich, 283, 333
Korot, Beryl, 292
Koussevitzky, Serge, 201, 260
Kowalke, Kim, 246
Krasner, Louis, 248
Krause, Martin, 126
Krebbers, Hermann, 152
Kreisler, Fritz, 95
Kremer, Gidon, 34, 67, 69, 302, 305, 307, 309
Kubelik, Jan, 141–42
Kubelik, Rafael, 160

Labadie, Bernard, 72
La Chapelle de Québec, La, 72
La Chapelle Royale, 129
Landowska, Wanda, 42, 53–57
Langridge, Philip, 244
L'Archibudelli, 76, 137
Large, Brian, 140
LeBoulaire, Jean, 266
Leiferkus, Sergei, 143, 144
Leigh, Janet, 283
Leighton-Smith, Lawrence, 289
Leister, Karl, 134, 135
Leningrad Philharmonic Orchestra, 147
Lenya, Lotte, 245
Leonhardt, Gustav, 42, 55
Leopold II, 63
Les Arts Florissants, 9, 10
Lesur, Daniel, 265
Les Violons du Roy, 72
Levin, Robert, 72
Levine, James, 81, 83, 162, 164, 165, 247, 249
Lewis, Richard, 86
Liadov, Anatol, 145
Liddell, Nona, 244
Lieberson, Goddard, 238
Ligeti, György, 285, 334
Lin, Lucia, 316
Lincoln, Abraham, 240
Lindberg, Magnus, 313
Lindsay String Quartet, 76

Lipovšek, Marjana, 144–45
Liszt, Franz, 97, 124–26, 131, 163, 201, 204, 227
Lithuanian Chamber Orchestra, 307
Llobet, Miguel, 218
London, George, 129
London Sinfonietta, 244, 310, 312
London Symphony Orchestra, 51–52, 61, 134, 160, 274, 276, 289, 294, 296, 302
London Symphony Orchestra and Chorus, 271
Los Angeles Philharmonic, 282
Ludwig, Christa, 165, 167
Ludwig, Christian, 30
Luening, Otto, 289
Lully, Jean-Baptiste, 27
Lutosławski, Witold, 285
Luxon, Benjamin, 244, 273

MacDowell, Edward, 239
McFarland, W. D., 50
McGegan, Nicholas, 51
Machaut, Guillaume de, 4–6, 8
Mackerras, Sir Charles, 115, 133
McNair, Sylvia, 38
McNally, Terrence, 111
Mahler, Alma, 175, 248
Mahler, Gustav, 77, 162, 170–78, 204, 225, 230, 327
Manahan, George, 296
Mangoré, Chief Nitsuga, 219
Mann, Robert, 184
Manzoni, Alessandro, 165, 166
Marcon, Andrea, 60
Maria Barbara, Princess (later queen of Spain), 56
Marriner, Sir Neville, 153–55
Márta, István, 334
Marx, Karl, 262
Mary, Queen, 27
Massenet, Jules, 216, 270
Massine, Leonid, 213
Masur, Kurt, 233
Mathias, Georges, 194
Meiningen Court Orchestra, 134
Melos Ensemble, 135, 271
Mendelssohn, Felix, 77, 115–17, 122, 153, 249, 324
Mengelberg, Willem, 171, 176, 201
Menotti, Gian Carlo, 241, 243, 244, 290
Menuhin, Yehudi, 34
Messiaen, Olivier, 264–66, 285, 334
Meyer, Paul, 262
Miaskovsky, Nikolai, 255
Miles, Alastair, 19, 167

Milhaud, Darius, 268, 292, 297, 332
Milstein, Nathan, 34, 95
Milton, John, 81
Milykova, Antonina, 148
Minter, Drew, 51
Minton, Yvonne, 70
Mitropoulos, Dimitri, 253
Moll, Kurt, 81
Monoyios, Ann, 19
Monteverdi, Claudio, 19–26
Monteverdi Choir, 38, 73, 83, 167
Montreal Symphony Orchestra, 185, 186
Moreschi, Alessandro, 17
Moret, Ernest, 270
Morley, Thomas, 15, 16
Mozart, Constanze, 71–72
Mozart, Wolfgang Amadeus, 39, 56, 61–73, 74, 77–78, 79, 85, 88, 105, 108, 115, 136, 138, 141, 163, 171, 257, 323
Mravinsky, Evgeny, 147–50
Mühfeld, Richard, 137, 138
Müller, Wilhelm, 103, 104
Munch, Charles, 93, 164, 243
Mundy, William, 321
Munich Capella Antiqua, 5
Munich Chamber Orchestra, 262
Mussorgsky, Modest, 143–47, 150, 151
Muti, Riccardo, 233
Mutter, Anne-Sophie, 61, 247, 249, 250

Nagano, Kent, 302, 305
Naglia, Sandro, 19
Napoleon, 89
National Conservatory of Music, 158–59
Nazareth, Ernesto, 267
NBC Symphony, 242
Neidich, Charles, 240
Neilsen, Carl, 327
Nelson, Judith, 35, 37, 48
Neubauer, Paul, 316
Neumann, Václav, 141
Neveu, Ginette, 180
New Philharmonia Orchestra, 170
New York Chamber Symphony, 316
New York Philharmonic, 91, 114, 129, 147, 158, 159, 160–61, 171, 180–81, 189, 190, 192, 225, 228, 230, 231, 235, 241, 242, 243, 250, 253, 279–82, 289, 290, 291
Nielsen, Carl, 170, 285
Niemann, Edmund, 292, 293–94
Nienstedt, Gerd, 70
Nietzsche, Friedrich, 201
Nijinsky, Vaslav, 209, 210
Nono, Luigi, 286
Nordraak, Rikard, 153, 154

Ockeghem, Johannes, 321
O'Conor, John, 99
Oelze, Christiane, 129
Ogden, Robert, 45
Ohlsson, Garrick, 118, 119
Oistrakh, David, 253–55
Onofri, Enrico, 60
Onslow, Georges, 106
Opalach, Jan, 35, 37
Orchestra of St. Luke's, 302
Orchestra of the Enlightenment, 115,
    116–17
Orchestra of the 18th Century, 92
Orchestre de la Société du Conservatoire,
    164
Orchestre de la Suisse Romande, L', 196, 198
Orchestre des Champs Elysées, 129
Orchestre National de la Radiodiffusion
    Française, 267
Orchestre Révolutionnaire et Romantique,
    167
Orgonasova, Luba, 167
Ormandy, Eugene, 253, 259
Overton, Hall, 292
Owen, Wilfrid, 272

Paganini, Niccolò, 220, 325
Page, Tim, 38, 40
Paine, John Knowles, 233–34
Pan American Association of Composers,
    229
Paniagua, Gregorio, 305–6
Panufnik, Andrzej, 277
Paris Opera, 216
Parker, Horatio, 232, 234, 239
Parker, William, 51
Parrott, Andrew, 6, 26–29
Pärt, Arvo, 307–9
Partridge, Ian, 244
Pasquier, Etienne, 266
Paul, Thomas, 38
Paul V, Pope, 20
Pavarotti, Luciano, 167, 310
Pearlman, Martin, 72
Pears, Peter, 271, 272, 273
Péladan, Joséphin, 194
Pennicchi, Marinella, 19
Perahia, Murray, 105, 119
Percussion Group the Hague, 294, 296
Pérès, Marcel, 6
Pergolesi, Giovanni Battista, 213
Perkins, Anthony, 283
Perle, George, 97, 183
Perlman, Itzhak, 156, 158
Persichetti, Vincent, 292, 313

Petersen Quartet, 262
Petrarch, 24
Petrucci, 7
Philadelphia Orchestra, 242, 253
Philharmonia Baroque, 51
Philharmonia Hungarica, 80
Philharmonia Orchestra, 170, 180
Philharmonia Orchestra and Chorus, 165
Philip Glass Ensemble, 296, 297, 299, 303
Phillips, Daniel, 69
Picasso, Pablo, 213
Pinches, Jack, 73
Pinnock, Trevor, 42, 55
Piston, Walter, 290
Plato, 24
Playford, John, 306
Pleeth, William, 134, 135
Polish Radio Symphony Orchestra, 276
Pollini, Maurizio, 99, 288
Ponce, Manuel, 219
Popp, Lucia, 155
Poppen, Christoph, 262, 263
Poulenard, Isabelle, 168
Poulenc, Francis, 39, 165, 215, 332
Prades Festival Orchestra, 107
Prégardien, Christoph, 102
Preston, Simon, 48, 162, 164, 271
Prêtre, Georges, 164–65
Prey, Hermann, 101
Prokofiev, Sergei, 224–28, 255, 274, 331,
    332
Proust, Marcel, 216
Puchberg, Michael, 68
Pujol, Emilio, 218
Purcell, Henry, 17, 26–29, 44, 274

Quasthoff, Thomas, 102

Rachmaninoff, Sergei, 224–28, 329
Ramuz, Charles-Ferdinand, 214
Rangell, Andrew, 42
Raskin, Judith, 170, 174
Rattle, Simon, 176
Rautavaara, Einojuhani, 171, 312–15
Ravel, Maurice, 145, 146, 190–92, 195, 197,
    198, 215, 268, 270, 329
Reggio, Godfrey, 299
Reich, Steve, 292–96, 302, 335
Reich, Willi, 173
Reiner, Fritz, 93, 95, 160, 201, 259, 260,
    261
Respighi, Ottorino, 213, 329
Ricci, Ruggiero, 95
Richter, Johanna, 174
Richter, Karl, 42

Richter, Sviatoslav, 146
Riesman, Michael, 296
Rifkin, Joshua, 35–38
Rihm, Wolfgang, 250
Riley, Terry, 292, 302, 334
Rimsky-Korsakov, Nikolai, 143, 145,
    150–52, 198, 208
Rippon, Michael, 244
Roberts, Marcus, 236
Robson, Nigel, 19
Rodrigo, Joaquín, 332
Roerich, Nicolai, 209
Roger-Ducasse, Jean, 169
Rolfe-Johnson, Anthony, 273
Rooley, Anthony, 12, 15
Rorem, Ned, 335
Ross, Scott, 55
Rossini, Gioacchino, 85, 163, 165–66, 166
Rostropovich, Mstislav, 107, 253–55
Roussel, Albert, 195
Royal Concertgebouw Orchestra of
    Amsterdam, 77, 78, 111, 150, 152, 178
Royal Philharmonic Orchestra, 51, 64, 66,
    178, 180
Royal Philharmonic Society of London, 163
Royal Scottish National Orchestra, 315
Rubinstein, Arthur, 117–20, 119, 120, 121,
    124, 126, 187, 268
Rubinstein, Ida, 191, 214
Rudolph, Archduke of Austria, 10
Ruggles, Carl, 231, 233–34, 239
Rutter, John, 170

Saariaho, Kaija, 313
Saffer, Lisa, 316
Saint, Eva Marie, 281
Saint-Saëns, Camille, 162–65, 332
Sallinen, Aulis, 313
Salomon, Johann Peter, 78, 81, 82
Salonen, Esa-Pekka, 282, 285, 313
Sand, George, 118, 119
Sanderling, Kurt, 148
Sanz, Gaspar, 306
Satie, Erik, 193–95
Satoh, Somei, 308
Savall, Jordi, 84, 85
Sawallisch, Wolfgang, 121
Say, Sazil, 236
Sayão, Bidu, 270
Scarlatti, Domenico, 53–57
Schickele, Peter, 336
Schiff, Andras, 42
Schiff, Heinrich, 105, 106
Schiller, Henryk, 91
Schindler, Anton, 90

Schippers, Thomas, 241–44, 253
Schneider, Alexander, 106
Schnittke, Alfred, 307
Schoenberg, Arnold, 39, 108, 183, 189–90,
    203–7, 208, 229, 247–48, 283, 286, 303,
    330
Schönberg Ensemble, 294, 296
Schreier, Peter, 101
Schubert, Franz, 77, 85, 96, 97, 99–111,
    136, 174, 184, 324
Schuller, Gunther, 334
Schuman, William, 171, 240, 241
Schumann, Clara, 95, 131, 153
Schumann, Robert, 89, 95, 115, 120–24,
    128, 153, 288, 325
Schütz, Heinrich, 128
Schwarz, Gerard, 316
Schwarzkopf, Elisabeth, 101, 165, 167
Scorsese, Martin, 285
Scott, John, 168
Scottish Chamber Orchestra, 133
Scriabin, Alexander, 328
Seefried, Irmgard, 129
Seeger, Charles, 234
Seeger, Mike, 234
Seeger, Peggy, 234
Seeger, Pete, 234
Seers, Mary, 168, 169
Segerstam, Leif, 312, 315
Segovia, Andrés, 217–18, 220
Senancour, Etienne Pivert de, 126
Senfl, Ludwig, 9
Serkin, Peter, 264–66, 316
Serkin, Rudolf, 99
Sessions, Roger, 313
Setzer, Philip, 258
Shaffer, Peter, 62, 70, 71
Shakespeare, William, 16, 101, 112, 216,
    223
Shankar, Ravi, 297
Shaw, George Bernard, 116
Shaw, Robert, 37–38, 127, 128–29, 273
Sheng, Bright, 316
Sherry, Fred, 264
Shostakovich, Dmitri, 39, 76, 145, 148, 171,
    250–56, 257, 260, 277, 307, 318, 331,
    334
Sibelius, Jean, 72, 170, 178–81, 312, 313,
    314, 328
Simpson, Marietta, 38
Sinfonia of London, 170, 222
Skigin, Semion, 143
Skinner, John York, 14
Slatkin, Leonard, 241
Slovik, Eddie, 214

Smetana, Bedřich, 138, 263
Smith, Michael, 26
Smithson, Harriet, 112–13
Solti, Sir Georg, 130, 132–33, 167, 259, 272
Sondeckis, Saulus, 307
Sor, Fernando, 220
Sousa, John Philip, 233
Spence, Patricia, 51
Spitta, Philip, 132
Spivakov, Vladimir, 60–61
Staatskapelle Dresden, 200
Stalin, Joseph, 251, 255
Steiner, Max, 283
Stern, Isaac, 106
Steve Reich and Musicians, 296, 303
Stillwell, Richard, 127, 129
Stock, Frederick, 201, 225
Stockholm Chamber Choir, 81
Stockholm Radio Chorus, 81
Stokowski, Leopold, 171, 201
Stoltzman, Richard, 264, 289, 291
Stone, William, 38
Stösslová, Kamila, 182–83
Stover, Richard, 219
Strauss, Richard, 39, 200–202, 203, 229
Stravinsky, Igor, 172, 198, 207–14, 268, 285, 289, 291, 318, 330
Stuttgart State Orchestra, 307
Süsskind, Walter, 180
Süssmayr, Franz Xaver, 70, 71–72
Sutherland, Joan, 167
Szell, George, 86–92, 146, 160, 170, 172, 174, 213, 259
Szell, Marion, 141–42
Szigeti, Joseph, 260

Takemitsu, Toru, 334
Talich, Václav, 140, 141
Tallis, Thomas, 222
Tallis Scholars, 12
Talvela, Martti, 167
Tan Dun, 317
Tárrega, Francisco, 218
Tashi, 264–66
Tasso, 10
Taub, Robert, 286, 287–88
Tavener, John, 308
Taverner Choir, 6
Taverner Consort, Choir and Players, 26
Taylor, Cecil, 287
Tchiakovsky, Modest, 148
Tchiakovsky, Peter Ilyich, 147–50, 208, 214, 223, 326, 331
Te Kanawa, Kiri, 280
Telemann, Georg Philipp, 75, 323

Temirkanov, Yuri, 148
Tennstedt, Klaus, 121, 176
Terfel, Bryn, 19, 102
Tetzlaff, Christian, 32–34, 34
Thomán, István, 260
Thomas, David, 14, 26, 28, 48
Thomas, Dylan, 290
Thomas, Jeffrey, 51
Thomas, Mary, 244
Thomas, Michael Tilson, 234, 241, 294, 296
Thornton, Barbara, 3
Three Tenors, 310
Thurber, Jeanette M., 158–59
Tilles, Nurit, 292, 293
Tilney, Colin, 55
Tolstoy, Leo, 182
Tortelier, Paul, 107
Toscanini, Arturo, 92, 241
Tower, Joan, 335–36
Trondheim Soloists, 61
Truffaut, François, 285
Tucker, Mark, 19
Tureck, Rosalyn, 42
Twelve Cellists of the Berlin Philharmonic, 307

Uchida, Mitsuki, 108–11, 109–10, 111, 119
University of California Berkeley Chamber Chorus, 51
Upshaw, Dawn, 310, 311, 312

Valery, Paul, 148
van Eyck, Jacob, 306
Varcoe, Stephen, 45, 170
Varèse, Edgard, 228–31, 233, 237, 268
Vasks, Peteris, 335
Venice Baroque Orchestra, 60
Verdi, Giuseppe, 17, 165–67
Verlaine, Paul, 216
Vienna Opera, 175
Vienna Philharmonic, 93, 134, 145, 147, 160, 167
Vienna State Opera Chorus, 167
Vieuxtemps, Henri, 326
Vignoles, Roger, 215, 216–17
Villa-Lobos, Heitor, 267–70, 332
Viñes, Ricardo, 191
Violons du Roy, Les, 72
Vishnevskaya, Galina, 271, 272, 273
Vivaldi, Antonio, 58–61, 201, 237, 249, 250
Voces String Quartet, 85
Volkov, Solomon, 252
von Dohnányi, Christoph, 231, 233–34
von Fricken, Ernestine, 122
von Fürnberg, Count Karl, 75

von Keyserlingk, Count Hermann Carl, 40
von Meck, Nadezhda, 149
von Otter, Anne Sofie, 73, 102, 167
von Spanheim, Jutta, 1
von Spaun, Josef, 104
von Stade, Frederica, 170, 174
von Swieten, Baron Gottfried, 81, 82
von Walsegg-Stuppach, Count Franz, 71
von Zemlinsky, Alexander, 203

Wagner, Richard, 90, 131, 163, 200, 203, 204, 272
Walter, Bruno, 129, 171, 172, 176
Warfield, William, 241
Watkinson, Carolyn, 48
Weber, Karl Maria Friedrich Ernst von, 138
Webern, Anton, 108, 247, 248, 262, 330–31
Weelkes, Thomas, 15, 16
Weill, Kurt, 244–47
Weissenberg, Alexis, 165
Welles, Orson, 283
Western Wind Vocal Ensemble, 299
Westminster Choir, 129
White, Willard, 73
Whiteman, Paul, 236
Wickham, Edward, 7–9
Widor, Charles-Marie, 229

Wieck, Clara, 122, 124
Wieck, Friedrich, 122, 124
Wiley, Roland John, 149
Willcock, Sir David, 170
Williams, Janet, 51
Williams, John, 136, 217–21
Williams, Ralph Vaughan, 171, 222–24, 314, 327
Williams, William Carlos, 295
Wilson, John, 15–16, 16
Winbergh, Gösta, 81
Wistreich, Richard, 26
Wood, Natalie, 280
Woolley, Robert, 26
Wunderlich, Fritz, 101
Wuorinen, Charles, 287

Yakar, Rachel, 228
Young, LaMonte, 292, 302
Yo-Yo Ma, 67, 69
Ysaÿe, Eugène, 95, 157–58, 326

Zamkochian, Berj, 164
Zhou Long, 317
Ziegler, Delores, 38
Zimbalist, Efram, 95
Zinman, David, 310, 311, 312

About the Author

ALLAN KOZINN is a classical music critic for *The New York Times*. Before joining the staff of the *Times* in 1991, he was a contributing editor for the classical music magazines *High Fidelity, Opus,* and *Keynote,* and he was the music critic for the *New York Observer.* He lives in New York City.